WAGE SETTING, SOCIAL PACTS AND THE EURO

CHANGING WELFARE STATES

Processes of socio-economic change – individualising society and globalising economics and politics – cause large problems for modern welfare states. Welfare states, organised on the level of nation-states and built on one or the other form of national solidarity, are increasingly confronted with – for instance – fiscal problems, costs control difficulties, and the unintended use of welfare programs. Such problems – generally speaking – raise the issue of sustainability because they tend to undermine the legitimacy of the programs of the welfare state and in the end induce the necessity of change, be it the complete abolishment of programs, retrenchment of programs, or attempts to preserve programs by modernising them.

This series of studies on welfare states focuses on the changing institutions and programs of modern welfare states. These changes are the product of external pressures on welfare states, for example because of the economic and political consequences of globalisation or individualisation, or result from the internal, political or institutional dynamics of welfare arrangements.

By studying the development of welfare state arrangements in different countries, in different institutional contexts, or by comparing developments between countries or different types of welfare states, this series hopes to enlarge the body of knowledge on the functioning and development of welfare states and their programs.

EDITORS OF THE SERIES

Gøsta Esping-Andersen, University of Pompeu Fabra, Barcelona, Spain
Anton Hemerijck, the Netherlands Scientific Council for Government Policy (Wetenschappelijke Raad voor het Regeringsbeleid – WRR)
Kees van Kersbergen, Free University Amsterdam, the Netherlands
Jelle Visser, University of Amsterdam, the Netherlands
Romke van der Veen, Erasmus University, Rotterdam, the Netherlands

PREVIOUSLY PUBLISHED

Jelle Visser and Anton Hemerijck, *A Dutch Miracle. Job Growth, Welfare Reform and Corporatism in the Netherlands*, 1997 (ISBN 978 90 5356 271 0)

Christoffer Green-Pedersen, *The Politics of Justification. Party Competition and Welfare-State Retrenchment in Denmark and the Netherlands from 1982 to 1998*, 2002 (ISBN 978 90 5356 590 2)

Jan Høgelund, *In Search of Effective Disability Policy. Comparing the Developments and Outcomes of the Dutch and Danish Disability Policies*, 2003 (ISBN 978 90 5356 644 2)

Maurizio Ferrera and Elisabetta Gualmini, *Rescued by Europe? Social and Labour Market Reforms from Maastricht to Berlusconi*, 2004 (ISBN 978 90 5356 651 0)

Martin Schludi, *The Reform of Bismarckian Pension Systems. A Comparison of Pension Politics in Austria, France, Germany, Italy and Sweden*, 2005 (ISBN 978 90 5356 740 1)

Uwe Becker and Herman Schwartz (eds.), *Employment 'Miracles'. A Critical Comparison of the Dutch, Scandinavian, Swiss, Australian and Irish Cases Versus Germany and the US*, 2005 (ISBN 978 90 5356 755 5)

Sanneke Kuipers, *The Crisis Imperative. Crisis Rhetoric and Welfare State Reform in Belgium and the Netherlands in the Early 1990s*, 2006 (ISBN 978 90 5356 808 8)

Wage Setting, Social Pacts and the Euro

A New Role for the State

Anke Hassel

Amsterdam University Press

The publication of this book is made possible with a grant of the GAK-Foundation (Stichting Instituut GAK, Hilversum).

Cover illustration: The "Kearsarge" at Boulogne, 1864, Édouard Manet (1832-1883)

Cover design: Jaak Crasborn BNO, Valkenburg a/d Geul
Lay-out: V3-Services, Baarn

ISBN-13 978 90 5356 919 1
ISBN-10 90 5356 919 7
NUR 754

“Statutory or voluntary, it [incomes policy] may not
have many positive virtues; but the alternative –
leaving it all to the slow-acting and uncertain treatment
of tight fiscal and monetary policies – is even less appealing.”

THE ECONOMIST, 11 FEBRUARY 1978

Table of Contents

Figures and Tables

Figures

Tables

Preface

This book project has lasted for a period of eight years. It started in summer 1998 when the German Social Democratic Party, SPD, announced it would set up an Alliance for Jobs with the unions and employers' organizations in case of a change of government. Becoming interested in the renewal of corporatist decision making, I prepared a small comparative study on social pacts in Europe that became the foundation for this book.

By the time this book is published, the German attempt to strike a social pact – the Alliance for Jobs – will have been dead for at least four years and another change of government has taken place. The new corporatist phase has contributed more to the demise of social partnership in Germany than to its renewal. Thankfully, I did not start a project on the effectiveness of this new mode of governance. Rather, my attention was grabbed by the underlying motivation of governments to enter such pacts including soft forms of incomes policy in an era when these types of policies had generally been written off. Though this is a new variation on an old theme, I hope that the readers will take new insights from it for studying the political economy of wage bargaining in Europe.

Writing this book met a couple of profound challenges, of which I would like to mention two. One was my ten-month stint to Manila, capital of the Philippines, in 2000-2001. Writing about the finer details of European monetary integration and wage regulation on a beach on the tropical island of Boracay overlooking turquoise sea or being stuck in a city of extreme social inequality was a challenge. Erich Kästner writes in the foreword of the famous German children book *The flying classroom*: "It is understandably very difficult to write a Christmas story in the warmest days of summer. One cannot just sit down and write 'it is freezing cold, the snow is pouring down...' when one feels like a joint of roasting meat... waiting for a heat stroke" (Kästner, 1998 [1933]: 10; my translation). Some similar problems arise when you think about the nitty-gritty of European wage increases for well paid skilled workers while living in a country where the vast majority of the population lives on one dollar per day.

The other challenge has been changing jobs three times in three years. My interest in governments' motivations when dealing with trade unions led to me spending a year in the planning division of the Ministry of Economics and Labour to observe policy decisions in the making. This was followed by appointments at the International University Bremen and finally at the Hertie School of Governance – all institutions I am very grateful to have been, and to remain, associated with. But with every new workplace, it takes time to adjust to new perspectives.

This book would not have been produced without the generous support of all these institutions. Most important of all has been the Max Planck Institute for the Study of Societies in Cologne. I owe an enormous debt to Wolfgang Streeck, who has been so tolerant towards and supportive of a project with which he disagreed in many ways. In the course of revising the book I have taken up many of his suggestions and understand many of his concerns, in particular the danger of using technical language and explanations for a deeply political process. Special thanks go to Jelle Visser, who encouraged me to offer the manuscript to Amsterdam University Press and who helped a great deal when I revised it. Moreover, he did not even blink an eye when I confessed that I had lost his notes on the manuscript at Budapest airport.

Thanks also to the Sociology Department of the Ruhr-University Bochum that accepted the manuscript as a habilitation thesis. In particular to Rolf G. Heinze who managed the process smoothly, but also to the department staff, Barbara Oetelshofen and Mechthild Bauernschmidt, as well as the faculty members who served on the habilitation committee. The two other reviewers of the thesis, Ulrich Widmaier and Klaus Armingeon, have provided extremely valuable comments on how to improve the arguments. Thanks also to the Science Center Berlin (WZB) for hosting me for eight months and the Volkswagen Stiftung that financed a one-year exchange to the planning division of the Federal Ministry of Economics and Labour.

My colleagues at Cologne and elsewhere have been crucial for discussing my work and this project, by inviting me to present my work, by sharing their time, their political and academic perspectives and thoughts and/or even their office space with me: Sabina Avdagic, Lucio Baccaro, Pablo Beramendi, Tom Cusack, Bernhard Ebbinghaus, Werner Eichhorst, Henrik Enderlein, Maria Funder, Steffen Ganghof, Peter Hall, Bob Hancké, Martin Höpner, Sven Jochem, John Kelly, Bernhard Kittel, Philip Manow, David Marsden, Philippe Pochet, Martin Rhodes, Fritz W. Scharpf, Wolfgang Schröder, Thorsten Schulten, Nico Siegel, David Soskice, Christine Trampusch, Sig Vitols and Stephen Wood.

Precious insights into the thinking and working of government administrations I gained from Henri Cordes, Britta-Maria Loskamp, Kirsten Neu-Brandenburg, Stefan Profit and from countless discussions with Oliver Villwock at the Ministry of Labour and Economics, which have deeply informed and thereby changed my understanding of political bureaucracies.

The prize for the best research assistants in the world should go to Sebastian Gröbel and Moira Nelson; followed – in no particular order – by Yorck Großkraumbach, Nele Kampffmeyer, Marina Krestinina, Lena Riedel, Irina Shames and Malgosia Skorek.

Finally, I have to thank my family. I thank Lucas for not taking the slightest interest in any of our work and pointing out to us the really important things in life. And Hugh for never stopping to support whatever I was doing and for hanging in there with me in all the emotional and intellectual turmoil I went through. It is not lost on me.

1 The Political Economy of Adjustment in Europe

Western European economies have undergone a major adjustment process over the last 25 years. They have had to adjust to the challenges of the effects of the oil shocks of the mid-1970s, to major effects of the process of European monetary and economic integration, to structural burdens of highly developed welfare states and decreasing labour market participation rates, and to an ever increasing degree of international penetration of markets, especially financial markets.

While processes of economic internationalization and financial liberalization have affected all advanced countries, Western European countries have faced a particular challenge. European economic integration processes have increasingly taken away economic policy tools, such as national competition law and national subsidies for certain industries and companies and employment protection in nationalized industries, which traditionally played an important role in Western European economic policy-making. In addition, European monetary union has progressively ruled out external adjustment via the exchange rate to compensate for losses in national competitiveness. Monetary integration in Western Europe has also meant universal adherence to the German model of restrictive monetary policy, which was the role model for the European monetary system. Moreover, convergence criteria and the Stability and Growth Pact have tightened fiscal policy. The fundamentally liberalizing nature of European economic integration has robbed national governments of important ways of cushioning and mediating necessary economic restructuring.

The external constraints on economic policy-making have crept into Western Europe on a gradual basis. Capital controls were lifted during the 1970s. The volume of international financial transactions increased dramatically between the 1970s and the late 1990s. Monetary integration started immediately after the collapse of the Bretton Woods system with the currency snake in 1973. It became an effective exchange rate mechanism for a small number of European countries with the setting-up of the

European Monetary System (EMS) in 1978. Devaluations still took place until the 1980s but were increasingly discouraged and avoided. After the EMS crisis in 1992, major devaluations were virtually ruled out. The Maastricht Treaty not only laid down the fight against inflation as a precondition for monetary union, but also put an end to further expansion of public expenditure by introducing ceilings for public debt and deficits. European governments chose to adopt the policy of financial restrictiveness and public austerity at different speeds and in different ways. Countries with previously high inflation and high unemployment, such as Italy and Ireland, joined the monetary club at an early stage, while most of the Scandinavian countries were more reluctant. They had opted for a strategy of competitive devaluation combined with real wage restraint as a temporary adjustment tool. In most cases, the adoption of the German role model required a major shift in economic policy-making. Inflation and devaluation had become the accepted means of adjustment to balance of payment difficulties. But from the early 1990s onwards, European governments had tied their hands tightly in favour of a restrictive monetary and fiscal policy, liberalized markets and strict competition policy.

One of the major consequences of monetary and economic integration of the European Union member states has been that it has shifted the burden of adjustment to economic imbalances and economic shocks increasingly and unilaterally onto the labour market. To the extent that external adjustment via the exchange rate is not available any more, that previously sheltered economic sectors are now open to international competition and that currencies are traded on international finance markets, changes in the competitiveness of national economies and regions have to be compensated for by the adjustment of real labour costs and, in many cases, of real wages. Tightening external economic conditions has required an increase in wage flexibility or the capacity for wage restraint in order to maintain current levels of employment.

While restrictive monetary policies and tighter fiscal policies were adopted almost universally in Western Europe,[1] the approaches towards wage flexibility remained contested. Whereas restrictive monetary policies were designed to discipline price and wage setters by highlighting the negative externalities of excessive price and wage increases, the conditions under which this policy would be most effective were still an open question.[2] European labour markets were highly regulated and wage bargaining institutions in many countries were centralized. Different views prevailed over the most beneficial relationship between monetary policy and wage bargaining institutions.

For most economists, labour and product markets produce the best results when governed by the rational expectations of workers and firms under competitive conditions. The credible threat of restrictive monetary policy can cause all economic actors to expect low price and wage increases, thereby controlling inflationary tendencies automatically. Competitive labour markets allow for the adjustment of imbalances between sectors and firms. Unregulated labour markets with decentralized wage formation procedures would therefore always outperform solutions of institutionalized wage formation because centralized forms of wage setting carry the costs of large and oligopolistic price and wage setters and frequently entail the intrusion of public policy into a private market domain. Two developments helped to strengthen this view throughout the 1970s and 1980s. Firstly, in economic theory, the dissemination of the role of *rational expectations* as the main guiding formula in macroeconomics separated monetary policy from the real economy. Economists emphasized the role of monetary policy for fighting inflation without being held responsible for welfare effects. Secondly, experiments of government intervention in wage bargaining as a response to the high inflation period of the mid-1970s failed utterly in many European countries. These experiences showed that governments were failing the markets, not *vice versa*.

During the 1970s and 1980s, a body of principles on macroeconomic policy-making spread throughout the Western world, which was based on the assumption of the neutrality of monetary policy for economic effects. On the basis of rational expectations, it was argued that monetary policies would only have price effects but not welfare effects. Non-competitive markets for goods and labour caused welfare effects – in particular unemployment. The theory of the neutrality of monetary policy introduced a clear distinction between the world of monetary and fiscal policies dealing with prices and the world of real economic activities. Previous beliefs about a trade-off between changes in prices and unemployment (the Phillips curve) were shattered. In the long run, the consensus in macroeconomics was that there was no relationship between inflation and unemployment. As a consequence, monetary policies – aimed at stabilizing prices – would not have an effect on the real economy. Consequently, disequilibria within the real economy such as unemployment had to be dealt with by improving the competitive conditions in the markets for goods and labour.

Hence, by the beginning of the 1980s, government economic advisors tended to recommend the deregulation of labour markets and the introduction of more market mechanisms into wage formation. For instance, the council of economic advisors in Germany argued from the mid-1980s in favour of deregulation of the German labour market (Sachverständigenrat 1987). The OECD jobs study introduced a range of measurements to combat labour market rigidities and judged the performance of countries on the extent that they tackled these rigidities (Armingeon 2003; OECD 1994 a and b). For most economists, labour market rigidities rather than restrictive macroeconomic policies were at the heart of the continuously low performance of European labour markets.

Incomes policies, on the other hand, were a popular, but not very successful, tool of economic policy throughout the 1960s and 1970s. Incomes policies were only rarely recommended to governments by economists who accepted the given state of the economy as being dominated by large-scale price and wage setters.[3] The increase in labour market regulation and wage formation throughout the 20th century stemmed from the traumatic experience of the Great Depression for economic policy-makers. Regulation and economic planning were the lessons learned from low growth, low demand and economic volatility. In addition, war efforts had led to a further integration of the labour movement into policy-making. In all industrialized countries, the 1930s were followed by a period of increasing institutionalization of centralized wage bargaining, usually encouraged by government support. A new deal was struck on the labour market, with trade unions being accepted as responsible bargaining partners for employers and governments alike. The approach of regulated wage formation was carried over to the post-war period and was in place throughout the 1950s and 1960s. In the immediate post-war period, wage growth was moderate and capital stock was built up. However, already by the 1960s, European economies were in a very different position compared to the inter-war period. Rather than a lack of demand, governments faced the problem of tight labour markets and inflationary pressures. Governments experimented mostly unsuccessfully with different forms of incomes policies as guidelines to wage and price developments. Although the experiences of the 1960s were not seen as successful at the time, governments turned to various policies to influence the wage setting behaviour of firms and trade unions (incomes policies) during the 1970s when the post-war model was put to the test. Again it failed in many countries. In the UK, Italy, Ireland, the Netherlands and Denmark, governments were frustrated about the lack of commitment shown by unions towards cooperating in economic management.

Moreover, the US administration made a clear shift in its policy of economic adjustment in 1978/79, preferring to pursue a new trend towards a political economy based on deregulation, rather than defend the principle that wages should be not just factually but also rightly taken out of competition (Streeck 1992: 108). The Federal Reserve responded to the second oil price shock with drastic increases in interest rates and – given the internationalized nature of financial markets – forced the industrialized world to follow the policy of high interest rates.

Nevertheless, despite the turn in theoretical thinking, previous experiences and the US role model, the recommendations by economists came to no avail. The majority of Western European governments did not leave wages to the market. Quite the opposite; incomes policies – as an active intervention of governments in wage formation – were practised by a number of European governments in one form or other throughout the 1980s and 1990s, albeit in different forms compared to the 1960s and 1970s. The turnaround of French economic policy in 1982 was accompanied by a four-month price and wage freeze imposed by the government, rather than left to the market to sort out the consequences of the high wage increases induced by the government only a couple of months earlier (Hall 1986; Levy 2000). Wage freezes were also either imposed or threatened in Belgium, Denmark, Finland, the Netherlands and Portugal (Hassel 2003). Governments pleaded frequently for voluntary wage restraint. Tripartite wage agreements with governments that were also involved at the bargaining table and as a signatory party to wage agreements were to be found in the majority of the EU member states throughout the 1980s and 1990s.[4] In Belgium and Finland, the traditional role of governments bargaining over centralized wage agreements continued. In Spain and Portugal, traditional government-led incomes policies were temporarily abandoned but then resumed and reorganized in the run-up to EMU. In the Netherlands and Denmark, previous conflictual incomes policies of the 1970s were turned into tacit understandings between governments and the social partners of voluntary wage restraint and decentralization.

In Ireland and Italy, new central agreements led to a reorganization of the relations between governments and social partners and sought a more coordinated rather than deregulatory approach. This included the transformation of wage bargaining institutions at a more central level (O'Donnell and O'Reardon 2000; Perez 2000a and b). In Sweden – the country in which employers were most determined to abandon corporatist involvement in the 1980s – a number of government commissions sought to install new pay formulas and introduce the methods of an incomes policy.

In Austria and Germany, the two countries where monetarism struck first, adjustment took place in 1974 and was from thereon enshrined as "institutionalized monetarism" (Streeck 1994). The conduct of wage bargaining was enshrined to serve monetary stability and national competitiveness in close interaction with public policies. The burden of German unification, however, led to new adjustment pressures and an increased role for governments in wage bargaining from the mid-1990s onwards. It was only in the United Kingdom that monetarism was accompanied by a deliberate government policy to decentralize labour market institutions and leave wages to the market. Strict monetary policy, fiscal austerity and market clearance of the labour market were the explicit policy of the British government for more than two decades.

In many countries, the re-emergence of cooperation between governments and trade unions took the form of social pacts. Governments in Ireland, Finland, Portugal, Spain, Germany and Italy signed explicit tripartite agreements containing clauses on wage formation. Tripartite summits were held in France, Belgium and Sweden. Even in countries where governments were outspokenly hostile towards trade unions during the early 1980s, such as Denmark, the Netherlands and Ireland, corporatist approaches, rather than attempts to deregulate the labour market, re-emerged in the later part of the 1980s. Again, the United Kingdom is the only example where the government broke drastically and ultimately with all traditions of coming to negotiated solutions with organized labour. The British example is, however, very untypical of the rest of Europe, including in particular the Irish experience, where the most centralized arrangement of wage setting evolved throughout the latter half of the 1980s and the 1990s.

On an aggregate level, comparative studies have pointed out that corporatism has been extremely stable in most European countries (Ferner and Hyman 1998b). Only in Sweden and Denmark was wage bargaining decentralized to a lower level. In both cases, this process was driven by employers rather than by governments. Decentralization here took the form of moving from the national to the sectoral level of bargaining rather than to the plant level.[5] In countries where stable relationships between governments and the social partners existed, they generally remained (Ferner and Hyman 1998b; Traxler 1997).

With the exception of the British government and the Swedish employers' association in the early 1980s, in no West European country were corporatist institutions or forms of policy-making actively dismantled during the 1980s and 1990s. For instance, in Austria – still the most corporatist country in Western Europe – the chamber system has remained intact until today and has only recently come under limited attack from the right-wing coalition partner, the FPÖ. In Germany, Belgium, the Netherlands and France, patterns of an institutionalized interaction between the government and the social partners remained intact throughout the period. No major institution that embodied corporatist policy-making, such as the Federal Employment Office (*Bundesanstalt für Arbeit*) in Germany, the Socio-Economic Council (*Sociaal-Economische Raad,* SER) or the Labour Foundation (*Stichting van de Arbeid,* STAR) in the Netherlands, or the National Labour Council (*Nationale Arbeidsraad*) in Belgium, was dismantled.

Government intervention into wage bargaining was not part of a social democratic strategy; in fact, it was not explicitly tied to any political faction. From the 1980s to the mid-1990s, conservative and liberal parties dominated most governments in Western Europe. If deregulation of the labour market was associated with partisanship, we should have seen a clearer tendency towards decentralization. Instead the opposite occurred: centralized agreements on incomes policies were often struck between conservative governments and trade unions. For instance, in Ireland, the Netherlands, Denmark and Spain, a new approach towards a more organized form of wage bargaining was only possible after the stalemate that had developed between left-wing governments and trade unions over wages had been broken by conservative governments. These governments were often firmly committed to following the new macroeconomic policy paradigm of conservative monetary policy and the liberalization of labour markets. In practice, however, conservative economic policy-making often went hand-in-hand with new corporatist negotiations on incomes policies.

Even more puzzling is that the return to corporatism seems unrelated to the level and evolution of trade union strength in these countries. In general, trade union strength was in decline throughout the 1980s and 1990s. Trade unions were unable to gain substantial new membership in any of the countries studied (Ebbinghaus and Visser 2000). However, successful examples of the new corporatism can be found not only in countries with weak and declining trade unions such as the Netherlands, but also in countries with strong and thriving trade unions such as Finland. Even countries with strong but fragmented trade unions such as Ireland and Italy experienced successful forms of tripartite concertation. The notion that working-class strength or even working-class defence against the spread of neo-liberal policy-making could be at the heart of the reinvention of corporatist practices seems inadequate at first glance.

Faced with increasingly hard external economic constraints, most Western European governments turned towards negotiations on income policies with their social partners and not towards the market. Income policies of some sort not only persisted throughout the 1980s and 1990s, but they also emerged in places where they had not been found previously and where they certainly had not been expected.[6] Wage bargaining institutions continued to matter and were even strengthened by governments rather than weakened. This is not only in contrast to economic thinking but also in contrast to the experiences in the non-European countries of the OECD where labour market regulation and collective bargaining coverage continuously declined.

Why have European governments continued and sometimes increased their intervention in wage formation processes, while at the same time committing themselves to strict monetary conservatism? Why have they not relied on the rational expectations of economic actors that monetary restriction will automatically dampen wage demands? Why did governments engage in negotiations with trade unions at a time when their legitimacy and membership strength were increasingly undermined?

The limits of neo-corporatist analysis

Neo-corporatist approaches have explained the interaction between governments and interest groups by pointing to the mutual gains of a close-knit division of labour between them. Public policy can try to ensure that interest groups articulate and position their interests in a more publicly desirable way by inviting them to influence public policies. Interest groups can restrain from upsetting government policies and thereby gain access to the formulation of other policies. Governments can offer organizational security to interest groups by granting representational monopolies or state funding. Centralized and monopolistic interest groups are more suited to neo-corporatist exchanges than pluralist ones. Over time, interdependence and mutual interpenetration of public policy and associational governance increase and reproduce distinct neo-corporatist patterns of policy-making.[7]

In the past wage bargaining was traditionally at the heart of neo-corporatist arrangements.[8] In particular the ability of centralized trade unions and wage bargaining institutions to restrain wages enabled national economic policy-makers to adjust their policies accordingly. Policy options available to governments depended to a considerable extent on the ability to restrain wages at will. Countries where trade unions were able to offer governments wage restraint adopted a different strategy of economic policy than others (Scharpf 1991). In exchange, governments tried to ensure high levels of employment by pursuing expansionary economic policies. Moreover, trade unions gained access to a variety of political decision-making procedures.

However, the neo-corporatist literature has been unable to anticipate the continuity and re-emergence of political exchanges. Most of the scholars were taken by surprise by the developments of the 1980s and 1990s (Schmitter and Grote 1997). Authors expected the erosion of the decision-making capacity of corporatist arrangements and a general decline in the regulation of labour markets. This was mainly because they assumed that corporatist institutions had become inadequate under a more internationalized and liberalized market environment.

There were different reasonings behind the scepticism (Wallerstein and Golden 1997; Wallerstein, Golden *et al.* 1997): From the employers' perspective, it was thought that more flexible production systems would require greater differentiation of pay and a stronger connection between individual performance and rewards (Katz 1993; Streeck 1993; Iversen 1996; Pontusson and Swenson 1996). This would give companies a greater interest in locally designed pay systems rather than central wage agreements. Since the centralization of wage bargaining systems has distributive consequences as well, distributive struggles would be unleashed once centralization lost its dampening effect on labour costs (Iversen 1999). Centralized wage bargaining institutions strongly correlate with a low degree of wage dispersion. Low wage dispersion, however, is becoming increasingly dysfunctional for companies when dealing in an internationally constrained open economy. Companies would force employers' associations to push for decentralization or would opt out of the bargaining arrangements.

From the trade unions' perspective, the fragmentation of trade union membership was expected to reduce the capacity of trade unions to act collectively. New groups on the labour market would undermine the dominant position of blue-collar workers. Less cohesion on the side of labour would reduce the ability of peak associations to achieve industrial peace or wage moderation in centralized bargaining systems. Central wage bargaining institutions would become increasingly dysfunctional (Calmfors 1993; Moene, Wallerstein *et al.* 1993; Lange, Wallerstein *et al.* 1995).

The main reason for scepticism, however, was based on the – often implicit – assumption that corporatist arrangements were embedded in the sovereign economic policy capacity of governments to offer some sort of expansionist policies in exchange for trade union concessions. "As much as these systems may otherwise have differed, under the rules of corporatist bargaining a state that cannot with any reasonable prospect of success promise to apply its fiscal and monetary policy tools to alleviate unemployment cannot possibly hope to gain concessions from unions or to influence settlements between unions and employers by, for example, offering to improve the terms of the bargain through a corresponding economic policy" (Streeck 1992: 109).

That the capacity for expansionary economic policy was a precondition for political exchanges was also assumed by the political economy literature on the politics of growth (Lange and Garrett 1985). Strong trade unions were cooperating with left-wing governments in order to sustain full employment and induce investments (Cameron 1984; Lange and Garrett 1985; Alvarez, Garrett *et al.* 1991). The mutually beneficial strategic interaction between left-wing governments and trade unions was based on the assumption that strong trade unions would be willing to exercise wage restraint only under the condition that the government would ensure high investments and economic growth. Where unions were weak and labour markets decentralized, a conservative government, based on liberal market principles, would best provide economic performance. In countries without such 'congruent' regimes (strong labour/left-wing government or weak labour/right-wing government), either union militancy or inefficient 'adjustment policies' would dampen investment and growth (Lange and Garrett 1985). It follows that one should not expect an understanding between governments and trade unions on voluntary wage restraint if the required union trust in a government policy of economic growth no longer exists. External constraints arising from increasing international interdependence of national economies and the deflationary bias of the international economy should thereby rule out trade union cooperation.

Europeanization itself was also seen as contributing to the expected demise of national corporatism (Streeck 1992: 110; Streeck and Schmitter 1991). European economic integration meant the loss of national sovereignty over economic policy-making *per se*, since decision-making rights were transferred to the European level. Interdependence did not allow national deviation from the path of monetary austerity for very long, as the French example showed. Moreover, the lack of institutional regulation at the European level was a promise that was made by governments to business so they would give up the request for national protection. In the context of European integration, governments were neither able nor willing to concede to trade union concerns.

In addition, it was argued that granting concessions to trade unions in exchange for voluntary wage restraint was superfluous in the new international economy. Cooperation between social democratic governments and trade unions on wage restraint was only necessary in the context of a Keynesian economic policy (Scharpf 1991). Only in a Keynesian economic environment would governments make themselves dependent on the goodwill of trade unions to engage in voluntary wage restraint. If, however, the government switched towards a monetarist strategy, wage restraint would no longer be based on the encompassing structure of the trade union organization or the wage bargaining institutions. In a monetarist context, excessive wage settlements are immediately punished by unemployment. Unemployment, unlike inflation, is experienced not as a collective evil but as an individual risk to every single worker. Trade unions have to respond to the increasing economic insecurity and will lower their wage claims accordingly.

Therefore, there should be no need for negotiated wage restraint under the condition of monetarism, but wage restraint should follow automatically. This argument was the most direct application of the 'rational expectation' approach of economics in the political sciences. Rational actors would recognize the economic constraints and internalize their likely effects. The previously-held view on the importance of organizational and institutional structures that mediate individuals' concerns and the behaviour of collective actors would become irrelevant once economic insecurity increased and the mere threat of unemployment was signalled clearly enough.

According to the neo-corporatist literature, under the condition of liberalized markets, the dominance of restrictive monetary policies and of increasing economic and monetary integration were detrimental to corporatism. Exchanges between the government and trade unions were less likely to come about and more likely to decline due to the lack of compensation and sovereignty. Nor were these exchanges really necessary, due to the immediate disciplinary device of restrictive monetary policies. Even among the non-economists, the neo-corporatist sociologists and political scientists, the general expectation was a policy shift towards the deregulation of labour markets after the American and British model.

The approach of this book

This book makes two claims, one with regard to our understanding of the interaction between governments and trade unions and one with respect to the substance of the issue. The first claim of this book is the need to move on from the classic understanding of neo-corporatism as the effects of the organization of wage bargaining on policy-making towards an interactive approach between policy-making and institutions by taking a stronger problem-driven approach (Baccaro 2003; Molina and Rhodes 2002). To be fair, there have been previous approaches to corporatism as forms of governance that have emphasized the process of policy-making rather than the organizational structures of interest associations.[9] These approaches have seen the interaction between governments and interest associations as a mode of governance of complex societies. However, these approaches have remained largely conceptual and have not provided an explanatory framework for why corporatist exchanges have changed over time. The original aim was to produce a general theory about the relationship between the state and private actors that was based on exchanges.[10] Therefore the focus of these studies was less on the underlying problem that gave rise to this interaction.

The aim of this book is to argue that a comprehensive understanding of the evolution of the interaction between governments and social partners must entail an assessment of the problem that governments are addressing when dealing with associations. The book tries to combine the notion of governance with an understanding of problems that governments are attempting to solve when negotiating over wages. Therefore the book makes a number of references to the body of political economy literature[11] on the changing conditions of wage formation in internationalized economies. The argument wants neither to diminish nor to overcome the existing literature on neo-corporatism. It rather adds to our knowledge by emphasizing that organizational structures and established institutions offer opportunities for actors to pursue their interests, while with the changes in problems and in the perception of problems actors adapt by adjusting institutions or setting up new ones.

At the heart of the problem is the incorporation of trade unions into the political systems of Western Europe that occurred in the context of accommodating the employment and wage expectations of workers in the Keynesian welfare state. In advanced Western democracies there was an increasingly influential view among the population – also nurtured by the socialist countries where unemployed had 'disappeared' – that governments were responsible for high and stable employment rates. Survey data, for instance, shows that in the Western world more than 26 per cent of the population held the view that governments are definitely responsible for providing jobs. In Western Europe, this view was shared by 36 per cent of the population (Armingeon 2001, table 4).[12]

Underlying the interaction between governments and trade unions on wage formation issues are the wage expectations of trade unions. The relationship between governments and social partners varies with the institutional context. In the post-war period, the accommodation of labour into the Keynesian welfare state occurred both through trade union organizations becoming incorporated into corporatist institutions and through governments and social partners negotiating on wage formation. The institutional design left deep traces on both the capacity of wage bargaining actors to respond to the new economic situation and the opportunities for governments to negotiate with trade unions on wages. However, in this book it is not assumed that the institutional design determines this interaction completely.

When moving towards a hard currency regime, governments interfere in wage bargaining in order to adjust trade unions' wage expectations. Trade unions are usually in control of wage developments and have an interest in securing real wage increases for their members. Depending on their expectation of the government's economic policy, trade unions will set their wage preferences accordingly. Moreover, depending on their organizational structures, trade unions will tend to combine real wage increases and employment protection as they see fit. Governments interact with trade unions to bring the wage expectations of workers into line with government needs. On both sides, the actual degrees of wage demands or restraint are not fixed but dependent on a range of other factors that cannot easily be determined *ex ante*. Employment and the inflationary effects of wage settlements are not easily recognized since the competitive position of a country depends on external factors and monetary policy decisions. Productivity increases vary the room for manoeuvre in wage bargaining. The structure of the labour market determines the threat of unemployment for the individual. The extent to which wage settlements are seen as appropriate is therefore subject to interpretation on both sides.

Both sides are also conditioned in their attempts to frame wage expectations by organizational constraints. Governments are constrained by weak majorities or coalition partners. They have to consider the impact of their policies on their relationship with trade unions and employers' organizations. Moreover, they have to take into account reputational and electoral effects. Trade unions, for their part, have to consider the potential political competition or wage competition of individual affiliates and the discontent of workers with their standards of living. While the immediate preferences of both sides can be assumed *ex ante* (governments prefer wage restraint; unions prefer real wage increases and employment security), the pursuit of these preferences depends on a number of factors that lie beyond the pure organizational and institutional environment.

What is more, the capacity of institutions does not simply evolve; it may also decline. As with other institutional arrangements, tasks evolve over time and capacities degrade. Actors have and develop diverging views about external constraints and the purpose of the institutions themselves creating a need for political adaptation. Even highly centralized wage bargaining arrangements were not at all times and under all conditions geared up to the task of evenly mediating between wage expectations and distributive equality on the one hand, and economic constraints on the other. The pressure on governments to react to balance of payment deficits, soaring inflation rates and devaluation pressure has prompted numerous interferences with wage bargaining institutions. Rather than relying on the institutions to produce the required results, governments try to push wage bargainers to restrain wages.

Wage bargaining institutions were put to a severe test in the period of the late 1960s and early 1970s. The post-war commitment of governments to strive for full employment encountered the cracking of the international economic order aggravated by the oil shock. In most countries, collective bargaining institutions were not up to the test. Full employment, high rates of economic growth and rapid company restructuring made it more difficult for wage bargainers to respond to economic downturns. High wage expectations could not be contained by trade unions and social unrest pressured their leaders to ensure real wage gains.

This book argues that the dynamic of government-union relations is rooted in the *mismatch* of wage bargaining outcomes and government economic policy. Therefore it tries to identify the mechanisms that better determine the responsiveness of wage bargaining institutions. It is particularly important to understand the capacity of national institutions to deliver wage restraint and how this has changed over time. For instance, why were the Scandinavian wage bargaining institutions responsive to economic constraints in the context of a soft currency policy but not in the context of a hard currency policy? Why were the Dutch trade unions willing to engage in extreme wage restraint during the 1950s, but developed strong wage pressures during the 1960s? Which mechanisms keep wage pressures in check and which produce high real wage expectations?

It transpires that the divergent reactions of wage bargaining actors and governments to the crisis of the 1970s and the subsequent challenges of monetary internationalization can only be explained when the gradual decline in the responsive capacity of wage bargaining institutions in many Western European countries is taken into account. For instance, quite independently from the organizational structures of the wage bargaining system, wage indexation systems which fixed workers' expectations on real wage increases had been introduced in a number of countries (often in the 1930s) (Braun 1976). This tended to increase the mismatch in those countries much more vividly than in countries where the notion of real wage protection never existed, but rather where wage increases were always seen as a function of competitiveness.

For the reasons outlined above, this book therefore focuses on the relationship between governments and trade unions as the key variable for their interaction. In contrast to recent trends in the political economy literature to highlight the role of business and employers' organizations as key actors, it assumes that government policies *vis-à-vis* wage bargaining primarily address the expectations of workers.[13] Companies and employers obviously participate in wage bargaining and often have powerful veto positions, but the dynamic of the interaction takes place around the issue of the legitimate role of organized labour in economic policy-making.

With regard to the *substantive* issue, this book makes the claim that the internationalization of financial markets and the subsequent shift in economic policy has not rendered obsolete a negotiated approach between governments and trade unions in Western Europe mainly for three sets of reasons. Firstly, it argues that even under the condition of internationalized markets the conduct of wage formation is based on the organization of the labour market. Depending on the institutions that govern the labour market, wage bargainers have different incentives to internalize negative employment effects or not. While restrictive monetary policy will discipline the wage bargaining behaviour in the long run, a complete market-driven approach in a labour market that is dominated by powerful trade unions that are, however, insufficiently responsive might lead to high costs in terms of employment losses.

The institutions that govern labour markets also include the capacity of the social partners to control wage formation in the labour market. In decentralized collective bargaining institutions, there is no single collective actor in a position to set the going rate for wage increases. Instead, wage formation is based on local labour market conditions. Therefore, there is no direct access for centralized decisions on wage formation. In highly coordinated or centralized bargaining systems, these opportunities are more accessible since one single actor or a small number of actors have at least some control over how wages will develop. The Western European countries in this book have wage bargaining systems that are sufficiently coordinated for governments to possess the capacity to influence wage bargaining behaviour. There is therefore an incentive for governments to use centralized wage bargaining structures in order to exert a higher degree of control over wages.

Secondly, the economic costs of high unemployment have political implications. The post-war consensus in Western societies entailed the notion that governments are held responsible for the employment performance of their economies. Governments can only turn a blind eye to the performance of wage bargaining institutions if they reject their responsibility for employment performance. In the Western European context, the economic performance of a government is, however, still judged on its employment record. If governments see their involvement with the social partners on wage bargaining as a potentially useful tool to ease the friction between a tight monetary context and employment performance, they still have an incentive to bargain over wages.

Thirdly, the interaction between governments and the social partners is based not only on the institutions that govern the labour market, but also on the political linkages that tie trade unions to political parties. The choice of governments to push for further labour market deregulation in order to make institutions more responsive to market pressures or to negotiate with social partners depends on the *political* relationship between parties and unions; in particular on the parallels between the structure of the party system and the trade union system. In general terms, in competitive majoritarian political systems, trade unions have less of a political rooting than in consensus-based political systems. In the former case, a decision in favour of deregulation might be easier, while in the latter negotiations might be unavoidable.

Hence, as a starting point, this book tries to integrate the reasoning in the political economy literature about the interaction between monetary policy and wage formation. It is assumed that incomes policies in the form of the involvement of governments in wage formation are still perceived as having the potential to make a positive contribution to a government's performance on employment. As long as the disciplinary force of monetary policy is not directly translated into the automatic adjustment of wages in a highly decentralized context, governments have the scope and the incentive to engage in wage bargaining procedures.

Since the developments in different European countries over the last two decades diverge, the book seeks explanations for differing outcomes. Given the fact that the explanatory model is based on the interaction of the role of monetary policy, wage bargaining institutions and the political costs of unemployment for governments, the variance in these factors is used to explain different government behaviour. It is argued that governments prefer to seek negotiations with trade unions on wages if the monetary regime does not have the credibility that it will punish excessive wage settlements, if the government is politically dependent on the social partners and if the wage bargaining institutions are not responsive.

Finally, it should be pointed out what this book does *not* try to do. It does not give an account of the role of the welfare state and fiscal policy in the interaction between governments and trade unions. The expansion of the welfare state has been an important tool for accommodating trade union wage demands; it has also increasingly sheltered unions from the pressure of the markets and thereby impacted on the wage-employment trade-off. Similarly, expansive fiscal policy has been employed by governments to improve their employment record and thereby to alter trade unions' wage bargaining behaviour. However, for the sake of clarity and brevity neither social policy nor fiscal policy has been addressed systematically here.[14]

The book also does not try to give a comprehensive account of the evolution of corporatism and social pacts in Western Europe. Its focus is much narrower, centred on the interests of the government when negotiating with trade unions over wages. Recent literature on social pacts generally has a wider focus across different policy fields.[15] At the core of my argument is not concertation *per se*, but the specific mechanism of interaction between governments and trade unions when it comes to wages and wage bargaining institutions in the context of EMU.[16]

Lastly, this book does not attempt to contribute to the broad literature on the impact of labour market institutions on economic and employment performance.[17] While I draw many insights and concepts from this literature, I only use it to put forward an argument that focuses on the relationship between governments and trade unions. To the extent that the impact of wage bargaining institutions is of importance for this relationship, they will be discussed and considered accordingly. The overall aim and focus is, however, of a different nature.

Methodological issues

In comparative research, the standard approach is to investigate the effects of institutions on economic or political performance that can be quantified on a metric scale. In this case, however, the focus of the studies is government behaviour, which cannot easily be translated into performance indicators. The aim of the book is therefore not to test the effects of the corporatist responses of governments to economic crises, but to explain their behaviour *per se*. The dependent variable is a behavioural variable of the interaction between governments and wage bargaining actors – in particular trade unions. This variable interacts with the institutional design of each case, and is therefore difficult to operationalize.

I try to tackle this problem in a number of ways. Although this is a book covering 13 countries, I have limited the number of cases so that substantial material about the countries could be used.[18] In particular, in chapter 7 I present empirical material on the interaction between wage bargaining institutions and government intervention. The narrative presentations on the country cases help to compensate for the limits of the quantitative analysis. The case studies not only illustrate the political processes that took place and that could only be hinted at in the preceding chapters, but they also underline the causal connections between the independent and dependent variables.

Secondly, the statistical tools I have used are basic in order not to take out too much information from crude variables (see below). Thirdly, I have also aimed to define the dependent variable in a narrow way. While governments and trade unions have negotiated over a number of issues including social policy and other economic policies, this book focuses exclusively on governments' policy towards wages.

The comparative method

This is a comparative study of 13 Western European states, namely the pre-2004 member states of the European Union, with the exception of Luxembourg and Greece. Both countries were left out for pragmatic reasons of data availability. The book attempts to build a bridge between quantitative studies that try to maximize the number of cases and the case study approach that empirically investigates fewer cases in a detailed manner. The design of the book aims to draw benefits from both approaches: it aims at including enough cases to make some basic statistical operations possible, while limiting the number of cases so that statistical relationships can be traced in selected illustrations.

The choice of cases was based on two contextual variables. Firstly, the focus on Western Europe allowed the study to build on a shared understanding of the role of labour in industrialized societies after World War II that was unique to Western Europe. In no other part of the world has organized labour been able to exert such a high degree of influence over public policy, with the exception of the smaller states of the former British Empire – New Zealand, Australia and Canada – where different economic circumstances have applied.[19] Secondly, Western European countries particularly were confronted with the challenges of European monetary integration, even though not all countries joined EMU. The EMS and preparation for EMU restricted government policy in particular ways. Compared to other OECD countries that had flexible exchange rates and autonomy over their fiscal policy, European governments were especially hard hit by the tightness of the economic policy framework they had chosen for themselves.

By holding EU membership constant, it was possible to choose similar cases with respect to post-war traditions and types of economic challenges. By including as many as 13 Western European member states, dissimilar EU members were compared as well. At the same time, the choice of countries and the treatment of the empirical material explicitly reflect the fact that the member countries of the EU are increasingly interdependent and cannot be seen as discrete cases.[20] Within the European economic context, some countries play dominant roles due to their economic and political power and thereby affect the room for makeover of other countries. These interdependencies are usually not taken into account systematically, especially not in pooled time-series analysis. In effect, the choice of countries reflects a combined approach of a similar country versus dissimilar country design.

Data and data analysis

The book is based on a large database comprising the historical statistics of the OECD, existing databases on political institutions and wage bargaining institutions, and my own measurements of the extent of government negotiations. Most data was collected for the period between 1970 and 1999 on an annual basis.

The data was employed, however, using rather simple statistical tools. In most cases, only bivariate scatterplots and correlations based on averaged data across decades were produced. In some cases, compared means tests and cross-tabulations were employed to take advantage of annual data points. The main reason for not employing more sophisticated methods of pooled time-series analysis concerned the crude nature of the dependent variable that did not allow for systematic testing in a more elaborate statistical way.[21] Government intervention in wage bargaining procedures is only a very loose proxy for the behaviour of governments towards wage bargaining actors, a behaviour that cannot reasonably be assumed to be based on a metric scale. A degree of government intervention is a rough relative measure, but not sufficiently differentiated to be sensibly employed in regression equations. Simple linear regression equations were only used in the wage equations found in Chapter 6.

The data was accompanied by material on the country cases. Case studies in the extensive literature on industrial relations and social pacts in individual countries were supplemented with newspaper articles and documents. Particular aspects of country studies were chosen selectively, mainly in order to illustrate specific mechanisms that have previously been identified with the data. Therefore, the aim of the case studies was not to arrive at a comprehensive understanding of each case, but to trace the process by which the independent variables identified in the statistical section relate to the dependent variable.

The plan of the book

Figure 1.1 summarizes the structure of the book. Chapter 2 – which is not found in the figure – addresses the theoretical issues as they are discussed in the current political economy literature. It explains from a theoretical point of view why government involvement can be explained as it faces the interaction of monetary policy and wage bargaining institutions. Chapter 3 introduces the measure of government intervention in wage bargaining as the political answer to accommodating trade union power. It establishes the dependent variable for the remainder of the book. Chapters 4 to 6 present the three contextual factors that can explain the variation in government behaviour during the 1980s and 1990s. Chapter 7 brings the issue of Chapter 6 forward by looking at the interaction between the responsiveness of wage bargaining institutions and government intervention. Finally, Chapter 8 summarizes the different themes that are laid out in the chapters and makes some tentative remarks about how the dynamic relationship between governments and wage bargaining institutions might move ahead under EMU.

Conclusion

In the preceding sections I have argued in favour of an alternative approach to the classic corporatist theory that is entirely based on the organization of the labour market. The theoretical shift is motivated by the necessity to move from a linear view of corporatism, which interprets institutional efficiency as a product of the centralization of the organizational structures of interest associations, to an interactive approach, which includes processes of adjustment to a new economic and political environment, institutional mismatches and feedback processes. A linear assumption about the effects of the organization of the labour market on economic performance and political behaviour has left us too often with rather crude reasons for the expected decline in corporatist decision-making under the influence of internationalization and harsher economic constraints. Moreover, it cannot account for new forms of corporatist policy-making where organizational structures of the associations do not support such behaviour.

When setting out to study the relationship between governments and trade unions in Western European countries, we must begin by establishing the theoretical assumptions that prompt governments to engage in regulation of the labour market rather than leave it to market forces. Governments do not wish to intervene in wage bargaining in order to increase their political power or expand their policy fields. In general, governments in market economies do not see the formation of wages as a public policy issue. Rather, governments engage in wage bargaining because the present organization of the labour market produces outcomes that do not respond to the economic situation or to their economic policy. But they choose to intervene in rather than deregulate labour markets because they either need or want to protect the existing trade union organizations and institutions that regulate the labour market. Corporatist policy responses are part of the political compromise of including organized labour in the political systems of Western democracies. This basic political commitment in favour of strong wage bargaining organizations has become enshrined and institutionalized in a whole range of social and labour market institutions that are not easily dismantled or changed.

Beyond the political commitment by governments towards organized labour and the institutional forms this has taken, the responsiveness of wage bargaining institutions to changing economic conditions plays a central role in the analysis. The responsiveness of wage bargaining institutions is, however, shaped by a number of factors that mediate the effects of the centralization of wage bargaining institutions. Therefore I argue that the centralization of wage bargaining institutions as such is not a sufficient factor to explain the changing behaviour of governments towards wage bargaining.

The approach taken in this book consequently does not negate the importance of institutional design. The degree of efficiency of institutions has an important impact on the behaviour of political actors towards them. The failure of institutions to deliver the outcomes political actors need influences the attitude of those actors towards the institutions. Actors in turn intervene in the workings of these institutions and thereby influence the institutions themselves. Institutions are not seen as coherent and closed systems of rules and norms. Rather, they are open for external influences and adjustment to apparent mismatches. Institutional settings can produce outcomes that are satisfactory for all actors involved and thus create a situation of equilibrium. These periods of equilibrium, however, are short and frequently disturbed by external events and the subsequent reorientation of actors. There is a continuous process of adjustment and recalibrating of actors' interests and interaction that is at the heart of wage setting and labour market regulation in general.

Figure 1.1 **The structure of the argument**

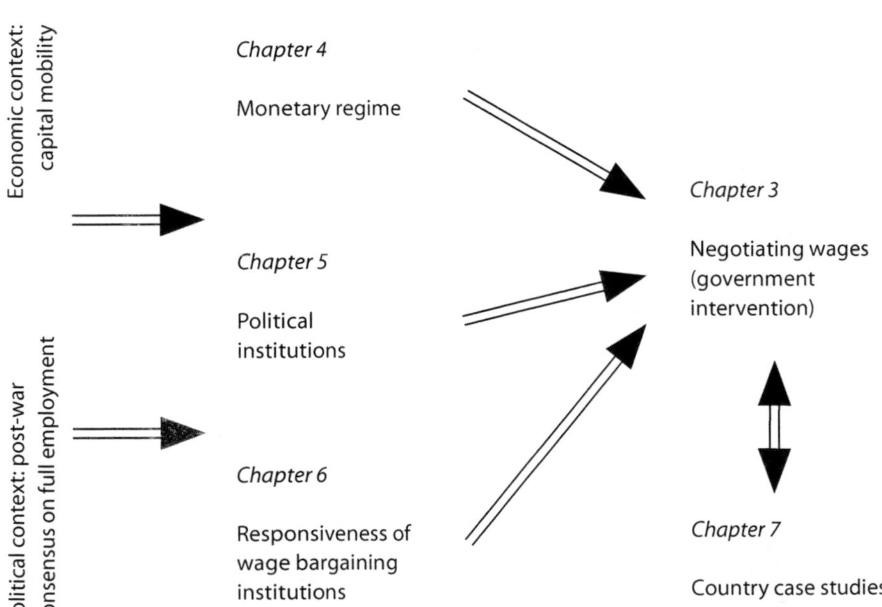

2 Governments and Wages – A Theoretical Framework

Economically speaking, it is not obvious why governments have started to use intervention into wage formation processes as a tool in economic policy-making. In the neo-classical world of economic policy, monetary and fiscal policies are the two main instruments a government can and should employ in order to strengthen economic stabilization during the business cycle. Wages and, in particular, the assumptions about the rigidity of wages have been important factors when assessing the potential of fiscal and monetary policies respectively. The Keynesian revolution in economic thought held out the prospect of full employment secured through the creation of aggregate demand by public authorities, rather than through reduction of costs by private enterprises under the pressure of competition. The Keynesian scenario was based on the assumption that nominal wages were rigid and could not easily be adjusted to economic imbalances. But even under Keynesian assumptions, the classic instruments of governments were traditionally confined to monetary and fiscal policy. Moreover, monetary and fiscal policies were legitimate policy fields over which governments had complete control.[22] Wage bargaining was either in the realm of independent associations or left to the market. Nevertheless, in practice, governments since World War II have employed policies on wages as an important tool in economic policy.

This chapter lays out a theoretical explanation for this apparent contradiction. The argument centres on the following assumption, which is the main guiding hypothesis on which this book is based: the incentive for government intervention into wage bargaining arises when it appeared to the government that intervention could potentially reduce the political and economic costs of a perceived necessary disinflationary policy. Thus governments have tried to avoid the negative consequences of the interaction of a non-accommodating monetary policy and non-responsive wage bargaining institutions, which can potentially carry high costs in terms of unemployment, loss of real output and interference with growth. A more effective disinflationary policy – as pursued by governments – has aimed at clearly indicating to wage bargaining actors that harmful effects of excessive wage increases will be punished.

The chapter is divided into four sections. The first section traces the history of the relationship between government economic policy and wages, and concludes that, in terms of previous experiences and economic theory, there is little or no reason for governments to intervene in wage bargaining. Section two develops a general hypothesis about the incentives for governments to employ incomes policies, based on established arguments in the political economy literature about the relationship between wage bargaining institutions and monetary policies. This includes a comparison of incomes policies pursued in the 1960s and 1970s with those more recently pursued by governments under monetarist conditions. The third section lays out the factors that influence the government's decision whether or not to negotiate with trade unions, focusing on monetary regimes, political institutions and the responsiveness of wage bargaining institutions. Several conclusions are outlined in the fourth and final section.

Policies on wages

Before World War II, governments generally had no policy on wages. The liberal world economic order of the 19th century was based on the flexibility of wages and prices. The role of the government was to protect the market mechanisms that could ensure flexible adjustment of labour markets to the requirements of the gold standard (Simmons 1994). Wage and price freezes that were decreed by governments were only used in very specific situations such as during the war economy. It was only in the 1950s that governments started to play an increasingly influential role in wage bargaining. A crucial reason was that the economic, social and political landscape had changed so fundamentally in many advanced countries that a tolerable degree of price stability could not be achieved by reducing demand, since the potential costs of demand reduction in terms of unemployment, loss of real output and growth had grown to a level that would not have been supported by the electorate and the public as a whole.

Economically, the European post-war economies did not resemble the inter-war situation. In the first decade after the war, wage growth was moderate and capital stocks were built up. After demobilization and recovery, "the main difficulty of the post-war economies was not slack demand, relative overproduction or insufficient investment, but an ungovernable tendency of demand to outrun the economy's capacity to meet it without inflation and price rises" (Postan 1967, 17). Rather than stimulating demand further, governments soon faced the task of reducing inflationary pressure.

Socially and politically, the fundaments of economic policy had changed drastically. During World War II, economic mobilization and the governance of the war economy required the collaboration of trade union leaders, who in many countries came to be co-opted into positions of quasi-public authority. Soldiers were promised a better life in a fairer society upon their return from the battlefields. In many countries, the traditional elite were replaced in the aftermath of war by liberal or socialist governments. The democratic capitalism of the golden age after World War II entailed the legal recognition of trade unions, an increase in welfare provisions and a promise of economic policy-making in favour of the working people. Full employment had become the priority for all governments (Streeck and Hassel 2003).

The relationship between unemployment and inflation became one of the core policy issues in economic policy-making, and wage bargaining processes were the most important factor influencing this relationship. Western governments in the post-war period faced a situation that was perceived as a trilemma of domestic objectives, of full employment, price stability and free collective bargaining, in which any pair could be achieved only by sacrificing the third goal. The trade-off between employment and price stability – the Phillips curve – thus depended on the conduct of collective bargaining. Accordingly, high employment levels could be achieved by governments letting money supply grow, stimulating demand and consequently allowing prices to rise. Under the given institutional design of a regulated labour market and free collective bargaining, a decrease in unemployment would lead to an increase in inflationary pressure (Ulman and Flanagan 1971: 2-4; Flanagan, Soskice *et al.* 1983). Policy-makers came to believe that price stability could only be achieved at the unacceptable price of increasing unemployment. The obvious solution to the trilemma was the active involvement of governments in the wage formation process. Governments thought they could protect employment by securing a moderation of real wages through voluntary wage restraint instead of through disinflation. As Braun observed: "An incomes policy is often presented as a means of improving the trade-off between unemployment and price stability" (Braun 1975: 2).

The rationale of incomes policies

Incomes policies were initially pursued in combination with expansionist demand management. Expansionist demand management combined with simultaneous wage restraint, it was believed, would prevent real wages from rising, stimulate an increase in employment and protect profitability and competitiveness from declining. This is the Scandinavian scenario as described in the Lange and Garrett article on the 'Politics of Growth' (Lange and Garrett 1985). Working in cooperation, the social-democratic government and the centralized trade unions used a combination of wage restraint and fiscal expansion in order to promote economic growth.

During the first two decades after the war, governments regularly employed incomes policies in almost all advanced economies in order to deal with increasing inflationary pressures of the time. Incomes policies were used to urge trade union leadership to assume a more moderate attitude towards wage bargaining. When wage bargaining systems were not sufficiently centralized or coordinated to take into account the effects of their wage settlements, governments tried to compensate for this defect by striving to influence wage bargaining behaviour through either giving tax incentives for wage restraint or imposing wage freezes. Assuming a Phillips curve type of trade-off between price stability and unemployment, governments hoped to steer the curve in favour of employment by maintaining price stability. If governments had to choose, most observers were convinced that they would prefer inflation above unemployment: "Clearly, no Member country would be willing to accept high levels of unemployment in order to hold its prices in check", the OECD pointed out in a report on the problem in 1962 (OECD 1962, 25).

Under these conditions, the use of restrictive monetary policies for stabilizing prices was not only seen as politically unacceptable, but also, for a number of reasons, practically impossible. Monetary policy had not helped to avoid the Depression in the 1930s; and as a result its reputation was severely under attack. The result was that governments had no disciplinary device *vis-à-vis* trade unions when negotiating over wages, but instead relied completely on the use of persuasion and the possibility of a statutory imposition of wage settlements and price freezes.

At the same time, the statutory imposition of wages and prices was much harder for governments to pursue since these policies lacked political legitimacy. First of all, trade unions had fought hard for the right to free collective bargaining and were not prepared to surrender this right to government-imposed incomes policies. But even in practical terms, a statutory incomes policy immediately raised the question of distributive equality in societies and was politically contested. As Shonfield points out when observing the debate on incomes policies during the 1960s:

> There was a curious unrealism about the fervent expectations which suddenly came to be attached to the pursuit of an incomes policy in a variety of Western countries during the 1960s. It was talked of by practical hard-headed men as if it offered an immediate short cut to an ideal economic world of steady price and uninterrupted growth. It was alleged by some to be the precondition for effective economic planning (Shonfield 1965: 217).

Indeed, there was a certain enthusiasm for incomes policy as the new economic policy device. In the United States, the newly elected President Kennedy issued his 'guideposts for non-inflationary wage and price behaviour' in order to pre-empt inflationary pressure in the course of expansionary fiscal and monetary policies that the Kennedy government had planned. The newly-founded OECD published a whole range of largely favourable reports on the conduct of incomes policy in its member countries during the 1960s (OECD 1962, Suppanz and Robinson 1972; De Wolff 1965). In contrast to the war-time direct wage controls, incomes policy was defined here thus: that "the authorities should have a view about the kind of evolution of incomes which is consistent with their economic objectives, and in particular with prices stability; that they should seek to promote public agreement on the principles which should guide the growth of incomes; and that they should try to induce people voluntarily to follow this guidance."

The OECD discovered that "in this broad sense, it appears that many Member countries are trying to evolve incomes policy" (OECD 1962, 23). In general, it was hoped that wage increases in line with productivity increases would enable non-inflationary economic growth and could potentially avoid major exchange rate adjustments between countries. Economists were working on a tax-based incomes policy that aimed at introducing an economic base for the concept.[23]

According to Shonfield, the lack of realism on the part of policy-makers stemmed from the misguided assumption that union leaders would perceive the division of wealth as basically fair. One only had to agree on the way in which the annual increment of national production was to be distributed (Shonfield 1965: 217). This was based on the belief that economic growth could be taken for granted and that a highly competitive economy existed where one had to treat capital well: "Labour is really asked to give its consent to a particular type of social order. There is no reason why it should do so – or for that matter why the owners of capital should positively assent to any alternative proposed. All this is another way of saying that a practical approach to a more rational wages policy must be deliberative and extensively political. It seems unlikely that people in a democratic society will accept a policy of wage restraint unless the composition of all other domestic incomes which affect costs, however remotely, is brought under close and expert scrutiny" (Shonfield 1965: 218-9).

The failure of incomes policy in the late 1960s and early 1970s was due to a range of factors that were not all linked to the political problems that were raised by Shonfield in the mid-1960s.[24] International price levels had started to rise from mid-1968 onwards. The US economy had induced a growing demand for imported manufactures and incurred large budget deficits. This coincided with an increase in raw material prices. Moreover, most economies operated under full employment from the mid-1960s onwards and labour markets were tight. Thirdly, the conduct of collective bargaining in many countries had instituted an expectation that workers would be protected against real wage losses. An increase in price rises was automatically translated into wage rises despite the tradition of incomes policy. And fourthly, the labour protests of 1968 had consisted of unrest on the shop floor against centralized wage bargaining and had shifted the bargaining power from the central level to the local level. In many cases, national union officials were not able to implement the agreements they had settled at a national level. The years between the late 1960s and early 1970s were "an exceptionally unpropitious period for incomes policy" (Braun 1975: 14; see also Soskice 1978).

In other words, the first generation of incomes policies had helped to increase the profitability and competitiveness of companies, but it had not helped to lower the real wage expectations of the workforce. On the contrary, real wage protection was the basis on which incomes policy in many countries rested and real wage expectations were high due to full employment and increasing levels of social spending.

The shift in economic policy-making

It was only after the first oil shock in 1973 that governments started to seriously use disinflationary policies against the imminent stagflation of the 1970s, combined with a new generation of incomes policies. The context of government intervention had thus changed. Under the condition of restrictive monetary policies, governments can always leave the effects of wage bargaining on employment to the market and rely on monetary authorities to achieve low inflation expectations. Rather than being dependent on trade union support in wage bargaining, governments regained monetary policy as an instrument if wages got out of control. On the other hand, monetarist adjustment could potentially carry high costs in terms of employment if trade unions were not responsive to monetarist policies. Restrictive monetary policies combined with aggressive wage bargaining could lead to exceptionally high increases in unemployment. Rising unemployment would eventually discipline trade union wage demands, but it was worth avoiding.

The 1977 McCracken report produced by the OECD already recognized this change of discourse on the responsibility of governments for securing both real wages and employment (OECD 1977). When assessing the role of incomes policy, the report states that it supports the idea that governments should regularly discuss the general evolution of prices and wages with trade unions and employers. It suggests that if governments are going to take this line, they must at the same time be prepared to indicate to those responsible for wage and price determination what kind of behaviour on their part would be consistent with the monetary and fiscal policies they intend to follow. The report then states:

> This idea is not new. What is new is the context within such discussions takes place after a major inflationary recession. Five years ago, it was understandable that representatives of business and labour might take it for granted that governments had it in their power to ensure high levels of sales and employment. They may well have felt that the warnings against the dire consequences of irresponsible behaviour on their part need not be taken seriously. All this has now changed (OECD 1977, 215).[25]

In other words, during the incomes policy of the 1960s, governments faced two distinct issues. On the one hand, they openly had to adopt a policy position on distributive issues when engaging in incomes policy since this tended to take the form of strict wage guidelines and was discussed in a political forum. At the same time, governments had no disciplinary device *vis-à-vis* trade unions that would indicate to the unions the consequences of a failure of incomes policy. Moreover, when incomes policies failed, governments were nevertheless held responsible for ensuring high levels of employment via expansionist economic policies.

After the first oil shock, this situation changed. The effects of the recession and the vulnerability of the world economy had become apparent to all economic and political actors. Financial liberalization had reduced the effectiveness of monetary expansion and started to penalize high inflation. Although the use of restrictive monetary policy varied widely within the OECD between the mid-1970s and the late 1980s, a trend was set in motion that would eventually spread. The new incomes policy that had started to operate from the 1980s onwards would ease the way for introducing tight monetary policy, rather than serve as a means to avoid it, while at the same time it would be based on a new understanding of economic policy.

In addition to the changing economic environment, the new understanding of economic policy had been theoretically and argumentatively prepared by a shift in macroeconomic theory. Rational expectations were introduced into economic modelling. The theory recognized that people's expectations are highly responsive to policy and hence that expectations matter for assessing the impact of monetary and fiscal policy. In two major contributions, Friedman (1968) and Phelps (1967) explained how a sloping short-term Phillips curve would transmute, once expectations begin to adjust, into a vertical (or even backwards-bending) Phillips curve. The vertical Phillips curve showed that there could be any level of inflation at a given (natural) level of unemployment. If governments wanted to lower unemployment, they had to raise money wages above the rate of real wage expectation:

> There is always a temporary trade-off between inflation and unemployment; there is no permanent trade-off. The temporary trade-off comes not from inflation *per se*, but from unanticipated inflation, which generally means from a rising rate of inflation. The widespread belief that there is a permanent trade-off is a sophisticated version of the confusion between 'high' and 'rising' that we all recognize in simpler forms. A rising rate of inflation may reduce unemployment, a high rate will not. (Friedman 1968: 11)[26]

Therefore, rising inflation rates or surprise inflation might still create surplus employment, but a steady rate of rising prices would not. A vertical Phillips curve also implies that there is a natural rate of unemployment that cannot be reduced by means of an expansionary monetary and fiscal policy.

The policy implications of this newly accepted line of arguments have been particularly important for monetary policy. The role of monetary policies was downplayed in the first two decades after World War II mainly due to the dismissive assessment made by Keynes when addressing the role of monetary policy during the Great Depression. Monetary policy was seen as a largely ineffective tool of economic policy. Post-war monetary policies therefore focused on the provision of cheap money. A most telling illustration is the article by John Hicks, in which he argues that in the early post-war period the previous gold standard was replaced by a labour standard in which "monetary policy adjusts to the equilibrium level of money wages so as to make it conform to the actual level" rather than the other way round (Hicks 1955: 391).

In the mid-1970s, however, this view had reversed again. If there is no trade-off between unemployment and inflation, the best monetary policy for central banks to adopt is to pick an inflation target and to stick to it. If there are long-term negative effects on employment and growth, these were not due to monetary policies themselves, but to rigidities in the market. Monetary policies should aim to keep the growth of aggregate demand stable in order to prevent fluctuations. Using the arguments derived from the rational expectation revolution governments' approaches towards economic policy had thereby changed towards focusing on the effectiveness of disinflationary policies rather than on the need to control wages.

The effect of this change of assessment for the relative importance of economic policy by governments is a shift in emphasis. Since the mid-1970s, economic advice on the persisting problem of inflationary pressure has been that, rather than use incomes policies to dampen wage demands, governments should improve the effectiveness of monetary policy. If restrictive monetary policy is more effective, its negative externalities on the real economy might be reduced. The emphasis has been placed in the main on the credibility of the policy. It is thereby assumed that a disinflation policy will have lower short-run costs if the general policy of the monetary authority is effective.

At first glance, the rational expectation assumptions imply that an increased emphasis on monetary policy should reduce the role of wage bargaining institutions in general, as has also been argued by Fritz Scharpf (Scharpf 1991). If monetary policy can fight inflation effectively by disciplining wage bargaining actors through a reduction in demand, the role of wage bargaining institutions should become less important. It should also curb the inclination of governments to intervene in wage bargaining processes too. The question therefore arises as to why governments nevertheless intervene in wage formation processes, even when monetary policy shifts towards a more restrictive regime.

Monetary and wage bargaining regimes in the political economy literature

The answer to this question, and the basis of my assumption that governments aim to reduce the costs of disinflationary monetary policies by intervening in wage setting processes, derives from the interaction between wage bargaining institutions and monetary policy. This interaction is a well-established part of the political economy literature, and will be outlined below.[27]

Since the arguments of the literature are complex, I summarize the conclusion of the literature review upfront. The literature has so far concentrated on establishing the effects of wage bargaining institutions on economic performance and has established a negative impact of a mismatch of restrictive monetary policies and decentralized wage bargaining institutions on outcomes (in particular Iversen 1999; Hall and Franzese 1998; Adolph 2004). It argues that a disinflationary policy is more effective in countries that have somewhat coordinated wage bargaining institutions rather than decentralized bargaining systems.[28]

However, despite being driven by equilibrium assumptions, the literature has not taken into account that an institutional environment that is not responsive to restrictive monetary policy will give governments the incentive to increase the effectiveness of monetary policies and to adjust their bargaining institutions to their economic policy approach.[29]

If the main mechanism of disinflationary policies is the enforcement of the effectiveness of a restrictive monetary regime – as has been emphasized in the macroeconomic literature – it makes sense for a government to foster the effectiveness of their monetary regimes by making their wage bargaining institutions more receptive to the change in the monetary regime. Government intervention is therefore an adjustment policy adopted by governments in order to promote the responsiveness of wage bargaining institutions towards monetary regimes. In the following sections, I will lay out this argument step by step, starting with the assumptions of the effect of monetary regimes and moving to the institutional foundations of wage bargaining.

Monetary regimes and central banks

According to the assumptions of rational expectation, the most important tool of achieving an effective monetary policy is the credibility of monetary agencies.[30] If the monetary agency can credibly commit to a restrictive monetary policy, the expectation of economic actors with regard to inflation will be low. If the expectation of inflation is low among economic agents, there is little need to push up wages. It is only under the condition of insecurity about the inflation target of the government that economic actors have an incentive to increase wages and, with them, prices, and thereby reinforce inflationary pressures.

To clarify, it was argued that uncertainty about the conduct of monetary policy tends to provide wage bargaining actors with the incentive to anticipate safeguards for higher inflation and thereby provide higher wage settlements than necessary. If wage earners cannot be sure about the level of inflation due to an erratic monetary policy, their interest will likely err on the side of higher settlements. If they can, however, be assured by monetary authorities that prices will remain stable, their fear about losses in real wages and real returns will be reduced and they can settle for lower increases than they would otherwise have done.

Credibility can be achieved in a number of ways. One way is to announce a clear monetary policy with regard to the money supply. Since the money supply is seen as the single most important factor that determines inflation, a rule-based monetary policy centred on the money supply can reinforce the expectations of low inflation. Governments that publicly adhere to a certain policy rule on restrictive monetary policy and are prepared to implement the rule should be able to lower inflation without creating adverse effects on the economy.

The second – and in the literature seen as the most promising – way of achieving a higher degree of credibility for monetary policy is the independence of central banks.[31] The argument is that, in a political environment, politicians have an incentive to produce surprise inflation in order to boost employment for short-term electoral reasons. Because wage bargaining actors know about the electoral pressures and the electoral gains of surprise expansionary policies in the political business cycle, they will nevertheless push for higher wage settlements in order to guard against higher inflation. When governments can institutionalize an anti-inflationary monetary decision rule by delegating the policy-making power to an independent agency, they can automatically increase the credibility of their policy and have an anti-inflationary effect without any costs. As Grilli *et al.* pointed out: "...having an independent central bank is almost like having a free lunch; there are benefits but no apparent costs in terms of macroeconomic performance" (quoted in Iversen 1999: 21).

A third way of increasing the credibility of monetary policy is by pegging the currency to a non-inflationary anchor currency (Iversen and Thygesen 1998). If a currency is pegged and capital mobility is high, the monetary authority – whether independent or not – has to follow the policy of the authority of the non-inflationary currency in order to keep the pressure from the exchange rate. If a devaluation of the currency is ruled out, the monetary policy of the country that pegged its currency automatically increases its credibility *vis-à-vis* domestic economic actors.

In whatever way the credibility of the monetary policy is enhanced, the degree of credibility of a monetary regime is nonetheless always based on passing on information and influencing other people's expectations. The credibility of a policy needs to be assured by making it understood to the relevant actors. As Hall and Franzese point out:

> If credible signals are sent from the bank, and the relevant economic actors are able to coordinate their behavior in the light of them, nominal wage-price settlements will be lower than they would otherwise be, and the bank can pursue the monetary policy it has announced without dampening the economy. On the other hand, if these signals do not inspire appropriate wage-price behavior, either because they lack credibility or because the relevant actors cannot coordinate on appropriate behavior, the monetary policy announced by the bank will occur in a context of relatively excessive nominal wages and prices, thereby dampening the economy and generating unemployment (Hall and Franzese 1998: 507).

Putting the emphasis on the credibility of monetary policy in order to dampen wage expectations therefore raises the question of the mechanism that ensures that the policy is understood and taken into account by economic actors. The effects of monetary policy thus depend on the presence of an institutional arrangement that provides actors with a basis for making a credible commitment and for monitoring each other's behaviour (Hall and Franzese 1998: 508). In the political economy literature, this transmission belt of the credibility of a central bank has been the wage bargaining system – the main forum where wages are set in most advanced economies.

Wage bargaining institutions as the transmission belt of credible monetary policies

A substantial literature has argued that the organization of the labour market and, in particular, the wage bargaining institutions have an effect on wage bargaining behaviour and thus on economic performance.[32] Put very generally, specific properties of wage bargaining institutions provide incentives for wage bargaining actors to consider the effects of their wage settlements. The most important property of the bargaining system is the degree of centralization of decision-making on wage demands of trade unions. In decentralized settings, local bargaining units do not have to take into account the externalities of their behaviour for others. If a small bargaining unit negotiates over a wage agreement, it only considers the interests of its own members and ignores the effects of the resulting price increase on other groups of workers. Other externalities can be the loss of employment and the consequences following from this (Flanagan 1999).

In contrast, where centralization is high, the leadership of a trade union has to make sure that the effect of a wage agreement is not harmful to its membership; it internalizes negative externalities. The most important effect of centralization is therefore the moderation of wage demands. The leadership of trade unions in centralized settings is careful not to drive wage demands too high since this might affect the employment of other groups of workers. Therefore, they tend not to employ their full bargaining potential and thereby to have a comparatively positive effect on performance.[33] This argument assumes a linear negative relationship between the centralization of bargaining and the level of unemployment and real wages. More centralized collective bargaining systems produce lower unemployment rates, *ceteris paribus.* A similar effect can be achieved when labour market institutions are completely decentralized and wage bargaining units operate under conditions of perfect competition. The result is a hump-shaped relationship with highly decentralized and highly centralized wage bargaining institutions having the best results (Calmfors and Driffil 1988).

When it comes to the interaction of wage bargaining institutions and credible monetary policies, the situation is as follows. For wage bargaining actors it is important how the policy of the central bank affects the perceived costs of wage increases. It is only in centralized wage bargaining systems that the union leadership contemplates the trade-off between real wages and unemployment. In decentralized wage bargaining institutions, the union will not react to monetary policy for three main reasons (Hall and Franzese 1998). First, in decentralized bargaining situations, local unions aim at protecting themselves from real wage losses by seeking inflation increments on top of the real wage they desire, because they cannot anticipate the outcomes of other wage settlements. Second, in decentralized settings bargaining units do not take into account the effects of their settlements on other bargaining units. Third, none of the decentralized bargaining units will be held responsible for disinflationary policies by the monetary authorities if their settlements turn out to be inflationary.

In centralized bargaining arrangements, however, the trade union leadership will assume a trade-off of unemployment against real wages. The policy of the central bank becomes important because it can affect the trade-off and act as a deterrent to high wage increases (Calmfors 2001: 333). If the unions anticipate that wage increases which threaten the central bank's goal of price stability will trigger a more restrictive monetary policy, and therefore negatively affect employment too, they will have an extra incentive to restrain wages that they would not have had otherwise. Centralized trade unions and bargaining institutions should therefore be particularly responsive to the monetary policy regime.

When unions are very centralized however, this effect should decline, because highly centralized wage bargaining institutions have to internalize other negative externalities and an anticipated monetary policy reaction might not make much of a difference (Calmfors 2001: 334; Corricelli, Cukierman *et al.* 2000). Therefore, the strongest effect of interaction between monetary policy and wage bargaining institution's should take place when bargaining is centralized at an intermediate level.

Empirical studies support these assumptions. Hall and Franzese (1998) found that higher central bank independence increases the level of unemployment when wage bargaining is decentralized. Cukierman and Lippi (1999) found that higher central bank independence reduces unemployment with intermediate centralization, but increases it with decentralization. This effect, however, decreases at higher levels of centralization. Bernhard Kittel (2000) reports that labour cost increases are inversely related to monetary restrictiveness, but positively related to higher levels of centralization of wage bargaining and union density. Iversen (1998 and 1999) and Traxler, Blaschke *et al.* (2001) report a positive impact of an intermediate level of centralization when it interacts with restrictive monetary policy.[34] Since the number of observations of different combinations of wage bargaining institutions and monetary policy is very small, the interaction effect, however, is not really robust (Calmfors 2001: 334).

In any case, the theoretical and empirical political economy literature gives some reason to believe that the effectiveness of monetary policy indeed depends on the institutional arrangements of wage bargaining. Restrictive monetary policy is no free lunch, as some economists have claimed it to be, but is contingent on institutional preconditions. Different institutions react differently to a change towards tighter monetary policy. The link between monetary policy and wage bargaining is the sharing and passing on of information about the credibility of tight monetary policies. It is only in coordinated or centralized wage bargaining systems that bargaining actors are receptive to this information and will, moreover, take it into account when engaging in wage bargaining.

The rationale for government intervention in wage bargaining and incomes policy under restrictive monetary regimes

If the conduct of wage bargaining can make a contribution to the process of lowering inflationary pressures and pre-empting restrictive monetary policies on its own, then the government may try to influence the bargaining behaviour of trade unions.[35] By reducing the wage claims of trade unions, governments can use incomes policies in order to achieve a trade-off between higher employment and lower real wages. Incomes policies that focus on the effect of employment are therefore not immediately distinguishable from other institutional effects of wage bargaining systems such as centralization of bargaining.

If wage bargaining institutions are relevant for conveying the credibility of monetary authorities and the likely impact of a tight monetary response to wage bargaining actors, the same argument can be made for the role of the government in wage negotiations. If high levels of credibility of monetary restrictiveness work best where bargaining actors are responsive towards the effects of their wage settlement on economic performance, governments still have an incentive to influence trade unions towards voluntary wage restraint. Therefore, even without the assumptions of the Phillips curve, governments face the dilemma between the negative effects of disinflationary policies on employment, on the one hand, and the wage expectations of workers, on the other. If wage bargaining institutions cannot adjust the wage expectations of workers to the economic situation, but trade unions and employers are nevertheless important bargaining actors on the labour market, governments might be tempted to increase the effectiveness of their disinflationary policies and ease the frictions between the expectations of workers and the economic reality by negotiating with the social partners directly.

Moreover, the shift of attention towards the credibility of monetary policies as the main policy tool for ensuring low inflation might lead to particularly restrictive monetary policies, especially during the period of transition from an accommodating monetary regime to a tighter one. Since the main mechanism for ensuring low inflation is the expectation of ordinary people that the monetary authority will guarantee low inflation no matter what, monetary authorities have an incentive to prioritize price stability above all else, even if they are officially committed towards economic growth and employment as well. The importance of the credibility of monetary authorities has only been recognized in the literature and in policy-making in the last two decades. In many countries, central banks have only recently gained a higher level of independence from governments. In those countries in particular, there needs to be a conscious process of redirecting the expectations of wage bargaining units towards a new policy framework.

But the capacity of governments to negotiate with trade unions over wages also varies, depending on the organization of the labour market. In very decentralized wage bargaining systems, the capability of governments to meaningfully influence wage bargaining behaviour is restricted. Local bargaining units might not be impressed by the government's efforts and may not be able to overcome their local competition. Governments might choose to further deregulate the labour market rather than seek interventionist solutions. In highly centralized bargaining arrangements, bargaining units might be sufficiently responsive to changes in the economic environment anyway. Therefore, governments are most likely to intervene in the wage bargaining process where bargaining units are sufficiently organized but not highly centralized.

The argument here – in line with arguments that have been made about the importance of wage bargaining institutions under credible conservative monetary authorities by Streeck (1994), Hall and Franzese (1998), Iversen (1999) and Traxler, Blaschke *et al.* (2001) – is therefore that the credibility of monetary policies needs *institutional mechanisms* to convey collective expectations to wage bargaining units. Centralized wage bargaining institutions can be the conveyors that internalize the effects of a credible conservative monetary institution and thereby dampen the negative real effects of disinflation. Another mechanism can be the intervention by governments to persuade wage bargaining actors to settle for lower wage claims, in order to pre-empt these expected negative effects. In this way government intervention can try to avoid the potential negative impact of disinflationary policies on the real economy by closing the gap between the wage expectations of workers and the expected restrictive monetary policies of the monetary authorities.

A summary of the argument is given in figure 2.1. Rather than let credible monetary policies take effect by themselves, governments have an incentive to use restrictive monetary policies and interventionist wage policies in tandem if wage bargaining institutions are not in themselves sufficiently responsive. Credible monetary policies ensure low inflation; negotiating wage restraint can help to smooth the negative effects of otherwise harsh disinflationary measures.

The credibility of the government: from political exchange to imposing a new policy paradigm[36]

In the neo-corporatist literature, the political relationship between trade unions and governments has been predominantly described by the notion of political exchange (Pizzorno 1978). While governments had to respect free collective bargaining, union compliance with the need of national economic policy was a matter of political exchange (Streeck and Ken-

Figure 2.1 Negotiated wage restraint: policies of government intervention

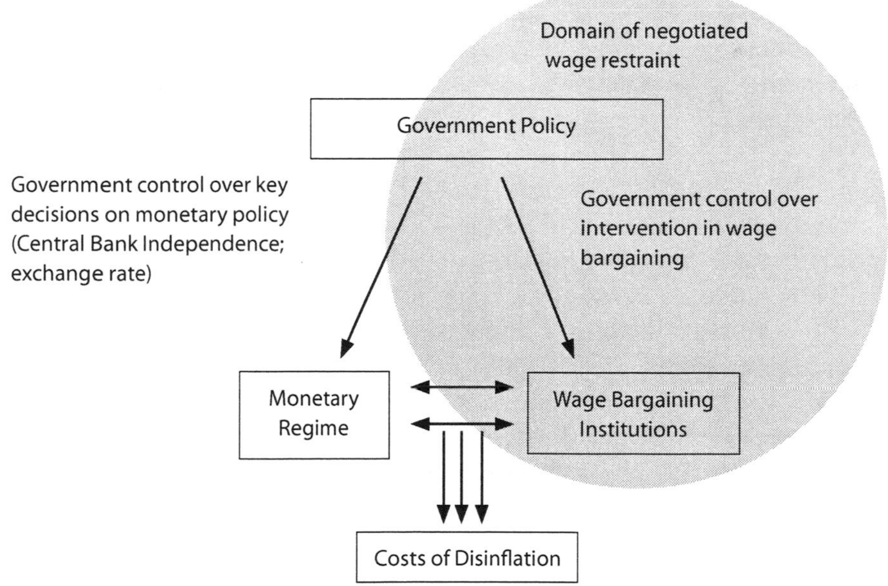

worthy 2005: 9). Political exchanges were based on the conversion of industrial into political power, which trade unions could trade for a wide variety of concessions from governments, such as industrial, regional and educational policy programmes, thus wielding extensive power over public policy (Headey 1970; Lehmbruch 1984; Schmitter 1977). The concept assumed the existence of centralized unions that command strong bargaining power. It assumed economic situations where the outcomes of collective bargaining are decisive for macroeconomic performance, especially with respect to monetary stability and employment, and where the political survival of the government depends on such performance (Streeck and Hassel 2003).

The onset of tight monetary policy has changed the nature of the exchange between the government and trade unions on incomes policy. In contrast to the assumptions of the Keynesian version of incomes policy, there is no master plan with which governments intend to tackle the crisis, but an incremental adjustment to external constraints. Furthermore, governments have a deliberate choice between negotiating an incomes policy or letting a conservative (or non-accommodating or restrictive) monetarist policy take its course in order to reduce wage pressures. During the exchanges of the 1970s, for instance, monetary policy was an underdeveloped tool. Finally, trade unions are in principle aware of the fact that the room for real wage increases is tightly constrained by hard currency policies.

Government intervention in the context of tight monetary policy is not based on an economic policy in which the pay-offs are clearly defined. During the 1970s, left-wing governments committed themselves to high spending in order to maintain employment levels if trade unions exerted wage restraint. In that context, government intervention in wage setting went hand in hand with higher public expenditure as a result of a political exchange (Lange and Garrett 1985). This strategy was not only seen as viable but also regarded by some observers as superior in terms of economic growth (Cameron 1984; Lange and Garrett 1985).

However, fiscal expansion has become equally constrained as monetary accommodation. Open economies, rising levels of public debt and rising costs of public debts due to high interest rates have restricted the ability of governments to offer fiscal expansion in exchange for wage restraint. Since the turnaround in economic policy by the French government in 1983, public-spending commitments have been discredited as economic policy and there has been no 'labour-friendly' demand strategy presented for resolving the crisis.

Also, since the early 1980s, all governments have understood the monetarist alternative for controlling wage pressure. Rather than being dependent on union approaches in wage bargaining, governments can turn to other instruments if wages get out of control. Conversely, monetarist adjustment without the cooperation of trade unions can potentially carry high costs in terms of employment if trade unions are not responsive to monetarist policies (Scharpf 1991). Restrictive monetary policies combined with aggressive wage bargaining can lead to exceptionally high increases in unemployment, as can be seen in the case of the United Kingdom in the early 1980s. In most countries, high and/or rising unemployment is not only politically unpopular, but also fiscally expensive.

While governments have a choice on how to approach wage bargaining, trade unions face the fact that the pressures will increase either way. Trade unions can either commit themselves to voluntary restraint or they will have to face the consequence of higher employment losses if they do not. Since there is no longer a Keynesian scenario in which inflationary wage pressures can be accommodated by monetary policy, the scope for wage increases has diminished. Higher employment losses will eventually drive wage increases down. If unions opt for a negotiated incomes policy, they can try to bargain over a price for wage restraint.

From the trade unions' perspective, the crucial question remains the extent to which the government or the central bank will actually punish the wage bargainers for wage agreements that they see as excessive. If the government has a very clear line on tight monetary and fiscal policy, trade unions have to expect an impact of wage bargaining on employment via tighter monetary policy. If, however, welfare provisions in the form of unemployment programmes and early retirement schemes take care of the unemployed, the impact is likely to be less severe. Trade union vulnerability to the effects of high wage settlements therefore depends on both a tight macroeconomic policy and the provision of welfare.

The politics of new incomes policy under tight monetary control therefore hinge on the resolve of the government to display its commitment to a non-accommodating policy rather than on the willingness of the government to compensate trade unions for wage restraint. In the past, not only had central banks accommodated inflationary wage settlements, but fiscal and social policies also took care of the negative effects of wage increases. Expansive fiscal policies counteracted the negative impact of tight monetary policy when employed for disinflation. Moreover, welfare programmes and employment schemes protected the trade unions and their members from the hardship of the market.

The disciplinary force that stems from a tight monetary policy *vis-à-vis* the trade unions is therefore contingent on the position of the government *vis-à-vis* other policy fields – independent from monetary policy itself. Wider government policies are therefore an important contextual factor for the effectiveness of monetary policy. If governments are willing to accommodate the negative effects of a tight monetary policy rather than pass them on to the labour market, trade unions will not be affected in their bargaining strategies. On the other hand, if governments are prepared to pass on the effects and do not accommodate further pressures by means of social policies, trade unions can be expected to adjust to the new situation more rapidly. Governments are expected to be more likely to intervene in wage bargaining when they cannot credibly make a commitment to a non-accommodating position. In other words, the more clearly the government can display its pursuit of a non-accommodating policy, the less likely it is to intervene in bargaining processes.

As in the case of the reputation of the central bank, it is argued here that the new politics of government intervention rest on the credibility of the government to convey a new policy paradigm to wage bargaining actors. The crucial issue is that strategic behaviour does not depend on the compensation that is offered in exchange for wage restraint, as is implied in the traditional notion of political exchanges. The strategic approach by the government concerns the limitation of the bargaining scope of the wage bargaining actors. Unlike the wage bargains under accommodating economic policies, incomes policy in the 1980s and 1990s did not offer a compensation for wage restraint in the form of a political exchange. Governments intervene in wage bargaining processes in order to change the rules of the game of the bargaining procedures themselves, by introducing the new economic framework. It is therefore expected that, in those political institutional contexts where the government cannot display its new commitment by itself, governments are more likely to intervene. The key explanatory variable for the politics of incomes policy under tight monetary conditions is therefore the ability of governments to display their own commitment to non-accommodation.

This does not mean that there is no compensation for trade unions when agreeing to voluntary wage restraint, but the compensation is not vital to the interaction between governments and trade unions. While governments might concede tax reforms, delays in social policy retrenchment or the installation of new committees on labour relations, the capacity for compensation does not determine the approach by the government *vis-à-vis* wage bargaining.

The implications of this line of argumentation are twofold. First, the new type of incomes policy should be expected to be less statutory and thereby avoid many of the problems of political legitimacy that Shonfield raised already in the mid-1960s and that manifested themselves in many countries in the strike waves of the late 1960s. Governments are concerned to ensure that the trade unions understand the externalities of their wage bargaining behaviour. Within the context of a tight monetary framework, governments will refrain from using intervention as an immediate tool to fight inflation as they did before. Inflation is fought by monetary policy, but if incomes policy can help the wage bargaining actor to adjust to the new framework, it can lower the transition costs with regard to employment. Being under less immediate pressure to achieve wage moderation for fighting inflation *per se*, governments can use their influence more indirectly.

Secondly, incomes policy should not be based on the support of the relationship between friendly governments and trade unions, but on a clearly defined division of labour in a framework of economic policy set by governments and of wage bargaining performed by the social partners. Wage bargaining institutions continue to mediate the effects of tight economic policy on the labour market; by intervening in wage formation procedures, governments aim to push wage bargainers into accepting responsibility for these effects and into internalizing government economic policy choice as a fixed parameter in wage bargaining procedures.

Explaining policy choices

Despite the shift in economic policy approaches after 1980, most governments in Western Europe did not abandon their attempts to influence decisions by wage bargaining actors, but continued to negotiate over wages. Yet in the period from 1980 to 1999, governments displayed varying degrees of activity when engaging in negotiations with trade unions and employers. Why did some countries actively pursue a new type of incomes policy, while others either rejected any cooperation with trade unions or kept it to a strict minimum? This section briefly outlines a set of factors that influenced the behaviour of governments. The factors are: the type of monetary regime; a country's political regime; and the responsiveness of wage bargaining institutions. A full theoretical explanation of these factors can be found in the relevant substantive Chapters 4 to 6.

The monetary regime and wage bargaining institutions are directly linked to the theoretical assumptions found in the political economy literature. Since the interaction between the monetary regime and wage bargaining institutions determines the effect on economic performance, both factors individually are also likely to influence the government's decision to negotiate on wages. The third factor refers to national political institutions and their effects on the propensity of government to negotiate over wages. As will become clear in the more detailed operationalization of the factors in subsequent chapters, the monetary regime and the political regime are characteristics of countries that are fixed in the short run and do not vary much over time. For the period of the 1980s and 1990s, these factors can therefore be seen as given by the political actors and thus out of their reach. The responsiveness of the wage bargaining institutions, however, varies over time and is also the aim of government intervention. Government behaviour is therefore prompted by the responsiveness on the one hand, while wage bargaining responsiveness also interacts with government behaviour on the other.

The monetary regime – central bank independence

The monetary regime determines the context in which the government's economic policy takes place. In general, a restrictive monetary regime will narrow the room to manoeuvre of any government on economic policy. Fiscal expansion that leads to public deficits and public debts will be more severely punished under a restrictive monetary regime than under a monetary regime that is subject to government control. To the extent that negotiated wage restraint has traditionally been embedded in a more accommodating economic policy, a restrictive monetary regime curtails these options considerably.

Moreover, a restrictive monetary regime disciplines wage bargaining actors directly and will control inflationary pressure no matter what. In coordinated wage bargaining systems, the restrictive monetary regime will contribute to the responsiveness of wage bargaining actors. However, the monetary regime in itself will also enhance the governments' commitment to economic stringency and reduce its propensity to negotiate with trade unions.

Political institutions – consensus democracy

The process of disinflationary adjustment under non-responsive wage bargainers can carry with it high economic and political costs. Governments that enjoy a stable parliamentary majority and are not dependent on coalition partners may be sufficiently secure to commit themselves to a strict line on economic policy without being tempted to negotiate a wage restraint with trade unions. Governments that are built around many coalition partners in complex political systems, on the other hand, often have short life spans and are unlikely to take risks. Thus the nature of the political system, in particular the distinction between majoritarian and consensus-based political institutions, can give governments the incentive to rely either on their own parliamentary strength or negotiate with trade unions respectively by determining the capacity of governments to hold out without union support. Unstable and consensus-seeking governments can also try to strengthen their position through finding an agreement with trade unions on the conduct of economic policy in general and on a negotiated wage restraint in particular. The broader the social support for economic adjustment, the less painful the experience might be for a generally weak or divided government.

Moreover, in political systems that produce multi-coalition governments, trade unions often have a higher number of access points to the government and can use the competitive nature of political unionism to lobby for their interests in a way that again prompts governments to negotiate with trade unions rather than confront them with restrictive economic policy.

The responsiveness of wage bargaining institutions

The responsiveness of wage bargaining institutions describes the capacity for wage bargaining actors to adjust and is therefore the basis for governments to worry about wage formation. If wage bargaining institutions respond to changing economic developments, there is little reason for governments to engage in negotiations with trade unions on wage adjustment. Coordination and adjustment take place tacitly and indirectly. In some cases, responsiveness of wage bargaining institutions is strongly embedded in the political system itself and direct intervention might be unnecessary. However, the lack of responsiveness of wage bargaining institutions will provide an incentive for governments to negotiate over wages in order to bring wage formation in line with the demands of the economic situation.

Conclusion

The aim of this chapter was twofold. Firstly, it presented a hypothesis of why governments intervene in wage bargaining processes even under the conditions of tight monetary policies. This hypothesis counteracts the expectations found in the neo-corporatist literature that political exchanges are based on the capacity of governments to compensate trade unions for wage restraint with expansive fiscal and monetary policies. As has been argued here, this is not necessarily the case because governments seek cooperation even when they pursue tight economic policies. They do so because the effectiveness of disinflationary policy, similar to expansionist economic policy, varies with the organization of the labour market. Both expansionist and contractionist demand policies by governments are mediated by the responses of wage bargaining institutions towards them.

This chapter has fleshed out the different contexts of incomes policies when employed under expansionary or contractionary economic policy conditions. When governments use intervention in wage bargaining in order to enhance the effectiveness of disinflationary economic policy, they have alternative disciplinary devices *vis-à-vis* trade unions that they do not have under expansionary policy conditions. The difference in context has implications for the form of the intervention as well as for the politics on which it is based.

Secondly, the chapter has laid out the factors that determine whether or not a government chooses to engage in negotiated wage restraint with trade unions. In the following chapters, these implications will be spelt out in more detail and the differences between national cases will be made apparent. Chapter 4 will discuss the role of monetary policy and the independence of central banks, while Chapter 5 will address the political institutions that determine the approach taken by governments and the role of partisanship. Chapter 6 will deal with the responsiveness of wage bargaining institutions as the main institutional precondition. In order to give the argument an empirical base, Chapter 3 presents a measurement of government intervention in wage bargaining processes that will be used throughout the remainder of the book.

3 Policy Options and Institutions: How Governments Respond

Politically, the origins of negotiations between governments and trade unions lie in the new balance of class power that emerged in the settlement that followed World War II.[37] The promotion of Keynesian welfare state policies guaranteed trade unions the right to free collective bargaining while committing governments to ensure high employment levels. Combining full employment with secure and free collective bargaining rights raised the welfare expectations of workers and in turn created demand for institutional and political tools for adjusting these expectations to enable balanced economic growth. Collective bargaining institutions mediated between the welfare expectations of workers on the one hand and the transformation of the economic environment on the other. Operating within the framework of these institutions trade unions gradually adjusted their wage bargaining behaviour – often pushed by governments.

Chapter 2 discussed the relationship between monetary policy and wage bargaining institutions and the incentives of the government to influence this relationship. It argued that, even under restrictive monetary policies, wage bargaining institutions retain a functional role to the extent that the government remains able to influence the performance of these institutions. This chapter looks at the choices open to governments from the perspective of their institutional environment. The neo-corporatism literature[38] has introduced a sharp dichotomy between the institutional endowments of political economies with respect to the relationship between governments and trade unions. Depending on the form and type of trade union organizations, the relationships of trade unions with governments have taken markedly different developments.

Starting from this dichotomy between corporatist versus non-corporatist countries, this chapter argues that patterns of *negotiations* between governments and trade unions are situated between the institutional accommodation[39] of trade union demands, as in the corporatist case, and the market-based or liberal form of addressing trade union wage demands, as in the pluralist case. In other words, negotiations are an expression of attempts to reconcile conflicting institutional settings which, on the one hand, only insufficiently respond to the government's economic needs but, on the other hand, embody a commitment by the government to a political approach that makes a more liberal response by the government neither acceptable nor feasible.

This chapter aims to move on from a research perspective that derives the notion of accommodation primarily from the organizational structures of trade union organizations and wage bargaining systems to a more dynamic view of the interaction of institutions and policy responses. In order to do so, it introduces a measure for the negotiated response, which will hereafter be referred to as government intervention.[40] This measure will then be used in the remainder of the book as the key dependent variable.

Secondly, it will show empirically that the behaviour of governments towards wage bargaining in Western Europe during the 1980s and 1990s is not systematically related to the institutions of wage bargaining systems or the corporatist traditions of individual countries. In other words, whether a government tries to negotiate with trade unions on wages or not is ***not solely*** determined by the corporatist or non-corporatist tradition of the country. In the first section, I will discuss the different conceptual backgrounds of the institutional accommodation of trade unions in terms of corporatism and wage bargaining centralization and government intervention as a form of political accommodation of trade unions. In the second section, I will introduce the operationalization of the variables. The third section contrasts the relationship between the institutional embedding of trade unions and government behaviour towards wage bargaining. The final section comprises the conclusions.

Policy options towards the redistributional power of trade unions: market responses and negotiations

Adopting a stylized view of the post-war situation, there were two institutional configurations that influenced how governments responded to the question of how to accommodate the redistributional power of labour in the framework of the post-war Keynesian welfare state – the corporatist and the pluralist setting. Corporatism or pluralism were not policy approaches chosen by governments, but were fundamental structures of government-trade union relations based on the organization of the labour market, in particular on the organizational structures of trade unions.

Corporatist settings comprised the institutional integration of trade union organizations into the political system and on the labour market. Centralized trade union organizations, able to monopolize the conduct of collective bargaining, gained exclusive access to political decision-making and collective bargaining rights. In turn, they were willing to accept the responsibility for moderate wage demands. Incorporation and centralization of trade union structures took place in the inter-war or immediate post-war years, often with heavy involvement by governments. At other times, centralization and the autonomous regulation of wage bargaining by the social partners were aimed at keeping the government at bay. Once centralized structures and monopolies were set up, they functioned as an integrative force, since trade unions had to mediate competing interests between groups of workers internally rather than pursue local wage gains.

The pluralist setting was based on a trade union structure that was organized in a decentralized way, with weak organizational control over wage bargaining procedures and wage formation outcomes. Where trade unions and wage bargaining structures had their roots in early industrialized economies, they were decentralized and often dominated by traditional craft unions that did not have close relationships with the political arena (Streeck and Hassel 2003). In these cases, the institutional accommodation of trade unions was more superficial and fragile since trade union structures and public policy-making were largely incompatible even though, in many cases, benevolent governments tried to set up consultation procedures that included trade union participation.[41]

In the immediate post-war period, these two basic settings endowed political actors with a set of responses to mismatches between the economic environment and the role of trade unions in wage formation: an institutional response, a market response and a negotiated response. The *institutional response* represents the reliance of political actors on the capacity of existing corporatist institutions to adjust to a changing environment. Economic imbalances were addressed by political actors working to realign wage bargaining actors' behaviour to fit within the imperatives of existing bargaining institutions. This is accomplished by indirectly adjusting the otherwise stable institutional set-up of centralized wage bargaining, for instance by stabilizing wage bargaining actors or giving support to moderate wage claims through social policy expansion. It was built upon the pre-existing set of corporatist wage bargaining institutions.

The *market response* broke with the post-war consensus of political integration of trade unions. It rejected the legitimate claim of trade unions to organize the labour market and thereby exert a political influence over economic policy-making. This response included policies towards the deregulation of the labour market, the curtailing of rights of regulation by trade unions and the political exclusion of trade unions. The market response was based on the pluralist tradition of arm's length relations between public policy-making and trade unions.

The mismatch between the expectations of employees and the economic environment of firms introduced a third type of response that was, in some cases, able to reply to shifting needs in a way that the two previous responses could not. The *negotiated response* was the attempt of governments to negotiate with trade unions over wage restraint in a variety of institutional settings. Where institutions were not conducive to accommodating trade union wage demands due to a fragmented wage bargaining structure, as was frequently the case in pluralist countries, and where governments were nevertheless committed to the consensus of the Keynesian welfare state that guaranteed trade unions a high degree of influence over wage bargaining procedures, governments tried to influence the wage bargaining behaviour of the unions.

Figure 3.1 illustrates the argument. The two ends of the bottom line are the ideal types of government-union relations that are embodied in the neo-corporatist literature. Corporatist institutions at one end take care of adjusting trade union wage expectations to the economic reality. Pluralist settings at the other end do not presuppose a positive role of coordinated labour market institutions and see the decentralization and deregulation of the labour market as the policy baseline of governments. Negotiations occur when institutions fail to deliver the required economic outcomes but governments are nevertheless committed to a powerful and institutionally embedded role for trade unions on the labour market. They are therefore not an ideal type of political response that corresponds to either a corporatist or a pluralist approach; instead, they reflect responses that, on the one hand, seek to reconcile the conflicting aims of institutional accommodation and acceptance of the political role of trade unions while, on the other hand, actively addressing an economic imbalance that is based on a maladjustment of wage bargaining behaviour by trade unions. In other words, negotiations reflect *tensions* between the politically accepted role of trade unions and their inadequate behaviour in wage bargaining procedures.

In practice, the two responses of negotiation on the one hand and negotiated accommodation and deregulation on the other were not mutually exclusive, but often overlapped, just as corporatism and pluralism tend to overlap. After World War II all advanced countries started with a process that attempted to incorporate trade unions into the political decision-making process while simultaneously introducing a much higher degree of government intervention in the economy than ever before (Streeck and Hassel 2003). Deliberate attempts by governments to incorporate trade unions often took the form of consultation on wages and economic policy within the framework of tripartite economic and social councils. More indirect incorporation addressed the organizational status of trade unions. Trade unions received legal entitlements for the protection of their organizations, which in some cases granted them monopoly representation and the guarantee that they alone should control wage formation procedures.

At the same time, government intervention extended over the whole period between 1945 and 1970, with only its form and policy goals varying. In the first three decades after the war, there was no *laissez-faire* approach by governments, but purposeful economic policy that included a strategy towards prices and wages. All governments in advanced industrialized countries at one point or another either decreed wage and price freezes or had discussions with unions and employers about the appropriate wage policy. While the influence of trade unions over economic policy-making was seen as a legitimate political process, the management of wages was seen as a legitimate tool of economic policy-making.

In contrast to the institutional setting that is described by corporatism, the approach to negotiate the accommodation of trade unions describes the government *policy* towards wage bargaining. Negotiated accommo-

Figure 3.1 Institutional settings and policy options

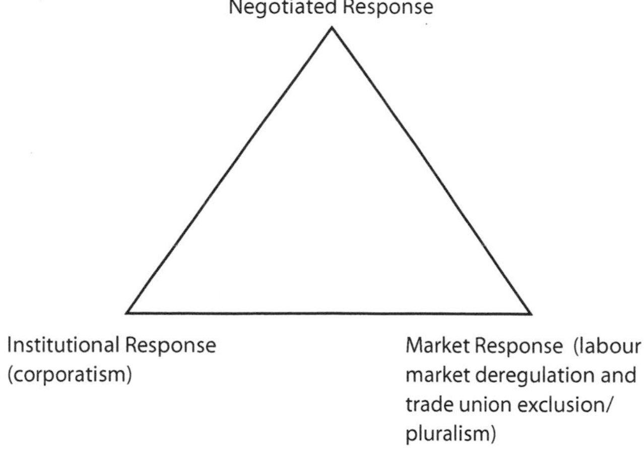

dation is not based on the institutionally mediated cooperation between governments and trade unions, but on the attempt of governments to push trade unions towards a more responsible position in wage bargaining than they would otherwise have adopted (Headey 1970). It is therefore the result of a *mismatch* of the interplay between institutions and the needs of the government in economic policy-making. The need for negotiated accommodation, in other words, arises when the institutionally produced outcomes do not square with the aspirations of the government. Negotiations are aimed at mending the frictions in the interplay between economic policy and wage bargaining behaviour.

Conceptualization of the corporatist institutions and negotiated policy response towards trade unions' redistributional power in the neo-corporatist literature

Corporatism and the centralization of trade union organizations and wage bargaining institutions can be regarded as characteristics of the institutional approach to the challenge of containing the new role of labour in the post-war order. The expanding regulative and integrative task of the modern state requires prior aggregation of opinion, which only singular, hierarchically ordered representative monopolies are able to provide, as Schmitter has described it. In his conceptualization, corporatist interaction as an "osmotic process whereby the modern state and modern interest associations seek each other out leads, on the one hand, to even further extensions of public guarantees and equilibration and, on the other, to even further concentration and hierarchic control within these private governments" (Schmitter 1979: 27). The interaction between the state and private associations is thereby founded primarily on the capacity of the associations to deliver the control over their constituencies and the representation of group interests.

Based on these assumptions, the literature on neo-corporatism focused on the role of organizational structures and institutions as a precondition for virtuous interaction between associations and the state. The organizational structure of trade unions and employers' associations was at the centre of attention, in particular the question of whether they conformed to a corporatist pattern or not and what the effects of a more fragmented and pluralist structure of interest associations were.

In some parts of the literature, however, corporatism has been conceptualized both as a form of policy formation and as a form of interest intermediation. With regard to policy formation, designated interest associations are incorporated within the process of authoritative decision-making and implementation. As such, they are officially recognized by the state not merely as interest intermediaries but as co-responsible 'partners' in governance and guidance (Schmitter 1981: 295). Interest intermediation, on the other hand, describes the mode of arranging the political process based on a system of centralized and concentrated interest groups. The two forms of corporatism are not synonymous: corporatist policy formation can take place when corporatist interest mediation is not present. However, corporatist theory argues that corporatist bargaining is more susceptible to collapse under the stress of exogenous shocks if "unprotected by firmly rooted institutions" (Katzenstein 1985: 89). The centralization of interest associations thus gives rise to a number of other characteristics of corporatism, including a tendency towards corporatist policy formation. As Philippe Schmitter points out:

> There is, nevertheless, considerable evidence of an elective affinity, if not a strong element of historical causality, between the corporatization of interest intermediation and the emergence of 'concerted' forms of policy making. It is not an accident that virtually all the authors using different definitions of corporatism agree on the countries and policy arenas they chose as exemplars for theory building or cases for hypothesis testing (Schmitter 1981: 296).

The elective affinity between corporatist interest mediation and policy formation rests on the incentives that a corporatist structure of interest intermediation presents to governments. Corporatist interest intermediation would lead to a political process which included the major interest associations as important social actors and by which they acquired a stake in the policy formation even if they were dissatisfied with its outcome. Interest groups would participate in the formulation and implementation of policies that go beyond their specific sectoral interests to include such broad political objectives as full employment, economic stability and growth as well as the modernization of industry (Katzenstein 1985: 92).

The whole process would generally be embraced by an ideology of social partnership that is shared by business and trade unions alike and is expressed in national politics. Corporatism contributes directly to the cooperative and non-conflictual behaviour of trade unions and business, and therefore manifests itself in low levels of industrial conflict. Hibbs found that strike levels were greatly reduced in those countries that were later classified as the smaller corporatist countries in Europe, namely

Denmark, the Netherlands, Norway and Sweden (Hibbs 1977). In a number of studies, therefore, the level of industrial conflict has been used as an indicator of corporatism (Cusack 1995).

In general, the different types of conceptualization of corporatism as the specific relations between civil society and the state produced very similar lists of countries that were described as corporatist. Comparisons of corporatist typologies showed a great deal of overlapping (see, for example, Crouch 1993b; Kenworthy 2003; Wilensky 1976; Wilensky 2002). The distinction between the organizational bases and the policy approach of concertation mattered only at the level of conceptualization and the reasoning why these interactions would occur. At the empirical level – with a few exceptions such as Switzerland and Belgium – both approaches of neo-corporatist analysis came to similar conclusions.

In these approaches, corporatism is more pronounced in small states than in big states and is – for historical reasons – characteristic of continental Europe. In continental Europe, a set of 'ancient associations', which were inherited from guild privileges and other involuntary associations, were transformed into bodies of corporatist interest mediation with the growth of capitalist market societies and civil liberalism. Depending on the extent of the spread of liberalism, intermediate organizations were sometimes completely abolished; in other cases where the period of liberalism was short and incomplete, the remnants of interest associations were transformed from medieval corporations into modern interest associations. In small countries in particular, the challenges of the inter-war years led to a more cooperative form of intermediation between the state and interest organizations. Under the condition of the rapid expansion of the global economy, this form of cooperation within small states was reinforced. The social and political cohesion of small states with a historical legacy of strong social organization supported the evolution of corporatist intermediation.

Among the big states in Western Europe, Germany has the strongest corporatist structure. As Katzenstein puts in: "West Germany's corporatism derives as much from openness, dependence and a sense of vulnerability brought about by the diminished size of the Bonn Republic after 1945 as from the implantation of its political parties in fresh democratic soil" (Katzenstein 1985: 201). For the other large industrial states, corporatism is not a useful way of responding to the risks and opportunities of the international economy. Since large countries generally have a longer time span in which they can adjust their economies and a more heterogeneous mix of industries stemming from size, corporatism is naturally less developed in large states.

Policies on wage bargaining

Government policy towards wage bargaining has been a core focus of neo-corporatist conceptualization because it cuts across the boundaries of public policy-making and the regulatory responsibility of associations in the labour market. Wage bargaining is not a policy domain of public policy. In contrast to monetary and fiscal policy, wage formation is not seen as a part of public policy but rather as a private activity on the labour market that is governed by private associations. Decision-making on wages is therefore not based on public force but on the strength of the associational actors themselves, while it is always constrained by macroeconomic policy decisions and monetary policy in particular. In the area of industrial relations, public policy generally only has direct interventionist power under very special circumstances. For example, public policy provides a legal framework of substantive and procedural rules. This includes basic standards in the labour market, such as a minimum period of paid holidays or a maximum working week. In addition, public policy also prescribes procedural rules, as in the cases of early retirement and redundancies.

Despite the vast literature on neo-corporatist policy-making, the conceptual tools for distinguishing and identifying the political forms for accommodating trade union wage bargaining positions have remained underdeveloped in the literature. There are a few political science studies on incomes policy that have attempted a conceptualization, notably by Headey (1970), Armingeon (1982 and 1983) and Marks (1986).

In the neo-corporatist literature, most concepts of political exchanges (Marin 1990; Crouch 1993b) or of modes of governance (Lehmbruch 1984) have generally remained within the framework of the pre-eminence of political and economic institutions. The notion of political exchanges assumes that unions are paid by governments for their cooperation (Streeck and Kenworthy 2005). Incomes policies, on the other hand, are government attempts to give incentives and other reasons to trade unions to restrain wages. They can be part of a political exchange, but the two processes are not synonymous.[42] Approaches that focus on political exchange therefore tend to overlook the broader nature of incomes policy. For instance, Crouch has used the concept of political exchange as a function of centralized trade union organizations and trade union strength (Crouch 1993b). On the other hand, the generalized political exchange as conceptualized by Bernd Marin has abandoned the primacy of the structural and institutional preconditions, while remaining vague about the substantive mechanisms that encourage political exchange in weakly institutionalized settings (Marin 1990 and 1991).

Similarly, in the new literature on social pacts, attention has been drawn to the fact that corporatism has to be seen as a "variable and constantly evolving phenomenon" if we are to understand the interaction between governments and the social partners without having the benefit of clear conceptual guidance on how to proceed (Molina and Rhodes 2002: 322). While it has become empirically obvious that the relationship between the state and associations have been developing in ways that were not theoretically in line with corporatist theorizing (Schmitter and Grote 1997), the literature has tended to dwell on the substantive issues, such as reform of the regulations of the labour market, in order to gain theoretical insights from the cases. For instance, recent contributions on social pacts in Western Europe by Fajertag and Pochet (2000), Regini (2000) and Rhodes (1998 and 2001a), with the exception of Baccaro (2003), have tended to pass over a theoretical explanation for these changes in order to assess thoroughly the substance of the reform changes.

A more policy-based approach that systematically includes the substantive issues and seeks to explain the diversity of developments in the relationship between governments and associations has therefore not received much attention in the literature. The sheer institutional variety has tended to obfuscate the distinction between governmental policy on wages and the institutional accommodation of trade unions. For a long time, institutions and policies were seen as complementary: countries with corporatist institutions tended to employ policies of negotiations, while pluralist countries tended to deregulate. The tensions between institutions that did not comply with the needs of governments and policies that did not fit in with the institutional set-up were not fundamentally addressed.

In sum, institutional and negotiated forms of accommodation are interrelated but distinct responses to the issue of labour inclusion in modern economies. Negotiated accommodation responds to the imperfection and mismatches of institutional outcomes. In order to assess the dynamism of the evolution of corporatist interaction between governments and interest associations, it is also useful to distinguish these two approaches empirically.

The operationalization of variables

In order to test the assumptions of the preceding chapter, we need a measure of the government intervention in wage bargaining. Here we face the problem that the corporatist literature is vast while, in contrast, the developed measures of corporatism tend not to be time-sensitive, but based on the structural properties of wage bargaining institutions. The literature has produced numerous national corporatism indices derived from diverse information such as bargaining structures, centralization of trade union organization, union density etc. These indices measure what has been conceived of as the precondition for corporatist interaction, but not the degree of the interaction itself. Measures of such corporatist interaction or government-trade union negotiations, on the other hand, hardly exist.[43] This section presents a proxy for measuring corporatist responses that is both time-sensitive and comparative.

It takes the perspective of government intervention rather than cooperation between governments and trade unions as the starting point for tracing a stronger or weaker degree of corporatist response. Government intervention in the wage bargaining process – although often disliked by the social partners and often only used by governments as an instrument of last resort – can be seen as a powerful indicator of the willingness of a government to engage in a negotiated adjustment process rather than in a process of deregulation and decentralization.

Measuring government intervention

The measurement of government intervention needs to be independent from the institutional design of the corporatist tradition of countries. It also has to be time-sensitive and comparative. In contrast to the vast number of studies and different measures of the degree of centralization and coordination of wage bargaining institutions, there is very little recent work on government intervention in general, and there is no recent measure of the degree of government intervention in particular. Even during the 1960s and 1970s, when incomes policies were prevalent throughout the industrialized world, there were descriptive comparative studies on wage freezes and incomes policies, but only a few quantitative measures of the degree of government intervention.[44]

Accordingly, the means available to governments to influence wages will vary. The policies are obviously situated in an institutional context of wage bargaining institutions and the general economic policy tools of the government. Centralized wage bargaining institutions enable centralized negotiations with trade unions to take place and ensure that pay norms are implemented, while decentralized wage bargaining institutions may preclude this outcome. Particular legal or constitutional settings might forestall active government involvement or might encourage it. In the past, there have been four distinct approaches that governments have used:

- Tax-based incomes policy. Tax-based incomes policies were designed by economists during the 1970s in order to offer permanent tax incentives for wage restraint. The government thereby introduced tax-relief for low wage settlements.
- Setting of minimum wages. Where governments are in control of setting minimum wages, the rate of increase of the minimum wage might provide a guideline for wage bargaining; in particular if wage bargaining institutions are otherwise weak.
- General negotiations with trade unions on wages. Governments can opt to pressurize unions or negotiate with them candidly on wages, with the results being implemented in wage agreements. Negotiations can include rewards for wage restraint in the form of tax relief, working time incentives or other institutional rewards. Trade unions are nevertheless free to accept and implement these settlements.
- Setting wage norms for the private sector. In some cases, governments can also set wages directly either in the form of wage freezes or the statutory imposition of wage increases. A statutory wage policy will override wage settlements.

There are two main problems with measuring government intervention. The most obvious is that, empirically, the involvement of governments in wage bargaining interacts greatly with the wage bargaining institutions and corporatist traditions in general. In many countries, wage bargaining institutions have developed in the shadow of the state. In some cases, state regulation has enabled trade unions to pursue strategies of bargaining coordination and centralization by granting them monopolies of membership. Monopolies over membership enable trade unions to centralize their wage bargaining structures. These have been established by legal means in Germany and Austria. The active involvement of the state in the conduct of wage bargaining in these two countries, however, is low.

Depending on the historical evolution of the relationship between wage bargaining institutions and the state, the interaction can take many different forms that are not easily categorized in a hierarchical measure. For instance, centralization of wage bargaining arrangements has sometimes occurred in order to exclude the state from the domain of collective bargaining. The Swedish Agreement of Saltsjöbaden of 1938 was an active measure adopted by the social partners to pre-empt government intervention in the wage bargaining system (Fulcher 1991). This pattern has continued until today, with wage bargaining behaviour on the part of the social partners becoming more responsive when government intervention is looming.

The Wassenaar Agreement enacted in the Netherlands in 1982 is an important turning point in Dutch wage bargaining that was prompted by the radical shift in the manner in which the new government related to unions (Visser and Hemerijck 1997). The agreement in itself and the process leading up to it were not characterized by government intervention, but rather by an indirect threat by the government to radically alter its attitude towards the unions if wage bargaining outcomes did not change. Compared to the interaction between governments and wage bargaining of the late 1970s, the degree of government intervention in 1982 was lower than before. The major change in the Dutch bargaining procedure was the lack of government intervention rather than increased involvement by the government. Therefore, government intervention does not necessarily have to take place in order to be effective. As in the case of Sweden, the Dutch experience shows that it is often the *threat* of intervention that influences wage bargaining behaviour.

In other countries, centralization and coordination of wage bargaining has traditionally taken place under the active involvement of the state. In Finland, for instance, the government has traditionally participated in wage bargaining. In Portugal and Spain, the incorporation of trade unions into the political systems via economic councils was an important part of the transition to democracy. Here, government involvement was part of the normal wage bargaining procedure and was not a specifically designed incomes policy.

Also, in countries with decentralized bargaining systems, processes of decentralization were often state-induced. In the UK, the Thatcher government enacted legislation that decreased the capacity of trade unions to coordinate their bargaining activities. In France, the Auroux Laws that were introduced in 1982 were meant to strengthen bargaining activities by giving trade unions the right to bargain at plant level. They led to a further increase in wage bargaining at plant level at the expense of the sectoral level and thereby increased decentralization. In general, therefore, government intervention in wage bargaining systems has to be judged against the backdrop of existing wage bargaining institutions.

The other measuring problem is that government intervention in wage bargaining has several dimensions that are not easily collapsed into one measure. The most important distinction here is the scope of the intervention with regard to the impact on wages *vis-à-vis* the process of intervention itself. In some cases, such as Belgium, governments have persistently intervened in the wage bargaining process by legislating upper limits to wage agreements. This is a rather severe measure of government intervention, comparatively speaking. Since wages in Belgium are generally indexed to changes in prices and the potential scope of wage bargaining only applies to the increases above indexation, the scope of the intervention is however relatively small. In other cases, such as the United Kingdom from 1975 to 1978, governments appeared to be fairly reluctant to intervene directly and instead pleaded with the unions to restrain wages voluntarily; the scope of the intervention, however was large since it implied an initial substantial decrease in real wages.

Moreover, not every measure developed by the state falls into the category of government intervention in wage bargaining. Governments have developed a number of measures that extend the effects of wage bargaining and agreements beyond the constituencies of the social partners. *Erga omnes* clauses apply wage agreements to segments of the labour market that do not participate in wage bargaining.[45] Giving workers the entitlement to a union wage even if the employer is not part of the wage bargaining system can also increase the coverage rate. These provisions strengthen the self-regulation of the wage bargaining institutions and should, strictly speaking, not be regarded as active involvement of the state in wage bargaining processes.

The only existing quantitative measure of the role of governments in wage bargaining, the government involvement index, was developed by Miriam Golden, Peter Lange and Michael Wallerstein (Golden, Lange and Wallerstein 2002). The score ranges from 1 to 15. The lowest score indicates that the government is entirely uninvolved in the wage formation process; the highest score measures the imposition of a wage freeze by the government with a prohibition on supplementary bargaining (table 3.1).

The Golden-Lange-Wallerstein government involvement index runs into some of the problems mentioned above. Conceptualized as an index with an ordinal scale, not every step of the index measures an increase in government involvement in wage bargaining. The extension of agreements could be seen as an indicator of governments restraining from intervention rather than engaging in it. The establishment of a minimum

Table 3.1 Index of government involvement in wage setting by Miriam Golden, Michael Wallerstein and Peter Lange, and government intervention index

Government Involvement Index	Government Intervention Index
1 Government uninvolved in wage setting. 2 Government establishes minimum wage(s). 3 Government extends collective agreements. 4 Government provides economic forecasts to bargaining partners. 5 Government recommends wage guidelines or norms. 6 Government and unions negotiate wage guidelines. 7 Government imposes wage controls in selected industries. 8 Government imposes cost of living adjustment. 9 Formal tripartite agreement for national wage schedule without sanctions. 10 Formal tripartite agreement for national wage schedule with sanctions. 11 Government arbitrator imposes wage schedules without sanctions on unions. 12 Government arbitrator imposes national wage schedule with sanctions. 13 Government imposes national wage schedule with sanctions. 14 Formal tripartite agreement for national wage schedule with supplementary local bargaining prohibited. 15 Government imposes wage freeze and prohibits supplementary local bargaining.	1 No role of government in wage setting. 2 Government influences bargaining by providing an institutional framework of consultation (includes the German concerted action or the Parity Commission in Austria). 3 Government determines wage bargaining outcomes indirectly (includes the minimum wage setting by the French government and the Wassenaar Agreement in the Netherlands). 4 Government participates in wage bargaining (as in Finland and Spain until 1987). 5 Government negotiates social pact or imposes private sector wage settlements (direct legislative measures such as in Belgium).

Source: for the government involvement index, Golden, Lange and Wallerstein (2002).

wage by the government, on the other hand, is in some cases, such as France, a powerful tool used by governments to control overall wage development. (See for annual data table A1.) The setting of the minimum wage, which is ranked on position 2 in the index, is in any case a more interventionist measure than providing the social partners with economic forecasts. Equally, the provision of sanctions is a higher degree of intervention in the freedom of the social partners than the distinction between arbitration and tripartism.

In order to deal with these problems of ranking different degrees of government involvement, a number of caveats are in order concerning the measurements of government intervention in wage formation. Firstly, it is assumed that governments generally prefer not to take part in wage negotiations directly. For good political reasons, no government has sought a direct role in wage formation procedures. Even in countries where governments have in the past been very active towards wage bargaining, such as in Denmark and Finland, governments have frequently withdrawn from wage bargaining procedures if the circumstances allowed them to do so. Governments prefer indirect measures to direct involvement. As a consequence, the direct participation of governments in wage bargaining processes, both in the form of participating in negotiations or in the form of issuing guidelines and imposing pay freezes, can be recognized as strong political interference and should not be regarded as traditional behaviour in these countries. Secondly, assessing government behaviour on an annual basis requires a broader set of categories at the expense of more detailed information. Similarly, the active behaviour of governments can take different forms that are entirely related to their institutional environment and not significant in themselves. And, thirdly, one should not try to assign too much of a statistical status to these crude assessments, but rather see them as a reflection of a particular position adopted by governments in their relations to wage bargaining processes that compare countries and change over time, without being applied in too strict a way.

Due to the conceptual and methodological difficulties associated with measuring government intervention in wage bargaining I have developed an alternative index that uses substantial parts of the Golden, Lange and Wallerstein data but tries to combine a number of variables and provides a broader categorization of cases. Using broader categories obviously implies a loss of differentiation in the data, but this seems justified since the data does not appear to allow a great deal of differentiation anyway. The government intervention index is scored from 1 to 5, with the lowest score indicating no involvement and the highest score the imposition of a wage settlement on the private sector. The three categories in between classify the increasing intensity with which governments try to influence the bargaining behaviour of trade unions. The categories are sufficiently broad to summarize cases that are only formally distinct but substantially similar. Overall, the government intervention index correlates sufficiently highly with the government involvement index by Golden, Lange and Wallerstein (Pearson correlation coefficient = 0.69).

A particularly difficult aspect of operationalization is the degree of consultation between governments and social partners over wage settlements. In many countries, there are standing tripartite committees, such as economic and social councils, in which consultation over wage and price developments takes place. However, the presence of consultation committees in itself is not a sufficient indication that governments actively intervene in wage bargaining. Only when governments proceed to act against trade unions by suggesting an incomes policy or indeed by bargaining over one, should this be considered a measure of government intervention. The differentiation between governments determining and influencing bargaining outcomes aims to distinguish cases where governments in principle have tried to determine wage expectations through tripartite consultation, as in the German Concerted Action (which is in category 2), from those cases where governments have tried hard to influence lower wage settlements without being directly involved, such as during the Wassenaar Agreement (category 3).[46]

Table 3.2 illustrates the changing degree of government intervention in wage bargaining over a period of three decades. (See for annual data table A.1.) Longitudinal data is averaged across the decades, which are in turn demarcated by unique economic environments: the 1970s is marked by

Table 3.2 Government intervention in wage bargaining in Western Europe, 1970-99

	1970s	1980s	1990s	Δ 1970s-90s
Austria	2.0	1.0	1.0	-1.0
Belgium	1.4	3.8	4.6	+3.2
Denmark	5.0	3.2	2.2	-2.8
Finland	3.8	3.2	3.1	-0.7
France	2.0	3.0	2.4	+0.4
Germany	1.7	1.0	1.1	-0.6
Ireland	3.0	1.9	4.0	+1.0
Italy	1.0	2.4	3.8	+2.8
Netherlands	3.6	2.3	2.2	-1.4
Portugal	-	4.0	3.7	-0.3*
Spain	-	3.6	2.0	-1.6*
Sweden	2.0	2.2	2.9	+0.9
United Kingdom	3.4	1.0	1.0	-2.4
Mean	2.6	2.5 (2.3)*	2.6 (2.6)*	-0.19

Note: * Change from 1980s to 1990s; in brackets without Portugal and Spain.

the two oil crises and stagflation, the 1980s is a period of economic recovery and universal shift towards stricter monetary policies, and the 1990s is the period of the run-up towards monetary integration.[47]

A first glance at the data points of the government intervention index supports the classification of countries that will be discussed in more detailed in Chapter 6. In a comparative perspective, the index highlights the variety of responses by governments in different countries and at different points in time. The following remarks will illustrate the measurements and contrast them briefly with country-specific developments.

The development of government intervention

When comparing the evolution of government intervention, there has not been a secular decline in negotiated wage restraint across Europe, but rather divergent trends in the pattern of government intervention across countries. The clearest decline of government intervention in wage bargaining has not taken place in Britain, as might be expected, but in Denmark. Denmark ranked highest in terms of government intervention in wage formation during the 1970s because of its strong arbitration system that gave the government an indirect opportunity to set wages. Moreover, from 1975 onwards, the Danish government imposed wage settlements that included sanctions. Britain, in contrast, had a lower level of government intervention because the government only imposed wage freezes three times during the 1970s: in 1973, 1978 and 1979. The attempts to negotiate an incomes policy in 1971 and 1975 were of a voluntary nature. However, unlike Denmark, where the state still plays an important role today, the British government has declined since 1979 to interfere with wage bargaining.

Falling levels of government intervention can also be observed in the Netherlands, Germany, Finland and Austria. In Austria, the role of the Parity Commission has clearly diminished over the years, whereas in Germany, the Concerted Action was abandoned in 1977. The government had used the Concerted Action to discuss wage guidelines with the social partners informally. Thereafter, any attempt to influence the social partners to exercise wage restraint only re-emerged once, in the framework of the Alliance for Jobs in 1999. In the Netherlands, the conflictual rounds of negotiating an incomes policy during the 1970s were replaced by two important agreements by the social partners in 1982 and 1993, both of which were negotiated in the shadow of government intervention, but without active government involvement.

The countries with a strong increase in government intervention in wage bargaining were Belgium, Italy and Ireland; countries with a minor increase in government intervention were France and Sweden. In Belgium, the government did not involve itself in wage bargaining until 1974, although parliament frequently implemented the inter-professional agreements that the social partners concluded. In the latter half of the 1970s, the government encouraged wage restraint but did not massively intervene in the labour market. However, since 1981 the Belgian government has tried persistently to control all wage bargaining by imposing legislated wage guidelines on the social partners. A similar evolution can be found in Italy. Here, the government played a minimalist role in wage bargaining until 1984 when for the first time it was part of a tripartite agreement on the Scala mobile. Since then, the intervention of the Italian government has steadily increased. In 1992 and 1993, tripartite agreements incorporated wage norms and abolished wage indexation. These were subsequently followed by another social pact on growth and employment in 1998. In Ireland, the government had sponsored national wage bargaining during the 1970s, but abandoned this role during the first half of the 1980s. Since 1987, however, the state has participated in tripartite wage bargaining negotiations.

In France and Sweden, governments increased their role in wage bargaining but on a more moderate scale. In France, government tried to reorganize wage bargaining throughout the 1980s. But the most important source of influence by the French government has been its role in setting the minimum wage. By controlling minimum wages in an otherwise weakly regulated labour market, the French government has gained a high degree of control over wage developments. In Sweden, the government became more active in wage negotiations during the 1990s, but remained hesitant to embrace the idea of intervention. It was only in the late 1990s that the Swedish government really started to pressurize wage bargaining actors into adopting a new scheme of arbitration under government control.

Finally, the cases of Spain and Portugal show high degrees of government control over wage bargaining during the transition years. In Spain, government participation in wage bargaining had ceased in the mid-1980s due to rising conflict with the unions. Cooperation with the social partners re-emerged, however, in the 1990s through the reorganization of wage bargaining structures. In Portugal, the state battled with the unions over wages throughout the period, and only recently has it found a modus of adjusting Portuguese wages to the requirements of EMU.

The variety of trends over time also indicates, as assumed above, that government intervention cannot be seen as a traditional instrument for achieving wage restraint that state governments frequently rely on. Governments certainly use established and traditional instruments in policy-making more easily than new instruments. The legal and historical availability of government intervention in wage bargaining thereby facilitates the decision by governments to intervene. On the other hand, the drastic changes in the behaviour of governments over time show that the availability of intervention is only one factor among others that influence government choices. At least in the domain of wage bargaining, governments are able to break with traditional policy approaches more frequently than the popular assumptions about path dependent behaviour would have us believe (Pierson 2000). Major policy shifts by governments on the role and conduct of wage bargaining have taken place in the majority of the countries covered in this book. This implies that national cases move from high to low degrees of government involvement in wage bargaining, primarily because governments do not want to intervene if the situation does not require adjustment. They move from low degrees of intervention to higher degrees if the external environment and internal factors give cause to intervene in order to adjust to economic imbalances. There is only scarce evidence that governments tend to opt for a more or less interventionist approach on principle.

Measuring corporatism and wage bargaining institutions

Measurements of *corporatism* that rely on the structure of interest mediation as the driving force behind corporatism and focus on the organizational centralization and associational monopoly of trade unions place those countries in the category of corporatism where governments have enabled trade unions to take comprehensive control over wage formation. Table 3.3 presents the combined index on societal corporatism by Schmitter, which ranks the countries according to their degree of societal corporatism. In the corporatism ranking, Austria ranks highest together with the Scandinavian countries. Germany and the Low Countries rank in the middle, while France, Ireland, Italy and Britain are at the bottom. Peter Katzenstein analysed democratic corporatism in small European states and constructs a similar measure. He distinguished between liberal corporatism, which is dominated by business interests, and social corporatism, in which labour is the stronger force. Austria and the Scandinavian countries are classified as countries with social corporatism, while

Belgium, the Netherlands and, to some degree, Sweden follow a pattern of liberal corporatism (Katzenstein 1985: 125).

Another measure of the institutional accommodation of trade unions is the *centralization* of wage bargaining institutions or of trade union organizations themselves. Corporatism and centralization are closely related since, as argued above, the centralized nature of trade unions originally gave rise to the incorporation of labour. Measures on wage bargaining centralization and coordination are abundant and relatively similar to each other. Table 3.3 shows the data of the Kenworthy coordination index and the Iversen centralization index. The Iversen centralization index concentrates exclusively on the degree of centralization of wage bargaining systems.[48] Since wage bargaining centralization is closely related to the degree of corporatism, the Iversen index captures an intermediate measure of wage bargaining institutions and corporatism. In contrast, the Kenworthy index integrates government intervention in its measurement and can therefore be seen as not completely independent from the government intervention index. However, the Kenworthy index has more data points available than the Iversen index.[49] In table 3.3 I have supplemented the Kenworthy index with missing data on Portugal and Spain.

Below I will compare these measures of corporatism, wage bargaining centralization and wage bargaining coordination with the government intervention index in order to illustrate the interaction between institutions and policies.

The relationship between institutional and political accommodation

In this section, I will explore the relationship between institutions and the policy responses by governments. Table 3.4 displays the Pearson correlation coefficients of government intervention, wage bargaining coordination, the wage bargaining centralization index and the Schmitter corporatism index. Correlating the measure of government intervention with institutional measure has two aims. First, it aims to underpin the theoretical and empirical reasoning that underlie the measure of government intervention. Second, it aims to show that the policy of governments on wages is not predetermined by the institutional accommodation of trade unions.

Table 3.3 Indicators of corporatism, wage bargaining centralization and coordination

	Indicators of corporatism by Schmitter*			Iversen index**	Supplemented wage bargaining coordination index by Kenworthy			
	Organizational centralization	Associational monopoly	Societal corporatism		1970s	1980s	1990s	ΔD1970s-1990s
Austria	1.0	3.0	1.0	0.437	4.0	4.0	4.0	0.0
Belgium	3.0	9.0	7.0	0.338	3.8	4.5	4.6	+0.8
Denmark	8.0	1.5	4.0	0.467	5.0	3.6	3.4	-1.6
Finland	5.0	4.5	4.0	0.445	3.9	3.6	3.8	-0.1
France	10.0	14.0	13.0	0.114	3.3	3.2	2.3	-1.0
Germany	9.0	6.0	8.0	0.353	4.0	4.0	4.0	0.0
Ireland	13.0	9.0	11.0	-	4.0	2.2	4.6	+0.6
Italy	13.0	14.0	15.0	0.185	2.6	2.3	3.4	+0.8
Netherlands	2.0	9.0	6.0	0.392	4.1	3.8	3.8	-0.3
Portugal	-	-	-	-	-	4.0	3.9	-0.1*
Spain	-	-	-	-	-	3.4	2.6	-0.8*
Sweden	5.0	4.5	4.0	0.485	5.0	4.1	3.4	-1.6
United Kingdom	13.0	12.0	14.0	0.182	3.1	1.0	1.0	-2.1
Mean	-	-	-		3.9	3.3	3.5	-0.4

* The ranking of the Schmitter index is based on 15 countries. Canada, USA, Switzerland and Norway have been left out here while the ranks have been held constant.

** Average for 1973 – 1993.

Sources: Schmitter (1981: 294); Iversen (1999: 56); Kenworthy (2001a).

Table 3.4 **Pearson correlation coefficients of wage bargaining, corporatism and government intervention, 1970-99 (1980-99)**

	Wage bargaining coordination	Corporatism	Bargaining centralization	Government intervention
Wage bargaining coordination	1.000	-0.521** (-0.439**)	0.680** (-0.696**)	0.487** (0.464**)
Corporatism		1.000	0.796** (0.655**)	0.054 (0.019)
Bargaining centralization			1.000	0.191** (0.072)
Government intervention				1.000

** Correlation is significant at the 0.01 level (2-tailed).
* Correlation is significant at the 0.05 level (2-tailed).

Note: Measure on corporatism is time invariant; the Iversen index and the wage bargaining coordination index are based on annual observations. The Iversen index, however, only goes up to 1993.

Sources: Iversen (1999); Schmitter (1981); Kenworthy (2001a); own calculations.

As expected, the strongest correlation exists between the degree of government intervention and wage bargaining coordination. In general, a high degree of government intervention should contribute to wage bargaining coordination, since governments then foster organizational structures of wage bargaining that are conducive to centralization. When governments invite the social partners to participate in a tripartite forum to discuss wage developments and this forum recommends wage guidelines, it is likely that these guidelines will prompt them to transfer wage bargaining to a national level. An example of this process is Ireland, where wage bargaining was decentralized in 1980. When the government and social partners started to negotiate a tripartite agreement in 1987, it automatically meant that the main level of bargaining over wages was the national level.

This is not necessarily always the case, however. There are several examples where governments have tried to intervene in wage bargaining processes by negotiating over wage guidelines or by having tripartite summits without having a lasting effect of centralizing wage bargaining. This was particularly true in the United Kingdom in the 1970s and in France during the 1980s and 1990s.

The effect also works the other way round: governments have a higher incentive to intervene in wage formation processes in situations where they can be assured that wage bargaining actors are capable of implementing agreements. When bargaining is decentralized to a local or plant level, the problem arises that the national trade union confederation, which is the negotiating partner for the government, might not be in the position to assure that wage guidelines will be implemented. If this is the case, the incentive for governments to negotiate with them is rather low and such negotiations might even have damaging effects. When bargaining is coordinated, the bargaining authority lies with the regional or national leadership of a sectoral or general trade union which, at the same time, might be in a position to negotiate with the government over wage guidelines. In this case, government can be assured that the wage guideline that is negotiated with the trade unions will be implemented at the local level. A higher degree of bargaining coordination can therefore increase the incentive for the government to negotiate with the social partners.

When looking at the average degree of government intervention across countries over time, two different trends emerge (figure 3.2). The year 1975 was a peak in terms of centralization of wage bargaining and government intervention in wages. Low points were reached in the early and late 1980s. As could be expected, the degree of government intervention is more volatile than the degree of wage bargaining coordination. Institutional development of wage bargaining institutions is a long-term process that tends to change slowly over time. Government intervention in wage bargaining is, in many cases, an ad hoc decision made by the government in response to a looming crisis. But apart from the peak in the mid-1970s, the subsequent development is not closely correlated. Interestingly, and in contrast to expectations, wage bargaining institutions tended to decentralize throughout the 1980s and re-centralize in the 1990s. On average, the degree of centralization of wage bargaining in Western Europe was at the same level in 1999 as it was in 1970.

Government intervention, on the other hand, had two further peaks: in 1985 and in the early 1990s. In 1985, the peak can be attributed to government intervention in Denmark and Sweden. In Denmark the government imposed a wage settlement on the unions, whereas in Sweden centralized bargaining was reintroduced with the help of a tripartite forum. In the early 1990s, a number of countries saw the re-emergence of government intervention, again focused on the Scandinavian countries. In 1990, the Finnish government stepped up its negotiations with the trade unions, followed by Sweden in 1991 and Italy in 1992.

Figure 3.2 **Bargaining coordination and government intervention in 13 EU member states, 1970-99**

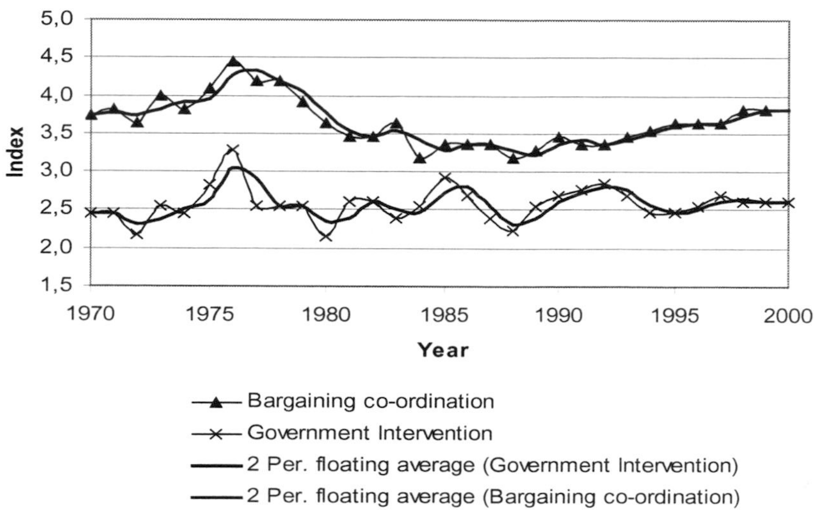

Source: as explained in text and appendix.

Further, the data shows the weak correlation of the government intervention index with bargaining centralization as measured by Iversen. The argument on which the Iversen index rests is based on the capacity of trade unions to internalize negative externalities in wage bargaining and so to exercise wage restraint. If one assumes, firstly, that government intervention emerges when and where wage bargaining institutions are not responsive to their external economic environment and, secondly, that the responsiveness of wage bargaining institutions is correlated with their degree of centralization and coordination, we should find a negative relationship between the degree of government intervention and the degree of wage bargaining coordination. Where wage bargaining is highly coordinated or centralized, governments should see less need to intervene in wage formation processes since the social partners are taking care of the externalities of their wage agreements themselves. Where wage bargaining is decentralized, the need for governments to intervene should be higher, since wage bargaining outcomes are less responsive to the economic requirements of governments. The weak positive correlation between government intervention and bargaining centralization might therefore reflect the contradictory effect of a higher degree of responsiveness due to centralization on the one hand and a stronger incentive to negotiate with centralized organizations on the other.

There is no correlation in table 3.4 between the degree of corporatism as measured by Schmitter and the level of government intervention.[50] I have used the Schmitter index on corporatism because it relies more than other measures of corporatism on the structural prerequisites for the institutional accommodation of trade unions, namely the centralization of trade union organizations. While the measure of corporatism – as expected – correlates positively with the degree of both wage bargaining centralization and coordination, it does not predict the behaviour of the government *vis-à-vis* the social partners during the 1980s and 1990s. Corporatist interaction, while still an important policy mechanism, has become detached from the institutional base on which it used to rest.

Negotiated responses by government intervention in wage bargaining processes have been used in both corporatist and non-corporatist countries. Governments in countries where the labour market is highly regulated are not *per se* more likely or unlikely to intervene in wage formation processes. For instance, among the Scandinavian countries, which are usually grouped together as highly corporatist, the relationship between government intervention and wage bargaining varied considerably. The Swedish government has been much more reluctant to engage in direct negotiations with the social partners over wages, and looming threats of intervention have often prompted reactions by the social partners to prevent an increased role of the state. In contrast, in Denmark and Finland, government participation has been much more accepted and widely used. In Finland, government has been involved in wage bargaining regularly since the late 1960s as a participating actor. In Denmark, governments have frequently intervened when either the social partners could not settle an agreement or the government was not satisfied with a potential agreement.

The Netherlands and Belgium have long been seen to be similar countries in terms of their industrial relations systems (Katzenstein 1985). Yet in both countries governments behaved very differently with regard to the possibility of intervention. In the Netherlands, the government switched from intervening directly in the 1970s towards an indirect position of simply threatening to intervene. Unions, anticipating intervention due to past actions of the government, responded with wage restraint. In this way, the government shifted from a Danish to a Swedish approach. In Belgium, the government has persistently intervened without a response from the social partners.

Countries which have been considered unsuitable for a corporatist labour market have equally shown remarkably different behaviour, even when they were seen to be rather similar in other ways. Italy and France have shared a history of politically fragmented unions, contestation and labour exclusion from World War II until the late 1960s. Since the mid-1970s, however, the behaviour of the Italian government has become more directly interventionist and more cooperative towards the trade unions. In France, on the other hand, labour exclusion has continued and the government has by now indirectly taken over wage setting without finding a closer cooperative relationship with the unions.

Lastly, the cases of Ireland and the United Kingdom show that the degree of centralization of wage bargaining structures is not a sufficient predictor of the level of government intervention. Both countries have a shared history of fragmented wage bargaining structures and a mixture of craft and general trade unions. Trade unionism in both countries is also similar since many Irish trade unions have British ancestors or are still part of a British trade union organization. In both countries, experiments with incomes policies and the introduction of a higher degree of coordination in wage bargaining failed utterly during the 1970s. However, in the late 1970s, the governments in the two countries developed opposing approaches towards economic policy in general, but also towards the role of trade unions in particular. While the British government decentralized wage bargaining, deregulated the labour market and strived for labour exclusion, the Irish government gave up decentralization in 1986 and since then has had a highly centralized wage bargaining system involving strong government participation.

In summary, the correlation between these four variables – coordination, centralization, corporatism and government intervention – provides some evidence for the proposition that, though government involvement increases coordination, institutional accommodation of trade unions does not forestall government involvement. The correlation of the variables also indicates that corporatism is not a sufficient condition for the internalization of negative externalities. Since government involvement only takes place if the autonomous regulation of wages by the social partners is insufficient or not satisfactory, there seem to be frequent occasions – even in centralized wage bargaining systems – when this involvement is required.

Conclusion

In this chapter, an empirical measure for the negotiated response of governments to the problem of accommodating trade union wage expectations was introduced. It was conceptually situated as a measure that tries to build a bridge between the political acceptance of the role of trade unions in the regulation of the labour market, on the one hand, and the need to adjust wage expectations to economic realities on the other hand. The measure for negotiated accommodation captured the degree of government intervention in wage bargaining. It was modelled as the behaviour of the government towards trade unions. Unlike other measures of corporatism, it did not attempt to capture the institutional design on which the action of the government was based, but argued that any interference by the government in wage bargaining processes can be interpreted as a political response to reconciling the conflicting aims of preserving the political role of trade unions and the need to adjust wage expectations to a new economic environment.

When compared to other measures of the interaction between governments and the social partners, an important observation emerged: corporatism was found to be the weakest predictor for the extent of government intervention over time. Corporatism was positively related to government intervention during the 1970s, with highly corporatist countries showing higher levels of government intervention. However, the corporatist structure of interest intermediation of the late 1970s does not predict the emerging pattern of the relationship between governments and the social partners for the following two decades. The quantitative empirical results here confirm observations that have been made on the basis of case studies in the literature, namely that the institutional context is increasingly ill-equipped to predict the behaviour of the actors (Royo 2002a; Baccaro 2003). The traditional assumptions of corporatist theory could not stand up to the empirical reality that negotiated responses between governments and trade unions spread throughout Western European during the 1980s and 1990s. For instance, Royo pointed out in his explanation of corporatism in Spain and Portugal:

> The institutional context is not able to explain the behaviour of the actors. This points to one of the main shortcomings of neo-corporatist theories: they fail to explain the actors' attempt to develop new solutions and change outcomes (Royo 2002a: 42).

The importance of theoretical distinction between different responses is that it allows us to systematically and exclusively distinguish between the different approaches towards adaptation of the power of trade unions to demand redistribution. In the past, it was assumed that a high level of institutional accommodation would be a sufficient indicator of the extent to which trade unions would internalize the negative externalities of wage bargaining. The active involvement of governments in wage bargaining procedures, however, shows that this effect could be partly conditional on the role of the government. In assessments of the role of labour market institutions in economic performance the extent to which wage bargaining behaviour has been systematically influenced and supported by the government has not been thoroughly investigated, however. In addition, these findings show that governments have in fact frequently used their power to intervene in wage formation processes when the need arose. This pattern was stronger during the 1970s when the shock of the oil crises tempted governments to freeze wages. But even during the shift towards tight monetarism and increasing levels of unemployment, most governments persisted in interfering in wage bargaining in order to restrain trade union demands. The degree of government intervention varied widely, not only between countries but also between time periods.

In the following chapters, the factors that influence the varying degrees of government involvement are discussed. As has been outlined in Chapter 2, governmental wage policies have been a tool to realign trade union wage expectations with the changing economic policy of the government. Chapter 4 addresses the shift in monetary policy as a major external factor that has prompted governments to negotiate over wages. Chapter 5 addresses the political preconditions for choosing between trade union exclusion approaches and negotiations. Chapters 6 and 7 focus on the responsiveness of wage bargaining institutions.

4 Striving for Conservatism: The Shift in Monetary Regimes

In the following three chapters I examine three potential explanations for the attempts made by governments to influence wage formation processes as discussed in Chapters 2 and 3. The present chapter focuses on the shift in monetary policy since the 1970s. The core argument is that governments have tended to employ corporatist policy approaches in order to strengthen the credibility of their monetary policy, particularly in situations where the preconditions for a credible monetary policy were weak. Government intervention thus serves as a policy instrument of governments for conveying a new economic policy. The argument is supported by a strong statistical correlation between an index measuring the legal independence of central banks and the index for government intervention developed in Chapter 3.

Over the last three decades, economic policy has undergone a major transformation in the Western world, both in its theoretical assumptions and with regard to the priorities of policy-makers. Across the world, policy-makers learned to believe in and act upon a version of economic policy that rejected the trade-off between inflation and unemployment and, instead, insisted on fighting inflation by focusing on the expectations of economic agents. This shift in policy-making was prompted by new developments in economic theory and facilitated by the increasing financial integration of the world economy that made economic policy measures sensitive to international capital movements.

This chapter argues that the role of governments *vis-à-vis* wage bargaining interacts with the institutional framework on which the new economic policy rests. All European governments since the early 1980s have attempted to shift their monetary policy towards conservatism. Monetarism – as pushed by mainstream economists since the mid-1970s – has filtered through into mainstream economic policy-making.

How government intervention as a policy instrument works for conveying a new economic policy is explained in the latter two sections of the chapter. In section three, evidence is presented for how governments in

Western Europe have attempted to increase the credibility of their monetary policy by using currency pegs. In section four, the relationship between credibility and government intervention is demonstrated empirically.

Before that, in the first two sections, I introduce the issue of credibility as a policy device as it is discussed in the economic literature with regard to central bank independence and monetary integration. In the second section, I examine European monetary integration as a tool for achieving central bank conservatism.

Credibility and the inflation bias

To understand the evolution of economic and, in particular, monetary policy-making, it is necessary to start by understanding some of the underlying theoretical issues. This is not because the contentions of modern economic theory are necessarily valid or even complete. Many assumptions on which theories of modern central banking rest are disputed in the literature, on theoretical as well as on empirical grounds.[51]

But even if one accepts as inadequate the argument that the independence of central banks, and thus the claim that signalling credibly one's commitment to a monetarist approach, is a potentially powerful economic policy device, it is nevertheless important to understand that many of the underlying theoretical claims have led to views on best practice in economic policy, which have in turn impacted on the realm of real-world policy-making. The role and conduct of monetary policy have changed tremendously over the last three decades, mostly in a direction recommended by the mainstream of economic theory. In many countries, central banks have introduced policy rules of inflation targeting or have been granted a higher degree of independence (McNamara 2002). In the design of the European Central Bank, strong emphasis has been placed on its formal independence from governments and the EU Commission in order to improve the reputation of the bank. Likewise, the designers of the new Bank of England or the Reserve Bank of New Zealand believed that changing the status of the bank in favour of greater political independence was an important step towards credibility.

Politicians believe this issue of central bank independence to be of central importance for policy-making and this belief is likely to have widespread policy ramifications. Economic ideas are powerful tools once the scientific community has accepted them.[52] Therefore, even if these tools are inadequate for theoretical or empirical reasons, there are reasons to believe that governments have nevertheless not only pursued them, but have also accepted the theoretical foundations of these approaches as policy guidelines.

The starting point for understanding the importance of the credibility of monetary policy-making is the claim of an inflation bias on the part of policy-makers.[53] If there is a short-term trade-off between unemployment and inflation, a discretionary policy-maker can create surprise inflation, which might reduce unemployment and raise government revenue. A politically motivated policy-maker, moreover, has reason to use this policy device, especially just before elections, in order raise the profile of the government. As the literature of the political business cycle argues, in a democracy a government will have incentives to pursue a policy pattern that starts with austerity in the early years and tends to become more expansive in later years (Nordhaus 1975).

If inflation is mainly created by the expectation of economic agents, a political business cycle is therefore in itself inflationary. Economic agents will expect a more expansive economic policy at the end of the electoral cycle and thereby expect a shift towards inflation. Individuals will understand the temptation of policy-makers and correctly forecast inflation. By internalizing these expectations, wage bargainers will tend to demand and settle higher wage increases than they would have done at a different point in time during the political cycle. Thus, any effect of inflation on employment will be neutralized. At the end of the day, inflation will have risen and the employment effect will not have taken place.

Moreover, the inflation bias is not simply based on policy-makers taking deliberate advantage of the short-term trade-off. To policy-makers, the argument of time inconsistency also suggests that a more accommodatory policy at that point in time is a sensible policy (Kydland and Prescott 1977). When economic policy-makers try to internalize the expectations of economic agents, agents can be expected to internalize these considerations as well. There is no reason why policy-makers should have a time advantage if these policy patterns are frequent. For instance, if inflation were on an upward path, people would expect a less accommodating policy. An optimal way to do this might be to accept the current high rate of inflation and promise that any future increases in inflation would not be accommodated. This would not entail any current loss in current output, and the promise not to accommodate any inflation in the future would moderate current wage and price adjustments.

However, if it is optimal for the new policy to accommodate today's inflation rate, then it will also be optimal to accommodate tomorrow's inflation rate, even if it is higher than today's. If people were rational, they would expect that policy-makers would behave this way and guess that policy will be more accommodating than promised. Hence the promised move to a less accommodating policy is not credible, even though everyone believes it would be superior relative to the more accommodating policy (Taylor 1982: 84).

Therefore, within this theoretical framework, for *any* policy-maker who cares about welfare in general, an inflation bias exists. Even if policy-makers do not wish to consciously exploit the potential of surprise inflation, the expectations of individuals towards monetary policy will always err on the inflationary side if welfare assumptions are likely to guide the monetary authority's action. The only way to solve this dilemma, the economic literature argues, is to place monetary policy in the hands of a central banker, who is not only independent from the political cycle and electoral pressures, but also more conservative than society (Rogoff 1985).[54] Only through the strong anti-inflationary reputation of the monetary authority can inflation bias be remedied.

There is an important lesson to be drawn from this argument that underlies all economic research into the independence of central banks and the role of monetary policy. The main effect of monetary policy-making by independent central banks is a reputation effect that the bank would react to inflation stronger than its politically controlled counterpart. It is the reputation of the bank that leads economic actors to anticipate reactions to inflationary behaviour.

In practice, monetary policy obviously affects the investment decisions of private business by setting interest rates and the supply of money. Tight monetary policy undoubtedly has a contracting effect on any economy. However, the necessity to use these monetary policy instruments depends primarily on the reputation of the bank. If the bank has a strongly conservative reputation and can thereby automatically reduce inflationary pressures by credibly committing itself to price stability, monetary policy in practice needs to be *less* conservative than when a bank has a less conservative reputation. According to these theoretical claims, we should not expect the actual policy of the bank to necessarily make a difference to the behaviour of economic agents; rather, the reputation of the bank or of the monetary authority will do so.

Therefore, when monetary policy-makers engage in a tighter monetary policy, the primary aim must be to strengthen the non-accommodatory *reputation* of the monetary authority. Monetary policy itself can be used for this purpose, but it is the reputation effect that is important for the effectiveness of monetarism in the medium and long term. This distinction between the reputation effect and the dampening effect of tight monetary policy is not trivial but important with regard to the indicators one can sensibly use to measure the tightness of monetary policy. For instance, it does not seem sensible to use measures that rely on actual monetary policy when assessing the role of monetary policy. Therefore measures of the legal independence of central banks, as have been attempted by Cukierman (1998) and Grilli, Masciandaro *et al.* (1991), more accurately gauge what central bank conservatism means for economic agents than do measures that emphasize monetary policy itself.[55] In other words, the effectiveness of monetary policy rests on the credibility of the monetary authority and not primarily on its policy choice. For this reason, the Cukierman index is used in figure 4.3 to investigate the relations between central bank independence and government intervention.

The role of central banks has not been constant over time, but is part of the moves towards European monetary integration. It is therefore necessary to examine this integration process in order to understand relations between monetary regimes and government intervention.

European monetary integration as a tool for achieving central bank conservatism

Monetary regimes have not been constant over time, but have shifted towards conservatism themselves. In this section, I will explore the role of European monetary integration in this process as an attempt by governments to increase the conservative reputation of their monetary regimes. European monetary integration has been the most important means of increasing monetary conservatism in Western Europe over the last two decades. Nevertheless, it is not absolutely clear at what point in time European monetary integration acquired the reputation of a conservative monetarist regime.

This section explores the role of monetary integration in the relationship between governments and trade unions. It argues that monetary integration was one integral instrument that governments used to swing the monetary regime towards conservatism. Governments aimed at monetary conservatism and used monetary integration as a tool to gain a reputation of credibility. Secondly, government intervention was used in order to underline and facilitate this process, but was not primarily used to meet the convergence criteria of monetary union itself. However, eventually, the effects of the convergence criteria of the Maastricht Treaty started to feed back into the adjustment process of increasing monetary conservatism and automatic wage deflation. European economic and monetary union thereby enhanced and supported a model of interaction between a conservative monetary regime and a coordinated wage bargaining system that had already been conceived in the mid-1970s and disseminated throughout the 1980s and 1990s.

Monetary integration and credibility

In economic theory, there are differing views about the usefulness of fixed exchange rate regimes. On the one hand, if they are accompanied by an anti-inflationary international monetary standard, they can be seen as one way of escaping the inflationary consequences of the time inconsistency problem of optimal discretionary monetary policy discussed above. On the other hand, these regimes imply other costs that emanate from the lack of freedom to react to previously unanticipated real macroeconomic disturbances (Alogoskoufis and Smith 1991; Alogoskoufis 1994: 195). In the economic literature on EMU, the latter problem is frequently discussed. Many economists argue that the advantages of a fixed exchange rate regime are outweighed by the disadvantage of sacrificing national monetary policy as a response to asymmetric shocks (Bayoumi and Eichengreen 1993). Moreover, given that EMU combines a centralized monetary authority with a decentralized political system, problems with identifying the relevant criteria for inflation targeting in a heterogeneous economic area lead to unsuitable policy positions (Enderlein 2001: 36).[56]

In this section, I will focus on the first aspect of monetary integration, as an anti-inflationary policy tool that has served as the driving force for pursuing the monetary union project, and will discuss briefly how, in economic terms, monetary integration relates to the issue of credibility.

When governments peg their currencies to a non-inflationary currency, the implications of such a move are similar to following a monetarist policy rule: “Any growth in domestic costs or inflation that threatens the government’s ability to maintain the current exchange rate in the medium term must be met by restrictive monetary and fiscal policy responses” (Iversen and Thygesen 1998: 63). Since economic agents know this, in a fixed exchange rate regime monetary authorities have to react to inflation differentials with the anchor currency; the hope of policy-makers is that the expectations of the agents will focus on the low inflation rate of the anchor currency and thereby adjust their inflationary behaviour accordingly. In other words, pegging one's currency to a low-inflation currency has potentially the same reputation effect as having an independent central bank. However, as in the discussion about the effect of central bank independence, the crucial question is the credibility of the exchange rate regime. The credibility of the exchange rate regime, in turn, depends on its potential to allow for depreciation.

If a government enters a fixed exchange rate regime with a low inflation anchor currency, the dampening effect of this move on inflation will depend on the capacity of the government to rule out any exchange rate adjustment. If the government allows depreciation despite its announcement that the currency is fixed, the credibility of the exchange rate regime will be low and there is no reason why inflation differentials should become smaller. At the same time, given the differentials in the real economy between two countries and differences in the historic record on inflation, currency traders will expect a currency adjustment if the differentials are too high and if the institutional credentials of the exchange rate regime are weak.

When looking at the different types of exchange rate regimes that have been implemented in Western Europe, we can judge them by the credibility of their exchange rate commitment (table 4.1). It turns out that already, from a theoretical point of view, one should expect the 'snake-in-the-tunnel' and the 'floating snake' to have low credibility scores since currencies could be adjusted and inflation differentials between the participating countries were high. Under the previous European Monetary System, exchange rates were still adjustable, but the commitments by governments to minimizing inflation differentials were stronger than before. They had

Table 4.1 Exchange rate regimes and credibility

	Snake: Fixed but frequently adjusted exchange rates	EMS: Fixed but adjustable exchange rates	EMU: Currency union
Period	1973-79	1979-99	Since 1999
Devaluation	Possible	Under certain conditions	Not possible
Credibility	Low	Dependent on negotiations on currency adjustment	Absolute

become even stronger with the convergence criteria of the Maastricht Treaty. But only monetary union reaches the level of absolute credibility of sticking to a low inflationary regime.

The credibility of European monetary integration

The idea of a European economic and monetary union has been on the agenda since the Werner Report whose recommendations were adopted as a goal of the European Community in March 1971.[57] It therefore preceded the spread of monetarist economic policy thinking, the return to monetary conservatism in Europe and also the massive increase in international capital flows that are all seen to have been the driving forces of European monetary union. The plans for a monetary and economic union were primarily politically motivated by the European integration process itself and by the aim to stabilize intra-European trade and the pricing system within the Common Agricultural Policy. Nevertheless, it would be wrong not to relate the further evolution of the European monetary union to the shift towards monetary conservatism in Europe.

The actual currency system that followed the Werner Plan in 1971 was soon redefined in its goals and ambitions. The Werner plan provided the intellectual justification for the 'snake' arrangement, which was instituted by the European Community in March 1972. The snake, however, was far from what was expected of a currency union, as it consisted only of an intra-EC exchange rate regime to which some non-EC members could peg their currencies. From the very beginning, the snake was seen as inherently unstable (Corden 1972). Since there was no pooling of foreign exchange reserves and no central monetary authority, there was no mechanism capable of ensuring the coordination of national policies. Individual members might choose to absorb real resources from the other members by running a balance of payment deficit with them (Cobham 1989: 204).[58]

The currency snake soon encountered fundamental weaknesses. National economies dealt with the different business cycles through adopting different approaches to monetary policies, which allowed for inflation differentials between countries. After a while, the responses by governments to the challenges of the first oil shock had become increasingly diverse; adjustment became pressing and ended in regular turmoil. Parity alignments were large and on occasions required the temporary closure of foreign exchange markets while the package of realignments was bargained over (Currie 1991). During the short life of the snake between 1972 and 1978, a pattern of frequent emergency adjustments of individual currencies emerged. The British pound only stayed in the snake for a couple of months during 1972, while the French franc left the snake twice in 1974 and in 1976. Without the membership of the big European countries and ongoing realignments and reshuffling, the snake quickly regressed into a 'permissive reptile', as *The Economist* mocked it.[59] Since these patterns could be anticipated and currency traders could speculate on currency adjustment, the instability of the system grew over time. In other words, the snake contributed more to the fragility of the international monetary system during the 1970s than to its strength. Although the snake was the beginning of increasing monetary integration in Europe, Gros and Thygesen estimate that "the mid-1970s marked the low point in European monetary integration" (Gros and Thygesen 1992: 20).[60] The snake never acquired a reputation for serving as a low inflation anchor.[61]

The policy shift towards monetarism

Despite the dismal failure of the snake to achieve exchange rate stability and to the surprise of many observers, the pursuit of monetary and economic union in Western Europe continued throughout the 1980s and 1990s. The European Monetary System (EMS) and its Exchange Rate Mechanism (ERM) were set up in March 1979. Since their institutions were similar to those of the snake, they were quickly dubbed the 'super-snake' and again met with universal scepticism from economists and public alike. Governments, on the other hand, not only pushed through the founding of the EMS but also soon engaged in the Single European Market programme. The German government of Helmut Schmidt made great efforts to get the EMS accepted by the other European countries in order to stabilize German exports. Moreover, and more importantly, there was also a decisive effort among various other national governments to make their participation in the EMS work better than in the snake.[62]

For instance, as has been documented by McNamara, the French government reacted to the failure of the French franc to remain within the snake with a radical policy shift. First, the French and the German governments had spent vast sums of money to keep the French franc within the snake in 1976 and until the last minute were finalizing new plans for reforming the snake.[63] Afterwards, President Giscard d'Estaing and Prime Minister Raymond Barre turned membership into a political question of top priority (McNamara 1998: 130ff.). In fact, unwillingness in late 1973 to follow Germany's lead and reduce its monetary growth drained France's foreign exchange reserves and prompted its departure from the currency bloc. "The snake could impose a discipline on us we may not be willing to accept," a senior official in the French Finance Ministry was quoted as saying.[64] This approach was only interrupted briefly by the expansionary economic policy of the early Mitterand government. When the Mitterand government had to choose between abandoning the French franc in the EMS and changing its expansive fiscal policy, the government reversed its policy.

The example of France illustrates how governments started to use first the snake and later the exchange rate mechanism as disciplinary devices to support their own weakly equipped monetary policy. This policy has since spread to all countries that are now member countries of the EMU. But more astonishing are those countries where an even sharper policy shift took place. The most prominent example here is Ireland. Ireland had the Irish pound fixed to the British pound sterling for 150 years. However, in 1978, the Irish government made a strong move towards joining the EMS because of the promise of currency stability, better trading conditions and extra EEC aid afterwards. The Irish government clearly feared that after the dismal record of the British economy during the 1970s, if they stayed outside with Britain they risked having to devalue, importing British economic troubles and facing new trade barriers set up by EMS members. Moreover, government ministers stated that they thought that "EMS membership may help them to keep down wages".[65] Throughout the 1980s, therefore, European governments tried to prepare their countries for stable participation in the EMS, because this was seen as a tool for the hard currency policy that had increasingly become the focus of economic policy-making.

The role of Germany within the EMS

In the general process of Western European governments moving towards a policy of 'sound money', the role of Germany is worth mentioning. By the mid-1980s, the German monetary regime had become the role model in Europe to which every other country and the European Commission oriented itself. The whole architecture of the EMU, the construction of the European Central Bank and the exchange rate mechanism were modelled on a strong and low inflation German currency. Without this role model to which all governments could aspire, European monetary integration would not have been feasible, since the lack of a dominant mode of central banking and monetary policy had been a major stumbling block to earlier attempts at economic and monetary union (McNamara 1998).

The dominant position of the German economic model was partly related to its economic importance for the smaller neighbouring countries. Austria has traditionally enjoyed strong economic ties with Germany and has not pursued an independent monetary policy. The Netherlands and Belgium have perceived themselves as dependent on the strong German market. As mentioned above, the French Barre government already took a strong liking to the German role model in the mid-1970s.

But the main attraction of the German model for those countries that were not direct neighbours was that the German model remained robust during the economic shocks of the 1970s and seemed to have succeeded in combining a stable currency and sound economic policy with moderate levels of unemployment and reasonable rates of economic growth. The example of Germany showed that a hard currency and a high level of employment were not incompatible. Germany was among those European countries that had recorded a reasonable economic performance in the 1970s and 1980s (figure 4.1). With regard to inflation, Germany outperformed all countries of the OECD; with regard to unemployment, only Sweden, Finland and Austria did better. Sweden and Finland, however, paid the price of above-average inflation rates.

Figure 4.1 Inflation and unemployment in Estern Europe, 1970-89

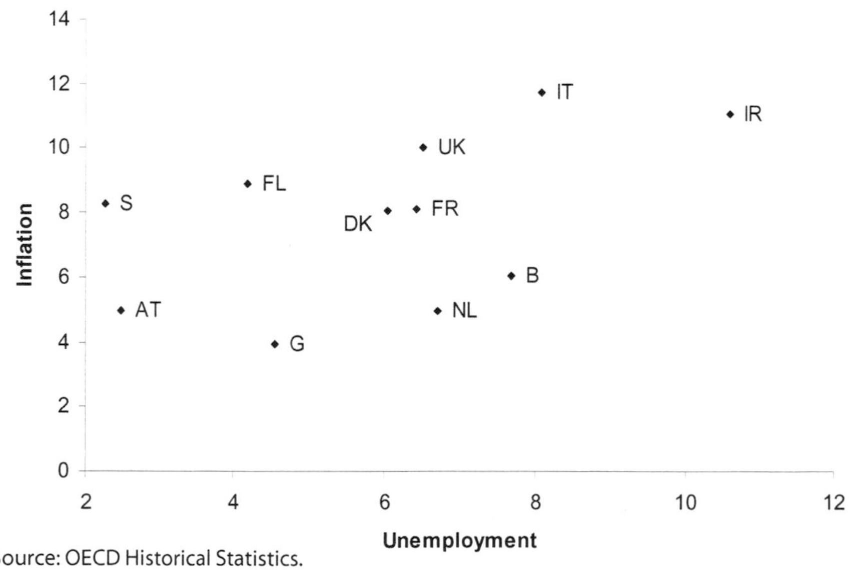

Source: OECD Historical Statistics.

Governments therefore hoped to import the non-inflationary reputation of the D-mark by pegging their currency to it. In contrast to its European neighbours, Germany stood out as successfully fighting inflation in the wake of the first oil shock. On average, German inflation rates between 1972 and 1980 remained at 5 percent, half the European average (McNamara 1998: 152). In the debates of policy-makers of the time, the successful fight against inflation was fully attributed to the monetary policy of the Bundesbank, not the government.[66] Associated with the non-inflationary reputation of the Bundesbank and endorsed by political commitment, German governments hoped that they had found a role model of economic policy-making that would deliver low inflation automatically.

In comparison, most other European governments found themselves in the position of being unable to control domestic distributive conflict, especially in the wake of the oil price shocks of the 1970s. The experience of stagflation across Europe changed the minds of European social democrats about how best to achieve wage and price stability, while also converting Europe's central bankers from soft Keynesians to hard currency advocates (Rhodes 2001b; Marshall 1999). The "brute reality of economic management in the 1970s and 1980s", as Martin Rhodes has called this process, was more decisive in driving a shift in the policy regime than the arrival of a neo-liberal paradigm or the spread of a sound monetary ideology (Rhodes 2001b, 3; quoted from manuscript).

Monetarism without credibility

The effect of monetary integration on national governments in the framework of the snake and EMS, however, was mixed. On the one hand, governments lost their national autonomy in monetary policy since monetary authorities had the primary task of ensuring that the currency was kept within the exchange rate mechanism. They were forced to follow the monetary policy of the anchor currency, the German mark, without being able to influence that policy. On the other hand, neither the snake nor the EMS was domestically credible enough to adjust the inflationary expectations of economic agents to those of the Germans.

The countries that experienced the dilemma of tight monetarism without credibility most painfully were those of the inner circle of the snake, the Benelux countries plus Denmark, France and, from 1978, Ireland. They were severely hit by the high interest rates of the Bundesbank without being able to convey their commitment to the exchange rate system to their wage bargaining partners. As a result, the core EMS countries suffered from higher unemployment and inflation throughout the 1970s and 1980s (Kurzer 1988 and 1993; Scharpf 2000; see also De Grauwe and Vanhaverbeke 1990).

During the 1980s, those countries that were openly committed to the exchange rate mechanism fared much worse in terms of employment than those that were not. The exchange rate commitment forced their central banks to deflate, but the credibility of the EMS had not been strong enough to adjust the expectations of their trade unions. Those countries moved only very slowly towards the beneficial reputational effects of monetary conservatism. At the same time, there was little alternative to the attempts made by governments to strengthen the commitment to the EMS. The core snake countries plus France were among the founding countries of the EC and therefore committed to European integration. Apart from France, they were among the small countries that had a strong interest in supranational frameworks, which gave them more influence *vis-à-vis* the larger member states. The early participants were also the governments of the smaller European countries that traded heavily with Germany. They were determined to maintain the parity with the D-mark, because if their currencies depreciated they would again be subject to inflationary pressures along rising import prices. Despite the negative effects, the early EMS participants were condemned to proceed further towards monetary integration rather than seek alternatives.

The credibility of EMU

By the late 1980s, the EMS had become a stable arrangement. Between April 1983 and January 1987 there were only four realignments, while between January 1987 and the EMS crisis in September 1992 there were no currency realignments (McNamara 1998: 162). At the same time, capital flows and market integration increased significantly over the same period. Policy-makers were satisfied with the working of the EMS as a system that had reached a certain degree of stability. For the first time, domestic policies and the requirements of monetary integration were supporting and reinforcing each other rather than being at odds.

Hence, in 1989, Jacques Delors re-launched the European Monetary Union and, in 1991, the Maastricht Treaty set out the route towards it. The Maastricht Treaty provided for the second stage of monetary union to start on 1 January 1994, by which date member states had to have taken measures to ensure the lasting convergence necessary for the achievement of economic and monetary union, in particular with regard to price stability and sound public finance. By the time the Maastricht Treaty was adopted, the German role model was disseminated throughout Europe to the degree that European Monetary Union was not only modelled on the German Bundesbank, but also central bank independence had become an important precondition for monetary union. As the European Monetary Institute pointed out in its convergence reports, central bank independence was seen as "essential for the move towards Monetary Union and thus a prerequisite for Monetary Union" (European Monetary Institute 1999: 20). In the run-up to monetary union, the member states were therefore required to increase the legal independence of their central banks, despite the fact that the EMS already required the central banks to employ monetary policies that would keep them in line with the currency bands. In order to guarantee a high degree of independence for the European Central Bank, the independence of national central banks was seen as a supporting pillar.

As can be seen in Table 4.2, both central bank independence and currency pegging are monetary policy devices that were adopted universally in all countries in Western Europe – independent of whether a country was an active member of the European Monetary System or not. All countries had accorded their central bank the status of legal independence, even the United Kingdom. The British government had notified the EU Council that it would not participate in the single currency and therefore was not required by the Maastricht Treaty to delegate a higher degree of independence to the Bank of England. Also the Swedish government, which did not participate in the ERM, amended several laws affecting the Sveriges Riksbank in order to increase its independence. At the same time, apart from the United Kingdom, all European countries participated in a form of exchange rate system. The Nordic countries had started to peg their currencies in the early 1990s. Finland joined the EMS after that.

An examination of the depreciation of national currencies *vis-à-vis* the German mark shows that credibility only emerged with the anticipation of the Maastricht Treaty and EMU. During the 1970s and 1980s, only Austria and the Netherlands were really in a fixed exchange rate system with the German mark. Belgium approached a fixed currency regime in the 1970s, but lost momentum in the 1980s. For all other countries, a serious commitment to a fixed exchange rate system only emerged in the 1990s, after the Treaty of Maastricht. It was only at the end of the 1980s, when the

Table 4.2	**Exchange rate pegging and central bank independence**	
	Currency pegging	Recent changes in legal independence of central bank
Austria	Officially pegged to DM in 1980, member of EMS and EMU	
Belgium	Member of snake, EMS, EMU	Legal independence in 1993
Denmark	Member of snake and EMS	
Finland	Markka pegged to ECU in 1991, member of EMU	Legal independence in 1998
France	Member of snake 1971-73, 1975-76, EMS and EMU	Legal independence in 1993
Germany	Member of snake, EMS, EMU	
Ireland	Member of snake until 1972; member of EMS in 1978 and EMU	Legal independence in 1998
Italy	Member of the snake until 1973, member of EMS and EMU	Legal independence in 1992
Netherlands	Member of snake, EMS and EMU	Legal independence in 1998
Portugal	Member of ERM-EMS in 1992	Legal independence in 1992
Spain	Member of ERM-EMS in 1989	Legal independence in 1994
Sweden	Associate to the floating snake until 1977 Krone pegged to ECU in 1990.	Legal independence in 1999
United Kingdom	Member of the snake-in-the-tunnel in 1971-72 and of the ERM 1990-92	Legal independence in 1998

Note: Central bank independence was assumed when score was 0.35 or higher on the Cukierman index (McNamara 2002: 49).

Sources: for currency pegging, Andrews (1994) and various sources; for legal independence of central bank, McNamara (2002) and European Monetary Institute (1999).

domestic policy shifts had reached a degree of monetary conservatism, that the tight convergence criteria that were attached to EMU became acceptable. Indeed, this led to the credibility of the exchange rate regime that governments had tried to achieve through the initial pegging of their currencies.[67] Of those countries that were signed up for monetary union, only Italy (1.56), Spain (1.69) and Portugal (3.47) still had considerable inflation differentials with Germany during the 1990s (see table 4.3). All the early EMS countries that had suffered under the strong D-mark during the 1980s had negative differentials. This was due in part to the relatively high

German inflation rate in 1994 and 1995 after unification, but the reduction of the large inflation differentials of the 1970s and 1980s eased the pressure on European currencies considerably.

Due to its economic importance within Western Europe and its economic record of coming through the 1970s in a reasonable shape, Germany had become the monetary anchor in Europe. The German government itself promoted monetary integration largely modelled on its own experience. But the important point is that, apart from the case of Austria, the anticipated effect of wage bargaining actors adjusting inflationary expectation – along the lines of the German model – did not automatically spread to other countries participating in the EMS. Nor did the credibility of the Bundesbank suppress inflationary expectations in other countries throughout the 1970s and 1980s. Since, on the one hand, governments were committed to keeping their currencies within the EMS while, on the other, domestic wage bargaining did not respond to these constraints, the net effects of the EMS were negative.

It was only when Economic and Monetary Union was finalized in the Maastricht Treaty – despite the massive speculative attacks on the Italian and British currencies in the EMS crisis in 1992 – that the credibility

Table 4.3 Depreciation of the national currency *vis-à-vis* the German mark (inflation differential with Germany, average per decade)

	1970s	1980s	1990s
Austria	-1.50 (1.16)	-1.20 (0.93)	0.00 (-0.12)
Belgium	15.70 (2.13)	33.00 (1.99)	-0.30 (-0.38)
Denmark	43.20 (4.53)	33.60 (3.99)	-0.90 (-0.42)
Finland	61.00 (5.56)	25.10 (4.41)	49.20 (-0.33)
France	46.50 (4.33)	65.80 (4.46)	-0.20 (-0.63)
Ireland	102.40 (8.29)	80.50 (6.43)	4.70 (-0.24)
Italy	161.00 (8.15)	150.00 (8.27)	133.40 (1.56)
Netherlands	8.60 (2.01)	3.30 (-0.05)	-0.10 (-0.06)
Portugal	225.30 (12.68)	718.20 (14.73)	151.90 (3.47)
Spain	97.20 (9.54)	118.10 (7.34)	106.80 (1.69)
Sweden	55.90 (4.07)	89.40 (5.07)	49.70 (0.98)
United Kingdom	79.20 (8.15)	83.90 (4.53)	3.50 (1.18)
Mean	74.50 (5.88)	116.60 (5.18)	41.50 (0.56)
Mean (without Portugal and Spain)	57.20 (4.84)	56.34 (4.00)	23.90 (0.15)

Sources: Deutsche Bundesbank; Monatsbericht January 1998, p. 74; own calculations.

effects began to filter through. Any reputation effects of monetary conservatism stemming from European monetary integration were therefore only to be expected from the 1990s onwards.

The effects of monetary integration and restrictiveness on wage bargaining: sharpening the conflict between employment and real wage protection

The shift towards fixed exchange rates and restrictive monetary policy as anti-inflationary economic policy devices had real implications for the external conditions and conduct of wage bargaining in Western Europe from the 1980s onwards. Monetary integration via the EMS and the lifting of capital controls facilitated and required tighter monetary policy in the EMS zone. Capital movements and the fixed but adjustable exchange rates forced the monetary authorities in all countries to follow the monetary policy of the most powerful monetary authorities, in particular the American Federal Reserve and the Bundesbank. In Western Europe, national central banks tried to diminish the inflation differentials between their own currency and the German mark in order to ease the pressure on them to depreciate their currencies.

Figure 4.2 Real long-term interest rates in Western Europe, 1970-99

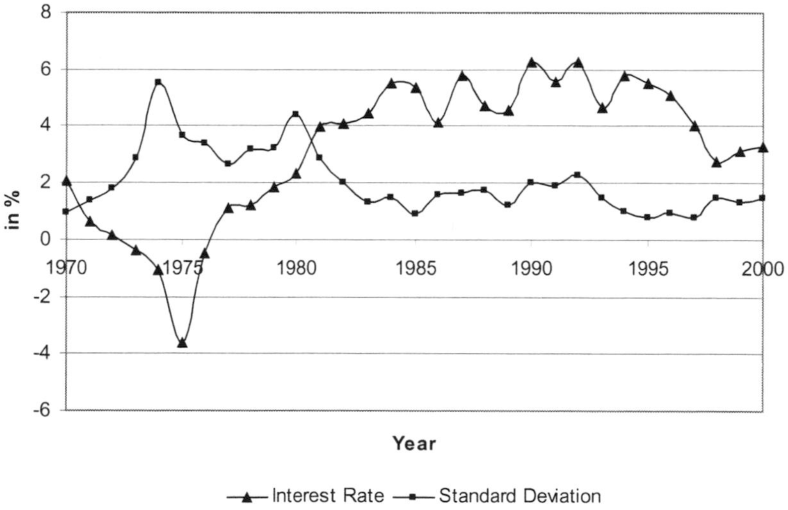

Source: OECD Historical Statistics.

As a consequence, from 1980 onwards, two major changes took place in the monetary policy of Western European countries: firstly, monetary policy became severely restrictive; secondly, policies converged. Figure 4.2 illustrates this development by showing real long-term interest rates as a measure of monetary policy. Between 1974 and 1984, the average real long-term interest rate in Western Europe increased from minus 1 percent to 5.5 percent. At the same time, the differences between countries diminished sharply (standard deviation declined from 5.5 to 0.9 in the same period). As an illustration: in 1974 real long-term interest rates varied from -11 per cent in Finland to 3 per cent in Germany. By 1985, the variation had decreased to 4.5 per cent in Austria and 7.1 per cent in Ireland. The period of vastly differing responses to the economic shock of the 1980s had been replaced by a standard response of restrictive monetary policy to inflationary pressures.

There exists a broad economic literature on the impact of surrendering monetary independence compared to fixed exchange rates, mostly with regard to the approach of EMU.[68] But, in fact, those countries that participated in the EMS had already abandoned a truly independent monetary policy by the early 1980s.[69] Even for those countries outside EMS, the differential in real interest rates to the Western European average was less than 1 per cent throughout the period. As pointed out earlier in this chapter, devaluations became scarcer and increasingly difficult to portray as acceptable within the framework of the EMS. Therefore, many of the implications that have been discussed in the literature on the impact of monetary integration on wage bargaining issues had in fact been relevant from the mid-1980s onwards and not only from the point at which EMU actually started.

There are two implications for wage bargaining and employment performance that stem from tight monetary policy and monetary integration.[70] Firstly, a tight monetary response to inflationary pressure has contractory effects on the economy and reduces output and employment. The speed of adjustment and further employment effects are – among other factors – dependent on the responsiveness of real wages to the level in unemployment. The responsiveness of changes of the real wage to unemployment is termed real wage flexibility.[71] A tighter monetary policy bears lower costs if real wage rigidities are low. It therefore has more severe employment effects in countries where real wage rigidities are higher.[72] A shift towards monetarism requires a higher degree of real wage flexibility if negative employment effects were to be minimized in the case of external shocks.

Secondly, increasing monetary integration in the past removed the possibility of using exchange rate adjustments to respond to inflation differentials. This change was particularly difficult for those countries that had used devaluations for boosting competitiveness. Changes in the exchange rate can alleviate balance of payments problems that are caused by external shocks or internal developments. Devaluations are a short-term adjustment of relative prices without rendering to the adjustment of wages. For instance, the increase of domestic prices can be balanced by a change in the exchange rate, which in turn changes the relationship between domestic prices and import prices. This prevents a shift in demand from domestic to imported goods. On the other hand, prices for domestic and imported goods may increase so that devaluations reduce the real wage (without touching the nominal wage level).

When devaluations are not possible because of fixed exchange rates, a differential in inflation rates will change the relationship between domestic goods and imported goods and induce a shift in demand. An adjustment of domestic prices will become necessary, frequently causing either a renegotiation of wage levels or changes in relative unit labour costs that produce changes in the real exchange rate. In both cases, under fixed or flexible exchange rates, the adjustment has to take place domestically. The adjustment of exchange rates can offer a short-term boost in competitiveness, while putting pressure on real wages. This might induce a pressure on wage bargainers to compensate for real wage losses. The difference of the impact of fixed and flexible exchange rates lies primarily in the form of wage adjustments (real wage losses versus money wage adjustments). In both cases, wages have to be adjusted eventually. However, in flexible exchange rate systems, devaluation offers a short-term opportunity to increase competitiveness via productivity increases (Mitchell 1993).

The effects of the increasing monetary integration and restrictiveness on the European countries therefore implied that the costs of different rates of inflation in different countries with stable exchange rates had to be compensated for by additional real wage adjustments. With the increasing effectiveness of the monetarist policy of bringing down inflation and nominal wage increases, adjustment also increasingly meant real wage losses. Moreover, the monetarist threat by central banks sharpened the trade-off between employment and real pay for trade union bargaining priorities. The loss of real wages, however, conflicted with established rules and traditions of wage bargaining procedures in many countries. The combination of monetary restrictiveness and monetary integration sharpened the distributive dilemma trade unions faced when they tried to protect real wages. The assumption here is that this affected different countries to different degrees and that the different effects led governments to intervene in wage bargaining processes.

Central bank independence, monetary policy and government intervention

How do the preceding arguments on monetary credibility and exchange rate regimes relate to the issue of government intervention? In Chapter 2, I assumed that governments use negotiated approaches towards wage setting in order to strengthen their shift in disinflation policy from voluntary wage restraint to monetarist policies by increasing the credibility of a conservative monetary policy. Because labour markets are organized by trade unions and employers' organizations, which serve as important information carriers, governments intervene in wage bargaining procedures in order to emphasize a shift in their monetary policy approach. During the golden years of the post-war period up to the mid-1970s, governments, banks and social partners developed patterns of interaction with regard to the stabilization of the economy. In many countries, this was based on an accommodating monetary and fiscal approach on the part of the government. When the economic policy by governments shifted towards monetarism, the government needed to convey its new approach towards the social partners without running the risk of negative deflation effects. Government intervention in wage bargaining can be interpreted as the attempts of governments to enhance the credibility of a monetarist deflationary policy.

If this is the case, we should be able to observe that, in those instances where central banks have a reputation for being conservative and independent, the need for governments to enhance their reputation should be lower than in cases where central banks do not have a conservative reputation. In other words, if the main effect of monetary policy as held in the literature is a reputation effect, one should assume that different degrees of reputation, in terms of banks' predisposition towards conservatism, prompt different government reactions to wage bargaining. The higher the credibility of a conservative central bank, the lower is the need for governments to boost that credibility by intervening in wage bargaining processes. I will examine this by testing the correlation between an index of central bank independence and the measure of government intervention developed in Chapter 3.

Central bank independence

Indices of central bank independence are almost as abundant as measures of wage bargaining coordination (Mangano 1998). The two indices most used and respected in the literature are the ones presented by Grilli, Masciandaro and Tabellini (1991) and by Cukierman (1998). Both indices are based on a set of legal characteristics of central bank constitutions. They emphasize the appointment procedures of the governor, the procedure for formulating monetary policy, and particular processes of monetary policies such as lending to governments etc. The two indices correlate highly (correlation coefficient = 0.84** for the countries studied here).[73]

In the following, I will use the Cukierman index of legal bank independence mainly for reasons of data availability.[74] The Cukierman index is a composed index made up of a number of variables that are designed to capture the legal independence of the bank. It measures both the independence of the bank from government and the "conservative bias" of the central bank as embodied in the law (Cukierman 1998: 377). It does not measure the actual monetary policy of the central bank in terms of changes in monetary supply or interest rates. Because the variables aim to measure the legal constitution of the bank, the index is basically time-invariant, although it was measured for different points in time. With regard to the countries of Western Europe, there was no change in the legal independence of central banks between 1950 and 1990. Only after the Treaty of Maastricht set forth criteria for European Monetary Union were steps towards increased legal independence adopted.

In Cukierman's ranking of central banks by overall legal independence, Germany and Austria rank among the highest of the 68 countries studied, after Switzerland, which leads the independence table (table 4.4). Among the countries studied here, Belgium ranks lowest. The Mediterranean countries of Spain and Italy also have low scores (both 0.21), followed by Sweden and Finland (both 0.27).[75] Unfortunately, no independence score exists for Portugal. Since the central bank of Portugal did not gain legal independence until 1992, it must have been below the independence threshold in the preceding years. During the 1990s, only Germany, Austria and Denmark did not change the legal regulation of their central banks in favour of greater independence. All three countries, however, already had the highest-ranking central banks in Western Europe.

The stability of central bank independence over time indicates that the measurement captures the reputation of the bank disseminated to politi-

Table 4.4 Legal independence of central banks, Western Europe

	Cukierman index
Austria	0.58
Belgium	0.19
Denmark	0.47
Finland	0.27
France	0.28
Germany	0.66
Ireland	0.39
Italy	0.22
Netherlands	0.42
Portugal	-
Spain	0.21
Sweden	0.27
United Kingdom	0.31

Source: Cukierman (1998).

cal and economic actors. Even if the laws on which the status of the bank rests were changed, the reputation might nevertheless persist for a long period of time. What is measured is therefore a general conservative attitude on the part of the political system towards economic policy-making, which is enshrined in legal foundations of the monetary authority and consequently not easily shifted.

In an important finding, figure 4.3 shows a strong correlation between the Cukierman index of the independence of central banks and the average degree of government intervention in wage bargaining over the period of the 1980s and 1990s (correlation coefficient = 0.72**).[76] The implication of the graph is in line with what could be expected from the theoretical assumptions: in countries with a central bank that is highly independent and therefore has the reputation of being conservative in its monetary policy, governments are less likely to intervene in wage bargaining processes. (If one controls for the degree of wage bargaining coordination, the partial correlation coefficient increases to 0.85**.) In other words, the conservative reputation of the central bank is strongly negatively correlated with the likelihood of governments to intervene in wage bargaining processes. During the 1980s and 1990s, governments were much less likely to intervene in the labour market in those countries where central banks were traditionally strongly independent and thus conservative.

Figure 4.3 Central Bank independence and government intervention in wage bargaining, Western Europe 1980-99

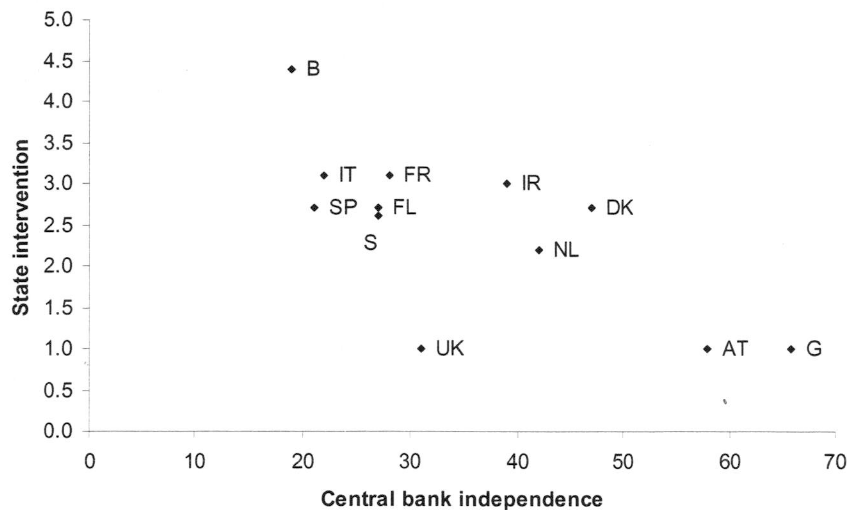

Source: Cukierman (1998) for central bank independence.

The only outlier in the otherwise stable and strong correlation is the United Kingdom. (If the United Kingdom is taken out of the correlation, the correlation coefficient increases to 0.87**.) The Bank of England was traditionally controlled by the government and has only recently gained legal independence. Independence of the central bank was advocated by a number of Chancellors of the Exchequer before it was finally put into practice. At the same time, the British case is also an outlier since the government not only adopted particularly stringent monetary policies after 1979 but was also exceptionally reluctant to engage in interventions into wage bargaining procedures for other – political – reasons. The British case, therefore, is an outlier on all accounts.

Monetary policy

As assumed above, an independent central bank does not have to pursue restrictive monetary policies in order to be credible. The credibility of the policies rests on the reputation of the bank for ensuring price stability. If the reputation of the bank is strong, the bank has even less need to employ restrictive policies since economic agents anticipate deflation and its consequences without the instruments being used. Therefore, while there should be a clear impact of central bank independence on inflation, there should not necessarily be any recourse to tight monetary policy. It is in this sense that economists have assumed central bank independence to be something of a free lunch. Where the reputation of the central bank is traditionally conservative, the use of tight monetary policies should be lower than in those cases where the reputation of the central bank is less conservative. In those cases, however, where governments and the bank itself try to create a more conservative reputation for the central bank, we should also expect to observe a higher incidence of government intervention set on making these policies more credible for the social partners.

Alternatively, one could assume that governments use monetary intervention in order to strengthen a particularly tight policy measure. When central banks engage in deflationary policies, either by keeping the money supply tight or by raising interest rates, governments will interfere in wage bargaining procedures in order to make these policy measures understood by wage bargaining actors. We can therefore test to what extent government intervention is related to the conduct of monetary policies.

In the following section, I will use two indicators for restrictive monetary policy. The first is long-term real interest rates. Long-term real interest rates indicate the real effect of the setting of interest rates by the central bank in a given economy. Changes in the money supply, on the other hand, are the direct mechanism with which central banks can influence the availability of money in the market. Table 4.5 shows the averages for both indicators over the 1980s and 1990s. The mean values show that, for both policy instruments, monetary policy became tighter from the 1980s to the 1990s, although the average changes in the money supply hide wide fluctuations between years. Moreover, the real shift in monetary policy took place from the 1970s to the 1980s. On average for the 13 countries, real long-term interest rates were negative during the 1970s, while the average change in money supply stands at 13 per cent compared to 9 per cent in the 1990s. There is a clear shift towards restrictive monetary policy.

My findings regarding the interaction between the reputation of the central bank, monetary policy and government intervention in wage bargaining processes are presented in tables 4.6 and 4.7. The tables are based on annual observations of monetary policy and government intervention, while remaining constant for central bank independence. No time lags have been assumed for the relationship between monetary policy and

Table 4.5 **Monetary policies by central banks, 1980s and 1990s, Western Europe**

	Long-term real interest rates (as a percentage)		Changes in money supply compared to previous year (as a percentage)	
	1980-89	1990-99	1980-89	1990-99
Austria	4.14	4.33	6.59	7.93
Belgium	5.98	5.05	4.18	3.12
Denmark	4.64	4.05	15.16	5.55
Finland	7.00	6.10	11.52	31.25
France	4.77	5.70	8.05	1.25
Germany	3.52	6.68	6.22	7.51
Ireland	2.57	5.70	8.14	13.49
Italy	4.23	6.58	11.63	5.71
Netherlands	5.61	4.96	6.82	7.76
Portugal	-	4.93	19.16	13.04
Spain	4.19	5.86	14.41	7.23
Sweden	4.07	5.30	7.27	2.59
UK	3.58	4.76	14.81	10.78
Mean	4.53	5.38	10.30	9.00

Note: data on Portugal on interest rates only available for 1993 and 1994.

Sources: OECD; IMF Financial Statistics.

Table 4.6 **Average government intervention by central bank independence and long-term real interest rates (observation per cell), 1980-99**

		Central Bank Independence	
		Low	High
Long-term real interest rates	Low	2.59 (54)	1.34 (35)
	High	3.02 (58)	2.42 (45)

Note: high central bank independence was assumed when CBI > 0.28.

Sources: for central bank independence, Cukierman (1998) and for long-term real interest rates, OECD.

government intervention. As seen before, when correlating central bank independence and the degree of government intervention on the basis of countries, government intervention is generally higher in cases where central bank independence is low.

The more interesting observation in this context, however, is that government intervention is particularly low where real long-term interest rates are comparatively low and central bank independence is high. Where central banks have a strong conservative reputation and do not need to prove this reputation with tight monetary policies, governments tend to intervene less in wage bargaining. On the other hand, government intervention is particularly high in those cases where central bank independence is low, but monetary policy is tight. Government intervention, in other words, goes hand-in-hand with tight monetary policy in situations where the institutional set-up does not provide a credible conservative reputation for the central bank.

This result is partly endorsed by the data on changes in money supply. Once again, government intervention is highest in cases where the conservative reputation of the central bank is low and the low expansion of the money supply indicates a tight monetary policy (on average 2.95 in table 4.7). However, with regard to the cases where the independence of the central bank is high, government intervention is lowest where monetary policies in terms of money supply expansion are also tight (on average 1.84). Again, given the volatility of the data, these results should be accorded less weight than the results on interest rates.

Table 4.7 Average government intervention by central bank independence and change in money supply (observation per cell), 1980-99

		Central Bank Independence	
		Low	High
Monetary expansion	Low	2.95 (65)	1.84 (51)
	High	2.63 (54)	2.12 (34)

Sources: for central bank independence, Cukierman (1998); for money supply, IMF (Financial Statistics).

Inflation

Finally, one counterargument needs to be explored. The main effect of independent central banks is to produce lower inflation. In empirical studies, the negative relationship between inflation, averaged over certain periods of time, and the legal independence of central banks has been shown (Alesina and Summers 1993; Cukierman 1998). If government intervention in wage bargaining is negatively related to the legal independence of the central bank, one might be inclined to argue that governments really react to inflation and not in dependence on the reputation of their central bank. In other words, the measure of central bank independence might not capture the reputation of the bank but more the inflationary pressure on a given country to which the government responds. Does government intervention in wage bargaining merely reflect efforts by governments to influence wage bargainers in order to fight inflation?

The data clearly shows that this is not the case. While government intervention is positively correlated with inflation as expected, this correlation disappears entirely when controlled for central bank independence. On the other hand, when the correlation between central bank independence and government intervention is controlled for inflation, the correlation becomes only marginally weaker.[77] The correlation is therefore driven by the independence of the central bank and not by the rate of inflation.

If one looks at the means of government intervention under different monetary regimes and different levels of inflation (table 4.8), this observa-

Table 4.8 Average government intervention by central bank independence and inflation (observation per cell), 1980-99

		Central Bank Independence	
		Low	High
Inflation	Low	3.01 (71)	1.69 (45)
	High	3.26 (34)	1.88 (57)

Source: for central bank independence, Cukierman (1998); for inflation, OECD (Historical Statistics).

tion becomes even more apparent. The row difference of government intervention between high and low inflation under the same monetary regime is only marginal, while the difference between columns, between a high and low degree of legal independence of central banks under the same impact of inflation, is substantial. Government intervention in wage bargaining processes is related to the reputation of the monetary regime. The fundamental constitution of the national economic and monetary policy framework matters for its policy behaviour and not the immediate policy pressure.[78]

Government intervention to foster monetary conservatism

Overall, the data gives support to the view that there is a systematic relationship between the reputation of the monetary authority and the behaviour of governments *vis-à-vis* wage bargaining institutions during a period when governments have shifted their economic policy towards tighter monetary policies. The underlying credibility argument is, moreover, intuitively reasonable in the context of the political economy literature: after World War II governments developed standard patterns of employment, monetary and fiscal policies that were in accordance with the institutional and organizational set up of the labour market (Lange and Garrett 1985; Scharpf 1991). Governments that had control over their central banks could use expansionary monetary policy in order to stimulate the economy and compensate trade union cooperation on wage restraint. Governments, which were not in control of monetary policy, had to adjust their economic policy accordingly. Wage bargaining actors learned to operate under a tight monetary framework.

In Sweden, the United Kingdom and Belgium, where the central banks were traditionally under the control of governments, the latter could force the banks to accommodate their economic policy, which was based on finding a compromise with trade unions on voluntary wage restraint. In Sweden, the interplay between a politically dominated Riksbank and highly centralized trade unions enabled a pattern of real wage restraint and frequent depreciation, which allowed for competitiveness and low labour costs (Lange and Garrett 1985; Scharpf 1991). In Germany and Austria, this option was not available and had not been pursued even by the social democratic governments of the 1970s. In both cases, the interaction between the social partners and the government rested on fundamental assumptions about the reaction of the other side to inflationary pressures. The independence of the central bank indicated the degree of opposition against accepting inflationary pressures. Where this opposition was constituted in the legal framework of the central bank, wage bargaining institutions had to accept this framework.

When a new economic consensus on monetary conservatism emerged among the political elite in the beginning of the 1980s, the interaction between governments and wage bargaining institutions started to change. This was particularly the case in those countries where the conservative reputation of the bank did not exist. Governments used their potential for intervention to adjust wage bargaining actors' expectations towards a new monetary regime.

In summary, it has not been the aim of this chapter to explain the shift by governments towards monetary conservatism, but to point out that this move in countries with highly regulated labour markets has prompted governments to intervene in wage bargaining procedures in order to adjust the expectations of trade unions and employers towards the new monetary regime.

That the relationship between economic policy and the attitudes of the governments *vis-à-vis* wage bargaining is primarily determined by a long-term preference for hard money on the part of the monetary authorities, rather than by the problems of the government, such as the public deficit, inflation or unemployment, might seem surprising at first glance. Government intervention and social pacts often occur under crisis conditions when several problems of public finance, inflation and external deficits coincide. However, we can observe that government intervention is not primarily a reaction to an increasing problem load, but more a long-term measure of the propensity of governments to directly influence wage bargaining outcomes averaged over decades. A long-term measure like the one used here, on the other hand, reflects the approach of governments to managing the issue of labour more generally, and is therefore seen as a better indicator of the general use of corporatist policy-making.

Finally, this chapter has argued that European monetary integration has been an instrument for achieving monetary conservatism, which in turn is based on the conservative reputation of the monetary authority. Since both the snake and the EMS were politically adjustable, neither exchange rate regime was able to achieve a conservative reputation before the mid-1990s. Only after the strong commitment to the convergence criteria under the Maastricht Treaty and after the survival of the Maastricht commitments following the EMS crisis in 1992 did the system finally gain the necessary reputation. By that time, many countries had already experienced a long period of trying to establish monetary conservatism – often without much success.

5 The Politics of Government Intervention

So far, I have considered the link between corporatist government intervention and monetary regimes. In this chapter, I will extend the line of explanation to the capacity of the government itself, examining how political institutions influence the decision of governments to intervene in wage bargaining procedures. Generally speaking, political decisions tend to be directed to preserve the *status quo* and governments have to overcome inertia and opposition from other political actors against change, which can use institutional devices in order to block political decisions.[79] Governments are primarily under pressure to avoid the political costs of a deflationary policy and aim to convince trade unions to commit themselves to wage restraint. Their ability to do so depends on the vulnerability of the government to the pressures from trade unions to be compensated for the negative externalities of restrictive monetary policy. This again is influenced by the political institutions themselves, the structure of the party system and the relationship between trade unions and political parties. The aim of this chapter is therefore to locate the political – rather than the economic – interaction between governments and social partners. Moreover, it aims to explain how weak governments and dependent political parties in particular use the means of government intervention to counteract economic crises that arise from the lack of adjustment of wage bargaining to a more restrictive economic environment.

Below, I will trace the political institutional factors that influence governments' behaviour. My argument is that governments have different abilities for dealing with the political costs of economic crises that arise when wage bargaining does not sufficiently respond to the new environment. High wage settlements under tight monetary policy can lead to major welfare losses since the reaction by central banks will reduce employment and thereby sacrifice growth. Governments therefore have, on principle, an interest in persuading trade unions to pursue moderate wage claims. On the other hand, when governments are able to display a strict non-accommodating economic policy, the adjustment of wage bargaining actors to the new conditions might take place faster without any further involvement on the part of the government. The choice is therefore between intervention in order to adjust trade union expectations or acquiescence to market forces disciplining wage bargaining actors.

The approach taken by the government of either intervening in wage bargaining or leaving wage bargainers to their own devices rests upon the ability of the government to make a credible commitment to disciplining wage bargainers. If a government cannot credibly commit itself to the discipline of tight monetary and fiscal policy, it will be more tempted to negotiate wage restraint in order to avoid the negative externalities of high wage settlements. Other actors will also shift their approach from accepting restraint due to the disciplinary force of the market compelling them to negotiate a price for wage restraint itself.

While restrictive monetary policy might solve the problem of high inflation, it does not furnish an answer to the equally salient question of losses in output and employment that follow from a deflationary policy. Governments either are strong enough to insulate themselves from the fall-out of bad economic performance or try to negotiate a mode of adjustment that decreases the economic costs. The strength of the government is accordingly based, firstly, on the institutions of the political system that translate votes into parliamentary majorities and the capacity of governments to act and, secondly, on the relationship between the governing parties and the trade unions themselves.

The chapter is divided into two sections. The main section examines the political institutional constraints on governments with regard to government intervention. It starts with a review of key aspects of the literature, followed by an examination of the relationship between relevant institutional factors and the measure of government intervention developed in Chapter 3. The main finding is that competitive types of governments in unified party systems have a low degree of government intervention, while strongly consensus-based governments in fragmented party systems have the highest degree of government intervention.

The next part presents an explanation for this pattern, drawing on an additional analytical element, the political fragmentation of trade unions. Finally, a more detailed case study compares the different government intervention outcomes in Belgium and United Kingdom, two countries with markedly different institutional constraint frameworks.

The second section considers another approach to the relations between political institutions and government intervention by examining the role of partisanship. The main finding is that, in general, right-wing governments tend to intervene less in wage bargaining procedures than left-wing governments. This was particularly the case during the 1970s, when incomes policy was seen as a suitable tool for supporting the Keynesian crisis management in many social democratic countries.

Institutional constraints on governments

The ability of governments to make a firm commitment on economic policy is shaped by the constraints that are embedded in the institutional design of political systems. Nations differ in their political institutions.[80] With regard to public policy, a whole range of studies has shown how political institutions determine the ability of governments to act.[81] The literature on political institutions has in recent years developed according to two diverging approaches: on the one hand, there have been increasing attempts to define the particular nature and interaction of veto players in political institutions in order to explain divergence in political outcomes by a particular set of veto players (Immergut 1992; Ganghof 2003; Tsebelis 2002); on the other hand, parts of the literature have attempted to classify national political systems into different categories by combining a large number of indicators into only a few dimensions (Schmidt 2002b; Lijphart 1999). While the first approach, regarding veto players, aims at answering the question of which type of veto player combination is responsible for which political outcome, the second, regarding consensus democracies, is more concerned with the general pattern of democratic institutions, while at the same time claiming that different types of democracies have distinctly different effects on outcomes (Lijphart 1999).

Veto players

The capacity of government to pursue and implement a policy can be hindered by the number of veto points a political system contains. Veto players are individual or collective actors whose agreement is necessary for a change in the status quo (Tsebelis 1999: 593; for a similar definition, see Tsebelis 1995: 301). Constitutional design can therefore be related to political outcomes. The veto player concept is thus particularly useful for studying the capacity of national governments to introduce substantial reforms in public policy (Schmidt 1996: 152). It identifies the number of hurdles a government has to take to introduce a shift in public policy in terms of legislative measures.

The literature on veto players and veto points has made two distinct points. Firstly, the veto point concept has been used to highlight very particular constellations of political institutions that can explain particular political outcomes. For instance, the access of organized interests to political decision-making has been explanatory for differences in health systems in a number of countries (Immergut 1992).[82] Secondly, the role of the German constitutional court can explain the particular situation of German tax reforms (Ganghof 2003).

The second use of the veto player concept has been a more general one. It has been argued that in political systems that are heavily affected by a large number of veto points governments are ordinarily impeded in exercising a major policy shift. This applies to a whole range of policies and seems to be unrelated to the type of policy. For instance, Tsebelis has argued that a large number of veto players can explain the lack of 'substantial' legislation or political decisions (Tsebelis 1999, 2002). Governments are, for instance, prevented from pursuing egalitarian economic and social policy (Birchfield and Crepaz 1998) or from following particular traits in welfare development (Huber, Ragin and Stephens 1993).

Veto player indices are usually composed of constitutional structures such as federalism, bicameralism, the role of judicial review, as well as the type of government and the independence of central banks (Huber, Ragin *et al.* 1993; Schmidt 1996; Lijphart 1999; Schmidt 2002a). Hence they often include elements of concepts of consensus democracies, as will be discussed below.

Consensus democracies

The most relevant distinction for the relationship between governments and the social partners is the distinction between majoritarian forms of democracy and consensus or negotiation-based forms of democracy (Lehmbruch 1979; Lijphart 1999).[83] Majoritarian democracies are defined by a strong degree of political competition between political parties that seek single-party or minimum-winning coalition governments. Institutional constraints on governments are minimal and governments have a great leeway for implementing their policies. Moreover, the influence of interest groups on public policy is limited and public policy is exclusively performed by public administration (Armingeon 2002a and 2002b: 81). Majoritarian democracies are also modelled on the Westminster model and predominantly to be found in English-speaking countries of the Commonwealth.

In contrast, consensus or negotiated democracies are based on deeply institutionalized political and social cleavages that prevent an open political competition on policy issues between parties. The majority party cannot and will not exploit its majority at the expense of minority interests because of either institutional or political constraints. Power is shared between different social groups and consensus is sought on major political issues. Consensus democracy is thus the reflection of the power structure and conflicts within societies that have turned into an institutionally based system of incentives that encourage the cooperation between political groups and minimize their competition.

Consensus democracies are closely related to consociational democracies and corporatism. Consociational democracies are discussed in the literature as a subtype of consensus democracy that in particular attempts to integrate several large minorities. They make greater demands on the division of power and the autonomy of segments of society in terms of the central decision-making bodies (Lijphart 1999: 41). Examples of consociational democracies are Switzerland, the Netherlands and Austria (Lehmbruch 1979). Consociationalism is also part of the veto player index of Manfred G. Schmidt (2002a).

Consensus and negotiated democracies, moreover, are often seen as complementary to corporatist decision-making. Lijphart and Crepaz (1991) and Lijphart (1999) have integrated the notion of corporatism into the measurement of consensus democracies, along with a wide variety of other indicators such as the independence of central banks, the balance of power between parliamentary chambers, and the power of the executive. The claim is that "corporatism is the interest group system that goes together with the consensual type of democracy and its opposite, the 'pluralist' interest group system, goes together with majoritarian democracy" (Lijphart and Crepaz 1991: 235). Under the very broad assumptions of a "structural affinity" between consensus democracies and corporatism (Keman and Pennings 1995: 274), the relevance of the extent of consensus societies and corporatist interventions by governments becomes immediately obvious, if not altogether self-evident. In consensus democracies, the political elites have reacted to cultural segmentation by including broad groups of society in decision-making processes. These elites have employed the same mechanism for "stabilizing and steering highly developed capitalist economies by promoting a new type of social integration" such as liberal corporatism (Lehmbruch 1979: 53). The literature on consensus democracy has therefore tended to include corporatist decision-making as one of its elements.[84]

The very broad and comprehensive approach adopted towards producing a measure of consensus democracy is, however, open to criticism (Keman and Pennings 1995; Armingeon 2002a; Schmidt 2000). In particular, the integration of corporatism into the executive party dimension of governments has been criticized on the grounds that the two phenomena are interrelated but empirically and theoretically distinct from each other (Keman and Pennings 1995). Empirically, it has been pointed out that there are important outlier countries that affect the correlation between the two concepts. For instance, Austria, Sweden and Norway are highly corporatist but not consociational or in other ways consensus societies. On the other hand, Italy can be classified as a non-majoritarian country, but not a corporatist one.

Theoretically, Keman and Pennings (1995) point to the fact that both concepts are based on different actors. "Consensus democracies represents a mode of institutionalization of political actors by referring to aspects of parliamentary democracy, whereas corporatist interest intermediation represents the incorporation of societal actors typically by means of non-parliamentary consultation in order to avoid zero-sum outcomes of policy formation" (Keman and Pennings 1995: 274). The concept of consensus democracies versus majoritarian democracies therefore presents an alternative classification of political institutions compared to veto points and veto players. It is theoretically distinct from the concept of corporatism but empirical observations point to parallels of consensus and corporatist systems of decision-making.

The choice of relevant institutional factors

The disagreements over definitions and the cohesiveness of indicators are not just academic debates. The question of how to resolve them is essential for the argument of how political institutions affect the economic performance and behaviour of governments. For instance, Arend Lijphart has repeatedly claimed that consensus democracies are kinder, gentler and better democracies which, moreover, show better political and economic performance in terms of political inclusion and inflation (Lijphart 2001 and 2002). In reaction, Liam Anderson (2001) has shown that the superior economic performance of consensus democracies is primarily due to the inclusion of the degree of corporatism and central bank independence as part of the index of consensus democracy. After having controlled for the degree of corporatism and central bank independence, he was able to show that the economic effects of the other indicators measuring consensus democracy are transformed into the opposite: consensus democracies are associated with higher inflation and higher unemployment. In addition, Klaus Armingeon rebels against the general claim that consensus democracies are superior and argues that consensus democracies are merely a form of government for segmented societies that does not necessarily lead to worse performance than majoritarian democracies (Armingeon 2002b: 99).

The various dimensions of consensus democracies examined in the literature, built on research on corporatism and veto player, will not be developed further in this analysis. Rather, I choose to focus on political institutional variables that are at the core of consensus democracies independent of their relationship to corporatism and veto players[85] and the degree of corporatism. In particular, I will argue that two of the key elements of consensus versus majoritarian democracies – whether a government is competitive or consensus-oriented, and the degree of fractionalization of the party system – can serve as potential predictors of governments' willingness to negotiate with trade unions over wages.

The argument, however, remains basically the same: a more competitive and unified political system that is at the heart of a majoritarian democracy reduces the likelihood of governments negotiating with trade unions, while a more fragmented and cooperative system increases the likelihood. The argument rests on the assumption that, firstly, a more unified and competitive political system will find it easier to give a clear signal to trade unions on its expectations of wage bargaining and thereby shift the responsibility for it more clearly into the wage bargaining arena and, secondly, the system will be generally less dependent on seeking a consensus with other parties.[86] It is thus generally assumed that a more fragmented party system reflects a higher degree of division of polities, and that in turn the dependency of political parties on trade unions will be higher in fragmented party systems than in unified systems. The overall effect of fragmentation and dependency of parties on trade unions is that which drives the attempts by governments to find a negotiated solution with the social partners.

The argument and findings therefore broadly support the approach taken by Lijphart and Crepaz in assuming a systematic relationship between the structure of political institutions and interest organizations in general (Lijphart and Crepaz 1991). It seems useful, however, to keep the individual indicators separate, since not all of the factors co-vary and not all the combinations of single factors work in the same direction. While there is a logical and structural affinity between the degree of political competition and the interest organizations which support the tendency of consensus democracies to find solutions in negotiations with the social partners, the aim in this chapter is to distinguish between the two arenas of political competition and interest group organizations.

Consensus versus majoritarian governments

In order to find a measure of consensus democratic political institutions that can be distinguished from the general degree of corporatism, I have only used partial indicators that are widely seen as indicating consensus democracy. In tables 5.1 and 5.2, two main indicators of consensus versus majoritarian democracies are depicted. The first measure is the type of government that distinguishes a competitive from a cooperative political system; the second is the fractionalization of the party system. The type of government and fractionalization of the party system do not necessarily co-vary. In principle, a more fragmented party system makes the forma-

Table 5.1 Effective number of parliamentary parties, 1970-98

	1970-79	1980-89	1990-98	1980-98
Austria	2.28	2.50	3.51	3.01
Belgium	6.53	8.46	9.63	9.05
Denmark	5.46	5.46	4.79	5.13
Finland	5.96	5.75	5.90	5.83
France	5.16	4.40	6.04	5.22
Germany	2.91	3.28	3.76	3.52
Ireland	2.80	2.96	3.88	3.32
Italy	3.83	4.37	6.80	5.59
Netherlands	5.99	4.08	4.92	4.50
Portugal	3.74	3.47	3.02	3.25
Spain	4.31	3.64	3.57	3.61
Sweden	3.54	3.53	4.21	3.87
United Kingdom	2.85	3.03	3.13	3.08
Average	4.28	4.23	4.86	4.54

Note: the effective number of parties carries the same information as the Rae index and is calculated from this index as follows: N=1/1-Rae. Index of fractionalization of the party-system according to Rae.

$Rae = 1 - \sum_{i=1}^{m} t_i^2$, were t_i is the share of votes for party i and m the number of parties.

Source: Armingeon *et al.* (2002).

tion of a winning coalition more difficult. The more parties participate in a political system, the more likely is a coalition government. In practice, while majority party governments are frequently associated with two-party systems and therefore have a lower score of party fragmentation, majority coalition governments are as frequently based in fragmented party systems as minority governments (Strom 1984: 206). Both indicators, however, can be used to show the propensity of the political institutions to find negotiated approaches rather than competitive unilateral ones.

The type of government divides the Western European countries into two relatively separate groups: those countries in which governments are based on either single party governments or minimum-winning coalitions. In the period between 1970 and 1998, Austria, Germany and the United Kingdom were the countries in which governments were always competitively organized; in Belgium, Ireland and the Netherlands governments were predominantly formed on a competitive basis. In the Scandinavian and Southern European countries, on the other hand, governments were primarily formed on a cooperative or consensus-seeking basis. Minority governments were to be found for most of the period in question in Denmark and Sweden; France, Finland and Italy had surplus coalitions. As expected, the United Kingdom had the strongest competitive political system, followed however by the two corporatist countries Germany and Austria.

This assessment is reinforced by the fractionalization of the party system as shown in table 5.2. Again the UK, Austria, Germany and Ireland are the countries with the lowest degrees of fractionalization of the the party systems, followed by Portugal, Sweden and Spain. Party systems were substantially more fragmented in Belgium and Finland, followed by Denmark, France, Italy and the Netherlands. The fractionalization of the party system increases over time on average and in most of the countries. Only in the transition countries, Spain and Portugal, and the Netherlands is the party system of the 1990s more unified than it was during the 1970s. There is a positive correlation between the type of government and the fractionalization of the party system, although it is not very strong (0.59, not significant).

What is the relationship between government intervention and the two measures discussed above? Based on the use of the government intervention index, table 5.3 displays the means of annual observations of government intervention by the type of government and the fractionalization of the party system.

The pattern of the data shows that both aspects of negotiated democracies positively contribute to the propensity of governments to intervene in wage bargaining procedures. Competitive types of governments in uni-

Table 5.2 Type of government, Western Europe

	Frequency of type of government, 1970-98					Minimal winning one party cabinet (%)
	single party government	minimal winning coalition	surplus coalition	single party minority	multi-party minority	1971-96
Austria	11	16		2		65.1
Belgium		26	3			28.8
Denmark		4		10	15	23.9
Finland		3	25	1		6.0
France		3	18	5	3	63.5
Germany		29				46.2
Italy		4	16	2	3	9.2
Ireland	7	15		4	3	57.3
Netherlands		21	6			37.3
Sweden	1	3		19	5	41.4
United Kingdom	27			1		93.3

Note: no data on Portugal and Spain available.

Sources: for columns 2-6, Armingeon, Beyeler *et al.* (2002) and own calculations; for column 7, Lijphart (1999).

fied party systems have a low degree of government intervention, while strongly consensus-based governments in fragmented party systems have the highest degree of government intervention. Both aspects of consensus democracies, the party system and the type of government, contribute to the propensity to intervene. Within unified party systems, the move from a competitive to a consensus type of government increases the average degree of government intervention from 1.38 to 2.58 throughout the period of the 1980s and 1990s. While all governments in fragmented party systems are on average more likely to intervene in wage bargaining, this effect is again increased by moving from a competitive to a consensus government. As expected, the pattern is stronger in the period between 1980 and 1998 than for the overall period. In that period, the move from a unified to a fragmented party system within the group of competitive governments has the strongest effect on government intervention. This effect indicates that the degree of party competition influences the position of governments *vis-à-vis* trade unions.

Table 5.3 **Government intervention by the competitive nature of the government and fractionalization of the party system (observation per cell), 1970-98 and 1980-98**

	Competitive governments		Consensus governments	
	1970-98	1980-98	1970-98	1980-98
Unified party system	1.72 (123)	1.38 (78)	2.14 (42)	2.58 (24)
Fragmented party system	3.16 (103)	3.00 (72)	3.21 (47)	3.45 (31)

Note: Portugal and Spain are not included due to data availability.

Sources: for party system fractionalization and type of government, Armingeon, Beyeler *et al.* (2002).

A combined measure of party system fragmentation and the type of government using the two Lijphart indicators can be found by simple factor analysis, which produces a standardized score for consensus government based on the two indicators.[87] The bivariate plot in figure 5.1 of the

Figure 5.1 **Government intervention and consensus democracy**

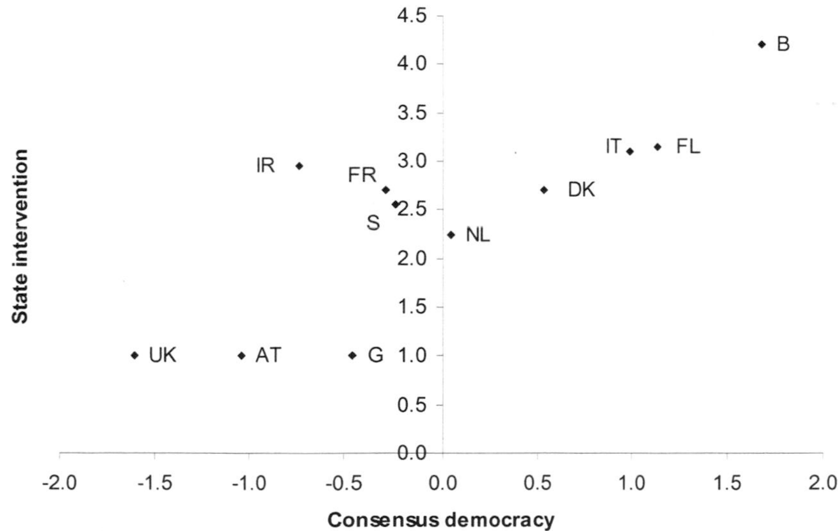

Source: explained in text.

standardized score of consensus government and government intervention for the period 1980-98 illustrates the relationship. There is a correlation between the standardized score on consensus democracy and the degree of government intervention of r = 0.77**. It shows that in stronger consensus democracies, governments are more likely to negotiate an incomes policy than in majoritarian democracies.

The shared roots of consensus democracy and corporatist responses: the political fragmentation of trade unions and the role of union-party relations

The fragmentation of party systems and the type of government are not directly related to the attitude of governments to wage bargaining. The assumptions made in the literature have been largely based on the general attitude of political elites in dealing with conflictual situations. Consensus orientation has evolved in segmented political systems in which large minorities that could not be circumvented or oppressed had to be integrated into decision-making (Lehmbruch 1979; Lijphart and Crepaz 1991). In a similar situation, it was argued, political elites tend to negotiate with trade unions over the need to restrain wages rather than merely confront them with a restrictive monetary policy alone.

In majoritarian countries, on the other hand, it is argued that political elites are accustomed to an approach of unilateral decision-making by the government that may or may not be restricted by other constitutional players, but not by other political actors within the parliamentary or party system. As a consequence, their approach towards organized interests would be more distant and not oriented towards negotiation.

In this section, another factor supporting the relationship between consensus democracies and negotiations on incomes policy will be introduced that has not been addressed systematically. The political fragmentation of party systems in Western Europe corresponds to the political fragmentation of trade union systems. The fragmentation of trade unions has two implications. First, as will be discussed in Chapter 6, it undermines the responsiveness of wage bargaining actors to the new economic environment and thereby gives rise to a more active role of the government in shifting workers' expectations. Second, the political fragmentation of trade unions is directly related to the fragmentation of party systems. Fragmented political party systems go hand-in-hand with fragmented political trade union systems, although not in all cases. The overlapping is high and not symmetrical. For instance, politically split trade unions are always reflected in the party system while not all political cleavages in the party system are mirrored by trade union organizations. This is due to the higher degree of dynamism of party systems that are generally more open to the formation of new cleavages.

The fragmentation on both sides gives rise to a negotiated approach by governments when dealing with difficult economic policy decisions, since there is no clear commitment from a strong majoritarian government to enforce the view of a reduced bargaining scope for wage bargainers. Rather, political conflicts between trade unions with different political affiliations and between different parties in coalitions that are tied to different trade unions hinder the necessary adjustment. Also, multi-party systems give trade unions more opportunities for access to the government and a greater bargaining power. The political divisions of trade unions increase not only the competition between the unions but also the degree of competition between those political parties that have to take into account the demands of individual unions to a greater extent than in systems where trade unions are a unified political actor.

Frozen landscapes of party systems and trade union organizations

In Western Europe, the historical evolution of trade unions is based on several cleavages that have led to a frozen landscape of several types of trade union organizations (Ebbinghaus 1993). Trade unions have followed the society-church splits of European societies and the political split on the left into socialist and communist camps. In many cases, these organizational cleavages within trade union movements have been matched by organizational cleavages in party systems.

Table 5.4 illustrates the party-union links and indicates the systematic pattern between fragmented party systems and politically divided trade union systems. As it turns out, the most politically unified trade union and party systems are to be found in countries as diverse as the United Kingdom, Ireland, Austria, Germany and to some extent Sweden. In Sweden, however, the party system is more fragmented due to a number of parties in opposition to the dominant Social Democrats. In all five countries, both the political parties on the left and the trade union umbrella organization enjoy a unified link with each other that is not threatened by competitive rivals.

The party-union linkage is most direct in the cases of Sweden and the UK. In both cases, the trade unions founded the social democratic party

Table 5.4 Political affiliations of major trade union confederations in Western Europe

	Union confede-ration	Affiliated party	Party-union link	Share of left party in gvt. (1970-2000)
Austria	ÖGB	SPÖ	No formal ties between the ÖGB and political parties; however trade union leaders frequently hold high-ranking offices within the SPÖ. Trade union is *ex officio* at party conferences.	68.1
Belgium	ABVV/ FGTB	BSP	Formal affiliation of the Socialist Union Confederation to the party.	33.2
	ACV/ CSC	CVP	Unions provide candidates for political offices.	
	ACLV/ CGSLB	VLD, PRL	No official link.	
Denmark	LO	SD	Formal ties between LO and SD. Union is automatically represented and provides financial support.	49.0
Finland	SAK	SDP	Informal ties between SAK and SDP in competition with Finnish Peoples' Democratic League.	40.7
France	CGT	PCF	Unions support PCF; General Secretary has a position in PCF political bureau.	37.2
	FO	PS	Informal links.	
	CFTC CFDT	MRP UDF	Personal links (CFDT).	
Germany	DGB	SPD	Unified trade union structure prohibits direct party affiliation. In reality, majority of unions are strongly related to the SPD, with only minor interconnection with CDU.	37.5
		CDU	Minor representation between CDU and DGB.	
Ireland	ICTU	Labour Party	Labour Party founded by unions; formal.	14.5

Table 5.4 Political affiliations of major trade union confederations in Western Europe

	Union confederation	Affiliated party	Party-union link	Share of left party in gvt. (1970-2000)
Italy	CGIL	PCI, PDS	Personal links, relaxed since the beginning of the 1970s; reorganization in 1992.	29.1
	CISL	DC		
	UIL	PSI		
Netherlands	FNV	PvdA	Union leaders often represented on executive boards of parties.	24.6
	CNV	CDA		
Portugal	CGTP	PC	Close ties.	25.5
	UGT	PSD/PS	Founded by PSD in 1979.	
Spain	CCOO	PCE	Close ties.	52.0
	UGT	PSOE	Personal links.	
Sweden	LO	SAP	Union involved in the founding of the party; union leaders have high influence over party leadership.	70.9
UK	TUC	Labour Party	Unions founded Labour Party. Individual unions are still affiliated to the party and have block votes at national congress; however, comparatively low influence on party politics.	30.0

Note: data on party in government for Spain 1977-98 and for Portugal 1974-98.

Sources: for Finland Arter (1987); for Ireland Hardiman (1988); for Spain and Portugal Magone (2001); for all other countries Ebbinghaus (1993), Ebbinghaus and Visser (2000), Western (1997: 69-70); for share of left governments Armingeon *et al.* (2002), and own calculations.

and traditionally exercised a high degree of control over the party leadership. In both cases, the strong integration has led to a strict division of labour between the role of the party and the role of the union. However, the internal organizational structures of the unions mean that there are different bases for this division of labour. In Sweden, the impact of a social democratic political understanding of an organized market economy and the cooperation between economic policy and wage restraint has been explicit. In the UK, however, due to the fragmentation of wage bargaining and the lack of control on the part of the trade union leadership, this understanding has never clearly developed.

Also, in Austria and Germany, the unification of the labour movement in the post-war period was matched by a unification of the political left. In both cases, due to the legal underpinning of the unification of the trade union organizations, political representation of other factions had to be organized within the framework of the trade union organizations. In Germany, at least one position on the executive board of the union is reserved for a member of the Christian Democratic Union (CDU). In Austria, the unions have internal political wings that compete in elections against each other. Therefore, within the unions and in their relations to the parties that carry the government, the political allegiances of the Austrian and German trade unions are less clear than in the cases of Sweden and the UK. In all four cases – but in particular in the case of Sweden and the United Kingdom – it can be assumed that government intervention is less likely to occur due to the clear and undisputed political linkages. If the social democratic party has wholeheartedly agreed to pursue a more disciplinary approach towards wage bargaining, it has no real need to negotiate with the unions about it, since the unions have no alternative political force that they can lobby instead of the social democrats. At the same time, for other political parties not on the left, the incentive to negotiate with trade unions is minimal because they will not enjoy the support of trade unions in electoral campaigns in any case and might have a higher price to pay for cooperation.

Ireland is an exceptional case since it emulates a number of the characteristics of the British political system, which are, however, overshadowed by the conflict over national independence from the UK. On the one hand, the Irish Labour Party was founded by the Irish trade unions and has been dependent on the unions in a similar way to the British Labour Party. On the other hand, the national conflict has become the overriding cleavage of Irish politics and has greatly reduced the influence of the Irish Labour Party. Among the countries here, the Irish Labour Party is the least influential left-wing party of all parties on the left.

In contrast, the remaining Western European countries all have to deal with political cleavages within the trade union organizations. The different political affiliations of unions to political parties that are represented in parliament make it more difficult for individual parties in government to forge a unified approach that can clearly display the implications of the new economic environment to the unions. Also, the political fragmentation of unions and parties can slow down the acceptance of the new environment by the unions so that more government intervention is needed to achieve any results.

A strong split of the political left into a social democratic and a communist camp of political parties and affiliated trade unions not only increases the fragmentation of the party system, but also fragments the political organization of the trade unions. In Finland, France, Italy, Spain and Portugal, the political cleavages on the left have had important implications for left-wing governments because the political rivalry among the left makes it more difficult for governments to pursue a more austere economic policy.

For instance, the French communist party (PCF) rejected any incomes policy as pursued by the French socialist party in 1982. The PCF, moreover, continued criticizing the socialist austerity policy until it left the government in 1984 over economic policy.[88] Therefore, the social democratic government found it more difficult to indicate to trade unions via its economic policy that wage restraint was essential for macroeconomic adjustment, but tended to adopt a more fuzzy mixture of tight monetary policy and looser fiscal policy. Trade union wage restraint was sought, but not requested, because of partisan-based constraints by social democratic clientele.

Examples of tense relationships between trade unions and social democratic governments on economic policy can also be found in Spain during the Gonzalez government (Gillespie 1990). The president of the socialist trade union (UGT), Nicholas Redondo, was not only a member of parliament for the social democratic PSOE but also almost became the leader of the socialist party in place of Gonzalez. During the Gonzalez government, Nicholas Redondo was among the fiercest critics of the government and led his trade union into many public sector conflicts over pay.[89] This conflictual relationship was not least rooted in the fact that the more oppositional communist trade union (CCOO) kept gaining ground on the socialist unions in workplace elections (Hamann 1998). A similar dynamic can be found in Italy between 1978 and 1992 when communist party-based opposition towards any concessions agreed by the CGIL put pressure on the other unions not to surrender too much ground in the negotiations over the Scala mobile. In Portugal, the establishment of a non-communist trade union in the late 1970s – supervised and guided by the governing social democratic party – was intended to undermine the militant opposition towards the government but first of all only succeeded in introducing further fragmentation into the political representation of the unions.

Finland has been the exception to the Scandinavian compromise and has had much more in common with the unstable democracies of mainland Europe. This was particularly apparent with regard to the split of the left in the immediate post-war period, which overshadowed most of the tripartite negotiations even after the cooperation between communist and socialist improved post-1969. As Arter has pointed out, comparing the politically more homogeneous Swedish situation: "In a historically divided polity like Finland it is not surprising that governments have had a vested interest in sustaining the incomespolicy system. In an obvious way it has appeared to strengthen the government, enabling cabinets to achieve a measure of stability and continuity in the industrial relations field. Whilst not a signatory to incomes agreements, the state has been interventionist in seeking centralized deals in a way that has not been the case (at least until recently) in Sweden, for example" (Arter 1987: 214).

Church-based cleavages continued to play a role after World War II in Belgium, France, Italy and the Netherlands (Ebbinghaus 1993: 85). In Austria and Germany, the thorough reorganizations of the unions diminished the role of Catholic trade unions. In Belgium and the Netherlands, a similar attempt failed due to the resistance of the Christian labour movements (Ebbinghaus 1993: 95). In the late 1960s, the two church-based trade union organizations in France, CFTC and CFDT, represented together 20 per cent of all trade union members. In Italy, the CISL had a third of all union members. Similarly, in the Netherlands NKV and CNV represented a third of all union members. In Belgium, the ACV had half of all union members.

The relations between Christian trade unions and Christian democratic parties has traditionally been looser than between socialist parties and trade unions (Ebbinghaus 1993: 93), but in all cases the Christian trade unions possess a political counterpart to which they are at least indirectly related.

In the most complex systems of party-trade union linkages, there are three different political constituencies in both the party system and the trade union organization that are systematically related: a social democratic or socialist, a communist and a Christian constituency. This combination could be found in Belgium and Italy until the early 1990s. Belgium and Italy are also among the countries with the highest degree of party system fragmentation and government intervention.

Comparing the United Kingdom and Belgium

In this section, I will illustrate the causal links between the type of political institutions and government intervention more directly by a closer examination of the two extreme cases, Belgium and the United Kingdom. The two countries are at opposite ends of the party system spectrum: Belgium has the most fragmented party system and weak short-lived multiparty governments, while the United Kingdom has the most unified party system and strong governments. At the same time, the Belgian government has been the most active on the issue of wage bargaining over the last twenty years, while the British has been the most restrained. The examples of Belgium and the United Kingdom show two important insights: firstly, that the various Belgian governments lacked the capacity, not the will, to adjust to the challenges and, secondly, that in the United Kingdom the absence of government-trade union coordination is not exclusively due to the weak organization of the labour market but also attributable to the majoritarian nature of the political system. It is not by chance that Belgium and the United Kingdom have been chosen by Arend Lijphart to illustrate benchmark cases of consensus versus majoritarian democracies (Lijphart 1999).

Belgium was first chosen by Lijphart to represent a classic case of a consensus model of democracy (Lijphart 1999). Starting as a three-party system in the late 1960s (with the Christian Democrats, Socialists and Liberals), the parties in Belgium have split over time along linguistic lines and several new parties have attained importance. About a dozen political parties have been able to gain seats in national elections; nine of them have participated in the government (Lijphart 1999: 36). During the 1990s, the fragmentation of the party system even increased with an additional split between Flemish and Walloon parties (Van Ruysseveldt and Visser 1996: 209). Governments usually consist of many parties although they rarely constitute a surplus or minority government. Due to the multitude of parties and cleavages, the average life span of a Belgian government is particularly short: between 1970 and 1998, there were eighteen changes in government. On several occasions over the post-war period, there have been governments of national unity in which all three of the major parties have participated.

Given the organizational links between political parties and trade unions as described in the previous section, Belgium's governments have found it difficult to govern in 'opposition to the unions'. At least one party with close ties to at least one segment of the labour market has been represented in the government for most of the post-war period (Van Ruysseveldt and Visser 1996: 211). On several occasions the unions have been able to form an alliance against governments that had begun to turn against the interest of the unions. Combined trade union opposition has also been able to bring about changes in the government.

At the same time, the trade unions have been in competition with each other. Competition between Belgian trade unions is played out in works council elections that are widely seen as indicative of the representative nature of the unions. Competition has been sharpened by the fact that the two biggest confederations, the ACV/CSC and the ABVV/FGTB, have exchanged dominance over time. While in the 1950s the FGTB was by far the strongest union with almost 60 per cent of the works council seats, with the CSC having 37 percent, this relationship had reversed by the mid-1990s. Independent of partisan considerations, the competition between trade unions *per se* has led to obstruction of government policies that could hurt trade union constituencies.

The relationship between government and wage bargaining actors is therefore characterized by mutual dependency. The two main political parties that alternated or shared in government throughout the post-war period were tightly linked to the labour movement. Even when the government realized the urgency of adjusting to the new situation in the early 1980s, no party managed to distance itself from the demands of the bargaining actors. In 1982, the centre-right government sought special powers approved by the Senate to impose wage decrees on the social partners rather than decouple the links between the Christian Democrats and trade unions.[90] Although frequently attacked by the trade unions, no Belgian government has really attempted to curtail or restructure the party-union relations in a complex multi-party system.[91]

The economic policy-making by wage decrees had the effect that necessary steps could be taken without the unions having to accept responsibility for the measures. The social partners could therefore shift the blame of adjustment from the wage bargaining arena to the government. Over time, a pattern evolved in which the social partners were increasingly unable to agree on adjustment since they were able to anticipate intervention by the government as a solution to deadlock (Van Ruysseveldt and Visser 1996: 218). Hence the government not only lacked the capacity to distance itself from the demands of the social partners but was also unable to confine their room for manoeuvre. The government was consistently forced to carry forward economic adjustment processes without shifting the responsibility for maladjustment of wages back into the wage bargaining arena. In consequence, negotiations about wages remained a government responsibility without the government ever having the option to deregulate wage formation.

In contrast, British Westminster democracy is the role model for all political systems in countries that have been under British control and that now form the group of majoritarian countries in Lijphart's study. The British party system is in effect a two-party system with the government alternating between two choices. The third party is represented by the former second large party, the Liberals, which merged with the social democrats in the late 1980s to form the Liberal Democrats. In practice, however, the third party does not play an influential role since the large parties frequently achieve almost 90 per cent of the votes and more than 95 per cent of the seats in parliament. In the post-war period, no third party has ever participated in government. Changes in government have alternated between the two major parties.

The dominant parties in the British political system are the Conservative Party and the Labour Party. Both parties enjoy exceptionally clear relations with the trade unions. Unlike the tradition of many Christian democratic parties or even liberal parties on the Continent, the British Conservative Party does not have any formal relations with the Trade Union Congress (TUC) or with its affiliated trade unions. There is no channel for influencing the Conservative Party from a trade union perspective. Since the Labour Party has been founded by the trade unions, the vast majority of trade unions have been officially affiliated to the party and have remained its main source of funding.

The two-party system, however, gives both political parties – not just the Conservative Party – a greater leeway in their positioning *vis-à-vis* trade unions. This is partly due to the electoral system that gives the governing party a larger than proportional majority in parliament and thereby frees the government from worrying about fringe demands. Secondly, the two-party system also allows Labour to be relatively negligent about trade union interests since there is no alternative political force that trade unions can potentially turn to. Whether or not a governing Labour Party pursues trade union interests has little effect on the traditional close relationship between the party and the trade unions.

Therefore, despite the tight links between the Labour Party and the trade unions, in effect the majoritarian political institutions insulate any government from the demands of any lobby organization, including trade unions and employers' confederations. This allows governments to take a clear stand on economic policy and wage bargaining issues and to shift the responsibility for labour market performance to the collective bargaining arena if it wishes to do so. In contrast, the incomes policy of the British government during the 1960s and 1970s – both Conservative and Labour governments – was based on the assumption that the British government should shoulder the responsibility for employment performance while accepting free collective bargaining. In these cases, the government pleaded for wage restraint with trade unions incapable of providing this, without being really prepared to concede much in exchange. Once the government effectively dropped this responsibility with the change of government in 1979, there was no need or incentive to ever deal with wage-related issues directly.

It is important to note that it is also the majoritarian nature of its political institutions that distinguishes the British case from other cases in this book – and not simply the country's strong degree of voluntarism and decentralization of wage bargaining structures. The low degree of centralization of British wage bargaining has been blamed for the collapse of incomes policy (Scharpf 1991; Regini 1984). While the British labour market has been exceptionally deregulated and voluntarist, there are a number of other European cases where trade unions also have only slight control over local wage bargaining issues, such as Italy and Ireland or, in some respects of wage drift, even Sweden and Denmark. The Irish industrial relations system has many parallel features with the British. However, the fact that the Irish and Italian governments have turned towards negotiation and the British government towards further deregulation and abstention is due to the country's political isolation from trade union pressure. Moreover, a number of other European governments would have liked to follow the British example of radically cutting their ties with the trade unions, but found themselves unable to do so.[92] Even the Belgian government of 1981 realized that major steps on the labour market were necessary if adjustment to the new situation was to occur.

After the change of government in 1979, the British government met fierce opposition from the trade unions. However, the unions were unable to deliver on this opposition in political terms. During the 1980s, the Conservative Party won elections with little more than 40 per cent of the votes and was able to achieve a large majority in parliament. The strong executive position of the government enabled a strong prime minister to be immune to further requests for social and trade union protection.

In sum, institutional constraints on governments directly influence their propensity to negotiate wage restraint with trade unions. These institutional constraints can be identified as the core attributes of majoritarian versus consensus democracies. A fragmented party system and multi-party governments are both conducive to open lobbying pressure by trade unions on the government to take up negotiations. The political institutional factors are particularly well suited to explain the shift in behaviour by the British government after the change of power in 1979. The majoritarian nature of the British political system allowed the British government to disregard political pressures by trade unions and thus opened the way to deregulation, which was not possible in consensual democracies.

The role of partisanship

Besides the institutional constraints that influence the capacity of a government, partisanship has been in the past a major explanatory variable for economic policy choice.[93] In this section, I test the extent to which – and over which time periods – a relationship exists between patterns of partisanship and of government intervention.

Partisanship theories of economic policy have frequently assumed that different political parties will tend to exploit in different ways the trade-off between unemployment and inflation in the short-term Phillips curve. The arguments used are ultimately based on the distinctions drawn by Hibbs on the relationship between voters and parties. Different classes of voters have different preferences in economic policy, prompting political parties that draw their support from these classes to respond to these preferences (Hibbs 1977). According to Hibbs, left-wing parties draw their support from working people who benefit from full employment and therefore favour expansionary policies in order to achieve high employment levels. Conservative parties, on the other hand, are more concerned about fighting inflation by focusing on a balanced budget and controlling the money supply at the expense of full employment.

While the partisanship argument of economic policy by Hibbs provides an elegant explanation for the 1960s, two major modifications have had to be made since. Firstly, the breakdown of the long-term Phillips curve in the 1970s diminished the scope for partisanship in economic policy. Because an expansionary economic policy as pursued by left-wing governments tended to become inflationary, workers would try to catch up with higher prices and thereby dampen the expansionary effect of the policy. The effects of an expansionary policy were anticipated by economic agents and quickly translated into rising prices. Left-wing governments could therefore attempt only in the short run to boost economic performance by expansion; in the long run, left-wing governments had to counteract the inflationary implications of their policies (Alesina, Roubini *et al.* 1997).[94]

Secondly, the effectiveness of expansionary economic policy was increasingly seen as being dependent on the organization of the labour market and the capacity of trade unions to engage in moderate wage bargaining (Scharpf 1991; Lange and Garrett 1985). Governments can only boost the economy if expansion is not undermined by inflationary tendencies. It was therefore argued that the responses made by trade unions were the precondition for a social democratic economic policy. If trade unions do not respond to an expansionary policy in a responsible way, even left-wing governments are eventually forced to return to deflationary policies rather than commit themselves to further expansionary approaches (Lange and Garrett 1985; Alvarez *et al.* 1991).

Therefore, the restrictions that are placed upon political parties when exercising their preferred economic policy are tight, and institutional preconditions for economic policy are important. However, at the same time, partisanship continues to matter on a number of policy issues and there is little reason to assume that the underlying preference order – of left-wing parties preferring employment over price stability while conservative parties have the reverse order of preferences – is completely obsolete (Widmaier 1989: 52; Schmidt 1996). Assuming that partisan preferences for full employment versus price stability are still salient, the institutional framework in which their economic policy operates makes the effectiveness of the policy dependent on the responses by wage bargaining actors and other economic agents. Nevertheless, a left-wing government, which is assumed to put a higher premium on employment than a right-wing government, faces stronger pressure to ensure that wage bargaining actors respond to its economic policy by showing wage restraint. One could therefore assume that, in principle and in any institutional setting, left-wing governments are more likely to intervene in wage bargaining procedures than right-wing governments. According to this view, government intervention becomes the functional equivalent to wage bargaining coordination.

My findings, presented in table 5.5, give some broad support for the partisan thesis. In general, right-wing governments tend to intervene less in wage bargaining procedures than left-wing governments. This was particularly evident during the 1970s when incomes policy was seen as a suitable tool for supporting the Keynesian crisis management in many

Table 5.5 **Partisanship of government and government intervention per decade (observation per cell), 1970-98**

	1970-79	1980-89	1990-98	1970-98
Cabinet dominated by non-left-wing parties	2.38 (65)	2.51 (95)	2.38 (86)	2.43 (246)
Cabinet dominated by left-wing parties	2.87 (45)	2.51 (35)	2.95 (57)	2.81 (137)

Cabinet composition based on Schmidt index: Cabinet dominated by right-wing and centre parties (gov_left<51); cabinet dominated by social democratic and other left parties (gov_left>50).

Sources: Armingeon, Beyeler *et al.* (2002); own calculations.

social democratic countries. But government intervention by left-wing governments was even more pronounced during the 1990s in the run-up to European Monetary Union. It was only during the transition period of the 1980s, when tight monetary policy diffused throughout Western Europe as an anti-inflationary device and concertation on wage formation had been seriously discredited in economic policy-making that left-wing governments did not intervene more frequently in wage bargaining than conservative governments.

Moreover, the data fits in with the 'congruence' thesis propounded by Lange and Garrett (1985) for the period of the 1970s in the sense that there is an interaction between the degree of corporatism and government policy towards trade unions. Since the economic policy by the government is contingent on the reaction by the trade unions, the interaction between the partisanship of the government and the capacity of trade unions to restrain wages can be divided into congruent and less congruent regimes. Lange and Garrett have assumed that an expansionary, employment-focused economic policy adopted by a left-wing government would be beneficial only under the condition that trade unions were encompassive and wage bargaining was comprehensive. If we assume that government intervention is an attempt to prompt trade unions to restrain wages where the conditions are not right for wage bargaining responsiveness, we should expect this strategy by a left-wing government to be most likely found in non-corporatist countries, since in corporatist countries centralized trade unions would find a more consensual way of entering into coordinated wage bargaining.

Table 5.6 **Government intervention by partisanship of government and degree of corporatism (observation per cell), 1970-99**

	Corporatist				Non-corporatist			
	70-79	80-89	90-99	70-99	70-79	80-89	90-99	70-99
Cabinet dominated by the left	2.70 (40)	1.90 (20)	3.13 (31)	2.67 (91)	4.20 (5)	3.33 (15)	2.73 (26)	3.09 (46)
Cabinet not dominated by the left	2.90 (30)	2.58 (50)	1.98 (46)	2.44 (126)	1.94 (35)	2.42 (45)	2.85 (40)	2.42 (120)

Cabinet composition based on Schmidt index: Cabinet dominated by social democratic and other left parties (gov_left>50). Cabinet not dominated by the left (gov_left<51). Corporatism by country classification: corporatist countries are Austria, Belgium, Denmark, Finland, Sweden, Germany and the Netherlands. Non-corporatist countries are Ireland, UK, Spain, Italy, Portugal and France.

Sources: Armingeon, Beyeler *et al.* (2002); own calculations.

The findings in table 5.6 present some evidence that right-wing governments are less affected in their policy choice by the degree of wage bargaining centralization, while governments that are dominated by left-wing parties change their approach towards trade unions depending on the degree of coordination of wage bargaining. In non-corporatist countries, governments are particularly active at persuading trade unions to moderate wage claims; in corporatist countries, they can assume more easily that trade unions will tend to comply with their economic policy.

There is, however, a trend in the data over the decades that mirrors the changing nature of the interaction between governments and trade unions particularly well: the strongest incidence of government intervention took place in the non-corporatist countries during the 1970s, reflecting the strong wish of left-wing governments to lure trade unions into cooperation even in countries that lack the necessary organizational preconditions in the labour market. The examples of the United Kingdom and Italy have been frequently analysed as unsuitable attempts by governments to engage with particularistic trade unions in corporatist exchanges (Regini 1984; Pizzorno 1978). The 1970s are therefore the prime example of the attempt by left-wing governments to find a solution to a 'non-congruent' situation by intervening in wage bargaining. However, over time, left-wing governments have become increasingly disillusioned with the attempts to discipline trade unions in non-corporatist settings and government intervention has declined. Conversely, for right-wing governments the trend is the opposite. While during the 1970s right-wing governments tended to refrain from political exchanges with trade unions, they tended to intervene increasingly in later years, albeit under the conditions of a non-accommodating economic policy.

In the corporatist countries, some evidence is found for the 'congruent argument' as well, though again this is conditioned by changes over time. In these countries, right-wing governments intervened more forcefully than left-wing governments during the 1970s, in particular in Finland, the Netherlands and Denmark. However, in the 1980s and 1980s, the right-wing governments in these countries tended not to engage in government intervention any more. Left-wing governments, on the other hand, were particularly interventionist in the corporatist countries during the 1990s, when previous adjustment attempts failed.

Consequently, when the potential for expansionary economic policies disappeared, the arguments of the 'congruency assumption' were reversed. In the 1990s, it was more likely for a right-wing than a left-wing government to intervene in wage formation in a non-corporatist country, whereas in corporatist countries left-wing governments intervened more strongly than right-wing governments. The assumption therefore that in corporatist countries the interaction between left-wing governments and trade unions is based on a shared strategy of expansion and wage restraint has clearly eroded. Since expansionary policies are only rarely available any more, left-wing governments in corporatist settings will intervene in wage bargaining in order to shift trade unions' expectations to the new realism of non-accommodation. To the extent that voluntary wage restraint also hits the public sector, left-wing parties in government might face partisan-based restrictions by their constituencies or parliamentary supporters. This plays out particularly convincingly in coalition governments comprising both left- and right-wing political parties, where the government's position on wage restraint might be torn between conservative and left-wing members of the cabinet undermining the government's resolve on the issue.

This task might be further complicated by the ambiguity of left-wing governments. Social democratic parties have remained highly ambiguous about their economic policies and have traditionally tried to shift the negative impact of tight monetary policies onto expansive fiscal policies that relied on public spending and employment schemes, even after public finances had deteriorated substantially. For instance, social democratic governments or governments with a considerable social democratic input were often unclear about the tightness of their economic policies even after they had adopted a strict hard currency strategy. The less likely it seems that the government would actually press ahead with tight monetary and fiscal policies, the more likely it is that trade unions might push up wages, the threat of unemployment being diminished.

A good example of the lack of government resolve on wage restraint is the Dutch centre-left coalition of 1981/82. Here, the stronger conservative party under Prime Minister Van Agt had been preparing significant public cuts in the budget after receiving strong criticism from the Dutch central bank on the question of public spending, while the junior social democratic partner in the government under ex-Prime Minister Den Uyl proposed a major employment scheme (Wolinetz 1989). When the two conservative parties in the government (the CDA and VVD) pushed through the spending cuts against the will of the social democrats, the latter left the government. As soon as the social democrats had left the government, the prime minister announced the abolition of wage indexation.[95] Almost exactly the same happened in Ireland in January 1987, when Labour left the coalition government with Fine Gael over spending cuts after experiencing ongoing disputes with public sector trade unions in preceding years.[96]

Conservative governments found it easier to display commitment to such restraint since their constituency would not be affected by wage restraint. Moreover, the distant relationship between conservative parties and trade unions enabled them to adopt a clear policy towards the trade unions.[97] Consequently, new tripartite agreements were struck after the government swung to the right in the Netherlands in 1982 and in Ireland in 1987, with the incoming governments being determined not to repeat the stalemates of the previous administrations (Visser and Hemerijck 1997; Hardiman 2002).

In contrast to accounts of political exchanges during the 1970s, government intervention in the 1990s was not based on an understanding between friendly social democratic parties and trade unions but rather on a mutually beneficial master plan. Trade unions would restrain wages if there were signals from governments that excessive wage settlements would be punished. Social democratic parties in government found it much harder to suggest and pursue a tight policy. Incomes policy based on the condition of tight economic policy might therefore be more attractive for conservative governments than for left-wing governments.

Conclusion: Negotiated adjustment and the role of political institutions

In the two realms of academic research on consensus democracies and neo-corporatism, there has traditionally been a great area of overlap. Political scientists who have studied political institutions have incorporated the role of interest associations as one indicator of consensus democracies. Those who have studied neo-corporatism and the interaction between interest associations and the capacity of the state and governments have long recognized that there is a close relationship between political institutions and neo-corporatism. However, the systematic study of the relationship between neo-corporatism and political institutions has in recent years subsided and the study of new forms of concertation between governments and the social partners has generally failed to focus on political institutions.

This chapter has aimed to draw attention to the fact that governments, when facing difficult economic policy choices, are restrained by the institutions of their political systems. I have attempted to show that there are systematic linkages between the type of government and the type of party system, and that these give incentives to governments to negotiate with social partners. The underlying argument has focused less on the traditional observation that in consensus societies the elite is generally socialized to seek consensus and more on the notion that governments find it difficult to display their commitment to a tight economic policy to the social partners if these are deeply intertwined with the political party system.

In addition, the chapter has shown that there is indeed a greater propensity for left-wing governments to start negotiating with trade unions. This observation was to be expected, since left-wing parties and Christian democratic parties generally have the closest links with trade unions. It has also been possible to show that this behaviour is especially salient in non-corporatist countries. This observation gives some credit to the congruency argument put forward by Lange and Garrett (1985): not with respect to economic performance, but with respect to economic policy choices open to left-wing governments

Finally, the chapter has pointed out the distinct role of the majoritarian political institutions in the British case, which enabled governments not only to keep trade union concerns at arm's length but also to abstain from negotiations. Despite the close relationship between the Labour Party and the TUC, it is the lack of competition between unions and parties over access that insulates the government from further trade union influence.

6 The Responsiveness of Wage Bargaining Institutions

Wage formation processes are embedded in the institutions that regulate the labour market. They are influenced by market developments on the one hand and mediated by institutional factors on the other. Market factors put pressure on wage bargainers to take into account the effects on the economy of changes in wages. External shocks, rising prices and high levels of unemployment alter the conditions under which wages are formed. Institutional factors are particularly strong in the labour market since wages determine the well-being of the majority of citizens. Concerns about social justice and the distribution of income are thereby integrally linked to the processes of wage setting. Since collective bargaining is carried out by wage bargaining institutions, the design of these institutions usually has a strong impact on the conduct of bargaining.

The shift towards restrictive monetary regimes has increased the role of market pressures in wage bargaining procedures. Previously, an accommodating monetary policy and changes in the exchange rate were policy instruments that buffered the trade-off between higher wages and employment performance. Incomes policies and wage restraint by trade unions operating in corporatist wage bargaining institutions were compensated for by an expansive economic policy. With the loss of these buffers, wage bargaining institutions had to internalize the effects of wage bargaining outcomes that had previously been taken care of by the government.

This shift in the external environment of wage bargaining process has altered the distributional conflict in the labour market. In wage bargaining, trade unions have to weigh up the interest of the membership in protecting and raising real wages on the one hand and the employment effects of wage settlements on the other. Members expect their trade union to raise the real wage, while the market pressure on firms imposes limits on their ability to pay without suffering losses in employment. This basic tension applies to any institutional wage bargaining setting. However, trade unions in coordinated wage bargaining institutions have tended to dampen real wage demands when facing high unemployment more than trade unions in decentralized wage bargaining settings. Trade unions have thereby sacrificed their potential to raise real wages in exchange for employment gains. Throughout the 1970s and 1980s, the capacity of wage bargainers to implement wage moderation in corporatist countries contributed to the relatively superior performance of economies with coordinated wage bargaining institutions compared to those with decentralized wage bargaining institutions. In non-coordinated wage bargaining institutions, trade unions tended to focus on real pay protection and were willing to sacrifice employment.

However, under the new competitive conditions of low productivity increases and tight economic policy, real wages have been constrained throughout the OECD since the mid-1970s. In all countries, real wage gains have been diminished and the previously big differences in real pay developments have converged. Corporatist bargaining institutions have thus lost their competitive edge *vis-à-vis* deregulated bargaining systems (Traxler 2001).

At the same time, in some European countries the established practice of centralized collective bargaining combined with the political integration of trade unions has led to expectations and rules in wage bargaining that have been highly focused on the protection of real wages. In particular, in those countries where previous periods of incomes policy facilitated the institutionalization of rules on wage indexation that fed changes in prices immediately into the wage formation process, wage bargainers have found it difficult to adjust downwards the real wage expectation of trade unions and their members.

In this chapter, I will argue that governments have tried to address in particular the issue of adjusting wage expectations to new external conditions when intervening in wage bargaining procedures. Intervention by the government aimed at stopping trade unions' focus on real wage protection when the policy of governments generally was to reduce the inflation differentials with Germany. This was particularly the case in those countries where the labour market was organized by centralized trade unions and employers' association but real wage expectations were based on the previous regime of accommodating monetary policy and fixed rules on wage indexation. By intervening in the wage bargaining process, governments tried to influence the real wage expectation of trade unions and their constituencies with regard to the new economic environment.

This chapter is distinct from the previous two chapters in that the factors discussed previously – monetary regimes and political institutions – do not change over time but are fixed factors that determine the room for manoeuvre for governments. In contrast, the relationship between wage bargaining institutions and the behaviour of governments is more fluid and interactive, and therefore offers greater scope for developing the understanding of how governments try to influence wage formation. As such, this chapter and the next, which highlights the interactions between wage bargaining institutions and government behaviour, are at the core of the argument of this book. In broad terms, the chapter seeks to use the established literature on the relationship between wage bargaining institutions and economic performance as a starting point. It does so by identifying a key element within this relationship – the responsiveness of wage bargaining institutions to their economic environment measured by indicators such as the level of unemployment – that helps explain national differences more fully. In this analysis, and unlike much of the political economy literature, the degree of responsiveness is not derived from the institutional properties of the wage bargaining systems but from performance indicators of wage flexibility under a given institutional regime. It turns out that countries with relatively similar wage bargaining institutions produce different degrees of wage responsiveness.

The innovations in this chapter fall into two areas. First, a statistical model of the responsiveness of trade unions to external factors in wage settlements adds to our understanding of why, for instance, Austrian unions respond significantly in such settlements to rising unemployment while their counterparts in the United Kingdom hardly respond at all. This is presented in the second section. Subsequently, the analysis of the institutional basis of wage responsiveness, in the third section, takes a fresh look at factors that influence this responsiveness by examining three such factors in addition to the core issue of the degree of wage bargaining coordination. In examining these factors – dissenting factions, exposure to the market and the role of wage indexation – special attention is paid to the latter aspect, as this has traditionally received little attention in the literature. The chapter starts with a brief review of aspects of the literature on the relationship between wage bargaining institutions and economic performance.

Theoretical assumptions about wage flexibility and the role of wage bargaining institutions

The neo-corporatist literature on the impact of wage bargaining institutions on the performance of labour markets is extensive and will not be summarized here.[98] In very general terms, the literature makes assumptions about how institutions shape the bargaining behaviour of trade unions when facing the trade-off situation of choosing between pay and employment. Depending on the bargaining strategy of the union, wages are more or less oriented towards promoting employment growth. Instead of presenting the different facets of the literature, three aspects that are of importance for the subsequent arguments will be highlighted.

The role of coordination

The coordination capacity of wage bargaining institutions is the primary factor influencing the responsiveness of wages to changes in the external economic environment. Since coordinated wage bargaining institutions internalize the negative externalities of high wage settlements, wage bargainers react sensitively to the level of unemployment when setting wages. In order to prevent employment losses, trade unions in coordinated or centralized bargaining institutions do not exploit their bargaining potential. In the corporatist countries, real wage moderation facilitated by centralized wage bargaining institutions has become a substitute for labour cost flexibility (McMorrow 1996: 12).

Economy-wide coordination mechanisms have been accepted as the most important factor influencing wage bargaining behaviour.[99] As has been pointed out by David Soskice (1990) and subsequently by Traxler, Blaschke *et al.* (2001), the coordination of wage bargaining can take place even in organizationally decentralized wage bargaining institutions. If decentralized wage bargaining is organized around a pattern-setter mechanism or replaced by other mechanisms such as government intervention, the lack of formal centralization can be compensated for.

If there is no coordination in the wage bargaining behaviour, local wage bargaining will always reflect the local conditions on the labour market and will not be sensitive to wider economic constraints. Moreover, local bargaining encourages leapfrogging with highly profitable companies influencing the expectations of workers in other companies. Local trade unions that are not embedded in a national bargaining system have to exploit their bargaining power since they do not have any reason to do otherwise (Soskice 1990; Flanagan 1999).

The centralization argument has always been countered by the bargaining power argument. The crux of the bargaining power argument concerns the effect of bargaining arrangements on the elasticity of the demand curve for union labour. Union bargaining power declines when wage increases threaten significant employment losses for union members. Decentralized bargaining structures tend to face highly elastic demand curves, since customers can easily shift their purchases to other companies if a collective bargaining settlement raises wages at one company (Flanagan 2003). As a result, in the economic literature, economists such as Calmfors and Driffil have hypothesized a hump-shaped relationship, where highly centralized and highly decentralized wage bargaining institutions outperform intermediate levels of centralization (Calmfors and Driffil 1988).

Distributive conflicts

The potential of distributive conflicts to upset wage bargaining responsiveness has been pointed out by Iversen (1999). He argued that real wage restraint under highly centralized bargaining structures is dependent on fiscal and monetary accommodation. This claim is based on the observation that highly centralized bargaining systems are based on a "coalition of diverse and conflicting interests" (Iversen 1999: 29). The internal dynamic of such a system depends on the successful reconciliation of these interests. If the confederal leadership has to work out a distributive compromise between high-wage unions and low-wage unions, this tends to result in an egalitarian wage policy because the low-wage unions can veto proposals that do not have redistributive effects. In practice, differentiation is achieved through an increase in the wage drift, which, however, increases inflationary pressures. Therefore, "the wage-inflationary effects of centralization clearly pose a challenge to the neo-corporatist emphasis on the dampening effects of centralization on wage claims" (Iversen 1999: 30).

In fact, the distributive conflict argument has turned the hump-shaped argument and, to some extent, the whole coordination argument upside down. According to Iversen, under a non-accommodating monetary policy, wage restraint will be highest under intermediate bargaining centralization, while high levels of centralization will lead to inflationary distributive struggles that will be penalized by restrictive monetary policy. On a more general level it should be pointed out, however, that an accommodating monetary policy can control any inflationary wage drift, whether it is due to distributive conflicts within centralized wage bargaining institutions or whether it is due to leapfrogging behaviour. Therefore, the potentially upsetting behaviour of sectoral pressure groups is not specific to the highly centralized Swedish model but must generally be integrated into the analysis of wage bargaining coordination.

Nominal versus real wage adjustment

Under monetary integration and low inflation rates, nominal wage adjustment has gained in importance, since the adjustment of the real exchange rate is increasingly dependent on the adjustment of the nominal wage differential. However, the connection between labour market institutions and the responsiveness of wages to changing prices (nominal flexibility) is much less clear and has been regarded differently by various authors. Theoretically, a high degree of nominal wage responsiveness is viewed as a sign of beneficial labour cost flexibility. On the other hand, in the empirical literature relating to the economics of the stagflation of the 1970s, a *low* degree of wage responsiveness to prices is seen to have been beneficial for avoiding the worst effects of the stagflation period since wages at the time did not try to catch up with inflation. As Bruno and Sachs (1985) have argued, as long as trade unions were generally competent in exercising real wage restraint and as long as rising prices did not immediately translate into wage increases through a high level of nominal wage responsiveness, a serious squeeze on profits could be avoided (Bruno and Sachs 1985: 241).

During the 1960s, wage indexation was proposed as an appropriate pay norm in the US wage bargaining system. Among economists like Milton Friedman, general systems of wage indexation were assumed to be technical formulae for reducing industrial strife and improving the responsiveness of wages (Braun 1976). Until today, the assessment of wage indexation in the economic literature has remained ambivalent.[100] On the one hand, indexation rules are seen theoretically as being welfare enhancing since they automatically adjust expectations in line with changing prices. Welfare gains can be made by reducing the level of uncertainty about future inflationary pressures. Since changes in wages can automatically adjust downwards if inflation goes down, indexation mechanisms were initially seen as an anti-inflationary device. On the other hand, this line of economic arguments has never been popular among policy-makers (Fischer and Summers 1989; Milesi-Ferretti 1994).

The different approaches towards nominal wage responsiveness derive primarily from the fact that a theoretical increase in nominal wage responsiveness is discussed in the context of an economic downswing in which nominal wages could potentially be decreased if flexibility were high. Here nominal wages are supposed to respond to deterioration in economic performance. In practice, however, a high level of nominal wage flexibility has traditionally meant that wages have adjusted rapidly to a change in prices that in itself is inflationary and puts pressure on economic performance. During the supply shocks of the 1970s, a low level of nominal wage responsiveness had positive effects because it helped reduce real pay, as the example of Sweden shows.

With regard to labour market institutions, nominal wage flexibility has been linked to institutional features of wage bargaining procedures such as the duration of collective agreements, the degree of wage indexation and the synchronization of wage bargaining (Bruno and Sachs 1985: 238; Layard, Nickell *et al.* 1991: 429). These institutional features determine how rapidly unexpected changes in the economic environment can feed through to nominal wages. If the duration of collective agreements exceeds one year, nominal wages cannot automatically adjust to changes in prices. On the other hand, wage indexation clauses introduce automatic adjustment into nominal wage formation. The synchronization of wage bargaining allows for a strategic adjustment of wages rather than pattern bargaining.

With regard to the relationship between the degree of wage bargaining coordination and nominal wage flexibility, the theoretical assumptions are not clear. Calmfors (2001) argues that wage bargaining coordination potentially has a positive effect on increasing nominal wage flexibility. Higher levels of wage bargaining coordination automatically increase the synchronization of wage bargaining. Moreover, since wage bargaining coordination rests on the assumption that trade unions base their decisions on economy-wide considerations, it is thought they might be willing to exercise nominal responsiveness in order to allow for the interests of labour market outsiders. On the other hand, there are indicators that wage bargaining coordination might reduce nominal wage flexibility. According to Alogoskoufis and Manning (1988) and Layard *et al.* (1991), wages tend to respond less to consumer price changes in a more corporatist wage bargaining system. Empirically, Bruno and Sachs do not find a relationship between nominal wage responsiveness and their measure of corporatism. "Interestingly, these two dimensions (corporatism and nominal wage responsiveness) are largely unrelated, so it appears that countries could benefit from one or the other of the favorable characteristics" (Bruno and Sachs 1985: 241).

Priorities of trade unions between employment and real wage protection in wage bargaining – an empirical measure

One way of establishing the relationship between the relative priority of real wage protection and employment is to estimate the impact of the change in consumer prices and unemployment on changes in nominal wages in a simple wage regression. I have done this by using a wage equation, with the findings presented in tables 6.1 and 6.2 and figure 6.1. The coefficients of the change in consumer prices and of the level of unemployment serve to indicate the conflicting priorities of trade unions in wage bargaining. A high and significant coefficient of inflation illustrates the attempt of the unions to protect real wages; a high and significant coefficient of the level of unemployment serves as a measure for the responsiveness to unemployment of the change in nominal wages.

The responsiveness of wage bargaining

Table 6.1 shows the coefficients of a simple wage equation that estimates the effects of the change in consumer prices and the level of unemployment on the change in the nominal wages of Western European countries between 1970 and 1999. The time span covers the period of the end of the so-called golden years up to 1974, the period of stagflation and the shift towards a tight monetary regime after the early 1980s. It does not allow for structural breaks.[101] The aim of the wage equation is not to present a model with a particularly good fit, but to indicate the different degrees of nominal responsiveness of wage bargaining in different European countries to a changing economic environment.[102]

As would be expected, in all countries a rise in consumer prices has a positive effect on wages, whereas a high level of unemployment has a dampening effect on wages. Both coefficients can only be used as rough indicators of the orientation of actors when taking decisions on which bargaining goals to pursue. In the equations, it is assumed that these orientations are long term and can be averaged over the lengthy period of 30 years.

Nevertheless, as can be seen in table 6.1, the degree to which trade unions decide either in favour of real wage protection or in favour of responding to unemployment levels differs substantially across Western Europe. Three groups can be distinguished. Firstly, there is a monetarist corporatist group, where nominal wages are affected by unemployment levels but not by changes in prices. Here, trade unions prioritize employment over real pay. Secondly, there is a real-wage corporatist group, where wages are affected by both. Trade unions are torn between two conflicting goals and only gradually come to prefer one to the other. Thirdly, we find a real-wage non-corporatist group, where nominal wages follow the aim of protecting real wages irrespective of employment effects.

One should note that the coefficients do not indicate how real wages have developed in these particular countries. Over a 30-year period be-

Table 6.1 Responsiveness of nominal wages of Western European countries, 1970-99

	Inflation	Unemployment	Productivity	Adj R2	Durbin-Watson
Responsive to unemployment					
Austria	0.23 (0.23)	-2.58*** (0.44)	-0.47** (0.20)	0.77	2.10
Germany	0.23 (0.16)	-0.88*** (0.12)	0.00 (0.06)	0.87	1.00
Non specified					
Sweden	0.27 (0.21)	-0.55 (0.27)	-0.71 (0.39)	0.62	1.27
Responsive to unemployment, but real wage protection					
Italy	0.82*** (0.09)	-0.98*** (0.22)	0.21 (0.25)	0.93	1.82
France	0.81*** (0.07)	-0.73*** (0.10)	-0.53** (0.23)	0.97	1.97
Belgium	0.89*** (0.09)	-0.63*** (0.10)	0.51** (0.20)	0.91	1.07
Netherlands	1.05*** (0.15)	-0.51*** (0.13)	0.47 (0.26)	0.86	1.18
Denmark	0.88*** (0.08)	-0.39*** (0.11)	-0.03 (0.04)	0.84	1.55
Spain	0.72*** (0.12)	-0.46*** (0.12)	0.48 (0.29)	0.96	1.51
Finland	0.93*** (0.17)	-0.37** (0.15)	0.16 (0.27)	0.81	0.93
Ireland	0.86*** (0.09)	-0.33** (0.14)	0.25 (0.24)	0.86	1.67
Real wage protection only					
Portugal	0.86*** (0.13)	-1.09 (0.77)	-0.18 (0.34)	0.69	1.27
United Kingdom	0.93*** (0.11)	-0.17 (0.20)	0.02 (0.31)	0.83	2.06

Note: Non-standardized Coefficients, ** p <0.05, ***p<0.001. Dependent Variable: change in nominal wages in per cent. Germany 1992 was excluded due to the high unification wage settlements.

* The Durbin-Watson test indicates that substantial autocorrelation of the residuals in the cases of Belgium, the Netherlands, Sweden and Portugal cannot be ruled out. In the cases of Germany and Finland there is evidence for autocorrelation. Coefficients were nevertheless interpreted since further specification of the models as shown in the appendix could justify this. However, the coefficients should be interpreted as loose indicators for general tendencies.
Independent Variables: change in consumer prices, level of unemployment, productivity (see Appendix).
Portugal since 1975, Spain since 1977 and Germany: 1992 excluded.

Source: see Appendix.

tween 1970 and 1999, the average increase in real wages in the United Kingdom was exactly the same as in Germany (2.2 per cent per annum) with Austrian real wages rising slightly faster (2.4 per cent per annum). The coefficients indicate to what extent a change in consumer prices can predict the nominal wage change in a particular country, not to what extent wage bargaining outcomes will raise the real wage.

Between 1970 and 1999, only Austria and Germany belong to the group of countries where wages reacted strongly to the requirements of a tight economic policy. The degree of responsiveness of wages to unemployment levels was high and the high levels of unemployment created constant pressure for wage restraint. Austrian trade unions behaved in a more restrictive way towards unemployment levels than German unions did. This partly reflects the comparatively lower unemployment levels in Austria. In fact, wage developments in Austria followed the German pattern of restrictive wage settlements despite the more favourable labour market situation. The coefficients are consistent with the interpretation that Germany was the first country that pursued a restrictive monetary policy from a credible and independent central bank that was immediately accepted by German trade unions (Scharpf 1991).

The second group comprises countries in which wage bargaining outcomes tend to react to both real wage protection and to unemployment levels. The group of ambivalent countries consists of most of the Western European countries. It is noticeable that all countries in this group have committed themselves to European monetary integration and thus to the German monetarist role model, although at different points in time. Within this group the tension between the real wage protection interest and the employment interest is greatest. Unfortunately, there are serious problems of autocorrelation in a number of countries, as the Durbin-Watson statistics highlight.

Thirdly, a real-wage non-corporatist type can be identified where nominal wage changes are highly influenced by the changes in price levels, but not the level of unemployment. This group comprises the United Kingdom and Portugal. The low degree of responsiveness of British wage bargainers to the changing employment levels is a classic example of the corporatist assumption of the effects of low wage coordination. Throughout the 1980s, the wage bargaining of British trade unions did not react to the steep increases in unemployment. Real wage growth in the United Kingdom was the highest of all European countries. In Portugal, a coordinated approach towards wage bargaining only developed from 1991 onwards.

Finally, in Sweden, nominal wages can be seen not to respond either to changes in consumer prices or to the levels of unemployment. The non-responsiveness of nominal wages in Sweden reflects the extent to which the unions focused on the Swedish model of extensive real wage restraint and the active labour market policy. The Rhen Meidner Model was a political model that operated irrespective of market pressures. However, it also shows how exceptional the Swedish wage bargaining practices were compared to the rest of Europe. This fact is also borne out by the responsiveness of real wages as shown in table 6.2. Here, Sweden, Germany and Austria are the countries where real wages are strongly negatively affected by an increase in consumer prices. In these countries, inflationary pressure signals to wage bargaining actors that they should prioritize real wage restraint in order maintain competitiveness. At the other end of the spectrum, real wage developments in the United Kingdom are influenced neither by inflationary nor by unemployment effects. Between the two extremes, we again find the majority of European countries, with mixed reactions. Inflationary pressure has had a negative impact on real wage growth in France and Spain, but not in the other European states.

From the perspective of adjusting wage expectations to the new economic environment, Austria and Germany are the countries where low nominal wage responsiveness created the least problems for a restrictive monetary policy. Sweden can be singled out for being capable of adjusting real wage expectations. Austria and Germany in principle outperformed Sweden, since nominal wages responded to unemployment levels as well. This result is in accordance with the assessment of the stagflation experience by Bruno and Sachs. They concluded: "High corporatism and low nominal wage responsiveness helped countries to avoid a serious profit squeeze and the worst of the stagflation of the last decade... Austria, Germany, Norway, Sweden and Switzerland come closest to having both sets of favourable institutions, while the Commonwealth countries Australia, New Zealand, and the United Kingdom have had the least favourable structures" (Bruno and Sachs 1985: 241).

Government intervention and the responsiveness of wage bargaining institutions

The responsiveness of wage bargaining institutions in the period between 1970 and 1999 can be related to the degree of government intervention during the 1980s and 1990s. In the following graph the coefficient of the

Table 6.2 Responsiveness of real wages of Western European countries, 1970-99

	Inflation	Unemployment	Productivity	Adj R2	Durbin-Watson
Responsive to inflationary pressure					
Austria	-0.77*** (0.23)	-2.58*** (0.44)	-0.47** (0.20)	0.55	2.10
Germany	-0.77*** (0.16)	-0.88*** (0.12)	0.00 (0.06)	0.66	1.00
Sweden	-0.73*** (0.21)	-0.55 (0.27)	-0.71 (0.39)	0.26	1.27
Spain	-0.28** (0.12)	-0.46*** (0.12)	0.48 (0.29)	0.39	1.51
France	-0.19*** (0.07)	-0.73*** (0.10)	-0.53** (0.23)	0.74	1.97
Responsive to unemployment					
Italy	-0.18 (0.09)	-0.98*** (0.22)	0.21 (0.25)	0.46	1.82
Belgium	-0.11 (0.09)	-0.63*** (0.10)	0.51** (0.20)	0.74	1.07
Netherlands	0.05 (0.15)	-0.51*** (0.13)	0.47 (0.26)	0.52	1.18
Denmark	-0.12 (0.08)	-0.39*** (0.11)	-0.03 (0.04)	0.35	1.55
Finland	-0.07 (0.17)	-0.37** (0.15)	0.16 (0.27)	0.18	0.93
Ireland	-0.15 (0.09)	-0.33** (0.14)	0.25 (0.24)	0.14	1.67
Non-responsive					
Portugal	-0.14 (0.13)	-1.09 (0.77)	-0.18 (0.34)	0.15	1.27
United Kingdom	-0.07 (0.11)	-0.17 (0.20)	0.02 (0.31)	0.09	2.06

Note: Non-standardized Coefficients, ** p <0.05, ***p<0.001. Dependent Variable: change in nominal wages in per cent. * The Durbin-Watson test indicates that as in table 6.1 serial correlation of the residuals cannot be ruled out in the cases of Germany, Sweden, Belgium, the Netherlands, Finland and Portugal.
Portugal since 1975, Spain since 1977 and Germany: 1992 excluded.
Independent Variables: change in consumer prices, level of unemployment, productivity (see Appendix).

Source: see Appendix.

change of consumer prices on the change in nominal wages will be used as a proxy variable for the responsiveness of national wage bargaining institutions to economic conditions. Changing consumer prices push trade unions to increase nominal wages in order to prevent real wage losses. A small effect of inflation on nominal wage development therefore indicates high degrees of responsiveness and a strong effect indicates low degrees of responsiveness. Correlating the proxy variable for responsiveness with

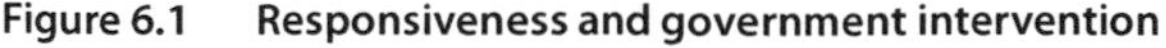

Figure 6.1 Responsiveness and government intervention

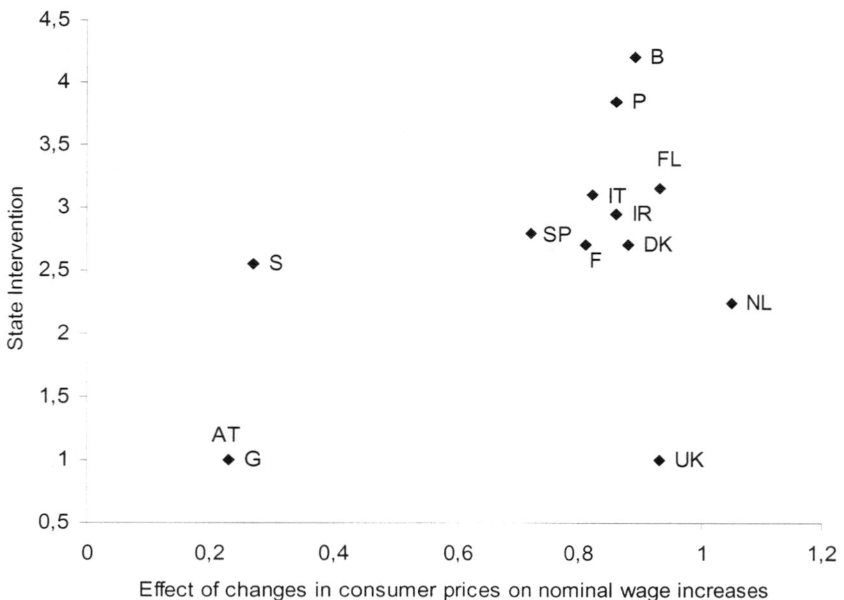

Source: Table 6.1 for effect of changes in consumer prices on nominal wages.

the degree of government intervention yields a correlation of 0.52 (Pearson correlation, non-significant). As can be seen in the graph, most countries cluster into an area where the effect of changes in consumer prices on nominal wages and government intervention are both relatively high, with the exception of Germany, Austria and the UK.

The countries that drive the correlation are Austria and Germany, where nominal wage increases did not react to increases in consumer prices, but primarily to an increase in unemployment (table 6.1), while at the same time state intervention is low. Sweden achieves a similar result for nominal wages, but shows higher degrees of government involvement. The correlation is weakened by the case of the United Kingdom. Given the low responsiveness of wage bargaining institutions, the expected degree of government intervention should be higher. If the United Kingdom is excluded, the correlation increases to 0.72 (Pearson correlation, significant).

The institutional basis of wage responsiveness

The trade-off between real pay protection and employment, as reflected in the notion of responsiveness presented and analysed in the previous section, is mediated by wage bargaining institutions. The framework of wage bargaining institutions influences the perceptions of wage bargaining participants about what bargaining goal to prioritize. In this section, I will explore the institutional and organizational factors that influence the decision-making process, particularly that of trade unions. I will introduce the degree of wage bargaining coordination as a precondition for any form of responsiveness of wage bargaining behaviour. At the same time, I will argue that the benefits of coordination have been influenced by other intervening variables, in particular by the role of dissenting factions within trade unions, by pay indexation mechanisms and by the role of the exposed sector in wage bargaining. Dissenting factions within trade unions and pay indexation schemes have inhibited wage bargaining actors from responding to external constraints by focusing their expectations on real pay protection. The strong role played by the exposed sector, on the other hand, has facilitated responsiveness.[103]

Wage bargaining coordination as precondition for responsiveness

In Western Europe, coordination of wage bargaining has been strong and widespread. Among the countries in this book, only the United Kingdom has no degree of coordination in wage bargaining at all (table 6.3). There was some coordinated voluntary wage restraint by British trade unions with the Social Contract of the 1970s and, as will be shown in Chapter 7, British trade unions at that time were able to restrain wages considerably. In all other countries, however, wage bargaining is generally coordinated. The types of coordination can be distinguished into those that rest on powerful wage bargaining institutions – either on the employers' or the trade unions' side – and others based on different arrangements. Coordination by powerful social partners is a particularly strong form of coordination since it assumes that the social partners can implement the wage settlements they coordinate with each other. Strong coordination can be found in Austria, Belgium, Denmark, Finland, Germany, Sweden and the Netherlands. Among these countries, coordination is strongest in Austria, Sweden and Germany because of their centralized trade union organizations. In the other countries, conflicts and fragmentation between the trade unions are more common. In the six remaining countries, the

Table 6.3 Wage bargaining coordination in Western Europe, 1970-99

	Type of coordination
Strong coordination	
Austria	Coordination through pattern setting
Belgium	Coordination through National Labour Council
Denmark	Coordination through centralized trade unions, some internal sectoral conflicts
Finland	Coordination through national wage agreements
Germany	Coordination through comprehensive sectoral bargaining
Netherlands	Coordination through Labour Foundation and Economic Council
Sweden	National coordination through centralized trade unions and employers
Weak coordination	
Ireland	Coordination through national wage agreements, little sectoral coordination
France	Coordination through government in public sector and nationalized industries
Italy	Informal coordination between major employers and within trade unions
Portugal	National agreements, no coordination
Spain	Weak sectoral coordination
No coordination	
UK	

Sources: Ferner and Hyman (1998a); EIRO-online various reports; Traxler, Blaschke *et al.* (2001); various sources.

forms of coordination rest either on agreements between large companies (Italy), on weakly developed sectoral negotiations (Spain) or on the pay coordination in the public sector (Portugal and France). Among the latter four countries, coordination is strongest in Italy, because of the strength of the unions, and weakest in Portugal, because of the absence of any wage bargaining pattern.

The degree of coordination explains to some extent the degree of responsiveness of wage bargaining outcomes. The complete lack of coordination in the United Kingdom under the condition of a hostile political environment can be seen as the main explanatory factor for the failure of British bargaining to respond to the changing environment. The degree of coordination does not explain, however, why even in the small corporatist states of Belgium, the Netherlands and Denmark responsiveness was comparatively low during the 1980s and 1990s, and government intervention was comparatively high. If the corporatist interaction in small states as described by Peter Katzenstein (1985) was particularly geared up for adjusting wage behaviour to external constraints, why did the majority of small corporatist states encounter intense conflicts between governments and trade unions over the adjustment procedure during the 1970s and 1980s? Why did coordinated wage bargaining institutions fail to internalize the new economic constraints? At the same time, why were, in the non-corporatist countries, new coordination mechanisms and institutions in pay bargaining developed in order to overcome existing frictions and a lack of pay adjustment?

Dissenting factions

Dissenting factions within the trade unions can upset the coordination of wage bargaining by voicing opposition to general wage agreements. Dissenting factions can either be organized along the lines of political or religious cleavages or arise as a sectoral or professional group within a trade union organization. Competition between major trade union organizations that negotiate alongside each other for the same groups of workers in the same industries can drive wage expectations up. Similarly, within a seemingly centralized organization, profession- or workplace-based bargaining structures can give incentives for leapfrogging behaviour when groups within trade unions compete against each other.[104] As the examples of Sweden and Denmark show, even highly centralized organizations cannot always ensure that dissenting factions can be disciplined and integrated into coordinated wage bargaining procedures. Opposition can be based on the potential bargaining power of the dissenting group exceeding the general settlement, or it can be based on the political competition that gives rise to ideologically grounded opposition to general rules. Depending on the organizational and interorganizational structures of trade unions, the role of dissenting factions can be minimized or pronounced.

As can be seen in table 6.4, it is only in Austria and Germany that there is no tradition of dissenting factions in collective bargaining. In Austria and Germany, comprehensive trade union organizations have an overarching monopoly position over collective bargaining with no internal group being able to voice dissenting views. In Austria, the comprehensive nature of the Austrian Trade Union Confederation is complete. Political factions are organized within the ÖGB but are not relevant to wage bargaining behaviour. In Germany, a weak competitive white-collar organization existed until 2000, but this was unable to dominate collective bargaining. Within the industry-based trade union organizations, no sector- or industry-specific pressure group has managed to organize effective opposition to general wage norms. Moreover, extensive legal regulation prevents competing groups from intervening in wage bargaining.

In all other countries, there have been dissenting factions intervening in wage bargaining procedures at least on a temporary basis. Fractionalization within centralized trade unions has become stronger in Denmark and Sweden, where an internal split has developed within the LO between the manufacturing and the public sectors. In Denmark, trade union organization has traditionally been more craft-based and therefore more

Table 6.4 Dissenting factions within trade unions

No dissenting factions	
Austria and Germany	Comprehensive integration of political and sectoral interests in sectoral organizations
Sectoral competition	
Denmark and Sweden	Sectoral competition between manufacturing and public sector
Politically and church-based competition	
Netherlands	Weak competition between Catholic, liberal and social democratic trade unions
Belgium	Strong political competition between socialist, liberal and Christian trade unions
Italy	Political competition between socialist and communist trade union with spells of cooperation
Finland	Some political competition between social democratic and communist trade unions
Portugal, France and Spain	Strong political competition between socialist and communist trade unions
Professionally based competition	
Ireland	Weak competition between locally organized trade union branches
UK	Strong competition between locally organized trade union branches

Sources: various sources.

fragmented. In both cases, the notion of a wage levelling policy combined with a strong increase in public sector employment has contributed to the emergence of a political rift between the two groups. Wage drift mechanisms that in themselves became inflationary were the safety valve that has let out the pressure from interorganizational conflict by restoring wage differentials.

In Belgium and the Netherlands, the organizational cleavages that occurred in the past between liberal, Christian and social democratic trade unions had less of a direct impact on the conduct of collective bargaining. However, as has been pointed out in Chapter 5, since in both countries the role of the government had traditionally been strong in wage formation, the affiliation of these religiously and politically rooted trade unions with political parties influenced the wage bargaining behaviour of the unions *vis-à-vis* the government. This was particularly the case when the government was dominated by a party to which the strongest trade union was affiliated. Examples of this were the period of social democratic rule in the Netherlands during the 1970s. In Belgium, the main trade union confederations (CSC and FTGB) were affiliated to the main governing parties for most of the post-war period. In Finland, the split of the social democratic party in 1956 into a social democratic and communist faction had serious knock-on effects for sectoral groups within the trade unions, which started to act more militantly with the support of the communist party.

In weakly coordinated wage bargaining systems, the role of dissenting factions has further inhibited the institutionalization of wage bargaining. In France, Italy, Portugal and Spain, strong political cleavages exist between social democratic and communist trade unions. In all the countries with a strong communist-party-based trade union organization, wage bargaining coordination has been traditionally weak or even largely absent. In Ireland and the UK, the pluralist nature of trade union organizations embodies the notion of different factions that legitimately pursue group-based interests.

Dissenting factions are particularly effective in wage bargaining systems that are otherwise highly institutionalized. Since wage bargaining institutions are aimed at finding a comprehensive wage solution for the economy as a whole, dissenting groups can strongly affect the process of compromising on a shared wage norm. This process is particularly pronounced in Belgium, since it combines a strong role for the state, an affiliation of political trade unions to the government party and political competition between the unions based on workplace elections that determine their relative strength within tripartite committees. This has caused tremendous tensions between the incorporation of trade unions into political decision-making on the one hand and political competition between trade unions on the other. In the Scandinavian cases, the conflicts were largely confined to the confederations themselves and their direct relationship with employers in wage bargaining.

The exposure to the market

The exposure of trade unions to international markets interacts with the pattern of coordinated wage bargaining. The coordination of wage bargaining only refers to the capacity to find a norm that can be applied throughout the economy. The exposure of trade unions to international markets contributes to the relative importance of the export sector. In coordinated wage bargaining institutions that are dominated by the interests of export or exposed-sector trade unions, the impact of wage settlements on the real exchange rate will inevitably play a role since it affects employment security in the export sector.

Figure 6.2 Share of trade union members in exposes sector and responsiveness

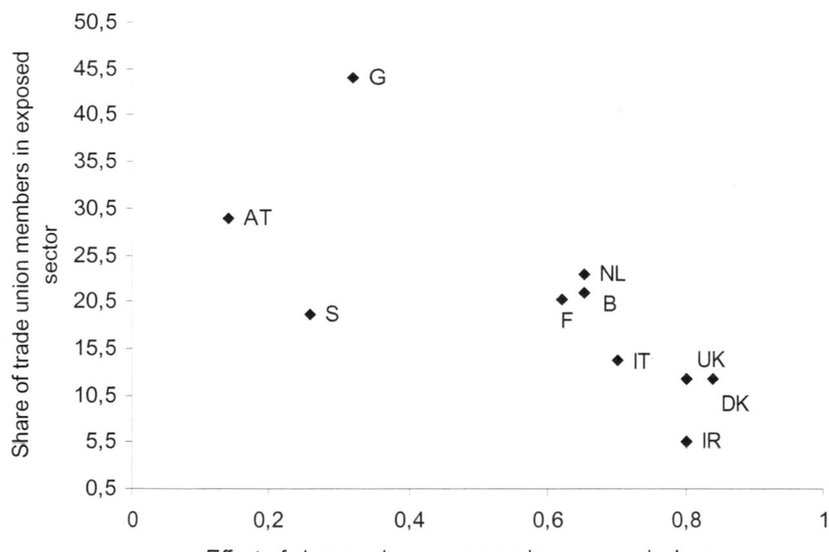

Source: Table 6.1 for effect of changes in consumer prices on nominal wages; Crouch (1993: 274) for share of trade union members in exposed sector.

Since international market conditions determine the price of goods and services, the competitiveness of national producers depends among other factors on changes in labour costs. In the public or sheltered sector, this relationship is weaker (Garrett and Way 2000; Franzese 2001). Employment security depends not so much on global competitiveness as on the preferences of the government and on the domestic consumption of the goods and services that are produced in the sheltered sector. Therefore one would expect trade unions that are dominated by the sheltered and public sector to push up wages more than trade unions that are dominated by the exposed sector. Trade unions that are heavily influenced by the exposed sector can be expected to be more responsive to changes in employment and prices.

Calculations for exposure to the market are presented in figure 6.2, which shows the relationship between trade union members in the exposed sector as a share of the main trade union confederation and the degree to which nominal wage increases are affected by changes in consumer prices. Low scores on the effects of changes in consumer prices indicate high levels of responsiveness. The Pearson correlation is -0.64. Again, Germany and Austria are the countries with the highest degree of responsiveness. They also have the highest share of trade union members in the exposed sector: Germany has 44 per cent of its trade union members in the exposed sector, and Austria has 29 per cent (Crouch 1993: 274). In contrast to what the literature on the role of public sector trade unions claims, the Scandinavian countries do not have the lowest share of trade union members in the exposed sector. Rather, it is the pluralist countries of Ireland and the United Kingdom that have a very low share of market exposure, which is also reflected in a low degree of responsiveness.

In Germany, the high level of exposure is tightly linked to the pattern setting procedure of wage bargaining. The key leading settlement takes place in the regional engineering wage round. Moreover, the leading region is often Baden-Wurttemberg, in which highly exposed companies are situated. The strong influence of the exposed sector means that negotiations centre on the changes in unit labour costs. However, since the settlement is likely to determine the general wage norm for that year, it also focuses on the likely impact of the settlement on the exchange rate. Wage bargainers are aware of the effect that inflationary wage settlements will have on the appreciation of the exchange rate and are therefore prone to moderate wages to avoid an appreciation (Soskice 1988).

The role of wage indexation

Wage indexation has been the main point of conflict in most of the cases where the relationships between governments and trade unions have been highly conflictual and where frequent government intervention has been necessary in order to bring the wage expectations of the unions more in line with the new macroeconomic constraints. In most cases, governments have engaged in lengthy battles in order to abolish wage indexation and replace it with new pay norms. In this section, the role of wage indexation is explored further. I will argue that in countries where wage bargaining has been insufficiently institutionalized, wage indexation has become a decisive instrument employed by the unions to strengthen their bargaining position. At the same time, with the increasing need for wage adjustments, indexation rules have also been a major stumbling block for economic adjustment. Government intervention reflects the struggle between the bargaining position of the unions reliant on indexation and the need to accept macroeconomic constraints.

The dissemination and practice of wage indexation has varied considerably among countries, irrespective of their wage bargaining institutions and the degree of coordination or centralization of their collective bargaining system (see table 6.5). Since rules on wage indexation do not require a particular wage bargaining set-up, but can be laid down either in law or as a general rule in decentralized wage agreements, they can be applied in any institutional environment. In some cases, wage indexation clauses have been a *quid pro quo* for contracts of a fixed duration and have thereby served as a form of compensation for trade unions in exchange for incomes policy and real wage restraint (Flanagan, Soskice *et al.* 1983: 664). In particular, immediately after the war and also in the high-growth period of the 1960s, governments throughout the OECD looked for ways to avoid industrial conflict. In many countries, wage and price controls imposed during the war were extended in the post-war period. In this period, there was an apparent expectation that centralized control over prices and wages would become an institutionalized factor of economic policy in a number of countries. This was reinforced by the implications of the Korean War, which created an upsurge in international prices and therefore also posed the first real challenge to the post-war approach to the management of wages.

In fact, in the majority of the OECD countries, including the non-corporatist countries of the USA, Canada, the United Kingdom, Ireland and Australia, some form of wage indexation rules were introduced in the 20th

Table 6.5	Wage indexation in Western Europe
Austria	No tradition of indexation.
Belgium	Since 1948, automatic indexation of 95% of wages. Suspended in the early 1980s by government decree, but reinstated in the mid-1980s. Real wage agreements are negotiated in national and sectoral wage bargaining.
Denmark	Indexation introduced in the 1920s including a flat rate component. Suspended by several rounds of incomes policy during the 1970s. Suspended in 1982 and abolished in 1983.
Finland	Full indexation between 1947-67; abandoned after devaluation in 1968; partially reintroduced after 1969. Suspended in 1991 and replaced by thresholds in 1992.
France	Indexation was widespread in the 1950s, but banned by law in 1958. Exception is the minimum wage (SMIC). Indexation clauses in the public enterprises and parts of the private sector in 1969 provided for automatic adjustment mechanisms following the Grenelle Agreement in 1968.
Germany	Wage indexation without authorization by the Bundesbank banned in the Monetary Law in 1948.
Ireland	Automatic indexation introduced in national agreement in 1970; reconfirmed in 1974 and 1975.
Italy	Automatic cost of living adjustment of wages since the war. Frequent renegotiations in the 1970s and 1980s; scope reduced by referendum in 1985, abolished in 1992.
Netherlands	Indexation since 1969, suspended by statutory incomes policy in 1974; abolished by the Wassenaar Agreement in 1982; disappeared from collective agreements in 1985.
Portugal	Introduced briefly in a pact between government and unions in 1987.
Spain	No tradition of indexation.
Sweden	No tradition of indexation.
United Kingdom	Long tradition of escalator clauses until 1966, when incomes policy abandoned them. Threshold clauses introduced in 1973-74. Afterwards abandoned.

Sources: Page and Trollope (1974); Braun (1976); various sources.

century. In British wage bargaining, escalator and threshold clauses existed until the early 1970s. Wage agreements were thereby made conditional on a particular inflation rate. If inflation moved upwards more quickly than expected, a new bargaining round was triggered.

In Ireland, wage indexation began in 1970 with the National Wage Agreements. The first three agreements contained a partial retrospective index-linked element. The onset of the oil price-led recession during 1974 meant that expectations regarding inflation were central to the agreement of 1975. The employers agreed to a one-year agreement involving quarterly phased increases linked to the consumer price index. The principle of indexation was also endorsed by the government White Paper 'A National Partnership'. Initially this was acceptable to employers as a means of containing the inflationary expectations of employees (Hardiman 1988: 59). However, in contrast to the assumptions by economists, wage indexation was soon to be regarded as a precious tool by trade unions for protecting the real wage, rather than for adjusting wage expectations downwards. Therefore, indexation rules were used as compensation devices in incomes policies. In France, wage indexation was part of the Grenelle agreements in 1968; in Italy, it took the form of the Scala mobile from 1975 onwards; and in the UK, there were the threshold agreements of 1973-74 (Flanagan, Soskice *et al.* 1983: 665).

Among the corporatist countries, there were two distinct approaches towards the relationship between wage indexation and collective bargaining processes. In some countries, wage bargaining institutions were embedded in a tight network of centralized labour organizations and sometimes in government-run tripartite institutions that were based on an understanding of responsibility for economic outcomes. In Austria and the Netherlands, the formation of wage bargaining institutions and the first generation of wage bargaining after the war took place under the tight control of government agencies. In Germany, wage indexation was outlawed, while in Sweden, highly centralized and political trade unions were not interested in sacrificing their autonomy for the sake of legislated guarantees of wage increases. Obviously, a change in prices always threatened the real wage, and wage increases were also based on protecting purchasing power. But the setting of wages was seen as an inherently political process that would respond to a number of different external factors that could not be replaced by an automatic mechanism.

In contrast, in other countries where the institutional control over wages by either labour organizations or tripartite bodies could not be ensured, direct rules on wage indexation were applied more easily. Among the traditionally corporatist countries, wage indexation rules played an important role in Belgium, Denmark, Finland and the Netherlands. In each case, wage indexation was introduced soon after the war in the context of price and wage controls. In some cases, indexation had already been established after World War 1 and was only reintroduced in the 1950s.

In Belgium, Denmark and Finland, the history of wage indexation goes back to the aftermath of World War 1. The Netherlands is a mixed case between an initially highly institutionally controlled system of wage bargaining – more like the Austrian system – and a system that ultimately moved towards wage indexation because the institutions could not contain local wage pressures during the 1960s. At the same time, the Netherlands is an example of how wage indexation had been discovered by trade unions as a means of ensuring real wage protection. The incorporation of trade unions in government-controlled institutions had been particularly harsh during the immediate post-war period. Dutch incomes policy had been prepared during the latter part of the war, when trade union officials and employers' representatives began secret deliberations on post-war reconstruction and set up an organization to ensure the smooth functioning of the labour market, the bipartite Labour Foundation. By 1954, the Netherlands was the only country in Western Europe in which there had been no increase in hourly wage earnings since 1948 (United Nations 1967: Ch. 4, p. 3). There was considerable discontent within the trade unions, to which the government did not respond. Instead, in 1959, the government instituted a new system linking pay to expected productivity increases. The discontent led to opposition by the unions and wages exploded throughout the 1960s. As a result, wage indexation clauses were introduced first at Philips and later, in 1969, into all collective agreements (Visser and Hemerijck 2000).

Wage indexation during the economic crisis

However, wage indexation was not an appropriate tool for the real incomes policy that was required from the early 1970s onwards. Indexation rules did not decrease inflationary pressure but increased it. When the oil crisis changed the terms of trade of the industrialized world with many countries requiring downward adjustments in wages in order to restore competitiveness, nominal wages were particularly sticky in countries that had firm wage indexation rules. The high increase in world prices had particularly negative effects on the price–wage spiral in countries with indexed wages. Through higher import prices, international prices entered the consumer price index and therefore directly into the wage index. Moreover, since wages were tied to prices, the rise in international prices had an immediate impact on the cost structure (Flanagan, Soskice *et al.* 1983: 666). In countries with a looser coupling of prices and wages, the upsurge in international prices could be counteracted with real wage restraint. "Despite – or because of – the real-wage protection goals of unions, however, every European country that introduced or extended wage-indexation systems as compensatory devices during the 1970s attempted subsequently to move in the reverse direction, and in countries in which wage indexation was already well established, the indexation arrangements posed difficult problems for incomes policy" (Flanagan, Soskice *et al.* 1983: 665).

In more decentralized and loosely regulated wage bargaining systems such as the British and the Irish, rules on wage indexation disappeared quickly. However in both countries, given the lack of institutionalization of wage bargaining procedures, protecting real wages remained the most important focus of trade union strategy in wage bargaining throughout the crisis. Therefore, in non-corporatist countries, wage indexation was discarded as official policy, but informally the changes in cost-of-living expenses remained the main guide for wage bargaining. For governments, the informal wage bargaining behaviour of trade unions, however, was out of their immediate control.

In other countries where wage bargaining institutions were more formalized, wage indexation rules tended to be ingrained in wage bargaining processes and sometimes in labour law. Trade unions, which originally were rather reluctant to accept wage indexation rules since they reduced their bargaining scope, had started to rely on them as a guarantor for protecting real wages in hard times. Moreover, since wage indexation had become a part of modern life in these countries, trade unions gained their legitimacy from bargaining on top of wage indexation. Wage bargaining in Italy, Belgium and the Netherlands in the 1970s was about the scope of increasing the real wage on top of inflation. Hence the expectations by trade unions of the potential pay increase were particularly far from what the economic situation required.

Wage indexation was not abolished in any of these countries during the stagflation of the 1970s. In Denmark, the Netherlands, Belgium and Italy, wage indexation was either suspended several times or the parameters of adjustments were renegotiated. Governments suggested that energy prices should be omitted from the price index in order to take into account the changing terms of trade. In other countries, the coverage and frequencies of adjustment were cut down. In Denmark, parts of the indexed wage increases were rerouted into the pension scheme (Flanagan, Soskice *et al.* 1983: 667). In Belgium, proposals were made to tax wage increases above the indexation rate. Later on in the negotiations for the Global Plan, the index was changed to a 'health index' with health-damaging contents being excluded from the index. Despite the guise of health-related issues, the primary task of the 'health index' was to push the process of further de-linking wage increases from price increases. However, the trade unions in all the countries in which indexation procedures were established managed to keep to these guidelines throughout the 1970s, even though they were sometimes reduced in scope.

Governments started to renegotiate wage indexation during the 1970s once the crisis set in. While the tinkering with existing mechanisms generally did not resolve the problem, indexation remained a bargaining issue. The problem worsened over time, since the employment situation in these countries deteriorated more rapidly than elsewhere. During the 1980s, unemployment rates in the indexation countries of Italy (9.5 per cent), Belgium (10.8 per cent), Denmark (8.9 per cent) and the Netherlands (9.7 per cent) exceeded the European average of 8 per cent.

The increase in unemployment, however, did not restrain trade union wage bargaining behaviour, but rather led to further conflict over wage formation. Trade unions already felt hard done by as a result of the worsening labour market performance and asked for more compensation for this hardship rather than be willing to make concessions. Instead of accepting the need for adjustment, they blocked any reform. The automatic protection of the real wage had become ingrained in the expectations of the trade unions and their members to the extent that every negotiation about indexation was perceived as an outright attack on the legitimacy of the unions. In all four countries, Belgium, the Netherlands, Italy and Denmark, unions had started to become dependent on indexation.

In Italy, wage indexation had become a powerful tool the trade unions could exploit in a situation which was characterized by weak bargaining institutions. In combination with the Workers Statute 1970, Italian unions started to build plant-level bargaining institutions, while at the national level they gained legitimacy from protecting wage indexation. But why were the trade unions in corporatist and consensus-based societies such as the Netherlands, Belgium and Denmark not in the position to give up indexation more easily when the need arose, and why in particular were social democratic governments under so much strain from the changing economic environment? The main reason was that wage indexation had become popular with working people and easily justifiable to the general public. With inflation eroding workers' incomes, indexation had become popular among trade union members.

In the early 1980s, Belgian workers had their wages adjusted four times a year. Every three months workers could expect a pay increase to catch up with rising costs of living. Among trade union members, indexation had become a precious good and unions were well advised to protect the mechanism. Policy-makers and trade unions for most of the 1970s lived under the impression that, because they cooperated in a corporatist, consensus-oriented, socially just society, economic adjustment should be possible on the basis of protecting what had been achieved so far. In the negotiations on incomes policy during the 1970s, trade unions therefore asked a high price in compensation for agreeing to wage restraint. Moreover, indexation had become a tool of redistribution towards groups of workers with low wages. Since indexation often guaranteed real wage protection more effectively for lower income than for higher income workers, it had also become a political instrument of redistribution within the working class.

Therefore, in order to adjust wage expectations downwards, the political pressure was increasingly directed at the indexation mechanism. This pressure derived initially from employers who had quickly recognized the rigidity of the current system. For governments, the issue was more difficult since they often defended the principle of indexation to secure the purchasing power of workers as justified and found it difficult to oppose this.

At the same time, the economic effects of indexation became more apparent and, increasingly, were openly addressed. For instance, at the European Summit of 1980, Belgium was advised to modify its "prejudicial system of wage indexation" if it wanted to stay in the EMS (Dancet 1988: 211). In Italy, indexation had long been identified as a major factor preventing economic adjustment. However, for the working population, indexation had become a form of insurance against the hardships of the market. As other forms of welfare rights came under pressure during the 1990s, the safeguarding of real pay was highly popular in these countries since they provided direct benefits to workers.

Eventually, indexation was abandoned in Denmark and the Netherlands in 1982 and in Italy in 1992. In all three cases, the abolition was a major turning point in the restructuring of the wage bargaining institutions in these countries. This indicates just how important indexation had become, since it took a major shift of approach in order for it to be abolished.

Establishing new wage guidelines

The adjustment of wage expectations under new economic constraints not only required abandoning all expectations that real wages could be safeguarded under any condition, but also prompted a search for new guidelines on pay. During the high growth decades of the 1960s, pay was easily determined by a compensation for cost of living and an additional rise stemming from productivity increases and economic growth. Under the new conditions of more fragile competitiveness, rearranged competitive conditions and, in particular, lower growth, new expectations on how pay should develop had to be shaped.

Therefore, in line with the increasing involvement of governments in the restructuring of wage bargaining, a search began for new pay guidelines, which might replace the old mechanism of cost-of-living adjustments and productivity (table 6.6). Pay guidelines were required in a situation where the new orientation was unclear or where decentralized bargaining units were to be directed onto a new course. No pay guidelines were issued in countries with largely deregulated wage bargaining institutions, such as France and the UK, or in countries where responsiveness was generally high, such as Austria. In France, wage bargaining had become oriented to the minimum wage increases that were set by the government. In the UK, wage formation had become completely decentralized. In Spain, after the collapse of tripartite incomes policy agreements in 1986, the issue of pay formation was largely excluded from tripartite talks.

In other countries, where wage bargaining remained coordinated and based on wage bargaining institutions, new rules on pay formation were issued for two reasons. First, wage guidelines were used in order to provide lower level wage bargaining actors with orientation guidelines. Second, wage guidelines were also issued as reconfirmation by the social partners of a newly emerging consensus on pay. For instance, the social partner declarations in the Netherlands (1982), Germany (1999), Belgium (1989), Sweden (1995), Portugal (1996) and Denmark (1987) confirmed the importance of safeguarding competitiveness for pay formation. On several occasions, social partners in the exposed sectors and governments both attempted to use the constraints of the exposed sector as the primary base for wage formation.

In Denmark, Sweden and the Netherlands, these pay guidelines have had a strong effect on wage bargaining behaviour and have generally been taken seriously. In the Netherlands, the rather vague declaration in the

Table 6.6 Wage guidelines for shifting expectations

	Year	Name	Content
Belgium	1998		Recommendation made by the Central Economic Council, which is composed of representatives of employers' associations and trade unions, plus six independent experts. Follows previous legislation on the Global Plan. Recommendation is based on the assumed average wage increases of Belgium's main trading partners, namely France, Germany and the Netherlands.
Denmark	1987	National tripartite declaration	Declaration recommends that the development of labour costs should not exceed the development of labour costs in competing countries.
Finland	1995	Agreement of the national tripartite incomes policy commission	Wage formula for 'non-inflationary wage cost development' recommends wage increases in line with the total sum of the inflation target of the central bank and the growth of productivity in the whole economy.
Germany	1999	Statement of the national tripartite 'Alliance for Jobs'	Recommends productivity growth as a guideline.
Italy	1993 1998	Tripartite agreements	Sectoral wage developments should be in line with the planned inflation rate and company-level wage bargaining should take into account the performance of the firm. Endorsed by the agreement in 1998; orientation is the average European inflation rate.
Netherlands	1982	Agreement of Wassenaar	Recommends wage moderation.
Portugal	1996	Strategic Concertation Pact	Promotes guidelines that are based on expected inflation and expected increases in productivity.
Sweden	1995 1997	Bipartite agreement in the industry sector	Edin-Norm 'European norm', according to which Swedish wages should not rise faster than the EU average, was recommended by the Economic Council.

Sources: Hyman and Ferner (1998); Hassel (2000); Schulten and Stueckler (2000); Schulten (2002); various sources.

Agreement of Wassenaar has led to a number of years of real pay losses. Similarly in Denmark, the period of the late 1980s, after the five-party declaration was signed, was characterized by particularly moderate wage settlements.

However, in a number of other countries, including Germany, Belgium and Portugal, the agreements on pay norms have played a more strategic role and have not influenced wage bargaining actors directly. This is not to say that in these countries wage bargaining outcomes have not fallen into line with the macroeconomic constraints of the 1990s. But with regard to the expectation of wage bargaining actors on wage formation, the new pay norms have been more a rhetorical concession in tripartite agreements rather than tending to reflect a shift in their bargaining goals. For instance, in Portugal, the productivity norm quickly lost its importance (Naumann 2000). In Belgium, the general issue of the relationship between competitiveness and wage indexation has still not been resolved in trade union wage bargaining strategies (Pochet 1999a). In Germany, a country with a high degree of responsiveness, the wage norm on productivity that was put forward by the *Sachverständigenrat* and within the Alliance for Jobs has deliberately left out the issue of cost-of-living adjustments.

In Germany, the role of the tax wedge and high non-wage labour costs was the more decisive issue for labour costs than wages themselves. Since the government has not managed to address this issue, the focus temporarily shifted back to pay; especially since the employers would have liked to see pay issues dealt with in tripartite agreements. The strength of the German system and the domination of the export sector in pay settlements have started to backfire with the increasing vulnerability of German export industries to union demands (Thelen 2000).

In most cases, the government has been directly involved in drawing up new pay guidelines. In the Netherlands the government of 1982 threatened a major intervention in the overall wage bargaining system if the social partners did not respond to its macroeconomic constraints. The Agreement of Wassenaar has therefore been seen as negotiated in "the shadow of hierarchy" (Visser and Hemerijck 1997). In Sweden and Belgium, the pay norms were designed by economic experts, but advocated by the government and state mediators at a later date. In Portugal, Italy, Finland, Belgium and Germany, the new pay norms were explicitly discussed in tripartite negotiations with government participation. By this means, governments deliberately pressed wage bargaining actors to adopt pay policies that were in line with the economic constraints they themselves faced.

In sum, wage indexation regulations have frequently been introduced both before and since World War II in order to ease the adjustment of wages to new economic conditions. In reality, the regulations fixed expectations on protecting the real wage. When these regulations were tied to otherwise highly institutionalized wage bargaining systems, wage indexation made these systems more rigid rather than more flexible. Despite good intentions, wage indexation at no time fostered adjustment.

Conclusion: Shifting workers' wage expectations

The wage expectations of trade unions and workers are largely shaped by the institutions under which wage bargaining takes place. In the post-war Western European countries, these institutions were shaped by four factors: by the degree to which wage bargaining could be coordinated across the economy, by the extent to which dissenting factions could establish themselves as competing forces within or outside trade union organizations, by the amount of exposure of the leading trade unions to the market, and by the level to which mechanisms of wage indexation had been established. Coordination and international exposure thereby increased the responsiveness of wage bargaining behaviour to changing external conditions, while wage indexation mechanisms and the presence of strong dissenting factions contributed to a lack of responsiveness. Depending on the institutional mix, wage bargaining outcomes displayed different degrees of responsiveness.

The four factors influencing wage responsiveness are interrelated: a strong tradition of dissenting fractions within trade unions has often forestalled a high degree of coordination. Only when factionalism was overcome has coordination been able to take place effectively. Similarly, a high degree of coordination might contribute to minimize the fractionalization of trade unions if coordination were to channel the organization of diverse interests and discriminated against others. The process of increasing institution building in a number of previously loosely coordinated collective bargaining systems, such as those in Italy and Ireland, has also minimized the conflicts between factions. On the other hand, where dissenting factions have been and continue to be strong, the competition between trade unions has forced them to insist on protecting the powerful instrument of wage indexation. In some cases, a higher degree of coordination and institutionalization has frozen existing patterns of political competition between trade unions. For instance, the tripartite councils in Belgium are based on the distribution of seats between the different politically divided peak associations. The representation within the tripartite councils thus strengthens the existing cleavages. The exposure of trade unions to international markets has had a greater effect where wage bargaining has been coordinated, since the competitive pressure that rests on the exporting sector has been able to be transformed into a generalized wage formula for the whole economy.

Building on the factors, one can identify different configurations of institutions that suggest a higher or lower degree of bargaining wage responsiveness (table 6.7). It becomes apparent that Germany and Austria have a combination of institutional features that are highly conducive to wage bargaining responsiveness. In Germany and Austria, the degree of dissenting factions within and outside trade union organizations is virtually zero. In both countries, trade unions are dominated by the exposed sector, wage bargaining is highly coordinated, and wage indexation has been ruled out either by law or by practice. At the other end of the spectrum, wage bargaining institutions in the United Kingdom do not suggest any form of responsiveness: coordination in wage bargaining is absent, local competition is encouraged by the organizational rivalry between trade unions, and the share of union members in exposed sectors is moderate. While wage indexation has not played an important role in wage bargaining since the mid-1970s, the main preoccupation of local wage bargaining in the United Kingdom has actually been to preserve the real wage.

Again, we find the majority of countries caught between the two extremes. Sweden comes closest to the model of Germany and Austria. The highly political nature of wage formation in Sweden makes an assessment of the responsiveness of wage formation difficult. Furthermore, high degrees of wage drift undermine the capacity of wage bargaining institutions to coordinate wage formation. The wage drift, moreover, is primarily due to distributive conflicts between different groups of workers belonging to the same umbrella organization, which in turn has not managed to find a solution to these conflicts and therefore allows them to find their expression in local bargaining. The other traditional corporatist countries are all affected either by some degree of factionalism within the trade unions or by wage indexation mechanisms. Denmark, the Netherlands and Belgium have subscribed to wage indexation that prevented real wage adjustments from being made via lower nominal wage increases. Among the coordinated countries, the worst combination of factors is to be found in Belgium. Here, strong political competition between trade unions pre-

Table 6.7 Summary of institutional foundations for wage bargaining responsiveness

	Coordination	Dissenting factions	Exposure to markets	Wage indexation	Responsiveness
Austria	high	none	high	none	high
Germany	high	none	high	none	high
Sweden	high	some	high	none	high
Denmark	high	some	moderate	yes	moderate
Belgium	high	some	moderate	yes	moderate
Netherlands	high	almost none	moderate	yes	moderate
Finland	high	temporarily considerable	moderate	temporary	moderate
Italy	low	temporarily considerable	moderate	yes	moderate
France	low	strong	moderate	some through public sector	moderate
Ireland	low	some	low	none	moderate
Spain	low	strong	low	none	moderate
Portugal	low	strong	low	temporary	low
United Kingdom	low	local	moderate	none	low

Sources: tables 5.3 and 5.4, figures 5.1 and 5.2.

vents the adjustment of an outlived wage formation model that is based on strict indexation criteria. While the high degree of coordination in Belgium theoretically could facilitate the adjustment of wages, in practice the interplay between the coordinating institutions, the rule of indexation and the competition between trade unions has reinforced a vicious circle of low adjustment and continuous contestation.

Low levels of responsiveness of trade union wage bargaining behaviour have prompted governments to intervene in processes of wage formation. Where responsiveness of wage bargaining has been high, such as in Austria and Germany, intervention has largely been absent. Where responsiveness has been mixed, intervention has been more pronounced. The more trade unions have emphasized the protection of real wages at the expense of responding to high levels of unemployment, the more governments have been tempted to use their authority to shift trade union wage expectations. In particular, governments have become active in abolishing systems of wage indexation in all countries where rules on indexation have been present.

In many cases, the adjustment of wage expectations has created the need for new mechanisms on which wage bargaining could be based. Where indexation has been abolished, the distributive conflicts between different groups have had to be minimized and more external pressure has been needed to contain wage expectations in the sheltered sectors. Hence governments and wage bargaining actors have been on the lookout for new distributive compromises. The solution as presented in a number of countries has been the adoption of pay guidelines.

The emphasis of new pay guidelines on competitiveness has strengthened the role of the exposed sector, particularly in countries where the exposed sector has not been strongly represented within the unions. By focusing on competitiveness rather than on the preservation of real pay or pay equality, wage bargaining institutions have shifted their responsiveness towards macroeconomic requirements at the expense of other priorities. They have enhanced their central quest for national competitiveness at the expense of delivering their traditional contribution to equity.

In this process, the interaction between governments and wage bargaining institutions has been crucial. Governments have been forced to act in order to increase the responsiveness of their bargaining systems. The imperative to act arises from both the high costs of poor adjustment, in terms of accommodating increasing numbers of unemployed in European welfare systems, as well as the responsibility of national governments to deal with the pressures on exchange rates. External openness and increasing capital mobility on the one hand and welfare expectation of working people on the other hand, put governments into a mediating role. Governments frequently filled this role by interfering into the wage setting process and thereby supported the adjustment process of wage bargaining institutions.

7 The Interaction between Wage Bargaining Institutions and Government Intervention

I now turn to the 13 country cases to discuss the interaction between wage bargaining responsiveness and government intervention. The analysis builds on Chapter 6, in which the responsiveness of wage bargaining institutions was assessed. In this chapter I go a step further, examining the interaction between wage bargaining institutions and the behaviour of the government.

The case studies themselves aim to synthesize the extensive literature on each of the countries and to do so in a way that places particular emphasis on developing a greater understanding of why, and under what conditions, governments intervene in the wage bargaining process. In this sense, this chapter reflects the overall approach of the book in combining, and at the same time seeking a balance between, approaches based solely on quantitative analysis and those based on qualitative country-based case studies.

The chapter is in four sections. The first section presents the responsive wage bargaining regimes of Germany and Austria. Section two considers corporatist countries with non-responsive wage bargaining regimes. These are divided into countries that have experienced massive intervention subsequent to declining economic performance (Belgium, Denmark and the Netherlands), and those that have moved from real to nominal wage restraint and monetary policies (Sweden and Finland).

The third section deals with non-corporatist countries with non-responsive wage bargaining regimes. The cases of France and the UK are characterized by de-institutionalization and decentralization as reactions to institutional failure, while in Italy and Ireland wage bargaining institutions have been built through government intervention. Finally, Spain and Portugal are discussed as cases where the building of responsive bargaining regimes followed government intervention. Figure A1 in the appendix accompanying the case studies shows wage formation over time through the relationship between unemployment and nominal wages. The fourth section presents conclusions derived from the case studies.

The guiding questions of the case studies are the following: How are wage expectations formed? Which incentives for wage responsiveness to external economic constraints are provided by wage bargaining institutions? Did government intervention occur as a reaction to an apparent decline in responsiveness in the wage bargaining institutions? How did government intervention interact with existing wage bargaining institutions?

The responsive wage bargaining regimes: Germany and Austria

The monetarist corporatist wage bargaining countries have been identified as those bargaining regimes in which the reality of external economic constraints had an immediate impact on the formation of pay while neglecting the priority of real wage protection. Austria and Germany are known as countries where labour entered the post-war period in a weak state. In both countries, the trade unions were organized along new lines after the war, disregarding older forms of workers' organizations. The new trade union organizations were highly centralized and, in both countries, the main trade union umbrella organization gained a near monopoly over the labour market. Nowadays, wage formation is dominated by sectoral concerns, while special arrangements are generally made for white-collar workers.

In both Germany and Austria, wage restraint is neither due to incomes policy nor to open political exchanges with the governments. Already in the mid-1960s, Kindleberger called the German wage bargaining systems an "incomes policy from below" (Kindleberger 1965: 248). The strategic capacity of wage bargaining institutions is particularly high in both countries (Hall 1986: 242; Scharpf 1991: 249). They are based on a system that diminishes distributive struggles between different groups of workers and sectors, while at the same time allowing for sector-specific adjustments. Moreover, they are dominated by the wage bargaining procedures in the exposed sectors that are highly vulnerable to the appreciation of the euro.

Sectoral bargaining is based on pattern bargaining that is usually led by the metal sector. In Austria, the sequence of sectoral bargaining is highly habitualized in that metal starts the annual bargaining round and the other bargaining units follow in a given order in the course of the year (Traxler, Blaschke *et al.* 2001: 171). In Germany, the pattern varies more since wage agreements are concluded for different periods of time which can lead to changing pattern setters other than the IG Metall. In both countries, there is an understanding between the trade unions and the employers' confederations that the pattern setter is not determining pay for other sectors but merely providing a model for other sectors to follow.

Given the lack of formal coordination procedures, informal coordination is achieved in two ways. The first manner in which informal coordination is achieved is through the competence of the pattern setter to establish a fine balance between the ability of companies to pay within the sector and the macroeconomic environment. On the trade union side, members' expectations in those companies which dominate the wage bargaining are usually informed by the specific company's ability to pay. On the company side, companies orient their willingness to engage in wage conflicts with reference to their own ability to pay.

At the same time, the pattern setters are based in the exposed sectors that are particularly vulnerable to the monetary policy of the Bundesbank. The comparatively high proportion of jobs in export industries and their relative role in the wage bargaining system has made the wage bargainers particularly sensitive towards the impact of their wage behaviour on a potential appreciation of the currency via restrictive monetary policy.

The second factor which keeps wage bargaining in a coordinated framework is the weakness of the sheltered and public sector trade unions in wage bargaining. Although trade unions in the sheltered and public sectors have less incentive to lower their expectations since they are not under the disciplining force of foreign competition (Garrett and Way 2000), they are not usually able to exploit their comfortable position of being protected from market forces. Rather, the pattern bargaining as set by exposed sector collective agreements helps these trade unions to pull wages in the sheltered and public sector up to a level which they would not achieve otherwise.[105] This trend exists even though union membership in the public sector is higher than in the manufacturing sector,[106] and as a result, trade unions find it difficult to achieve substantial wage increases under the condition of high public deficits. Within wage bargaining rounds, trade unions use the notion of catching up with manufacturing sectors as an argument. This is partly in order to evoke an argument about an equity norm in wage bargaining in the public debate and partly in order to keep the public sector as an attractive employer. At the same time, trade unions in the exposed sector have an interest in pulling the sheltered and public sector unions up to their level since a general wage increase for the whole economy can be used as a floor for future bargaining gains.

As a consequence, in Austria and Germany there is a high degree of institutional control over wage developments and little potential for group-specific distributional struggles undermining the strategic capacity of wage bargaining actors to react to changing external conditions. Both countries survived the test of time when, in 1975, a major adjustment in wage expectations was needed in face of double-digit inflation rates. The strong reaction by the Bundesbank led to immediate wage adjustments (Scharpf 1991). A similar adjustment of wage expectations took place in the immediate post-reunification phase in 1991. Business expansion to the east had led to high increases in prices and profitability, and trade unions aimed at participating in the boom by negotiating high wage increases in 1991 and 1992. A stark reaction by the Bundesbank again restricted the subsequent wage rounds.

Austria

In Austria, wage bargaining arrangements are tightly incorporated into the political system. From 1957 until 1994, a parliamentary committee on pay and prices (Parity Commission, or *Paritätische Kommission*) had the ultimate power to reject pay settlements. It had already started refraining from doing so, however, in the late 1970s (Traxler 1998: 246). The political incorporation of pay bargaining procedures stemmed from the immediate post-war period. Already in September 1945, the newly formed *Arbeiterkammer* approached the Chamber for Business (*Wirtschaftskammer*) and suggested a permanent committee be set up for consultation on wages. In the years that followed, the committee issued four price and wage agreements that kept wage increases under control. In 1950, after a violent strike by Austrian workers against the declining standard of living, the price and wage agreements were dropped. However, by this time, the exceptionally centralized chambers of labour and business along with the Austrian trade union confederation were firmly in control of wage developments (Talos and Kittel 1996).

While wage bargaining normally has taken place at a sectoral level, it was the Parity Commission which was accustomed to monitor bargaining procedures. The Austrian trade union confederation (ÖGB) had, in fact, to apply for sectoral negotiations to take place in the Parity Commission. This procedure gave the ÖGB a gatekeeper role *vis-à-vis* its own affiliates, since the ÖGB is free to decide when to apply for the negotiations to start. Since employees and employers were jointly represented in the Parity Commission, employers were also in control of the conduct of negotiations. In particular, during the 1950s and 1960s, the Parity Commission was an important instrument for coordinated wage negotiations. The ÖGB and the chamber of business could delay the start of negotiations and thereby dampen the wage expectations of the sectoral union leaders (Traxler 1982: 245).

By the early 1980s, the metal sector trade union had become the pattern setter in wage negotiations and the Parity Commission had lost in importance. Nowadays sectoral trade unions focus their expectations on the lead sectors. Nevertheless, the Parity Commission is still officially in control of the timing of negotiations and meets twice a month in order to discuss wages. If time is pressing, sectoral trade unions start negotiations before the Commission has officially cleared the way, and occasionally even wage agreements are settled before the Commission has officially decided on the conduct of the negotiations.

Coordination therefore takes place between the peak trade union confederation, i.e. the ÖGB, and the sectoral trade unions. Although the role of both the Parity Commission and the ÖGB has been reduced in recent years, both instruments are still present in the background of negotiations and could be evoked if necessary. Given the high degree of responsiveness of Austrian wage bargaining, these institutions played only a minor role in the public perception of wage bargaining. However, in conflictual situations, trade union leaders of the ÖGB can intervene in sectoral disputes in order to avert open conflict.

The high degree of wage bargaining responsiveness has been supported by the political institutions.[107] On the one hand, the close integration of the Austrian economy with the German one has implied adherence to the restrictive monetary regime of the Bundesbank, even though the Austrian National Bank has been more politically dependent than the Bundesbank. On the other hand, Austria's late membership of the European Union and the potential for monetary and fiscal expansion in contrast to the adjustment process in Germany have allowed for greater safeguarding of employment in Austria, which in turn has honoured the cooperation by the trade unions (Hemerijck, Unger *et al.* 2000). A challenge to the hitherto highly successful Austrian adjustment process only arose in the aftermath of the 1992/93 recession, when the Austrian economy was affected particularly badly. The government reacted to the recession with a tight economic policy that broke with the Austrian tradition of supporting wage restraint through an expansive economic policy. The trade unions complained about the government breaking with the tradition of implicit concertation and argued that their trust had been violated (Hemerijck, Unger *et al.* 2000: 204).

However, despite the complaints by the unions, wage bargaining responded to the worsening situation with only a minor delay. After unemployment rose to more than 5 per cent in 1996, which was exceptionally high by Austrian standards, the Austrian wage bargaining system reacted with real wage losses in two consecutive years, in 1996 and 1997 (see also figure A1). By 1995, therefore, the cooperation between the government and the unions on wage restraint had been restored again and the unions supported the restrictive budget policy of the government (Talos and Kittel 1999).[108]

Germany

In Germany, wage bargaining institutions were set up at arm's length from the political system, but with a high degree of legal regulation. In the immediate post-war period, labour was weak and had a stronger focus on political issues than on wages. It was only after the defeat in the co-determination laws in 1952 that German unions developed greater bargaining power with regard to wage formation (Lutz 1984; Scharpf 1991). The influx of foreign labour and the politically sensitive situation *vis-à-vis* East Germany restrained the role of the unions in the post-war period considerably (Flanagan, Soskice *et al.* 1983). Moreover, as has been described extensively in the literature, German wage bargaining reacted particularly smoothly to the restrictive monetary policy of the Bundesbank after 1975 (Scharpf 1991, Streeck 1994).

Compared to other European countries, Germany had been in a comparatively favourable position until the early 1990s.[109] Nominal wage developments spiralled out of control in the early 1990s when the unions claimed their dividend in the unification boom. The drastic wage increase of 1992 was only partly due to the lifting of wage levels in Eastern Germany but also consisted of an exceptionally large wage claim in Western Germany (figure A1 in appendix). The recession between 1992 and 1994 brought wage increases down to the average European level, but the competitive advantage of being able to agree wage settlements far below the European average had been lost. Given that private-sector wage settlements determine public sector pay to a large extent, the German government was facing similar economic problems that many Western European governments had faced since the early 1980s.[110]

However, in 1995 the Kohl government initially reacted to the problems in a traditional way and was rather reluctant to take up the offer from the metal sector union IG Metall to initiate tripartite negotiations. Klaus Zwickel, President of IG Metall, proposed wage increases in line with inflation for 1997 and agreed to lower wages for the long-term unemployed over a limited period of time. In exchange, the government should commit itself to refrain from further welfare cuts and to encourage companies to provide more and better training. The role of the employers was to provide 300,000 more jobs, 5 per cent more training and the promise not to make employees redundant for business-related reasons.[111] From the very beginning, the Alliance for Jobs was a sector-based initiative (EIRR 1996).

The proposal was discussed heatedly at the trade union congress of IG Metall, but was quickly picked up favourably by public opinion and policy-makers alike. It became the main topic at one of the 'Talks with the Chancellor' (*Kanzlergespräche*) on 22 January 1996. The 'Talks with the Chancellor', in which the government invited trade unions and employers' confederations for an informal exchange of opinion, had been taking place for some years since German unification (Lehmbruch 2000). After the meeting in January, a lengthy document was drawn up which listed eight pages of reform proposals, ranging from tax reforms via research and innovation to education and training as well as planning permissions to labour market and social policy. It is this process that became known as the Alliance for Jobs.

During the subsequent meeting in mid-February, an initial agreement was reached between the three sides on reform of the early retirement scheme. The previous highly popular and expensive early retirement scheme had expired in 1988, and both the trade unions and employers' confederations voiced their interest in a new scheme. Parallel to the Alliance talks, the government had pursued the route of parliamentary reforms. At the end of January 1996, the government published a 50-point programme entailing a range of detailed welfare cuts and labour market deregulation. Three important state elections took place in spring 1996. In all three elections, the liberal party (FDP), which was the smaller coalition partner, gained unexpectedly good results while the oppositional Social Democrats lost ground. After the elections, and with a strengthened liberal party that has traditionally been suspicious of corporatist policy-making, the government increasingly turned to the parliamentary route. It presented a list of cuts within the next round of Chancellor talks on 23 April, which included the de-coupling of benefits from wages, reduction of health benefits such as spa holidays, and an extension of fixed term contracts to 24 months. The list met with fierce protests from the trade unions (Bispinck 1997: 68).

The government, however, remained firm and presented to parliament in September 1996 those parts of the package that did not require the consent of the upper house. The trade unions pulled out of the Alliance for Jobs and started campaigning with parliamentary support from the left and moral support from the churches. In the following collective bargaining round, the trade unions focused on counteracting the changes in sick pay by having sick pay covered by collective agreements. Within a year, the unions were able to force employers in collective bargaining to continue with the previous statutory scheme (100 per cent rather than 80 per cent pay). Many other changes on the list of cuts were later reversed or reformed by the new government, which came to power in September 1998.

The initial proposal of the leader of IG Metall to exchange wage moderation for assurances of employment from the employers was never seriously discussed. Employers' federations quickly pointed out that they could not make any commitment to job creation on behalf of their members and that a halt to any business-related redundancies was not workable. Nevertheless, the collective bargaining round resulted in moderate wage agreements. Moreover, at the plant level, companies increasingly negotiated longer working hours and lower fringe benefits in exchange for investment promises with their works councils.[112] Yet negotiations never reached the level of far-reaching reforms, which is probably because labour costs fell. As a result, employers handled cost-cutting locally, but had no incentive to organize at a higher level. After the conflict between the government and the trade unions in autumn 1996, there were no further attempts to pursue the Alliance for Jobs at a national level. Nor did the trade unions and employers' confederations continue bilateral negotiations on the issue.

The new Schröder government relaunched tripartite concertation soon after it took office in September 1998. The first meeting in December 1998 presented a list of 11 major topics, all of which were to be dealt with in the tripartite negotiations. Compared to the programme in 1996, the list was both shorter and closer to the interests of the trade unions and employers' confederations. Despite the much more institutionalized set-up of the Alliance for Jobs and the high level of public attention compared to the first initiative in 1995, there has not been an agreement on a substantial reform proposal nor has there been any form of political exchange between the actors involved. Moreover, the proposed political exchange which was on the table focused once again on the extension of early retirement options.

The government had moved quickly to enact a number of reforms in the context of the topics of the Alliance for Jobs. In April 1999 it introduced a new environmental tax, which allowed the lowering of payroll taxes and thus lower non-wage labour costs. It also repealed some of the legislation of the old government on employment protection in small firms and extended social security to cover precarious employment. In a second step, the government addressed corporate taxation and lowered tax rates for companies considerably. By enacting these reforms, the government mainly acted in the interest of the associations, first in the interest of the trade unions and then in the interest of the employers.

The associations themselves resorted to rather vague wording in joint policy documents on the role of wage bargaining in the Alliance for Jobs. Officially, both sides strongly disagreed over the impact of wages on employment. None of the associations granted any concessions, apart from grudgingly accepting legislative changes in favour of the other side. The first and most contentious issue, which emerged as a joint discussion topic between the associations, was again focused on early retirement. The trade union side, led again by IG Metall, proposed that the retirement age should be reduced to 60 (*Rente mit 60*).[113] This new early retirement scheme was to be financed by a wage fund to be administered by the associations. Employers and employees were each to pay half a percentage of gross wages per employee into the fund. In exchange, IG Metall would exercise wage restraint for several years. The employers' federations, however, rejected a lower retirement age and any individual right to early retirement as a matter of principle. The government was initially interested in the agreement and offered to host a compromise, but soon found out that this would be an additional burden on public financing. Since no agreement could be reached in a meeting of the Alliance for Jobs in December 1999 and again in January 2000, the Chancellor sent the associations away to find a solution in the current collective bargaining round.

Behind the scenes, a deep political rift developed between the two major industrial trade unions in the metal and the chemical sector. While IG Metall publicly campaigned for a reduced retirement age, the chemical trade union had already agreed to a compromise with both the government and the employers, accepting improvements in early retirement legislation in order to pull IG Metall away from its more radical stance. To achieve this, the chemical sector settled the first major agreement on 22 March 2000, two months before the collective agreements in the chemical sector expired and well in time before the metal sector could seriously bargain over early retirement. A moderate wage increase in the chemical sector was accompanied by further improvements in partial early retirement by employers.

While the increasing role of the government in wage bargaining in Germany was initially due to a voluntary proposal by the metal sector trade union in the aftermath of the 1992/93 recession, the initiative was picked up by the new government in 1998, which started to use tripartite meetings to pressurize the unions into further wage restraint (Hassel 2001). Overall, however, the increasing involvement of the government in wage bargaining processes has yet to have any major impact on the wage bargaining institutions. The sectoral, export-based logic of wage bargaining procedures is still the main characteristic of wage bargaining in Germany.

The non-responsive corporatist countries

In most countries the struggle between the protection of real wages and the internalization of employment effects on wage bargaining procedures was not easily resolved. High growth rates and social unrest in the late 1960s created high wage expectations for the coming years; the external shock of the oil crisis, financial liberalization and the impact of monetary integration created pressure towards wage restraint. In traditional corporatist and non-corporatist countries, distributional conflicts erupted between the expectation of the government and the wage bargaining strategies of the unions. In both cases, these conflicts altered the relationship between the wage bargaining institutions and the state, as governments increasingly tried to bring the unions' wage expectations in line with the economic constraints they were facing.

Belgium, Finland, Denmark, Sweden and the Netherlands share a number of features of small open economies that have a corporatist legacy in which the state has traditionally played an important role in wage bargaining (Katzenstein 1985). In contrast to the countries in the preceding section, Austria and Germany, and with the exception of Sweden, the governments in these countries occupied a legitimate place in wage bargaining negotiations from a very early stage. Rather than resting on forms of self-regulation, corporatist wage bargaining took place under the close supervision of a state that frequently intervened if outcomes were not satisfactory in the eyes of the government.

In Denmark, strong collective actors emerged early after the September Compromise of 1899, which recognized trade unions and initiated centralized wage bargaining. General wage agreements for a two-year period had been concluded since the 1930s. Likewise, parliamentary intervention in wage bargaining had already emerged by 1933, when employers organized a nationwide lockout in order to achieve reductions in pay (Scheuer 1997: 151). Tighter corporatist structures only materialized in the 1960s, however, with the setting up of the Economic Council in 1962.

The Swedish national coordination of pay bargaining did not take place under active involvement of the government, but was rather a system of self-regulated centralization. The Saltsjobaden Agreement of 1938 between the LO and SAF was aimed at pre-empting the threat of government intervention. It was achieved by means of several national understandings on various policy issues agreed by the central organizations between 1946 and 1954 and was brought to completion with the centralized wage bargaining system that was set up in 1956. National wage coordination was based on the dominance of the blue-collar, private-sector trade union, LO. The LO had complete control over the wage bargaining activities of its affiliates (Iversen 1999: 123). Solidaristic wage policy supported the trend towards centralization by presupposing a tight top-down coordination of wages across industries.

Finnish corporatism emerged at a later date and was more fragmented than in the other Scandinavian countries. The first central agreement between the Finnish Trade Union Federation (FFC) and the Employers Association (AFC) was concluded after a general strike in 1956 (Elvander 1974: 432). Corporatist integration of labour, however, was undermined by a split within the left in the early 1960s, both within the unions and the Social Democratic Party, SDP, which impeded all further cooperation on incomes policy in Finland. Rather untypical for a corporatist society, Finland has a tradition of strong political contestation within the unions and also a high strike rate.

In the Low Countries, i.e. the Netherlands and Belgium, national wage bargaining coordination was embedded in corporatist agreements that were struck between trade unions and employers during World War II. In Belgium this was based on the National Solidarity Pact of 1944 and the Productivity Agreement made in 1952; in the Netherlands it was based on the agreement on the Labour Foundation (STAR) and later on the Socio-Economic Council (SER). In both cases, the new post-war settlement was conceived during the war when business and labour forged a clandestine alliance against German occupation. National coordination of wage bargaining was tightly linked to government intervention. For instance, the Netherlands was the only country in 1945 where pay settlements could be applied only with government approval and where approved pay settlements determined maximum as well as minimum pay (United Nations

1967: 9). Until the 1960s, the Netherlands had an administered wage determination system (Windmuller 1969: 392). The institutional framework was established immediately after the war at a time when "thorough regulation of almost anything was thought unavoidable or even natural" (Pen 1964: 183). As in Denmark, excessive agreements could be prevented by government action. But unlike Denmark, national coordination was a disciplinary device for trade unions that negotiated wages at the sectoral level. There was no overall coordination between the sectors on wage formation.

In Belgium, a similar process of tight government supervision over wage bargaining conduct was inaugurated. The Belgian wage bargaining institutions reflect the strong pillarization of the society combined with the urge to install consensus policies. Since social and political groups are divided not only politically (into socialist, Catholic and liberal camps) but also regionally and since governments have generally been inherently weak, a multitude of different concertation and bargaining institutions have been produced over time. Wage settlements are therefore embedded in a complex web of institutions that mediate between the sectoral affiliations of the national social partners and the national consultation institution with the prime purpose of involving a large number of different social groups.[114]

Among many institutions, the National Labour Council (NAR/CNT), set up in 1952, has become the body that was instrumental in settling inter-industry collective agreements. It also declares agreements as legally binding by royal decree, which gives the council quasi-legislative powers.[115] In the National Labour Council, representatives from both sides conclude the inter-industry collective agreements that establish the framework for employment relations in the private sector, including pay. On the basis of these agreements, sectoral agreements are concluded annually in Joint Committees. Sectoral agreements are thus bound by higher-level agreements. In order to implement the sectoral agreements, the Minister of Employment ratifies the agreements and thereby gives them legal force for the whole sector.

Massive intervention after declining performance: Belgium, Denmark and the Netherlands

Since Belgium, the Netherlands and Denmark all belonged to the founding states of the European currency snake they were confronted early on with the effects of the restrictive monetary policy of the Bundesbank. The year 1976 was therefore, in all three countries, a turning point that had severe implications for the relationship between the government and the social partners. Despite the long tradition of openness and corporatism – which was seen as being conducive to rapid adjustments to changing external environments (Katzenstein 1985) – the monetary policy shift led to major conflicts and frictions between the trade unions and the mainly social democratic governments. During the 1970s, all three countries had spells of incomes policies and wage freezes. Moreover, all three countries struggled with forms of wage indexation that turned out to be a major stumbling block for economic stabilization policy. In Belgium and Denmark, wage indexation had been introduced before the war; in the Netherlands it emerged during the 1960s. In all three countries, wage formation is based on an interplay between national agreements under the auspices of the government and sectoral implementation. Wage bargaining institutions are numerous and widely spread. However, the evolution of the relationship between the government and the wage bargaining process in the 1980s and 1990s turned out differently in each of the cases.

The Netherlands

Dutch wage formation during the 1960s was basically determined by the attempts of the government to maintain control over wage formation and increasing discontent in the unions with the extreme wage restraint.[116] The friction between the government and the unions was reflected in a temporary wage explosion that was, however, followed by a commitment on the part of the Labour Foundation (STAR) to reorganize itself. At the time, this was seen as an indicator of the tight corporatist structures: "Perhaps nothing illustrates the close integration of government and private organizations in the Netherlands industrial relations system so well as the willingness of the foundation to consult closely with government in overhauling its original constitution and its structure so as to equip itself for an administrative role" (Windmuller 1969: 308).

However, in the 1960s, the tension between tight government directives and union attempts to increase wages became apparent. The unions increasingly tried to break free from the tight state-controlled framework. One indication of the tension was the introduction of the New Wage Act in 1970. The government adopted the right to reject agreements which it deemed excessive. The new law was heavily criticized by the trade unions, in particular those that later were to become the FNV, and which withdrew from STAR and SER (Visser and Hemerijck 1997: 94). Between 1970 and 1982, the government suspended wage agreements on seven occasions (Visser 1997: 302).

Until 1982 the interaction between the government and wage bargaining actors in the Netherlands was rather similar to the Belgian situation. The employers responded to the shock of 1976 by protesting against escalator clauses. Pay indexation in the Netherlands had been adopted in the collective agreements of major firms that in the late 1960s had sought a formula for social peace by agreeing to automatic pay increases in line with inflation. Just as in Belgium, the system had spread across industries and to social security benefits by the mid-1970s (Visser and Hemerijck 1997: 98). And again as in Belgium, wage indexation had become an untouchable issue. The inflationary spiral of high inflation reinforced by high wage increases inflicted the same difficult economic situation on the Netherlands as it did on Belgium and Denmark. Like the Belgian and Danish governments, the Dutch government responded by intervening directly on several occasions in pay bargaining and wage freezes. Government intervention in wage setting went hand in hand with rising conflicts and political crisis (Hemerijck, Unger *et al.* 2000: 214).

In contrast to Belgium, the Dutch trade unions in 1982 modified their approach towards wages. Already in 1979, the Industries' Unions (IB) had proposed a similar agreement, which was, however, rejected by other affiliates of the FNV (Visser 1997: 279). In the Wassenaar Agreement (central recommendation concerning elements of an employment policy) of 24 November 1982, the unions recommended to their affiliated bodies that they accept wage agreements which kept wage increases lower than productivity increases and that they abstain from price compensation. This recommendation was immediately agreed to by lower level bargaining actors: "In less than a year, two thirds of all collective agreements were renewed, mostly for two years during which the payment of price compensation was suspended and a 5 per cent reduction of working hours took place. By 1985 cost of living clauses had virtually disappeared." (Hemerijck, Van der Meer *et al.* 2000: 262).

Afterwards, the relationship between the government and the social partners relaxed again, despite the fact that the government cut public sector pay in 1983. In principle, the shift by the unions had been accepted by sectoral bargaining. The Dutch unions repeated a period of exceptional wage restraint in the 1980s similar to the early 1950s, when the Netherlands was the only country in Western Europe with no increase in hourly wage-earnings since 1948 (United Nations 1967: Ch. 4, p. 3). The initial success of the policy supported further adjustment: "Over time, wage restraint allowed for a rather smooth interplay between wage setting and fiscal policy, stimulating economic growth while keeping inflation down" (Hemerijck, Unger *et al.* 2000: 254).

Since 1982 there has been no further intervention by the government and wages have developed in line with productivity growth. The Labour Foundation (STAR), which had been on the brink of being abolished, is now seen as a central element in the exchange of views between the government and the social partners on the future of economic and social policy. The pattern of tripartite agreements has strengthened during the 1990s. Several social pacts were concluded with wage restraint being traded for compromises on social policy retrenchment. In 2003, a two-year agreement was concluded that froze wages for 2004 and allowed for minor wage increases in 2005 (EIRR 2003b and 2005).

Denmark

As in the Netherlands, Denmark already had a history of incomes policy as a national emergency measure in the 1960s (Elvander 1974: 435).[117] In Denmark, the 'totality solution' was an emergency measure the government adopted in 1962, which included price and wage freezes. The solution had been prepared by the government in close cooperation with the main union, LO. The LO supported the government view that a wage freeze was necessary in order to stabilize the economy. Since the unions could not agree with the employers on the term of the wage freeze, the government decided to implement the programme by means of legislation (Elvander 1974: 420). The legislation on wages was not entirely new since the Danish government had often turned the results of mediation into law. At the same time, it remains the most comprehensive intervention since the war.

Throughout the 1970s, the government made frequent attempts to reach a general agreement with the unions on stabilization of the economy. In 1970, the non-socialist government proposed a package of wage restraint, price freezes and the abolition of wage indexation that was not accepted by the LO (Elvander 1974: 421). In 1975, the social democratic government under the former trade union leader Joergensen legislated moderate wage increases and a profit freeze. This was backed by a five-party declaration that promised to curb indexation and reduce costs (*The Economist* 1975a). However, despite a relatively slow growth in real wages, the emergency measures were not sufficient to stop the price–wage inflation in Denmark throughout the 1970s. In the late 1970s, incomes policy and wage indexation had become salient and even downright contentious political issues in parliament.

Furthermore, as in the Netherlands, the first step towards breaking the ice between the demands of the government and the unions was taken in 1982, when the new conservative minority government abolished wage indexation. Despite the political turmoil this issue had caused earlier, this move was not met with any major strike. Nor was this political move accompanied by an understanding between the social partners on the future conduct of wage bargaining. The trade unions were divided internally in the manufacturing sector, where the unions were increasingly unhappy with the leftist leanings of the Social Democrats, while the general workers' union, SiD, saw industrial confrontation as a way to topple the government (Scheuer 1997: 162). The de-indexation of wages therefore did not lead to wage restraint but to further political conflict (Benner and Bundgaard-Vad 2000: 439). The wage bargaining round in 1985 ended in a national strike and a legislated wage agreement by the government. However, by 1987 the position within the unions had changed: The trade unions and employers signed an agreement stating that "the level of costs in this country does not exceed that of the foreign countries" (Lind 2000: 139). Moreover, they agreed to a four-year agreement involving fixed wage increases per annum. In the years since, wage bargaining has remained conflictual in the face of a restrictive government policy, but stayed focused on wage moderation.

From the early 1980s onwards, wage bargaining institutions underwent a major restructuring process. Between 1933 and 1980, a system of biannual national wage agreements existed. The national employers' association (DA) and the union confederation (LO) settled an agreement for a going rate for the whole economy. Wage bargaining was highly synchronized, but not wholly comprehensive. Special groups outside the scope of the DA–LO negotiations were able to upset the whole system by failing to reach an agreement (Scheuer 1992). Since conflicts in one sector could have repercussions for the whole economy, particular negotiation deadlocks could prompt government intervention. A public conciliator would then propose a compromise that would tend to be similar to agreements in other sectors and then put the whole package to a collective vote (Iversen 1999: 122). This mechanism had a threefold effect: it introduced an early route for government intervention, it enforced coordination within the associations and it centralized decision-making. Moreover, deviating special interest groups were disciplined by government action if the associations themselves were not in a position to exert discipline.

The tensions over incomes policy translated increasingly into conflicts between different trade unions and the attempts of the employers to regain control over dissenting bargaining branches. Bargaining procedures were passed from the central level to the sectoral level. At the same time, the organizations on both sides were restructured. The number of affiliates of the employers' confederation DA was reduced from 150 to 33 by the late 1990s (EIRR 1994a). In 1991, the metal sector employers merged with the other manufacturing employers to form the Confederation of Danish Industry (*Dansk Industri*, DI). DI has become an important veto block within the overall employers' association. On the union side, LO attempted to design a new cartel structure. This led to conflict with the general workers' union, SiD, which would have lost out. Consequently, wage bargaining structures have now become more rationalized on the whole, at the expense of the left within the trade unions.

Belgium

In 1976, the Belgian government ended a 15-year phase during which the social partners autonomously concluded a whole range of bipartite central agreements on the construction of the welfare state. Between 1960 and 1974, the National Labour Council finalized numerous agreements on the representation of trade unions in companies, social security and other issues – agreements that had become law without much government interference. The active role of the Council rested on sectoral wage bargaining institutions that were crucial in providing the political support for central agreements (Vilrokx and Leemput 1998: 335). During this period, the government was very much absent from the regulation of welfare and labour issues.

However, in 1976, the government responded to mounting pressure from employers, increasingly radical demands from the unions and the rapid deterioration of the competitiveness of Belgian companies and public finances. As a first step, the government imposed a 'special levy' of 50 per cent on all contractual pay increases above those linked to indexation so it might finance a special fund for older unemployed workers. The decision provoked a national strike, jointly organized by the socialist and Christian unions, the first-ever strike undertaken by the latter against the government (Hemerijck, Unger *et al.* 2000: 235).[118]

From the very beginning, the issue of pay indexation was at the forefront of the struggle between the government and the unions. Belgium maintains a system of automatic pay increases linked to changes in con-

Table 7.1 **Incomes policy in Belgium, 1976-93**

Year	Policy	Implication
1976	Wage freeze	Imposed unilaterally
1982	Plan for Recovery	Negotiations failed. Pay freeze and suspension of indexation imposed
1989	Law on Competitiveness	Upper ceiling on wage increases
1993	Global Plan	Wage norm based on competitiveness

Sources: Vilrokx and Leemput (1998); Pochet (1999a).

sumer prices. This link was originally part of a collective agreement between trade unions and employers in the mining sector that was concluded immediately following World War I. Over time, pay indexation spread to all industrial and public sector wages and social benefits (EIROnline 1998).[119] Wage negotiations between trade unions and employers at the national and sectoral level therefore only ever applied to increases above inflation.

After 1976, a new pattern of negotiation between the government and the social partners emerged that steadily increased the role of the government in wage formation. Between 1976 and 1999, the government tried to negotiate wage restraint with the unions on many occasions, usually presenting this to both sides as a tripartite package. On several occasions, particularly in 1982 (Recovery Plan) and 1993 (Global Plan), the government proposed packages in which employers were asked to commit themselves to a reduction in job targets and working hours in exchange for wage restraint from the unions (table 7.1). The government was actually willing to increase spending on the subsidized reduction of working hours (Hemerijck and Visser 2000: 247-8; Hemerijck *et al.* 2000). In both cases, negotiations failed and were followed by a unilateral decision by the government to set norms for real wage increases. In 1982, the government decided to initially freeze wages and later on temporarily suspend the wage indexation mechanism. In 1993, it legislated an upper ceiling on wages that was based on a watered down indexation mechanism and a formula of wage comparisons with neighbouring countries.

The government intervention in 1976 also led initially to a suspension of the negotiations on wage agreements within the National Labour Council. Between 1976 and 1986, no central agreements were concluded.

Between 1987 and 1993, the central organizations resumed the negotiation of biannual wage agreements, but according to some observers these were "devoid of content and largely dictated by the government" (Vilrox and Leemput 1998: 340). After the failure of the Global Plan negotiations in 1993, no agreement was reached. However, the government introduced further legislation in 1996 (Law on Safeguarding the Competitiveness of Enterprises), which prescribed national bargaining on a biannual basis. This was to determine the pay margin for sectoral bargaining in order to forestall a government decree. In 1998 and 2000, central agreements were negotiated again. Both produced pay settlements that were within the framework of the law.[120]

Since the imposition of a wage norm in 1993, wage formation processes have been sandwiched from two sides. From below, the system of wage indexation continues to guarantee the protection of the real wage by adjusting wages to changes in consumer prices several times per year. Indexation has remained the primary source of wage expectations from workers and is defended by the unions at all costs. From above, a government-imposed norm sets a ceiling for all wage increases negotiated at the national and sectoral level in line with pay developments in other European countries. The government is determined to enforce this ceiling and has done so. As a result, the bargaining scope for trade unions and employer confederations is particularly small.

Rather than abandon the indexation mechanism the government has aimed at limiting its inflationary effects by dampening *real* wage increases. Negotiations between the government and the unions have therefore been trapped in a dilemma, according to which the unions have defended the floor because there is a ceiling while the government and the employers have argued in favour of the ceiling because they cannot abolish the floor. The expectations of those employed have remained firmly fixed on the protection of the real wage, which has been automatically adjusted several times a year.[121]

The stand-off between the social partners and the government indicates the fragility of the Belgian corporatist institutions. While the social partners reject interference in the autonomous regulation of the welfare state they had acquired, the move by the government did not lead to any closer cooperation between the partners that might prevent further government intervention. Being entrenched in a whole array of institutional safeguards, on the one hand, and part of a fierce political battle, on the other, the Belgian trade unions – in particular the socialist trade union,

FTGB – were unable to accept any concessions that the government requested with the aim of restoring the competitiveness of the Belgian economy.

From real to nominal wage restraint and belated monetarism: Sweden and Finland

In contrast to the other corporatist countries, Sweden and Finland share the position of switching late towards a more restrictive monetary policy, though for different reasons. Finland had been a latecomer to the Scandinavian model due to its agricultural and forestry background and its close ties to the Soviet Union. Stabilization measures had already become necessary in Finland in the 1960s and 1970s, and, from the first agreement on incomes policy in 1969 onwards, Finland developed a policy mixture of moderate negotiated wage restraint and devaluation. It was only after the deep economic crisis in 1991/92 and the collapse of the Soviet Union that Finland's economic policy converged on the central European hard currency model.

Conversely, the Swedish form of real wage restraint was based on negotiated monetary accommodation. In the interpretation by Torben Iversen (1999), based on similar assessments by Fritz Scharpf (1991), Walter Korpi (1983) and others (Martin 1985 and 2000; Stephens and Huber 1998), the solidaristic wage policy that the Swedish unions adopted in the 1950s led to a combination of a commitment to real wage restraint and a simultaneous accommodation of inflationary wage pressures. Real wage restraint in Sweden was only possible under the condition of an accommodating economic policy. In the words of Walter Korpi (1983: 228): "If the government cannot settle the distributive conflicts, at least temporarily, say, by increasing the money supply, they will appear in other forms, such as severe industrial disputes." Monetary and fiscal accommodation, in other words, were the precondition for real wage restraint.

Sweden

Real wage restraint was a successful tool in Sweden for responding to the external shock of 1975. In fact, Sweden and Denmark had the lowest increase in real wages during the 1970s in Western Europe. Between 1977 and 1979, real wages fell in three consecutive years following the devaluation in 1976. The same mechanism was employed between 1982 and 1984 when devaluation was followed by real wage restraint and a restoration of competitiveness (Martin 1985; Iversen 1999). Owing to the combination of real wage restraint after major devaluations and an expansive economic policy, employment could be protected and growth was stimulated (Lange and Garrett 1985).

Throughout the 1980s the economic and institutional basis for the Swedish model of competitive devaluation was increasingly eroded. The Swedish government could not insulate itself from the increasing liberalization of capital markets in the OECD and did not manage to regulate Swedish currency markets effectively (Iversen 1999: 145). Instead of introducing further regulation and controls, the government started to liberalize capital markets and to control inflation itself. All exchange controls were abolished in July 1989 and the krona was pegged to the ECU in 1990. The government thus committed itself to a restrictive monetary policy. At the same time, the institutional basis for the Swedish wage bargaining system came under attack from the employers who allied with the industrial sector unions against the dominance of the public sector. The central employers' organization SAF withdrew from national bargaining twice, in 1983 and in 1990. In 1991, SAF dismantled its bargaining unit and announced that it was no longer willing to play a role in bargaining (EIRR 1992).

Both policy shifts – the pegging of the krona and the stern refusal of SAF to engage in centralized bargaining any more – were arguably the most important economic policy changes in Sweden, since they marked the end of the commitment to full employment based on centralized real wage restraint and to an expansive economic policy. Nonetheless, the shift towards monetarist decentralization (Iversen 1999) did not automatically shift the wage expectations of the unions or the workers they represented towards nominal wage restraint. Instead, the adjustment of wage expectations took place over several stages during the 1990s, which were primarily initiated by the government.

First of all, new inflationary pressure in 1990 prompted the government to propose a two-year general pay freeze and strike ban that would have been the most far-reaching government intervention in Swedish wage bargaining, had it been implemented (Kjellberg 1998: 89; Martin 1995). However, after widespread protests against the proposals, the government resigned and the plans were abandoned. In place of the state-imposed wage freeze, the tripartite Rhenberg Commission was set up to persuade unions and employers to accept a two-year stabilization programme for 1991 and 1992. The stabilization agreement included a 1 percent increase for the low paid, a pay freeze for other workers and a ban on local bargaining that particularly upset the public sector trade union, the PTK (*Financial Times* 1991). In 1993, the same commission helped to coordinate a new round of stabilization agreements.

In the years that followed, state mediation took on an increasingly important role. The Rhenberg Commission had been centred on a national mediator who was commissioned to find a compromise solution for nominal wage restraint. Starting with the Rhenberg Commission, the role of state mediators became increasingly important. In 1995, for instance, the state mediator tried to push for the adoption of the Edin norm in sectoral pay negotiations. Since the LO tried to counteract this norm with its own 'strong norm', the bargaining round turned out to be the most conflictual since 1980 (Elvander and Holmlund 1997: 31).

The Edin norm had been developed by a commission of economists that had been delegated by the unions and employers without government interference. The proposal that the Edin report had come up with, however, was pushed strongly by the government. In 1997, the government exerted strong pressure on the social partners to reorganize the wage bargaining system. The government stated that if the social partners failed to come up with a formula before the end of March 1997, it would intervene in order to achieve its goal (EIRR 1997). The massive threat of intervention was followed by a commission report that recommended a stronger role for a new mediation authority. It was only after these threats that the unions and employers in the private sector agreed on a new cooperation agreement – the Industrial Agreement of 1997 – that took up a number of suggestions from the government report.[122] Over the next few years, a number of cooperation agreements were concluded in other sectors and, in June 2000, a national Mediation Institute was set up (EIRR 2001a and 2002a). The mission of the new Institute was to implement an 'efficient' wage policy that contributed to the stability policy of the Riksbank and promoted the so-called Euro-Norm, which was in fact a successor to the previous Edin norm.[123]

Among Swedish observers, the Industrial Agreement is seen today as the "most important innovation in Swedish industrial relations since the Agreement of Saltsjobaden" (Elvander 2002a: 197).[124] It parallels the Saltsjobaden agreement to the extent that, in both cases, a cooperative agreement between trade unions and employers aimed at averting further intervention by the government. For the first time since the early 1980s, both sides of industry are now committed once again to a cooperative and self-regulated approach towards the regulation of wage bargaining issues. However, unlike the post-war settlement, the room for accommodating distributive struggles is much narrower today than it was before. The associations alone have not been able to refocus expectations, and, as a result, the government has had to step in.

Finland

In Finland, the cooperation between the government and the unions on a common approach towards stabilization was briefer than in Sweden. After devaluation of the Finnish markka in 1967, a tight incomes policy was negotiated by a national mediator (Keijo Liinamaa). An agreement was reached between the government and both sides of industry that entailed minor wage increases below productivity rates. After the agreement was settled, parliament enacted an emergency law that gave the government the power to regulate wages and prices. The scale of government intervention was a novelty in post-war relations between the government and wage bargaining institutions.[125]

After the stabilization agreement, a national wage coordination scheme was established in 1968. The pattern of wage coordination was based on tripartite package deals with the government. At first, only the peak employers' confederation, the STK, and the main trade union SAK were part of the wage bargaining. But from the mid-1970s onwards, other federations were officially incorporated in the system (Lilja 1992). The outcomes of the Finnish wage bargaining institutions, however, were not binding for the member unions of SAK. Sectoral trade unions were entitled to break away from central agreements and could negotiate better agreements at the sectoral level. This became a weak point of Finnish wage bargaining since, at the same time, a political split had divided the trade unions, in which communist trade unions exploited workplace grievances and started to push up wages (Kauppinen 1994: 69).[126]

Tripartite wage agreements during the economic shocks of the 1970s were therefore under pressure from the left and grassroots activists, while the main trade union confederation cooperated in incomes policies. Performance improved in the early 1980s and, compared to the other countries that are studied in this book, led to relatively stable development. The economy was, however, dependent on trade with the Soviet Union and forestry exports. The link between government policy and wage bargaining was quite direct: in 1988 taxes were reduced by the same amount that pay increased (Kauppinen 1994, 66).

The economic recovery in the 1980s also led to the reintroduction of wage indexation in the tripartite agreement in 1984. Wage indexation had been a feature of Finnish wage bargaining until 1968 when it was abolished in the first stabilization agreement mediated by Keijo Liinamaa. At the time, it seemed surprising that Finland succeeded in eliminating indexation since this had become a deeply rooted system as in Denmark and Norway (Elvander 1974: 432). In the mid-1980s, however, with economic recovery at hand indexation reappeared.

In the 1990s, Finland encountered two major challenges that again were solved by striking tripartite wage agreements. First, the Soviet Union collapsed, prompting the deepest recession in Finland since World War II and, second, Finland joined the EU and aspired to join EMU. As in Sweden, the recession of the Finnish economy in the early 1990s was combined with a commitment from the government to avoid further devaluation. A comprehensive pact was negotiated with the national union to achieve this goal, which included a 3 per cent wage cut. Despite these efforts for a negotiated agreement, the agreement was rejected by the sectoral unions. The Finnish markka, which had been pegged to the ECU in June 1991, was devalued in November 1991. Following devaluation, a comprehensive tripartite agreement was adopted that included a pay freeze (Kauppinen 2000: 166).

In 1994, Finland acceded to the EEA and in 1995 it joined the EU. Again, the new challenge was met by a comprehensive tripartite agreement of September 1995. The government was assured of the support of the social partners, who were firmly committed to enabling Finland to join EMU. In 1997, a joint declaration confirmed this support and was turned into another pact. Both agreements were explicitly aimed at paving the way for European monetary integration.

The underlying dynamic of Finnish wage bargaining in the framework of tripartite agreements was the relationship between the national tripartite negotiations and the sectoral level of bargaining. National solidarity between the government and the unions could be evoked frequently under the impact of serious challenges. The Finnish social democrats and the social democratic strand of the trade unions were both firmly committed to cooperation. Since the mid-1960s, there were only four years in which the SDP was not in the government. The threat by the communist organizations in the late 1960s had strengthened their cooperation.

Sectoral wage bargaining emerged at times of recovery, when sectoral branches sought to catch up with sector-specific productivity gains, and during the years of the conservative government between 1991 and 1995, when no tripartite agreement could be reached.[127] In 1998 and 1999, on the basis of economic recovery, sectoral bargaining emerged again, when some of the industrial unions (the paper workers' union, the chemical workers' union and the electricity workers' union) refused to accept the terms of the new central agreement. While the sectoral breakaway was seen as a sign of the decline of the Finnish tripartite mode of adjustment, this is not necessarily the case. Rather, sectoral adjustments of relative wages could serve as a safety valve in an otherwise centralized and highly controlled wage formation process.

Adjustment of wage expectations in the non-corporatist countries with non-responsive wage bargaining regimes

The non-corporatist countries can be divided into three subgroups: the continental European countries of Italy and France, where contestation rather than cooperation characterized the post-war settlement between trade unions and the government; the Anglo-Saxon countries of the United Kingdom and Ireland with fragmented and pluralist trade unions; and the post-authoritarian countries of Spain and Portugal, which missed out on the post-war settlement altogether. The absence of corporatism in the post-war settlement did not mean, however, that labour was not integrated into the political decision-making. Political integration was merely impeded either by political conflicts or by the lack of institutional and organizational conditions.

As a case in point, economic planning in the United Kingdom and France in the 1960s took place under the active involvement of trade unions (Shonfield 1965). In the UK, the wartime cabinet was dependent on the goodwill of trade union leaders, who were supported by liberals like Beveridge and economists like Keynes. After the war, Clement Attlee headed the first Labour government in the United Kingdom to have a clear majority and was elected on its promises to the working people. Although this resulted in the National Economic Development Act of 1947, business organizations managed to block it in parliament.

In France, the country with the most detailed and formalistic type of economic planning, the role of trade unions in the planning process was limited because the real contact was between the government and business, with neither side being interested in seriously discussing their plans with trade unions (Barbash 1972: 149). In contrast to the United Kingdom, the role of labour was weak in France and Italy, and price controls were mainly directed at producers. In Italy, labour was excluded from political decision-making for most of the period of the 1950s and 1960s.

France and Italy share a tradition of labour exclusion, political contestation between communist and socialist trade unions, and weak institutionalization of wage bargaining up to the 1970s (Crouch 1978: 205; Flanagan, Soskice *et al.* 1983). In both countries, governments initially targeted their incomes policies on price controls rather than wage controls. Both countries have been at the core of European integration and were early members of the EMS. Both had to abandon the currency peg during the 1970s because of high inflation differentials in relation to the German mark.

Nevertheless, both countries displayed very different ways of adapting to the shift towards restrictive monetary policy in the 1980s and 1990s. While in Italy steps towards an increasing institutionalization of wage bargaining under the control of the government took place, wage bargaining institutions in France steadily disintegrated. Consequently, government intervention and tripartism in France only occurred with regard to welfare reforms, where trade unions still exercised considerable influence, albeit hardly over pay. National negotiations between the social partners on the framework of wage bargaining institutions in 1993 and 1995 resulted in further decentralization of bargaining. In contrast, in Italy, progressive institutionalization of wage bargaining procedures took place from the early 1970s onwards. While this process was held up and interrupted several times by political negotiations over wage indexation, it resulted in the adoption of a formal framework for pay bargaining in 1993 that was negotiated between the social partners and the government.

In a similar vein, the history of British and Irish labour relations was tightly coupled until 1979, when both countries went their separate ways. In 1979, the change of government ended the Social Contract in the UK, while the Irish government decided to abandon the fixed exchange rate with the pound in order to join the EMS. Until then, both countries shared a tradition of pluralist trade unions, voluntarist wage agreements and a close economic union, with the Irish punt pegged to the pound sterling, a constant flow of Irish workers to the United Kingdom and a steady stream of British goods into Ireland. Moreover, British trade unions organized a substantial minority of Irish workers in Ireland and as such reinforced a British view of trade unionism in Ireland.

At the same time, there were also important national differences in the institutions and political organizations that were partly reinforced by their ambivalent post-colonial relationship. These differences were mainly rooted in the role of the Catholic Church in Ireland, which propagated a notion of Catholic social integration into labour relations and their institutions, and the role of nationalism in the party formation after Ireland gained independence in 1922. The differences were reinforced by the asymmetrical relationship between the two countries, in which the United Kingdom was an overarching ex-colonialist world power and Ireland the ex-colony with a small, largely rural economy. Over time, when the economic and political institutions faced economic crises, these differences became more pronounced: Ireland turned to the central European corporatist approach while the United Kingdom moved firmly towards the Anglo-Saxon pluralist way.

In Spain and Portugal, the incorporation of labour was part of an authoritarian corporatist regime. Systems of national and centralized unions were established under the control of the government. Wages were set by statutory regulation and, particularly in Portugal, wages were often individually determined on the labour market (Barreto 1992: 453).

France and the United Kingdom: de-institutionalization and decentralization as a reaction to institutional failure

France and the United Kingdom both took a path of gradual de-institutionalization of wage bargaining institutions as a consequence of institutional failure. While in the UK institutions were deliberately abolished for political reasons, in France tripartite negotiations took place and labour market regulation remained strong. This, however, did not lead to a strengthening of the institutions. In both cases, there is a trend towards market based settlements of wages.

France

Attempts to institutionalize wage bargaining in France and improve the relationship between trade unions and the government have been rare.[128] Despite the tradition of economic planning, the government, the unions and the employers have rejected cooperation as in principle unhelpful. The state "agreed to such negotiations only when pressed by national crises of the sort generated by the steel strike of 1963 and the events following May 1968" (Hall 1986: 247). The communist trade union CGT took the view that cooperation with the government would be useful, but only "if it took place in a different society than ours" (United Nations 1967: Ch. 4, p. 21). The two biggest trade unions, CGT and FO, withdrew their participation from the preparation of the second economic plan (which began in 1953) and boycotted subsequent involvement until the eighth plan (Hall 1986: 158). The employers' behaviour was described as 'antediluvian', dominated by paternalistic and family-controlled companies that opposed innovation (Flanagan, Soskice *et al.* 1983: 567). In 1968, trade union rights were recognized in companies by law and trade unions have since been entitled to appoint trade union delegates (*délégués syndicaux*). They gained the power to negotiate and sign collective agreements. For these reasons, collective bargaining was virtually non-existent in France before 1968.

In contrast to Italy, this situation was not changed fundamentally by the social unrest in 1968, although the events of May 1968 sent a shock wave to the political establishment (Levy 2000: 320). The discontent on the shop floor led to a new initiative by the French president Georges Pompidou to build plant-level institutions and to expand trade union rights at this level. The employers' confederation CNPF increased its role in collective bargaining and started to negotiate national agreements (Flanagan, Soskice *et al.* 1983: 620). However, the spur of institutionalization came to a halt with the political conflicts between the unions and the persistent opposition of the CGT to any role in collective bargaining. Given political contestation and the industrial weakness of the unions, the government adopted a policy of price controls as a reaction to the oil shock. Moreover, the government used its close links with industry to make sure that a level of real wage restraint could be attained (Flanagan, Soskice *et al.* 1983: 640). The deflationary programme of the Barre government therefore worked via the pressure on industry rather than the imposition of an incomes policy.

As France struggled to remain within the EMS, real wage restraint was hardly sufficient. Until 1984 annual nominal wage increases hovered above 10 per cent. Moreover, the new Mitterand government initially raised the minimum wage substantially in 1982, driving wage inflation further upwards. When France was under threat of being forced out of the EMS once more in 1982, the government shifted its position. A four-month wage freeze was decreed in June 1982. France gained the edge through "competitive disinflation" (Fitoussi 1993). It became the priority of the Mitterand government to regain competitiveness by achieving a rate of inflation lower than that of its trading partners. "Toward this end, redistributive Keynesianism gave way to austerity budgets, wage indexation was abandoned and, most importantly, monetary policy was tightened, with real interest rates ranging from 5 to 8 per cent for over a decade" (Levy 2000: 324). After the compulsory wage freeze in 1982, the government no longer intervened directly in pay issues, but used the adjustment of the minimum wage as the focal point for influencing wage expectations in the private sector.

With regard to wage bargaining institutions, the cautious steps towards institutionalization in 1969/70 gained new relevance in the late 1970s, when the relations between the socialists and communists turned sour. The socialist trade union CFDT had traditionally been more open towards collective bargaining issues and had initiated new attempts to propose bargaining rights at the industry and company level. Given the temporary distance from the CGT, which still rejected cooperation, the proposals were able to find their way into the socialist party and became law under the new Mitterand government in 1982. The Auroux Laws imposed an obligation on companies to bargain over wages with trade unions on an annual basis (Goetschy 1997). By these means, Mitterand and his labour minister Jacques Delors had broken with the post-war government tradition of trying to weaken the union movement. They envisaged strengthening wage bargaining institutions and attempted to co-opt the unions by encouraging participation in bargaining.

However, the Auroux Laws did not help the situation of weak trade union organization and weak institutions. In the 1980s, the trade unions were already too weak and remained too internally divided to exploit their newly gained entitlement to bargain with employers. While new company agreements spread throughout the industry, the institutional basis was not strengthened. Wage bargaining remained fragile, lacking confidence in the ability of employers and trade unions to regulate labour affairs.

Since the trade unions were, however, a powerful political force, labour relations remained a political issue. The conservative governments of the 1990s held tripartite summits on employment in 1993 and 1996 to discuss working hours and labour market policy. In 1995, a summit of the social partners was called to discuss how bargaining might be better articulated. At the summit, a solution was found that enabled company bargaining to be carried out by mandated employees rather than union officials. The understanding also reversed the hierarchical order of bargaining: Company agreements could now undercut collective agreements (EIRR 1995). Although at first glance the summit showed the capacity of the social partners to deal with the restructuring of the wage bargaining system, the effects of the agreements contributed towards a further process of decentralization and also de-institutionalization of wage bargaining procedures.[129]

United Kingdom

The failure of incomes policy in the United Kingdom between 1961 and 1979 is generally ascribed to two factors: first, the lack of authority of the trade unions over their local constituency in wage bargaining and, second, the lack of interest by the government in protecting and sustaining the international competitiveness of the manufacturing sector.[130]

Unlike other countries that lost competitiveness in the 1960s, negotiated wage restraint in Britain was not used in combination with the devaluation of the currency. For twenty years (between 1950 and 1970), British policy-makers refused to devalue, except when forced to in 1948 and 1967. They consistently defended an exchange rate that by the end of the 1950s was seriously overvalued and, in doing so, generated a disruptive set of stop-go cycles. This policy served the perceived interests of financial capital. "At each turning point spokesmen for the City and the Bank of England pressed the government to deflate rather than devalue and in each instance their view prevailed" (Shonfield 1965; Brittan 1970; Hall 1986: 251).

For most of the 1960s and 1970s, incomes policies were based on a reluctant, but nonetheless voluntary, commitment by the trade unions to accept wage restraint. Governments and trade unions signed a declaration of intent that recorded the willingness of unions and management representatives to cooperate with the government on behalf of their members both in setting voluntary norms and procedures for reviewing such changes. Incomes policy became more rigorous in 1966 when the government introduced statutory penalties for breaches of its pay norms (Clegg 1979: 345). In 1973-74, statutory pay norms were imposed (see table 7.2).

At the same time, the practice of wage bargaining remained firmly based on a system that prioritized local bargaining arrangements and that was only partially encompassed by sectoral coordination. Neither the voluntary commitments nor the statutory policy prevented powerful bargaining groups from pursuing their own sectional interests. Standoffs between the government and the unions over the restructuring of the voluntarist and decentralized system of collective bargaining resulted in turmoil, lasting from 1970 until 1979. Despite the negative record of voluntary and statutory incomes policy, in 1975 the Labour government again tried to negotiate wage restraint in exchange for tax concessions and other benefits for labour. The Social Contract initially managed to reduce wage inflation considerably (see figure A1 in appendix). But it failed in the medium term due to distributional conflicts within the trade unions, sectionalist leap-

Table 7.2 Incomes policy in the UK, 1970-79

Year	Policy	Pay Content	Implication
1972-74	Incomes Policy	Several stages of low wage increases	Challenged by the miners' union
1975-1979	Social Contract	Several stages of voluntary wage restraint	First tacitly accepted by the unions, later challenged by the public sector

Sources: Flanagan, Soskice *et al.* (1983); Scharpf (1991); various sources.

frogging by major parts of the British trade unions and the lack of commitment from other parts of the trade unions to accept the concessions by the Labour government, in particular in the public sector.

With the change of government in 1979, all attempts to negotiate an incomes policy were replaced by a firm commitment to deregulate the labour market instead. A number of legislative changes removed traditional restrictive practices of wage bargaining and trade union organization. The scope and level of bargaining were considerably reduced. Tight monetary policy was deliberately employed to discipline wage bargaining (Rhodes 2000a and 2000b). After 1979, no British government attempted to directly influence or negotiate private-sector pay formation with trade unions. Tripartite bargaining or summits with governments and the social partners that occurred in all Western European countries in the 1980s and 1990s were deliberately absent from British policy-making, even when Labour returned to power in 1997. Labour market regulations are today the weakest in Europe, and with the exception of France, British trade unions also have the weakest role as wage bargaining institutions.

During the 1970s, real wage growth in the United Kingdom was among the lowest in Europe, matched only by the highly corporatist countries of Denmark and Sweden. Despite the weak institutional foundations, the Social Contract delivered real wage restraint and led to a substantial reduction in real wages in 1976 and 1977.[131] However, given the ailing manufacturing sector and a strong currency, real wage restraint was not even a temporarily sufficient instrument for economic recovery. With the outspoken hostility of the government towards labour from 1979 onwards, the trade unions engaged in protecting real wages. In contrast to the 1970s, real wage increases in the 1980s and 1990s were markedly above the European average. Despite rapidly rising unemployment during the 1980s, wage bargaining did not respond to economic needs, but trade unions rather tried to protect the immediate interests of their members. Since no shared view of a legitimate pay norm has evolved since 1979, wage bargaining has remained unresponsive to the economic policy of the government and is today largely accidental and contingent on local conditions and local power constellations.

The extent of the shift in the approach of British governments, however, cannot be explained solely by the failures of the wage bargaining system. As the other national examples show, adjustment failure was equally pronounced in a number of countries – both corporatist and non-corporatist. Similar problems to the British situation existed in Ireland, the Netherlands, Belgium, Italy and Denmark. In Italy and Ireland, wage bargaining institutions were similarly fragmented, with trade unions not prepared to sacrifice real wage losses for economic adjustment. Equally, many governments in the early 1980s shared the adversarial attitude towards labour. However, in a number of countries at the end of the 1980s, the adversarial approach had reverted to cooperation under new terms. The British government, however, has not returned to this position and wage bargaining institutions have continued to wear away throughout the period.

Italy and Ireland: building wage bargaining institutions through intervention[132]

While Italy started out in a similar position to France, the reaction of the unions towards the 'hot autumn' of wildcat strikes and social unrest of 1969 changed the situation from a tradition of a weakly institutionalized wage bargaining system to a steady process of institutionalization. This process took almost a quarter of a century to complete. It was in the tripartite Ciampi Agreement of July 1993 (*Accordo 23 luglio 1993*) that a legally binding collective bargaining framework was established that introduced a two-tier bargaining process similar to the German and Austrian model. In contrast to the German model, however, the Italian framework agreement included tighter rules on the wage formation process itself, by suggesting that inflation be used as a norm to guide sectoral bargaining and productivity be taken as the yardstick for plant-level bargaining. The 1993 agreement was accompanied by further action to strengthen the wage bargaining institutions at the plant level, by introducing a unity trade union representation (*rappresentanza sindacale unitaria*) that was mandated and dominated by the big three Italian trade union confederations.

Table 7.3	Tripartite agreements in Italy, 1970-98
Year	Policy
1978	EUR agreement
1983	Revision of Pay Indexation
1992	Amato agreement abolishing scala mobile
1993	Ciampi Protocol: Agreement on labour costs and collective bargaining system
1996	Employment Pact (Accordo per il Lavoro)
1998	Social Pact for Growth and Employment

Sources: Ebbinghaus and Hassel (2000); Regalia and Regini (2004).

The immediate effect of the social unrest in 1969 was to shift wage bargaining to the level of the plant. Plant-level bargaining reversed the role of the wage bargaining hierarchy; sectoral and national bargaining only generalized the agreements that were concluded in large firms in northern Italy (Regalia and Regini 2004). This was accompanied by the Workers' Statute in the 1970s, which gave Italian workers the most comprehensive body of individual employment rights in Europe (Ferner and Hyman 1992b: 534). In contrast to France, all the trade unions including the communist CGIL seized the opportunity to extend bargaining rights to the local level. The political motivation of the unions, however, had already contributed to a move towards centralized negotiations in the early 1970s. The trade unions forged an alliance – the Unitary Federation – and engaged in national negotiations with the employers' confederations and the government. The key achievement of the national negotiations was the agreement concluded in 1975 on the revision and extension of the pay indexation mechanism (*Scala mobile*) to the entire economy (see table 7.3).[133]

The extension of the Scala mobile at the time of strong external inflationary pressure exacerbated the shock to the Italian economy. The government reacted by forming a 'national solidarity' government in 1976, which included the communist party, PCI. In February 1978, the first tripartite agreement on wage restraint and social policy was negotiated during the so-called EUR union assembly (Ferrera and Gualmini 2000b). The cooperation between the Christian Democrats and the Communists did not last; nor did the agreement solve the economic problem.

As in Belgium and the Netherlands, pay indexation was the main bone of contention. The 'Unitary Federation' broke up over conflicting views on indexation. In 1983, an anti-inflation pact was signed that entailed some revision of the pay indexation scheme. Another attempt to revise indexation was made as early as 1984, but failed. The government was widely criticized for the generous compensation it offered to the unions, while the unions were split politically. The CGIL did not sign the agreement. In fact, the communist party campaigned against the agreement by demanding a referendum, which turned out to be a defeat for the communists.[134] Nevertheless, the experience forestalled further attempts at tripartite bargaining on pay indexation during the 1980s. For the remainder of the decade, the unions and the government stayed in their trenches and did not move.[135]

When the political situation changed fundamentally in the early 1990s a new approach could at last be adopted. In 1992, the old political system collapsed and the new 'technocratic governments' of Amato and Ciampi came to power. The signing of the Maastricht Treaty was followed by a serious fiscal and monetary crisis. Just as in the late 1970s, a national emergency situation mobilized the consensus required from the trade unions to abandon the pay indexation mechanism (Regalia and Regini 2004; Ferrera and Gualmini 2000b). In contrast to the emergency agreement (1978) and the agreement on pay indexation (1983), neither the Amato agreement nor the Ciampi agreement (1992 and 1993, respectively) was accompanied by further commitment from the government to public expenditure.

The Italian tripartite agreements[136] on the abolition of pay indexation and the restructuring of wage bargaining institutions of 1992 and 1993 parallel the agreements reached in the traditional corporatist countries of the Netherlands (1982) and Denmark (1987), where an adjustment in wage bargaining priorities took place under strong pressure from the government. In Italy, with its lack of a corporatist tradition, a similar move led to wildcat strikes in unionized companies and the temporary resignation of the leader of the CGIL, Bruno Trentin. But the agreement could not be undone by these signs of protest; on the contrary, it was further developed by the Ciampi agreement in 1993 and subsequent ones. The process indicates that the institutional evolution of Italian wage bargaining since 1970 has been strengthened rather than weakened – despite the political stand-offs that characterized the 1980s. This is partly due to the fact that, beyond the national and political cleavages between the actors, the relationships at the local level have been more cooperative. The contestation and political weakness of the 1960s has been replaced by workplace institutions, though often informal and limited to the formal economy.[137]

Ireland

Despite the voluntarist and pluralist nature of Irish trade unions, wage bargaining procedures have been surprisingly centralized for most of the post-war period.[138] National wage agreements were concluded during the 1950s and 1960s, though these were controversial: the national agreement of 1964 met with resistance in many plants and fuelled social unrest in the late 1960s (von Prondzynski 1992: 78). Strike rates in Ireland, too, have been comparatively high. Since Ireland, like the United Kingdom, encountered problems with high inflation rates in the 1960s, the government threatened to pass legislation on a statutory incomes policy (the Price and Incomes Bill) in 1970. In order to avert government intervention, the unions and employers' confederation reacted by setting up the Employers–Labour Conference, which was charged with negotiating national wages agreements.[139]

The national wage agreements, however, were unsuitable for coping with the oil crisis, but proceeded to follow the inflationary trend. In 1975, therefore, the government stepped in for the first time and promised the social partners budgetary concessions in exchange for lower wage settlements (von Prondzynski 1992: 79). The deal worked, at least temporarily, but by 1978 the trade union confederation took a vote not to continue with national bargaining. Again, in 1980, the government pushed the unions towards national negotiations, this time on the basis of a 'National Understanding' that was meant to replace the wage agreement and serve as a pay guideline. By this time, however, the employers were determined to abandon centralized bargaining and no further agreement was settled between 1981 and 1987.[140]

As in Denmark and the Netherlands, the shift in the government's approach took place in 1982. The continual political crises led to three general elections in 18 months in 1981 and 1982. For the first time, the government refused to comply with a pay agreement in the public sector because of macroeconomic considerations. By that time, public sector borrowing stood at almost 20 per cent and foreign debt at 40 per cent of national income. Inflation was around 20 per cent in 1981. In the meantime, however, Ireland had abandoned the currency peg with the British pound and had joined the EMS. In line with the slowdown of nominal wage increases in the EMS zone, Irish wage increases fell slowly, but not sufficiently to keep in line with the rest of the EMS. Between 1980 and 1986 unemployment rate exploded from 7.3 per cent to 17.4 per cent.

While wage bargaining moved to the plant level, the government nevertheless attempted to influence wage bargaining by issuing pay norms for the private sector or by trying to impose the public sector norm on other sectors. This, however, only worked in the early 1980s. On several occasions thereafter, to no avail, the government urged employers to implement wage freezes. In 1984, the trade unions offered incomes policy as an instrument for economic recovery, a move picked up by the National Economic and Social Council (NESC). The NESC prepared a study in which wage restraint, though not incomes policy, was a central element (Hardiman 2002: 8).[141] Only a change in government in 1987 enabled a breakthrough for a new agreement between the state and the social partners. The government invited the trade unions to talks and reached a consensus, which was then forced upon the employers' organization and the Irish Farmer's Association (Aust 1999).

With the Programme for National Recovery that was agreed upon in October 1987, a series of tripartite pacts were initiated that are widely seen as a major contribution to the recovery of the Irish economy (see table 7.4). The country not only escaped the deep economic, social and political crisis of the 1980s, but it also addressed its long-term development problems of emigration, unemployment, trade deficits and weak indigenous business development (O'Donnell and O'Reardon 2000: 239).

Four tripartite agreements were settled between 1987 and 2000, each of them lasting several years. Wage formation within the agreements took the form of graduated (usually annual) increases in the basic wage rate, plus provision for a locally bargained pay increase. Public sector pay tended to be treated separately, and this remained a point of contention. The range of bargaining issues broadened as the new agreements were negoti-

Table 7.4 Tripartite agreements in Ireland, 1987-2000

Year	Policy	Pay Content
1987-90	Programme for National Recovery	2% on balance
1990-93	Programme for Economic and Social Progress	10.75% over three years Local bargaining permitted up to 3%
1994-97	Programme for Competitiveness and Work	8% over 39 months
1997-2000	Partnership 2000 for Inclusion, Employment and Competitiveness	7.25% for 3 years local bargaining clause

Sources: Hardiman (2002), O'Donnell and O'Reardon (1997); various sources.

ated. The Programme for Economic and Social Progress (PESP, 1990-93) introduced a local productivity-related bargaining clause. Nevertheless, wage drift remained relatively low.

While the negotiations for each of the agreements were accompanied by conflicts and each time gave way to pessimistic forecasts that the time for tripartite pacts would soon be over, the agreements rested upon a number of factors that served the stability of the new bargaining arrangements. One aspect is obviously the immediate success of the initial agreement in 1987 that was contingent on an upturn in the international economy and a drop in inflation (Hardiman 2002: 9). Throughout the 1980s and 1990s, real pay increases in Ireland were higher than the EU average. Real wage restraint – which was the main feature of the traditional corporatist countries – remained difficult, with the Irish unions insisting on the protection of the real wage (Kavanagh, Considine *et al.* 1998). But equally important, the tripartite agreements very quickly moved from a general shared understanding of a macroeconomic strategy to addressing numerous supply-side issues (Roche 1997: 121). In particular, the institutional basis of wage bargaining was strengthened by introducing the Labour Relations Commission in 1990 (EIRR 1990). Wider social issues such as 'social inclusion and equality' and workplace representation were included in the agreements. Overall, the instrument of settling tripartite agreements has now reached such a level of political legitimacy in Irish economic policy-making in a period of exceptional economic success that they bind the actors together rather than letting them drift apart. However, during the period of 1987 and 2000, wage formation was dependent on the government agreeing to concessions to the social partners. To date, the institutional basis has not been strong enough to devise a wage formation procedure that is able to survive only by the support of the wage bargaining actors themselves.[142]

Spain and Portugal: building responsive wage bargaining institutions after government intervention[143]

In Spain, tripartite agreements including an incomes policy are so inseparable from the transition to democracy that the process has been characterized as 'pacted transition' driven by elite compromises (Hamann 1998 and 2001: 162; Heywood 1996). The actual transition to democracy in Spain was not only exceptionally smooth, compared with Portugal and Greece, but also amazingly well prepared by the outgoing Francoist government. The Political Reform Law of 1976 provided the necessary framework for the elections in 1977 and for a new democratic constitution (Heywood 1996: 147). The consensus and pact-based transition also included the relations with the social partners.

After the 1977 elections, the political parties that were represented in parliament signed an all-party agreement (*Pactos de la Moncloa*) in which the first post-authoritarian incomes policy was agreed (see table 7.5). In order to break the inflationary trend that had emerged in the mid-1970s (see figure A1 in appendix), wage growth was linked to monetary growth and not to past inflation. The leaders of the main trade unions, CC.OO and UGT, held seats in parliament and therefore assisted in ratifying the pacts (Perez 2000b: 344). The pacts were the basis for a number of tripartite agreements that regulated pay increases in Spain in the first decade after the transition until 1986. The early agreements committed the unions to wage restraint in line with inflation. From 1981 onwards, the Interconfederal Framework Agreement (AMI) permitted pay increases on the basis of productivity improvements at the company level. The agreements also dealt with a number of other labour-related issues, such as the legal regulation of industrial relations (the Workers' Statute) and the reduction of working time. Cooperation was fostered further by the attempted coup d'etat in 1981, which prompted the communist trade union CCOO to sign the 1982 agreement.

Table 7.5 Tripartite agreements in Spain, 1977-86

Year	Policy	Pay Content	Signatories
1977	Moncloa Pacts		Parliamentary parties
1979	Acuerdo de Base Interconfederal	13.0-16.0	UGT, CEOE
1980-81	Acuerdo Marco Interconfederal	11.0-15.0	UGT, CEOE, USO
1982	Acuredo Nacional de Empleo	9.0-11.0	Gvt., CEOE, UGT, CCOO
1983	Acuerdo Interconfederal	9.5-12.0	CEOE, CEPYME, UGT, CC.OO
1985	Acuerdo Económico y Social	7.2-8.6	Government CEOE, CEPYE, UGT
1986	Acuerdo Económico y Social	5.5-7.5	Government CEOE, CEPYE, UGT

Sources: Royo (2002b: 82); Hamann (2001: 158).

When the Spanish Socialist party won the election in 1982, the government was eager to continue with the agreements. In the first year of the socialist government, an agreement was signed that included both trade unions. Still, as early as 1984, a dispute between the government and the unions broke out over public sector pay and the introduction of fixed term contracts. Consequently, the communist trade union CCOO opposed the agreement. In 1985 and 1986, negotiations became increasingly strained. The expectations on both sides of the bargaining table, which supported cooperation through the transition years, had evidently diverged. The government perceived centralized agreements as increasingly disadvantageous and so assumed an increasingly uncompromising attitude towards the unions (Perez 2000b: 345). The socialist trade union UGT, on the other hand, became increasingly disillusioned with government policy. The conflict escalated in 1987 when the leader of the UGT, Nicolas Redondo, resigned from his PSOE party seat in parliament.[144] This move was followed by the first general strike in Spain for 58 years in 1988.

Between 1988 and 1996, the socialist government made several attempts to bring the unions back to the bargaining table. In 1991, a 'Social Pact for Progress' was proposed by the government, which would have tied wage increases to productivity increases for three years (Perez 2000b: 348). In 1993, another pact for employment was negotiated in the aftermath of the EMS crisis, which triggered the worst recession in Spain since the war. Both pacts failed to meet with the agreement of the unions, who blocked the minor labour market deregulations that accompanied the pacts. The government nevertheless implemented the labour law changes and thereby severed its relationship with the unions.

Since 1993, there has been no further tripartite attempt to effect wage agreements. As in the case of France, central negotiations have taken place on the issue of pension reform (1996) and on part-time and temporary work (1998). Between the social partners, a major agreement on the restructuring of collective bargaining procedures was reached in 1997, but without the involvement of the government. The agreement aimed in particular at reversing the move towards further decentralization of wage bargaining to the regional level that had been taking since 1994.[145]

Government intervention in Spain has therefore not responded to failures of the wage bargaining institutions but instead has preceded their evolution. Until 1977, there was a tradition neither of wage bargaining nor effective trade union organizations and employers' associations. In the first decade after the transition, wage bargaining was shaped by national tripartite agreements. Therefore, the primary problem of wage formation in Spain after the national agreements broke down was the lack of articulation and institutionalization of wage bargaining procedures. In the literature, the attempts made by the social partners in the mid-1990s to create better coordinated wage bargaining institutions are mainly attributed to the incapacity of the exposed business sector to control labour costs in absence of wage bargaining institutions. Despite overall wage moderation, sector-specific wage drifts have undermined the competitiveness of the export sector (Perez 2000a). In recent years, both social partners have been engaged in establishing a wage bargaining regime in which pay increases are in accordance with the macroeconomic policy of the government.

Nevertheless, an assessment of the wage bargaining system by the OECD concludes that "the system of wage bargaining has barely changed since the 1997 agreement between the social partners was adopted and remains complicated" (OECD 2000: 60). In particular, the overlapping nature of several layers of agreements is criticized, since in some sectors national agreements on wages are modified at the provincial level, and then possibly again at the firm level. In other sectors, negotiations are conducted at the provincial level, though certain recommendations on wage increases are passed down from national organizations. The problem of fragmentation and lack of articulation had already been addressed in a National Multi-industry Framework Agreement between the UGT and CEOE in 1980. This view has since been reinforced in the tripartite agreements and in the 1997 agreements. These issues have not yet been resolved and wage formation remains rather uncoordinated and subject to market pressures.

Portugal

In contrast to the Spanish case, the transition to democracy in Portugal was characterized by a period of constant political turmoil until 1979. The downfall of the regime in 1974 was followed by an attempted military coup by the far left in 1975. In subsequent years, a number of minority governments with brief tenure in office attempted to steer the country through continual crisis. Throughout the 1970s, wage bargaining by trade unions and employers was virtually non-existent.[146] This was due to the fact that the unions were largely dominated by the communist trade union Intersyndicat (later the CGTP), which sought political influence but not bargaining strength, and to fact that the Salazar regime lacked any real bargaining tradition.[147] The restoration of free trade unions coincided with communist dominance. For most of the 1970s transition period, there was a fierce struggle within labour organizations over the monopoly representation by the Intersyndicat. During this period, wages were regulated directly by the government which fixed the wage ceilings. It was not until December 1979 that the law that had set a ceiling on wage gains was repealed (Pinto 1990: 249). Even after the government withdrew from direct wage setting, it still played a key role in setting wages indirectly, through its involvement in the public sector and the nationalized industries.

From 1980 onwards, the approach by the government towards wage formation changed. This was due to several factors. First, a non-communist trade union emerged with the UGT in 1978, which enjoyed the support of the socialist (PS) and social democratic party (PSD). Secondly, from 1983 until 1985, the centre bloc parties (socialist and social democratic) formed a coalition government. And third, in the early 1980s, Portugal plunged into a deep economic crisis.

In this situation, while the government was forced to implement an IMF stabilization plan, it also conceived a new forum for consultation with the social partners, the Permanent Council for Social Concertation (CPCS). In subsequent years, the CPCS became an important tool for the government to use when trying to achieve wage restraint. The council could not agree on the deregulation of the labour market and the liberalization of labour laws, but did find it easier to reach an agreement on incomes policy. In June 1986, the first tripartite agreement on incomes policy was concluded (see table 7.6). The incomes policy contained a wage agreement that was tied to government inflation targets. In 1987, the targets for the year were met. In 1988, the political contestation between the unions relaxed and the communist trade unions that had so far boycotted the tripartite council took up their seats. But, already in 1988, the government had to deal with two problems. On the one hand, the relations between the communist unions and the employers were still highly conflictual. In the 1988 wage round, neither the Confederation of Portuguese Industry (CPI), nor the communist trade union, CGTP, signed the agreement. The CPI refused to sign the pact, regarding 6 per cent inflation and 5 per cent targets for wage increases as too high. The CGTP refused because it considered the wage targets too low.[148] On the other hand, the inflation targets on which the agreement rested were not met. When the government missed the target and inflation rose to 11 per cent, it even lost the support of the UGT. After a series of hefty conflicts and strikes, the government broke off its consultations with the unions and imposed a unilateral deregulation of labour laws (Financial Times 1989a and b).

Soaring inflation rates, despite moderate wage settlements, brought the actors back to the bargaining table in 1990. The government proposed a package to the unions, the Economic and Social Agreement, which included a working time reduction and a new version of a wage ceiling of 13.5 per cent. On this basis, a new labour pact was signed in the CPCS in 1991, but again without the support of the CGTP.[149] However, inflation in the early 1990s was still running in double figures and, with the entry of Portugal into the EMS in 1992, a further move towards wage discipline was needed. After months of negotiations, the government failed to agree a national wage pact for 1994. The centre-right government of Prime Minister Anibal Cavaco Silva tried to hold the unions to a 2 per cent wage-rise ceiling and set a tough example by stipulating a wage freeze for the public administrative sector. The unions opposed this. It was only after the escudo was devalued in March 1995 and the socialist party gained an electoral victory in the same year that a new consensus could be forged for signing another pact that included a public sector pay settlement of below 5 per cent.[150] The spell of the inflationary wage spiral was thus broken.

As in Spain, collective bargaining institutions in Portugal have remained weak. The political conflict between the unions, on the one hand, and the contestation between employers and unions, on the other hand, has not encouraged trustful relations at any level. In addition, high levels of inflation have created insecurity about realistic wage claims. In this book, Portugal has the strongest variation in increases in real pay, between 16 per cent increases in real pay in the mid-1970s and 4 per cent real pay loss in the late 1970s. Bargaining patterns have remained arbitrary and are largely confined to large companies. There is still no overall coordination of wage bargaining at the sectoral level, but lower-level agreements override agreements at the sectoral level.

Table 7.6 Tripartite agreements in Portugal, 1977-99

Year	Policy	Pay Content
1986-87	Agreement on Prices and Incomes Policy	7% wage increase
1988	Agreement on Prices and Incomes Policy	Not signed by CGTP and CIP
1991	Economic and Social Agreement	Wage guideline of 13.5%; not signed by CGTP
1996	Short-Term Social Dialogue Agreement	Cap on wage increases
1996-99	Strategic Social Pact	No reference to wages after 1998

Source: Royo (2002b: 85).

Conclusion: A comparative view on the dynamic between wage bargaining institutions and government intervention

A number of conclusions can be drawn from the cases above. As hypothesized, the countries with the most responsive wage bargaining institutions, Germany and Austria, have experienced comparatively little government intervention. However, by the end of the three decades, only Austria still has a successful model of monetarist responsiveness. In all other countries, wage bargaining actors have found it more difficult to adjust their wage expectations to the new challenges. In Denmark and the Netherlands, frictions in wage bargaining, already apparent in the 1960s, were exacerbated by the shock of the monetarist response of the Bundesbank in 1975. In Belgium, this process started in 1976. In all three countries, the main tension arose because wage indexation rules set the focus of wage bargaining firmly on protecting the real wage. In Denmark and the Netherlands, government intervention could finally abolish indexation rules; this did not happen in Belgium.

Finland and Sweden were both relatively unharmed by the crisis of the 1970s because government policy combined devaluation and real wage restraint, which was able, at least temporarily, to ease the economic pressures. In Finland, real wage restraint was weaker due to political conflicts on the left. Both countries, however, were challenged in the early 1990s when devaluation as an economic strategy had become unacceptable. In both countries, the corporatist base on which the real wage restraint had rested was also challenged by dissenting sectoral pressures. However, in both countries, a new interaction between national-level wage formation (in the case of Sweden through mediation, in the case of Finland through tripartite agreements) has since emerged that allows for a higher degree of sectoral differentiation in a national framework.

Germany was the last country to encounter a similar situation, in the latter part of the 1990s. In Germany, the increasing role of the government was prompted by the pressures of reunification in the 1990s, which coincided with a decline in the competitiveness of German industry (Hassel and Rehder 2001). The high productivity regime did not deliver the cuts in labour costs to stop companies squeezing the wage bargaining system. Since then, the social partners and the government have been under pressure to find new solutions to increase competitiveness.

In all five non-responsive corporatist countries, a process of restructuring of wage bargaining institutions can be observed that has attempted to find a new balance between macroeconomic constraints and sectoral and local differentiation. At the core of the restructuring has been the acceptance by wage bargaining actors of the tightness of these constraints. Even though at times painful, the limits of real wage protection have been recognized by the unions. In this process, the role of the government has been crucial and has gained in importance as the friction between the external environment and the wage expectations of the unions has increased.

In none of the corporatist countries governments have actively attempted to undermine existing coordinated wage bargaining institutions. Wage bargaining has transformed under the impact of new economic conditions, but has not been dismantled by government action. In Denmark and the Netherlands in 1982, the newly elected conservative governments indicated that they were no longer prepared to engage in political exchanges over incomes policy, as their predecessors had done during the 1970s. The British no-nonsense approach towards trade unions enjoyed some appeal but, by leaving the issue of wage formation to the social partners, the government was also dependent on trade union wage bargaining behaviour. In the Netherlands, the unions immediately gave in to the pressure from the government, while in Denmark internal rivalry between the SiD and the LO made adjustment more difficult. In both cases, the same conservative governments returned to the bargaining table, although under newly defined conditions.

All the non-corporatist countries started out with a weak institutional base for wage negotiations and wage bargaining responsiveness. However, Ireland had a tripartite structure from the 1970s onwards. While the Irish trade union structure resembled the British, the actual wage bargaining patterns in Ireland had always been more coordinated. Central wage bargaining failed during the 1970s, but the pattern served as a starting point in the severe economic and fiscal crisis of the early 1980s. Given its size and economic openness, Ireland would in any case have been a prime candidate for cooperative labour relations in the sense of Katzenstein's "small state in world markets" (Katzenstein 1985).

Similarly in Portugal and Spain, the history of tripartism served as a baseline for further negotiations at the peak level during the 1990s, although it encountered several difficult phases in Portugal and failed altogether in Spain in 1986. In Italy, the dynamic was somewhat different since the Italian trade unions engaged in more pragmatic workplace industrial relations while at the same time obstructing national negotiations. When the political crisis became a national emergency situation in 1992 with the collapse of the old political regime, Italian unions could draw on local support to organize a change of approach. In Italy, the shift in trade union approaches was also due to the strong labour leader of the CGIL, Bruno Trentin, who led his organization out of the stalemate.

The case studies support the theoretical claim made in the political economy literature about the close interaction of wage bargaining and monetary policy. In each case, on the one hand the shift in monetary policy responses created economic pressures for the government, while on the other hand, a clear traditional reputation of the monetary authority eased the transition towards a new regime provided that wage bargaining institutions were in control of wage formation. The transmission of restrictive monetary policy to wage formation processes was, however, only partly carried out by the social partners. In all cases, it was the role of the government to redefine and confine the room for wage bargaining by trade unions, either by refusing, like the British government, to accept responsibility for the employment effects of monetary policy or by pushing trade unions towards the acceptance of voluntary wage restraint.

8 Negotiated Adjustment – A European Approach

During the 1980s and 1990s, many observers assumed that corporatism in Western Europe had come to the end of its useful life. Economic internationalization, the changes in the labour market and the increase in unemployment after the oil shocks had changed the structure of European economies to such an extent that neither governments nor trade unions, it was believed, would be interested or able to engage in further forms of political exchange. Incomes policies had proven unsuccessful during the 1970s and forms of centralized wage bargaining seemed to lack support. To the surprise of many, the reality since has been different. Western governments, facing the constraints resulting from the oil shock, have pursued a double strategy of economic adjustment, combining elements that were previously seen as incompatible. They have firmly committed themselves to a non-inflationary economic and monetary policy within the European Monetary System and have further engaged in collaboration with their trade unions in order to adjust the wage expectations of workers to the needs of the economic and employment policy of governments.

The purpose of this book has been to explain government behaviour and to specify the conditions under which governments would choose either to negotiate on wage restraint or leave the effects of wage settlements exclusively to the market and to restrictive monetary policies. I have proposed three main factors that explain government behaviour. The first factor is the monetary regime that determines the room for manoeuvre and, moreover, signals to wage bargainers the strictness of the monetary response. In countries that have traditionally had a reputation for strict monetary policy, governments would be less likely to negotiate with trade unions over wages. The second factor is the political institutions that determine the capacity of governments to resist demands by unions. In consensus democracies, I have argued, governments are more closely intertwined with unions and, what is more, the governing parties offer access points for the social partners. In these cases, they are more likely to negotiate than to disregard trade union demands. The third factor is the responsiveness of the wage bargaining system that has created the necessity for trade unions to adjust their wage expectations in the first place. The responsiveness of wage bargaining institutions determines the extent of the necessary adjustments in the wage formation system. I have argued that the combination of these different factors in particular countries can explain the variance between different governments' behaviour.

The broader implication of this book is the argument that close interaction between governments and social partners on wages has survived and been revived for two reasons. Firstly, governments in a consensus democracy have not been able politically to abandon the post-war consensus on the role of trade unions in the organization of the labour market. In consensus democracies, governing parties are often too close to the demands of the social partners to openly pursue their exclusion. The fractionalization of party systems in consensus democracies combined with the access of political trade unions to competing parties makes it virtually impossible politically to neglect their demands.

Secondly, the wage bargaining institutions that the post-war settlements produced offered suitable starting points for negotiations about adjustment in the face of the effects of the internationalization of financial markets. Past governments generally attempted to cope with the increasing vulnerability and openness of their economies by seeking monetary stability without questioning the political and economic role of trade unions. These governments, moreover, used the increasing external constraints of monetary integration to draw trade unions further into the acceptance of long-term wage restraint.

As in the golden years of the post-war period, government intervention in wage bargaining has thus remained a double-edged sword for those involved. Governments can achieve a higher degree of control over wages but have to surrender autonomy and control over other policy issues; trade unions gain political legitimacy and influence but lose some of their autonomy in wage bargaining. Overall, an active role of governments in wage formation reproduces interdependency between governments and social partners. Although governments intervene in wage bargaining procedures, often with a clear intention of repelling trade union demands, this interaction legitimizes and often strengthens wage bargaining coordination along with trade union organizations themselves. The process of negotiated adjustment that could be observed in most countries in Western Europe throughout the 1980s and 1990s now feeds back on itself. This concluding chapter presents my main arguments and findings over five sections. The sixth section discusses the implications for adjustment under European Monetary Union.

Policy options towards trade unions' redistributional power

The post-war consensus on free collective bargaining and full employment posed for governments an extraordinarily challenging economic policy problem. While trade unions were free to pursue the wage aspirations of their members and of the society as a whole, the economic effects of high wage settlements had become a political problem of government. The Keynesian economic policy paradigm even encouraged the view that governments were capable and legitimately responsible for the performance of labour markets.

This combination created a trilemma of domestic objectives of full employment, price stability and free collective bargaining for governments, whereby any pair could be achieved only by sacrificing the third goal. The trade-off between employment and price stability – the Phillips curve – accordingly depended on the conduct of collective bargaining. Under the given institutional design of a regulated labour market and free collective bargaining, a decrease in unemployment would lead to an increase in inflationary pressure. Given the universal pledge by governments to aspire to full employment, the price of increasing unemployment in return for price stability was unacceptable. Given the universally accepted right of trade unions to bargain freely with employers and enjoy protection by law against their restraint, governments had no way of forcefully interfering with the organization of the labour market. At the same time, the effects of full employment on the position of trade unions in the economy had to be accommodated in order to keep wage expectations in line with the economic reality of low growth rates from 1970 onwards.

In an ideal-typical perspective, this accommodation could take three policy responses (see figure 8.1): accommodation by institutions, accommodation by negotiations or accommodation by the disciplinary force of the market. The institutional form was the corporatist integration of trade unions in the overall economic policy framework. The corporatist solution assumed that trade unions were given organizational securities, often in the form of labour market monopolies, while it was hoped that their wage bargaining conduct would be responsive to government needs. Trade unions gained the status of semi-public bodies and were involved

Figure 8.1 Political economy of monetary and incomes policies, Western Europe, 1980-99

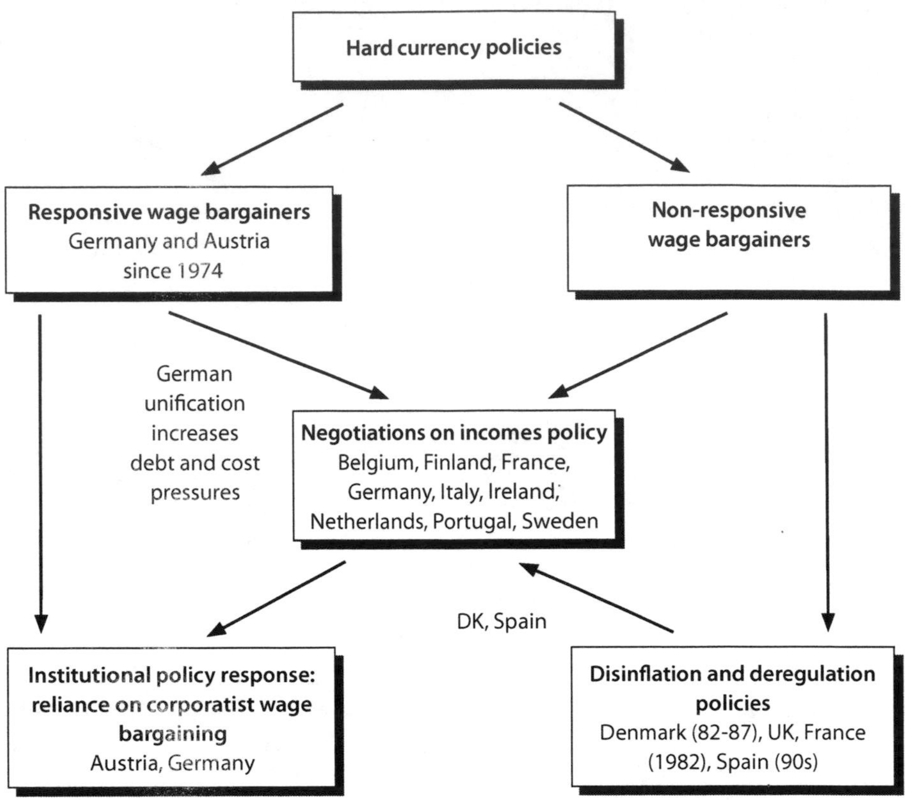

in the administration of social security programmes, training schemes and labour market policy. With the increasing levels of responsibility for economic policy, trade unions accepted this responsibility by adjusting their wage demands accordingly. The institutional incorporation of trade unions thus contributed directly to the responsiveness of wage bargaining. As the neo-corporatist literature on the effects of labour market organizations on economic performance shows, in the stagflation years during the 1970s, incorporation often led to better results than negotiation.

In other cases, the political and wage bargaining role of trade unions was not institutionalized in this form and governments had to negotiate with trade unions about their willingness to restrain wages. Negotiations, which in some cases took the form of imposed wage freezes, embodied the acknowledgment that wage bargaining outcomes were not in line with the needs of the government in its economic policy, but that the wage expectations of trade unions had to be adjusted.

The third way of accommodation was the market solution. By relying on the disciplinary force of the market, governments rejected the notion that it was their task to find a balance between the wage expectations of the employed and the need to maintain the competitiveness of its economy. The underlying idea was that competitiveness would be restored once the labour market had adjusted to imbalances and forms of centralized wage formation procedures had been removed.

In fact, the three policies were not clear-cut alternatives, but highly interrelated. When institutions failed to respond, but governments were committed to an economic policy that rested on the political inclusion of trade unions, most governments started to negotiate. In the process of negotiations, governments often used the pressure of market discipline to extract further commitments from the trade unions on wage moderation. There was, however, little overlap between the use of institutions and the use of the market. Where institutions were strong and responsive, deregulation was not pursued. Where deregulation and trade union exclusion were the primary policies, institutions could not be maintained. In this sense, negotiations are also a third way between powerful institutions on the one hand and market driven approaches on the other.

The pursuit of tight monetary policy as an anti-inflationary tool emerged primarily from the dissatisfaction felt by policy-makers in those countries where the institutional incorporation of trade unions was weak and negotiations on incomes policies had persistently failed – in particular the United Kingdom. After the experiences with the Social Contract and the 'Winter of Discontent' in contrast to the sharp reaction by the Bundesbank to the oil shock and the following wage settlements in Germany in 1975, conservative policy-makers in the United Kingdom prepared the return to restrictive economic policies and the deregulation of the labour market in order to discipline labour.

However, while governments in most countries turned towards monetarist responses to the inflationary threat, they were not so easily freed from the post-war commitment to labour inclusion. While monetarism promised low inflation without costs in terms of employment losses *in the long run*, governments still faced the pledge of restoring full employment – by then a universal demand of the electorates of any government. If the short-term negative employment effects of restrictive monetary policies could be alleviated by a voluntary wage restraint by trade unions, governments still had incentives to find cooperative solutions with them.

Therefore, as a theoretical concept, monetarism sought to disentangle the relationship between monetary policy and the real economy and, with that, the relationship between economic policies and the wage bargaining process, which had become increasingly interdependent during the first three decades after World War II. In practical terms, however, governments were still caught in the interlocking policy fields of wages and economic policy, to the extent that they could neither renounce their promises to work towards high employment levels nor forsake their commitment to leave the organization of the labour market to strong trade unions.

The return of tight economic policy as a disciplinary device (which had been used traditionally before World War I and in the inter-war period) and its dissemination in the process of European monetary integration have consequently increased the capacity of governments to fight inflation. It has not, however, been an adequate policy tool for easing the potential frictions between trade union wage expectations and the changing economic environment. In fact, quite the opposite is the case: tight monetary policies and fixed exchange rates require a higher degree of responsiveness from wage bargaining actors in order to allow for balanced economic growth. The responsiveness of wage bargaining outcomes and, equally, the institutions that govern responsiveness have therefore increased in their importance for economic performance. Since in post-war industrialized economies, governments are still held responsible by the electorate for employment performance, governments are more dependent on the responsiveness of these wage bargaining institutions than before. Hence, rather than letting monetary policy discipline unresponsive wage bargaining actors, a government's incentives to influence wage bargaining outcomes have tended to increase rather than decrease compared to earlier periods.

A pure market solution, involving no government interference and independent from the responsiveness of the wage bargaining system, has been a challenge too difficult for most European governments. Only the British government, which is strongly insulated from electoral and trade union pressure, could really afford the market solution. In addition, only the British Conservative Party under the leadership by Margaret Thatcher had the ideological strength to deny trade unions a legitimate role in organizing the labour market and influencing public policy.

In all other Western European countries, the combination of the full employment pledge, free collective bargaining by strongly institutionalized social partners *and* the use of tight monetary policies to achieve economic stabilization changed – and ultimately fostered – the interaction between governments and social partners on the issue of wage formation.

Countries with centralized bargaining institutions moved from the corner of responsive institutions towards negotiations in order to adjust to the changing monetary regime. Non-corporatist countries that could not abandon their commitments to the political integration of trade unions started to negotiate more seriously on wage restraint. Even in France, where trade union control over wages had become extremely weak and where government-union relations had been hostile throughout the postwar period, governments during the 1980s and 1990s still made repeated attempts to restructure wage bargaining procedures, organize tripartite summits and negotiate over wage formation.

In other words, restrictive monetary policy did not liberate Western European governments from their dependence on trade unions and collective bargaining decisions in economic policy as Fritz Scharpf had assumed (Scharpf 1991), but only altered the conditions under which the interaction would take place. Monetarism could only liberate governments from their dependence on trade union behaviour if they both disregarded the medium-term employment effects *and* were able to reduce the degree of labour market regulation by trade unions, as the British did. The majority of governments, however, were not prepared to go that far.

For continental European governments, an increase in market discipline through restrictive economic policy and monetary integration has led to intensification of the relationship between trade unions and the government, not to its diminishing. The disciplinary force of monetary policy has not been sufficient to replace previous attempts to accommodate trade union wage demands.

Moreover, politically, labour inclusion has not been abandoned as a tool for achieving political stability in the European political economy. This is particularly the case in the transition countries. In the post-authoritarian countries in the south of Europe, Portugal and Spain, the transition to democracy was built around a concept of including the trade unions into the new democracies. This process also took place in the post-socialist countries of Eastern Europe after 1989.[151] Tripartism and trade union consultation were used as a safety valve in these countries against the dissatisfaction of the population with economic hardship, and they spread rapidly throughout the post-socialist countries. This occurred even though the existing trade unions often did not represent substantial parts of the working population. Though a seemingly dated concept, the inclusion and institutionalization of labour has remained a cornerstone in the design of the European political systems throughout the last quarter of the twentieth century.

Therefore, apart from the UK, European governments were not successful in distancing themselves from trade union influence in the 1980s and 1990s. In Ireland and Denmark, the move towards deregulation of the labour market and decentralization of wage formation in the early 1980s did not work out, but instead put a strain on government economic policies. In Italy and Belgium, governments tried to negotiate away from the trade unions' acquired rights on labour market regulation, and failed. In the Netherlands, the threat to exclude labour led to a rejuvenation of corporatist concertation.

At the same time, the traditional corporatist solution of self-governance by centralized trade unions and employers' associations lost its strength in many cases. High degrees of responsiveness of wage bargaining actors based on the incorporation of trade unions only worked in Austria and, to a certain degree, Germany. In Sweden it was contingent on accommodating economic policies. When the Swedish model of expansive fiscal policy ran out of steam, only Austria remained as the role model for low unemployment in a tight hard currency framework. In Germany, the same was true in principle, but the German performance was burdened by reunification. In particular, the post-reunification boom in 1991/92 knocked the German wage bargaining off course. In the early 1990s, German wage bargaining was out of tune with the challenge that unification would pose to the German economy in the long run.

The other small corporatist states – Belgium, Sweden, the Netherlands, Denmark and Finland – all had particular aspects of wage bargaining institutions that had over the years started to undermine the institutions' capacity for restraining wage expectations. In Sweden and Finland, the late switch to a hard currency strategy made automatic adjustment difficult. In both countries, the adjustment to a hard currency policy required a more active involvement by the state. Moreover, in all the small corporatist countries with the exception of Austria and Sweden, institutionalized systems of wage indexation and rivalry between unions for membership shares deflected trade unions from their responsibility for wage restraint, on which the initial process of incorporation rested.

In the non-corporatist countries, tight monetary policies had an even more intense effect. While being tied to the post-war consensus on employment and free collective bargaining, the trade unions in these countries nevertheless had little tradition of responsible wage bargaining procedures. However, since in all countries but France they were in control of wage formation, governments had to try to influence their wage bargaining behaviour. Moreover, in France, Italy, Spain and Portugal, the tradition of political competition between unions and governing parties made a clear move by the government even more difficult.

As a result, a hard currency policy on its own was not a sufficient disciplinary tool for trade unions in political systems that were still well grounded in a post-war consensus of free collective bargaining, trade union responsibility for wage formation and government responsibility for employment performance. The monetarist solution might have been a sufficient disciplinary force for holding down inflation; it did not, however, have the potential strength to translate disinflation into employment-promoting wage bargaining behaviour on the part of the unions. While corporatist mechanisms were failing, negotiations on wages were gaining in importance.

The interaction of institutions and policies

According to institutionalist analysis, the organization of wage bargaining has been the main institutional factor influencing economic performance and the economic policy of governments. In the past, a high degree of organizational centralization was conducive to both economic performance and close cooperation with governments. Centralized wage bargaining was able to guarantee a level of wage restraint that was welcomed by governments. In turn, governments supported the trade unions through political inclusion. Without centralized wage bargaining, and therefore less responsive wage bargaining behaviour, governments had to turn to policies of labour exclusion and deregulation. Under these circumstances, the mutually beneficial interaction between public policy and interest associations did not emerge. The notion of corporatism describes the close interlocking relationship between governments and wage bargaining institutions. The mechanism on which this relationship rests is the political exchange. Trade unions achieve political power by converting their ability to strike in the market place into a tool that they can use *vis-à-vis* governments (Pizzorno 1978). By refraining to use the full extent of their industrial power, trade unions can ask governments for compensation, particularly in those cases where the political survival of governments depends on restraint.

When looking at the evolution of corporatism in a dynamic perspective, it emerges that the organizational dimension of corporatism only captures the potentially virtuous policy feedback circle of centralized wage bargaining institutions and government support. Over the past three decades, however, the forces of interaction that were responsible for the evolution of the relationship between governments and trade unions lied in the *mismatch* of wage bargaining outcomes and the economic policy constraints of the government. While the commitment towards labour inclusion created restraints for governments, which they tried to tackle by means of cooperation and persuasion of wage bargaining actors, the failure of wage bargaining actors to respond generated further interaction between governments and trade unions. Rather than assume that the responsiveness of wage bargaining institutions gave incentives for governments to incorporate labour, the opposite has been argued here, namely that the decline and lack of responsiveness in countries where labour inclusion was high led to the increasing involvement of governments in wage formation. In other words, non-responsive trade unions with a high degree of industrial power could insulate themselves from the forces of the market.

In this book, the responsiveness of wage bargaining institutions to changing economic conditions has been used as an indicator of the mismatch between governments' preference for wage bargaining and the actual wage bargaining outcomes. When looking at factors influencing the change of nominal wages, it has emerged that wage bargaining systems differ in their degree of responsiveness to changes in consumer prices and unemployment. Countries where changes in nominal wages have been significantly influenced by unemployment levels have been labelled responsive, whereas countries where changes in nominal wages have been largely dominated by changes in consumer prices have been termed non-responsive (see Chapter 6).

Only the bargaining institutions in Germany and Austria were responsive in the period between 1970 and 1999. In Finland, the UK, Ireland and Portugal wages reacted to consumer prices but not to unemployment. In the majority of continental European countries, wage bargaining institutions were caught in the middle: they were somewhat employment-sensitive and somewhat price-sensitive. In these countries, wage bargaining institutions were trapped in the conflict of ensuring real wage increases, on the one hand, and responding to the employment crisis, on the other. Only in Sweden were nominal wages affected neither by the change in consumer prices nor by unemployment levels.

It has emerged that responsiveness of trade unions is not exclusively determined by the centralization of trade union or wage bargaining institutions, as has been argued in most contributions in the literature. While the capacity of trade unions to control wage bargaining through either centralized bargaining structures or coordination is a necessary condition for responsiveness, it is not a sufficient one. This phenomenon has increasingly been recognized in political economy literature, as empirical studies have shown a declining effect of centralization of wage bargaining institutions on economic performance.

Moreover, this book has shown that, over time, wage bargaining procedures have been layered by a number of normative and institutional principles that influence their capacity to adjust wages to a changing economic environment. The first one is the expectation of wage bargaining actors of how the monetary regime will behave. As pointed out in Chapter 4, governments changed the monetary policy regime by pegging their currencies in the hope that wage bargaining actors would adjust their behaviour accordingly. However, throughout the conduct of the currency snake and the EMS, there was a chance in a number of countries that governments might react to economic imbalances with devaluation, which would have caused real wage losses. Often, the degree of non-accommodation of monetary policies, since this was action *ex post*, could not be assessed *ex ante* by the policy-makers themselves.

A government opting to adjust the currency rather than use tight monetary policies made it more difficult for trade unions to adjust wage agreements to changing economic conditions. The shift from an accommodating monetary regime to a non-accommodating regime required either prior consensus on wage restraint or a high degree of credibility on the part of the monetary regime to cause any change in the behaviour of wage bargaining actors. The potential to adjust exchange rates under the currency snake and the EMS blurred the expectation of wage bargaining actors as to the credibility of a non-accommodating policy while creating incentives to press for real wage increases. Even when a highly credible monetary policy was introduced, the adjustment of wage bargaining behaviour to the new monetary regime could have been potentially very time-consuming. Therefore, for the non-hard currency countries entering the snake and the EMS, the appropriate response to inflation differentials to the D-mark was not necessarily obvious, especially in cases where the effects of devaluation would be felt differently in separate economic sectors.

Secondly, past political exchanges had already affected the conduct of wage bargaining. Feedback processes had altered the pay-off for trade unions with regard to issues of real pay protection, pay equality and the social protection of workers. For instance, normative principles of wage formation had become engraved in wage bargaining procedures. The most important one of these principles in the Western European context was the indexation of wages to inflation, which basically ruled out any real wage reduction. In countries where strong elements of wage indexation had been institutionalized in wage bargaining procedures, such as in Belgium, the Netherlands, Italy and Denmark, adjustment was more difficult despite the sufficient organizational structures. Other factors were the exposure of trade union membership to international markets, the cohesiveness of trade union organizations and the potential for intra-organizational distributional conflicts. The extent to which wage bargaining actors were capable of responding to these conflicting pressures therefore depended to a large degree on the way in which *real* wage expectations had been incorporated in the bargaining institutions themselves.

In contrast, the responsiveness of German wage bargaining actors was largely explained by the fact that the principle decisions on wage formation were taken by industrial trade unions in the exporting sector, which measured their claims against the impact of labour cost increases on the competitiveness of their industries and the consequences of tight monetary policies for the revaluation of the D-mark. Moreover, being based on a system of cooperative workplace relations and one with the potential for high productivity increases, the unions could adjust their nominal wage claims to the economic situation and at the same time make real wage gains. Neither wage indexation nor wage equality ever became a guiding principle for German trade unions. Export orientation and a hard currency ensured that the unions were convinced that wage increases had to be earned before they could be delivered. The same observations can be made for the case of Austria.

The nature of negotiated adjustment: Reinforcing mechanisms of trade union incorporation

The main claim this book makes is that the evolution and persistence of negotiated adjustment, in preference to deregulation and market forces, is explained by the interaction between the responses of governments to wage bargaining outcomes and the political role of trade unions as linked to political parties. At the core of the evolution of corporatism lies the construction of the post-war settlement, whereby trade unions became fully integrated into the political system, class conflict was confined to the realm of collective bargaining through trade unions acquiring the legitimate role to regulate and organize the labour market, and governments meanwhile were made responsible for the economy in general and for achieving full employment in particular.

Political institutions that comprised the notion of consensus democracy provided incentives for governments to negotiate over wage restraint rather than leave the employment effects of high wage settlements to the market. In consensus democracies, party systems are more fragmented with trade unions affiliating to a variety of political parties. The competition between both parties in the electoral arena and trade unions in the wage bargaining arena diminish the strength of the government to pursue policies that were not trade union friendly. In turn, governments in political systems in which trade unions enjoyed several access points to political parties tended to negotiate with trade unions over economic adjustment rather than push the responsibility for employment performance onto the unions.

When economic imbalances arose, governments chose to approach trade unions and in the course of negotiating with them tended to offer incentives for wage restraint. Over time, however, all material gains for the unions – with the exception of tax cuts – were in effect seen as either detrimental to labour costs or inflationary or they were not acceptable to employers. The tightness of monetary policy reduced the room for governments to expand economic policy and thereby offer employment gains. Instead, the incentives for wage restraint became matters of organizational security. This process already started during the 1970s, when participation and co-determination became important union demands that were traded for wage restraint (Flanagan, Soskice *et al.* 1983; Esping-Andersen 1990: 176). Both the institutional incorporation of trade unions and the increasingly common negotiations with trade unions over wage restraint helped to secure the position of the unions on the labour market, though not necessarily their degree of responsiveness.

As a result, the incorporation of trade unions, whether in the form of corporatist structures, coordinated wage bargaining or persistent negotiations with governments, has had predominantly two effects. On the one hand, to the extent that these negotiations foster the coordination of wage bargaining and the adoption of moderate wage norms, they ease the frictions on the labour market over issues of wage formation. During the 1970s, the centralization of wage bargaining procedures was aimed at dampening wage expectations. During the 1980s and 1990s, government negotiations on wages also introduced further flexibility and differentiation (Visser 2002).

On the other hand, this process also reinforces the dependence of governments on the performance of trade unions in regulated labour markets and roots the unions further in the European political system. The Western European process of negotiated adjustment is thereby reinforced by the practice of negotiations. This is particularly apparent in comparison to the Anglo-Saxon alternative policy of deregulating the labour market. Rather than facilitating decentralization and deregulation on the labour market generally, the political effect of negotiations has been to strengthen the principles of negotiation and the legitimacy of the political role of trade unions.

Negotiations between governments and trade unions on wages – whether economically successful or not – have frequently tended to build new tripartite or bipartite institutions that at the time were thought to foster cooperation. In the corporatist countries, these institutions usually already existed and were rejuvenated by negotiations. In the Dutch case, Visser and Hemerijck called this process 'corporatism regained' (Visser and Hemerijck 1997). In the non-corporatist countries, for instance Ireland and Italy, institutions were newly established. Normally, the institutional support for tripartite negotiations helps to stabilize trade union organizations. As has been well developed in the literature on trade union membership and density, institutional factors have the strongest explanatory power with regard to the resilience of trade union organizations during times of economic distress (Western 1997; Ebbinghaus and Visser 1999; Visser 2002). The institution building aspect that evolves with continuous negotiations with the state has therefore not only fostered the political role of trade unions but also helped to establish organizational securities for trade unions that would not otherwise have come into being.

The German role model

Instead of embracing the approaches by the British government and US administration of labour market deregulation and labour exclusion, the German model of restrictive monetary (and fiscal) policy in conjunction with corporatist labour market regulation became the reference point of economic policy-making for its neighbouring countries during the 1970s and 1980s and, subsequently, for the European Union as a whole. By the mid-1970s, most European governments had realized that the impact of the oil shock was at odds with the wage expectations of European workers. Real wage expectations had become sticky, inflation endemic. All governments started to depress demand, but inflation and unemployment increased less in Germany and Austria than in other European countries. During the worst recession since the war, Germany remained "the world's over-achiever", in the words of *The Economist*.[152]

In neighbouring countries, the problem of inflation differentials became particularly pressing since these countries were trading heavily with Germany and losing their competitiveness. The German way of achieving non-inflationary economic adjustment was therefore particularly appealing. In the political debates of the time, Germany was held as an example of success. For instance, in France, the reference to the German model was quite explicit: the Barre plan of 1976 made direct reference to it (McNamara 1998: 131).

The main gateway through which the German model entered the adjustment process of most Western European countries was the currency snake. The European currency snake drew on the early Werner plan on European economic and monetary integration and was set up in 1972 in order to protect trade within the European Community from exchange rate volatilities and to stabilize the administration and financing of the Common Agricultural Policy. However, soon after the first oil shock, the European governments hoped to use the discipline of a stable exchange rate with the D-mark to force down inflation. The stringency of the Bundesbank, the lack of enthusiasm of the German government to engage in huge deficit spending and the responsiveness of the German wage bargaining institutions turned Germany into a successful model for the adjustment of wages to macroeconomic conditions without major negative consequences.

Through the currency snake, the participating countries imported the restrictive German monetary policy, but not necessarily its wage bargaining responsiveness or fiscal prudence (Scharpf 2000). In the core countries of the snake, apart from Germany and Austria, unemployment rose faster and problems of public finance were frequent. Governments had to comply with strict monetary policies in order to keep their currency in the snake, but tended to compensate for looming job losses through public spending. Even so, compared to the crisis-ridden examples of Italy and the UK, who had to ask the IMF to bail them out, the countries that managed to stay within the snake considered themselves better performers.

The dissemination of the German model of economic adjustment was particularly appealing to those small corporatist countries that already had a tradition of pursuing policies of combining economic flexibility and social inclusion (Katzenstein 1985). Economic openness had put pressure on the governments and interest associations of these countries to adjust flexibly to changes in the international economic order. Because small state corporatism was rooted in the notion of economic vulnerability and the national consensus of adaptation, the smaller countries had a tradition not only of economic openness and flexible adjustment but also of mobilizing the national consensus to support the necessary steps. In contrast, large countries have greater room for manoeuvre in economic adjustment and less capacity for forging a national consensus on economic flexibility.

The monetary straightjacket deriving from the snake and the consequent European Monetary System did not undermine small-state corporatism but rather presented a normal feature of vulnerability of the small and open economy in international markets. Governments in Denmark, Sweden, Belgium, the Netherlands and Austria had developed forms of national consensus policies to cope with changing economic environments since and through the political crisis of the 1930s and 1940s. But not even the small corporatist countries that were so used to adjusting to world market changes could meet the challenge easily. Apart from Austria and Switzerland, all the small neighbouring countries experienced difficult negotiations between governments and unions during the 1970s and 1980s.

For the big non-corporatist states, adjustment was more difficult. Italy, the UK and France had major adjustment problems and left the snake at some point during the 1970s. However, despite the failure of the snake to ensure currency stability, the mini-snake of Germany along with the Benelux countries and Denmark (with Austria in tow) had developed enough political momentum by the late 1970s to keep the French, Italian, Irish and even British governments aspiring to participate in some form of currency targeting and eventually in a European Monetary System. Under the impact of the increasing internationalization of financial markets, the stability of exchange rates and prices had become a priority for governments. Monetary integration was widely regarded as the suitable tool for achieving these goals.

Corporatism was not directly linked to the decision to use the German mark as the currency anchor for low inflation. In Ireland (1980-87), the Netherlands (1982) and Denmark (1982-87), for instance, tight monetary policies were initially accompanied by the rejection of incomes policies and concertation by governments. But the disciplinary force governments hoped to secure from currency pegging turned against them when and wherever trade unions refused to respond to the changed circumstances. Only after the tensions became acute did governments return to previously established corporatist practices in order to gain trade union acceptance of non-inflationary wage settlements. Meanwhile, the case of Germany could be used to show that in the strongest economy in Western Europe a reconciliation of low inflation, relatively high growth and a socially just form of labour market regulation was possible. For governments who were battling with inflationary tendencies and stronger pressure from trade unions, it was able to serve as a reference point for economic adjustment.

The German role model started to falter at the moment when its principles were finally accepted by the member states of the European Union in adopting the Maastricht Treaty in 1992 and the Stability Pact in 1997. The high costs of unification, the recession of the early 1990s and the increasing burden of facilitating wage restraint by encouraging early retirement policies took their toll. Frictions within the employers' camp over the future of coordinated wage bargaining had erupted since wage responsiveness had been bought by means of an increasingly expensive social security system (Streeck and Hassel 2003). Thus the role of Germany in disseminating a model of tight monetary policy and responsive wage bargaining had become a problem of adjustment in itself.

The German government reacted to the decreasing responsiveness of German wage bargainers in the same way as the other continental governments during the 1970s and 1980s. When the institutions failed them, they started to negotiate with the unions on further wage restraint. As in the other corporatist countries when governments aimed to modify union expectations, this process was slow and difficult. Unlike many of the other European examples, the negotiations ultimately failed due to structural problems of the social partners involved (Hassel 2003). They also failed because wage restraint could be achieved without negotiations and firms opted for concession bargaining at the company level.

The United Kingdom as the European exception

The British case is the main outlier in the pattern of negotiated adjustment in Western Europe. Despite the fact that the responsiveness of British wage bargaining was the weakest in Europe and the monetary regime did not have a reputation for non-accommodation, British governments after 1979 did not engage in further negotiations, as the theoretical assumptions of this book might lead one to expect. The book has shown that it was *not* just the weakness of British labour market institutions that prevented the government from negotiating further. While incomes policies in the UK were clearly unsuccessful in dealing with the crisis of the 1970s and while negotiations between trade unions and various governments in the 1960s and 1970s were particularly tense, these factors on their own are not sufficient to explain the stark reaction by the Conservative government against further negotiations with the trade unions. An analysis of comparable cases reveals this: Firstly, wage bargaining institutions in Italy were similarly weak during the 1970s (Regini 1984). Secondly, the trade union organizations in Ireland were equally pluralist and fragmented with the Irish industrial relations model being to some extent an expression of the prolonged dominance of British trade unions in Ireland. Thirdly, differences over incomes policies were just as conflictual in the Netherlands and Denmark during the same period. Fourthly, British trade unions were firmly rooted in the political and industrial arena of the British economy. Nevertheless, in all the other cases, governments did not abandon their propensity to negotiate a solution with trade unions. It was only in Britain that the government assumed an entirely uncompromising stance after 1979.

The British case, and with it the role of the UK in the European social model, cannot be understood without reference to the strong majoritarian nature of the political institutions that encouraged and allowed the Conservative government to pursue a vehement policy against the interest and political role of the British trade unions. The exclusionary attitude of British public policy towards the trade unions after 1979 contrasts starkly with all other European countries and is also attributable to political institutions. The key to the British case lies in the combination of the high degree of wage bargaining fragmentation *and* the majoritarian political system, which is based on a two-party system and strong one-party majority government. These features insulate British governments to a far greater extent than any other European government from the lobbying and influence of trade union organizations.

However, since the shift in government policy towards trade union exclusion, British trade unions have defended their position on the labour market and have become more focused on real wage gains than they had been before. As in the case of consensus democracies, the British case also displays mechanisms of reinforcement, in which an exclusion policy is followed by low responsiveness in wage bargaining, which again fosters exclusion. On the whole, the negotiated adjustment of continental Western European economies, on the one hand, versus the market-driven approach by the British government, on the other, has not bridged the gap between the two models. Even though, at the level of monetary policy, convergence has taken place in all countries, at the level of adjustment of labour market and wage bargaining institutions, strong differences remain.

Outlook: Implications for adjustment under EMU

Since the adoption of EMU in 1999, two aspects of the European political economy have changed. Firstly, under the regulations of European Monetary Union, monetary policy has to target the European average inflation rate and cannot be designed for particular countries or regions.[153] Secondly, in contrast to the EMS, there are no longer any conditional factors for membership of EMU since the member states that had signed up for EMU have now joined. National differences in public deficits and debts are controlled by the commitments of national governments to the Stability Pact. Therefore, there is a reasonable expectation that the incentives to cooperate might decrease under EMU. Governments might soften attempts for fiscal consolidation and might exploit the lack of strength of the Stability and Growth Pact. Trade unions, on the other hand, might go for more radical wage claims since their behaviour does not determine a reaction by the European Central bank. The moment for grand encompassing bargains might have passed since the immediate pressure has gone (Hancké and Rhodes 2005: 223).

However, as has been shown in Chapter 4, national monetary policy had already converged during the 1990s. From the early 1990s onwards, national monetary policy was no longer in the position to react to national economic developments, but instead was charged with securing the stability of the EMS. With regard to nominal wage adjustment – an asymmetric shock notwithstanding – the situation has not changed fundamentally, but rather sharpened the focus on nominal wage flexibility for adjustment to economic imbalances.

Therefore, as in the period of the EMS with its fixed exchange rates, the responsiveness of wage bargaining institutions to regional economic developments has remained of major importance. In particular, in the case of asymmetric shocks or regional imbalances, the European Union governments have no economic policy tools available that allow for a regional economic policy approach other than increasing the mobility of labour markets and the flexibility of pay. As a consequence, for governments the importance of wage bargaining responsiveness at the national level in the medium term is likely to persist.

Given this context, one should expect the interaction between governments and wage bargaining institutions to continue in the future. Governments committed to the Stability and Growth Pact are under strong pressure not to employ fiscal policy against economic downturns and therefore the role of wage bargaining will remain on the agenda. This claim is supported by the fact that in all the countries that have used the instrument of social pacts in the run-up to EMU, this instrument was further used after 1999. In the Netherlands, a wage freeze was agreed in 2003, in Denmark a new agreement including a three year pay deal was negotiated in 2003; in Belgium three pacts were signed in 2000, 2002 and 2005. In Finland (2002 and 2005) and Ireland (2003 and 2004) more pacts were signed too.[154] So far there has been no sign of a slackening role of the government in wage bargaining.

But in the euro-zone wage bargaining units are now smaller than the area for which monetary policy is made. While national control over wages might remain, there is no direct low-inflation incentive for each and every government and trade union anymore. Some governments and unions might be tempted to free ride on the low inflation behaviour of others. A remedy for this scenario would be stronger coordination of wage bargaining across countries. However, mechanisms of European wage bargaining coordination are only weakly developed. European wage agreements are not to be expected in the near future (Hassel 2004). How can coordination of wage bargaining under EMU be achieved?

This book has tried to shed some light on the determining factors for wage bargaining responsiveness and the propensity for smooth adjustment. It has claimed that the coordination of wage bargaining can still be regarded as a precondition for responsiveness, but has also pointed out intervening factors that in the past have undermined the responsiveness of otherwise coordinated wage bargaining systems. The degree of factionalism, the protection from international markets and the institutionalized rules on wage formation have had an impact on how wage formation has been able to respond to changing economic conditions. The adjustment process over the last two decades has also shown how governments have attempted to improve the responsiveness of their wage bargaining institutions. In most cases, this has involved a strengthening of coordinating mechanisms and the adoption of new and more flexible guidelines on pay. Compared to how wage bargaining was conducted two decades ago, these measures have brought wage formation closer to the requirements of the market and have introduced a substantial amount of flexibility without generally deregulating wage formation procedures. As the pressures on wage formation as the main adjustment tool continue, there is some evidence that wage bargaining institutions might become more rather than less responsive over time.

There are signs that EMU will contribute to a closer integration of wage bargaining procedures. Some countries have explicitly started to take note of wage developments in other countries. In the Netherlands, wage bargainers have been careful to keep wage increases below the going rates in Germany, which has resulted in complaints about a Dutch beggar-thy-neighbour strategy. In Belgium, the reference to wage bargaining in the neighbouring states (Germany, the Netherlands, France) has even been legislated on by the government. In Sweden, the Edin norm has been based on European pay developments.

If negotiated adjustment helps to sustain the coordination capacity of national wage bargaining systems within Europe, this might give rise to wage bargaining coordination between countries, leading to an informal European pay norm. As in the national wage bargaining systems, which have to accommodate a large number of different sectors with different productivity levels, a European pay norm would serve as a focal point and not determine pay for all. Deviation would be necessary to adjust pay development to nationally specific circumstances. As in national systems, there would be modifications of this at the lower level, reflecting national economic conditions and local labour market conditions. Subnational variety would be likely to continue albeit rooted in the straightjacket of pay guidelines.

Negotiation and coordination have for decades been the instruments for economic adjustment in Europe's political economy. Consensus-oriented political institutions that provide multiple veto points combined with high degrees of union incorporation and centralization contribute to an approach of small steps of rebalancing government policy with self-regulation by the social partners. This should not be interpreted as a sign of weakness and governments following this course should not be blamed for avoiding tough and radical decisions; rather governments' behaviour must be understood in the political and economic context in which they operate. At the same time, adjustment has taken place with regard to both monetary policy and wage setting. For researchers and politicians alike it is of crucial importance to understand the process of negotiated adjustment in general and the interplay between economic and political opportunities and constraints in particular in order to gear up European policy-making for the challenges ahead.

Appendices

Appendix to chapter 3

Bargaining Coordination Index: the index captures the overall level of coordination in national bargaining systems and includes state involvement in private-sector pay setting. Therefore countries with a high degree of government involvement in the form of national tripartite wage agreements tend to be classified as highly coordinated.

Coding: 1 = fragmented and firm-level bargaining; 2 = industry bargaining, no pattern setting; 3 = industry bargaining, pattern setting, only moderate union concentration; 4 = centralized bargaining or government imposition without peace clause or industry bargaining by centralized unions; 5 = centralized bargaining or government imposition with peace clause or extremely high degree of union concentration.

The coding of the index and a fair amount of the data are based on Kenworthy (2001a). Data on Portugal and Spain has been added and some countries have been reclassified. Data has been drawn from the European Industrial Relations Review, various issues, the European Industrial Relations Observatory website (www.eiro-online.ie) and Ferner and Hyman (1998).

Government Intervention Index: 1 = no role of government (govin 1, 2, 3, 4); 2 = government tries to influence (5, 6); 3 = government tries to determine indirectly (threat of intervention, attempts to negotiate pact); 4 = government is part of wage bargain; 5 = government imposes private sector wage (govin 7, 8, 11, 13, 11, 15).

The government intervention index is based on a recoding of the Golden-Lange-Wallerstein index (govin) combined with new information.

Table A1 Government Intervention, 1970-2000

Year	AT	B	DK	FL	FR	G	IR	I	NL	S	UK	P	Sp
1970	2	1	5	4	2	2	3	1	4	2	1		
1971	2	1	5	4	2	2	2	1	5	2	1		
1972	2	1	5	4	2	2	2	1	2	2	1		
1973	2	1	5	2	2	2	2	1	4	2	5		
1974	2	1	5	4	2	2	2	1	5	2	1		
1975	2	1	5	4	2	2	2	1	5	2	5		
1976	2	5	5	4	3	2	2	1	5	2	5		
1977	2	1	5	4	2	1	3	1	2	2	5		
1978	2	1	5	4	2	1	3	1	2	2	5		
1979	2	1	5	4	2	1	3	1	2	2	5		
1980	1	1	5	2	2	1	1	1	3	2	1	4	4
1981	1	5	5	4	2	1	1	1	3	2	1	4	4
1982	1	5	2	4	5	1	1	1	3	2	1	4	4
1983	1	5	2	2	3	1	1	3	2	2	1	4	4
1984	1	5	2	4	3	1	1	3	2	2	1	4	4
1985	1	5	5	4	3	1	1	3	2	4	1	4	4
1986	1	5	5	4	3	1	1	3	2	2	1	4	3
1987	1	1	2	4	3	1	4	3	2	2	1	4	3
1988	1	1	2	2	3	1	4	3	2	2	1	4	3
1989	1	5	2	2	3	1	4	3	2	2	1	4	3
1990	1	5	2	4	3	1	4	3	2	2	1	4	3
1991	1	5	2	4	3	1	4	3	2	3	1	4	3
1992	1	5	2	4	3	1	4	4	2	3	1	4	3
1993	1	3	2	2	3	1	4	4	3	3	1	3	3
1994	1	5	2	2	2	1	4	4	3	3	1	3	1
1995	1	5	2	3	2	1	4	4	2	3	1	3	1
1996	1	5	2	3	2	1	4	4	2	3	1	4	1
1997	1	3	2	3	2	1	4	4	2	3	1	4	3
1998	1	5	3	3	2	1	4	4	2	3	1	4	1
1999	1	5	3	3	2	1	4	4	2	3	1	4	1

Appendix to chapter 5

Table A2 Assignment of governing political parties to the left, centre and right

	Left	Centre	Right
Austria	Sozialistische Partei Österreichs (SPÖ) Kommunistische Partei Österreichs (KPÖ)	Österreichische Volkspartei (ÖVP)	Freiheitliche Partei Österreichs (FPÖ)
Belgium	Belgische Socialistische Partij (BSP, Flemish) Kommunistische Partij van België (KPB) Parti Socialiste Belge (PSB, Francophone)	Christelijke Volkspartij (CVP, Flemish) Parti Social Chrétien (PSC, Francophone) Front Démocratique des Francophones (FDF) Christelijke Vlaamse Volksunie (VU) Democratic Union (DU) Rassemblement Wallon (RW)	Liberal Party (LP) Partij voor Vrijheid en Vooruitgang (PVV, Flemish) Parti de la Liberté et du Progrès (PLP, Francophone) Parti des Réformés et de la Liberté de Wallonie (PRLW) Parti Réformateur Libéral PRL, Francophone) Independent Catholics (ICAT)
Denmark	Social Demokratiet (SD) Left Socialist Party (LSP) Socialistik Folkeparti (SPP, Socialist People's Party) Communist Party (COM)	Centre Democrats (CDM) Christian People's Party (CPP)	Venstre (LIB) Det Konservative Folkeparti (CON) Justice Party (JP) Det Radikale Venstre (RAD
Finland	Suomen Socialdemokraatinen Puola (SDP, Finnish Social Dem Party) Suomen Kansan Demokraattinen Liitto (SKDL, communist) Social Democratic League of Workers and Smallholders (TPSL) Vaemmisto Liitto (VAS, Linksallianz)	Keskustapuolu (KESK, center party) Liberaalinen Kansanpuolue (LKP, Liberal People's Party) Finnish Rural Party (FRP)	Kansallinen Kokoomus (KOK, National Coalition) Svenska Folkepartiet (RKP, SFP)

Table A2	Assignment of governing political parties to the left, centre and right		
France	Parti Socialiste Français (PSF) Parti Communiste Français (PCF)	Centre des Démocrates Sociaux (CDS) Parti Républicain et Radical Socialiste (RSP, Radical Socialist Party) Mouvement Républicain Populaire (MRP) Centre du Progrès et de la Démocratie Moderne (PDM) Union pour la Démocratie Française (UDF) Mouvement Réformateur (REF, Reformer's Movement)	Gaullistes (GAUL) Centre National des Indépendants (IND) Centre Démocratie et Progrès (CDP) Union pour la Nouvelle République (UNR) Rassemblement Pour la République (RPR) Mouvement des Radicaux de Gauche (RAD, MRG).
Germany	Sozialdemokratische Partei Deutschlands (SPD)	Christliche Demokratische Union (CDU) Christliche Soziale Union (CSU)	Deutsche Partei (DP) Freie Demokratische Partei Deutschlands (FDP)
Ireland	Labour Party (LAB) Democratic Left (DL)	Clann na Poblachta (CNP, Republican Party) Fine Gael (FG)	Clann na Talmhan (CNT, The People of the Land) Progressive Democrats (PD) Fianna Fail (FF)
Italy	Partito Socialista Italiano di Unità Proletaria (PSIU) Partito Communista Italiano (PCI) Partito Socialista Italiano (PSI) Partito Socialista Unificato (PSU) Partito Socialista Democratico (PSDI)	Democrazia Cristiana (DC) Partito Repubblicano Italiano (PRI)	Partito Liberale Italiano (PLI)
Nether-lands	Partij van de Arbeid (PvdA, Labour Party) Politieke Partij Radicalen (PPR)	Katholieke Volkspartij (KVP) Christen Democratisch Appel (CDA) Democratische Socialisten'70 (DS'70)	Volkspartij voor Vrijheid en Democratie (VVD) Christelijk Historische Unie (CHU) Anti-Revolutionaire Partij (ARP) Democraten'66 (D'66)

Table A2	Assignment of governing political parties to the left, centre and right		
Portugal	Socialist Party (PSP) Communist Party (PCP)		Popular Democrats, Social Democrats (PPD, PSD) Centre Social Democrats, Popular Party (CDS, PP)
Spain	Socialist Party (PSOE) Communist Party, United Left (PCE/PSUC)	Popular Alliance, Popular Party (AP/PP)	Centre and Unity (CiU)
Sweden	Socialdemokratische Arbetarpartiet (SDA)	Centerpartiet (CP, BF) Kristen Demokratisk Samling (KDS)	Moderata Samlingspartiet (MUP, Moderate Unity Party) Folkepartiet Liberalerna (FP, Liberal Party)
UK	Labour Party (LAB)		Conservative Party (CON)

Source: Armingeon *et al.* 2002.

Appendix to chapter 6

Wage equations are usually estimated when estimating equations for factors that best explain the rise or persistence of unemployment (Bean 1994; Layard *et al.* 1991; McMorrow 1996). In the context of this study, wage equations were used for specifying the choices of wage bargaining actors in particular countries in order to find an indicator for the responsiveness of wage bargaining institutions. The coefficients were used for indicating the orientation of the wage bargaining actors; the best fit of the model was not necessarily required. Nevertheless, due to autocorrelation problems, several models were estimated in order to ensure that the key determinants of the nominal wage growth in the countries were taken into account. Based on existing econometric studies on wage equations (McMorrow 1996; Grubb *et al.* 1983, Layard *et al.* 1991) the following variables were used:

Table A3 Description of the variables used in the regression analysis of nominal wage growth

Variable Name	Description	Source
Dependent Variable		
Nominal wage growth	Annual percentage in nominal compensation per employee, total economy	OECD, Historical Statistics
Independent Variable		
Unemployment	Standardized Unemployment Rate	OECD, Historical Statistics
Change in unemployment	Annual percentage change in the standardized unemployment rate	OECD, Historical Statistics
Productivity growth	Annual percentage change in real GDP	OECD, Historical Statistics
Inflation	Annual percentage change in the consumer price index	OECD, Historical Statistics
Inflation t-1	Annual percentage change in the consumer price index, lagged by one year	OECD, Historical Statistics

Since changes in prices and unemployment have different time spans no overall wage equation generally suits all countries (Flanagan, Soskice *et al.* 1983). The different wage equations show that time lags are important in some countries but not in others. On the whole, however, the degree of responsiveness of wage bargaining in particular countries is not changed by using different models. The model for Finland has satisfying results in the Durbin-Watson test when the lagged inflation rate is included. Germany has better results when the exceptional year of 1992, the first wage round after reunification, is included. Yet on the whole, the size and significance of the coefficients remain stable in different models. Based on these observations, the coefficients were used in the subsequent calculation for a combined index for wage responsiveness as shown in figure 6.1.

Table A4 Wage equations

Austria

	Model 1	Model 2	Model 3	Model 4
Inflation	0.23 (0.23)	-0.12 (0.22)	-0.28 (0.3)	-0.41 (0.26)
Unemployment	-2.58*** (0.44)	-3.24*** (0.41)	-2.58*** (0.4)	-3.16*** (0.39)
Productivity	-0.47** (0.2)	-0.51** (0.19)	-0.47** (0.18)	-0.54*** (0.18)
Change in unemployment	-	2.08*** (0.59)	-	1.78*** (0.58)
Inflation t-1	-	-	0.58** (0.24)	0.41 (0.22)
Adj R2	0.77	0.83	0.81	0.84
Durbin-Watson	2.10	1.43	2.17	1.55

Belgium

	Model 1	Model 2	Model 3	Model 4
Inflation	0.89*** (0.09)	0.85*** (0.11)	0.69*** (0.17)	0.68*** (0.18)
Unemployment	-0.63*** (0.1)	-0.63*** (0.1)	-0.67*** (0.1)	-0.67** (0.11)
Productivity	0.51** (0.2)	0.54** (0.21)	0.48** (0.2)	0.49** (0.21)
Change in unemployment	-	0.19 (0.35)	-	0.09 (0.35)
Inflation t-1	-	-	0.23 (0.16)	0.22 (0.17)
Adj R2	0.91	0.91	0.92	0.91
Durbin-Watson	1.07	1.03	1.04	1.03

Table A4 Wage equations

Denmark

	Model 1	Model 2	Model 3	Model 4
Inflation	0.88*** (0.08)	0.84*** (0.09)	0.67*** (0.17)	0.62*** (0.18)
Unemployment	-0.39*** (0.11)	-0.4*** (0.11)	-0.44*** (0.12)	-0.47*** (0.12)
Productivity	-0.03 (0.04)	0.21 (0.21)	0.07 (0.21)	0.14 (0.21)
Change in Unemployment	-	0.34 (0.24)	-	0.34 (0.24)
Inflation t-1	-	-	0.25 (0.17)	0.25 (0.17)
Adj R2	0.84	0.85	0.85	0.85
Durbin-Watson	1.55	1.77	1.58	1.83

Finland

	Model 1	Model 2	Model 3	Model 4
Inflation	0.93*** (0.17)	0.98*** (0.17)	1.52*** (0.24)	1.5*** (0.25)
Unemployment	-0.37** (0.15)	-0.31 (0.16)	-0.31** (0.13)	-0.3** (0.14)
Productivity	0.16 (0.27)	0.16 (0.27)	0.03 (0.24)	0.04 (0.25)
Change in Unemployment	-	-0.42 (0.29)	-	-0.13 (0.28)
Inflation t-1	-	-	-0.65*** (0.21)	-0.61** (0.23)
Adj R2	0.81	0.82	0.86	0.85
Durbin-Watson	0.93	0.95	1.61	1.58

France

	Model 1	Model 2	Model 3	Model 4
Inflation	0.81*** (0.07)	0.8*** (0.07)	0.66*** (0.12)	0.65*** (0.12)
Unemployment	-0.73*** (0.1)	-0.73*** (0.11)	-0.75*** (0.1)	-0.75*** (0.1)
Productivity	-0.53** (0.23)	-0.51** (0.24)	-0.51** (0.23)	-0.52** (0.24)
Change in Unemployment	-	0.12 (0.36)	-	-0.06 (0.37)
Inflation t-1	-	-	0.16 (0.1)	0.17 (0.11)
Adj R2	0.97	0.97	0.97	0.97
Durbin-Watson	1.97	1.96	1.82	1.82

Table A4 Wage equations

Germany (including 1992)

	Model 1	Model 2	Model 3	Model 4
Inflation	0.48** (0.22)	0.58 (0.34)	0.65 (0.34)	0.68 (0.39)
Unemployment	-0.7*** (0.16)	-0.65*** (0.22)	-0.68*** (0.17)	-0.66*** (0.23)
Productivity	0.04 (0.08)	0.05 (0.08)	0.05 (0.08)	0.06 (0.08)
Change in Unemployment	-	-0.21 (0.57)	-	-0.09 (0.62)
Inflation t-1	-	-	-0.18 (0.27)	-0.16 (0.3)
Adj R2	0.77	0.76	0.77	0.76
Durbin-Watson	1.29	1.27	1.26	1.25

Germany (not including 1992)

	Model 1	Model 2	Model 3	Model 4
Inflation	0.23 (0.16)	0.21 (0.26)	0.04 (0.27)	0.06 (0.17)
Unemployment	-0.88*** (0.12)	-0.89*** (0.17)	-0.91***	0.90*** (0.17)
Productivity	-0.00 (0.06)	0.00 (0.06)	-0.01 (0.06)	-0.01 (0.06)
Change in Unemployment	-	0.05 (0.41)		-0.07 (0.44)
Inflation t-1	-	-	0.18 (0.21)	0.19 (0.23)
Adj R2	0.87	0.87	0.87	0.87
Durbin-Watson	1.00	1.01	1.03	1.02

Ireland

	Model 1	Model 2	Model 3	Model 4
Inflation	0.86*** (0.09)	0.72*** (0.13)	0.87*** (0.2)	0.81*** (0.19)
Unemployment	-0.33** (0.14)	-0.49*** (0.17)	-0.33** (0.15)	-0.49** (0.18)
Productivity	0.25 (0.24)	0.25 (0.23)	0.25 (0.24)	0.27 (0.24)
Change in Unemployment	-	0.71 (0.51)	-	0.85 (0.56)
Inflation t-1	-	-	-0.01 (0.18)	-0.13 (0.19)
Adj R2	0.86	0.86	0.85	0.86
Durbin-Watson	1.67	1.57	1.68	1.61

Table A4 Wage equations

Italy

	Model 1	Model 2	Model 3	Model 4
Inflation	0.82*** (0.09)	0.83*** (0.09)	0.72*** (0.15)	0.65*** (0.16)
Unemployment	-0.98*** (0.22)	-0.97*** (0.22)	-1*** (0.22)	-0.98*** (0.22)
Productivity	0.21 (0.25)	0.24 (0.25)	0.29 (0.26)	0.4 (0.27)
Change in Unemployment	-	-0.48 (0.68)	-	-1.01 (0.76)
Inflation t-1	-	-	0.12 (0.14)	0.22 (0.15)
Adj R2	0.93	0.93	0.93	0.93
Durbin-Watson	1.82	1.83	1.7	1.68

Netherlands

	Model 1	Model 2	Model 3	Model 4
Inflation	1.05*** (0.15)	1.1*** (0.26)	0.84*** (0.28)	0.88** (0.37)
Unemployment	-0.51*** (0.13)	-0.48** (0.18)	-0.55*** (0.14)	-0.53*** (0.18)
Productivity	0.47 (0.26)	0.44 (0.29)	0.44 (0.27)	0.42 (0.29)
Change in Unemployment	-	-0.15 (0.58)	-	-0.12 (0.58)
Inflation t-1	-	-	0.23 (0.25)	0.22 (0.26)
Adj R2	0.86	0.86	0.86	0.86
Durbin-Watson	1.18	1.2	1.09	1.11

Portugal

	Model 1	Model 2	Model 3	Model 4
Inflation	0.86** (0.13)	0.84** (0.14)	0.20 (0.17)	0.20 (0.17)
Unemployment	-1.09 (0.77)	-1.11 (0.78)	-1.66** (0.55)	-1.66** (0.56)
Productivity	-0.18 (0.34)	-0.11 (0.36)	0.14 (0.25)	0.13 (0.26)
Change in Unemployment	-	0.69 (1.39)	-	-0.08 (0.75)
Inflation t-1	-	-	0.81** (0.17)	0.81** (0.18)
Adj R2	0.69	0.68	0.85	0.84
Durbin-Watson	1.27	1.28	1.56	1.56

Table A4 Wage equations

Spain

	Model 1	Model 2	Model 3	Model 4
Inflation	0.72** (0.12)	0.64** (0.12)	0.47* (0.17)	0.48* (0.17)
Unemployment	-0.46** (0.12)	-0.52** (0.12)	-0.47** (0.12)	-0.51** (0.12)
Productivity	0.48 (0.29)	0.17 (0.33)	0.50** (0.27)	0.31 (0.34)
Change in Unemployment	-	0.43 (0.25)	-	0.27 (0.27)
Inflation t-1	-	-	0.26** (0.13)	0.19 (0.15)
Adj R2	0.96	0.96	0.96	0.96
Durbin-Watson	1.51	1.39	1.35	1.28

Sweden

	Model 1	Model 2	Model 3	Model 4
Inflation	0.27 (0.21)	0.32 (0.22)	0.32 (0.24)	0.35 (0.25)
Unemployment	-0.55 (0.27)	-0.48 (0.3)	-0.58 (0.29)	-0.5 (0.33)
Productivity	-0.71 (0.39)	-0.67 (0.4)	-0.68 (0.4)	-0.66 (0.41)
Change in Unemployment	-	-0.35 (0.52)	-	-0.31 (0.56)
Inflation t-1	-	-	-0.09 (0.21)	-0.05 (0.22)
Adj R2	0.61	0.62	0.61	0.59
Durbin-Watson	1.27	1.3	1.32	1.32

UK

	Model 1	Model 2	Model 3	Model 4
Inflation	0.93*** (0.11)	0.89*** (0.13)	1.02*** (0.19)	1.02*** (0.19)
Unemployment	-0.17 (0.2)	-0.21 (0.22)	-0.14 (0.2)	-0.21 (0.22)
Productivity	0.02 (0.31)	-0.03 (0.33)	0.13 (0.36)	0.11 (0.36)
Change in Unemployment	-	0.21 (0.47)	-	0.48 (0.54)
Inflation t-1	-	-	-0.1 (0.16)	-0.18 (0.19)
Adj R2	0.83	0.83	0.83	0.83
Durbin-Watson	2.06	2.02	2.2	2.22

Figure A1 Evolution of wage formation, 13 Western European countries

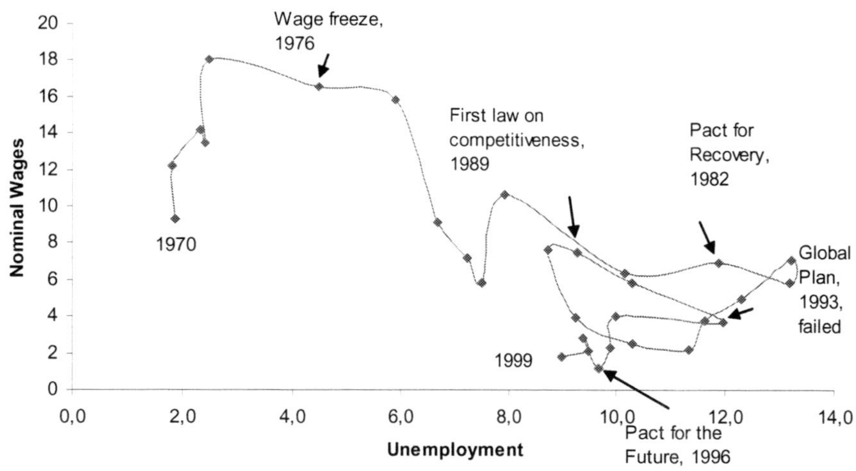

Figure A1 Evolution of wage formation, 13 Western European countries, continued

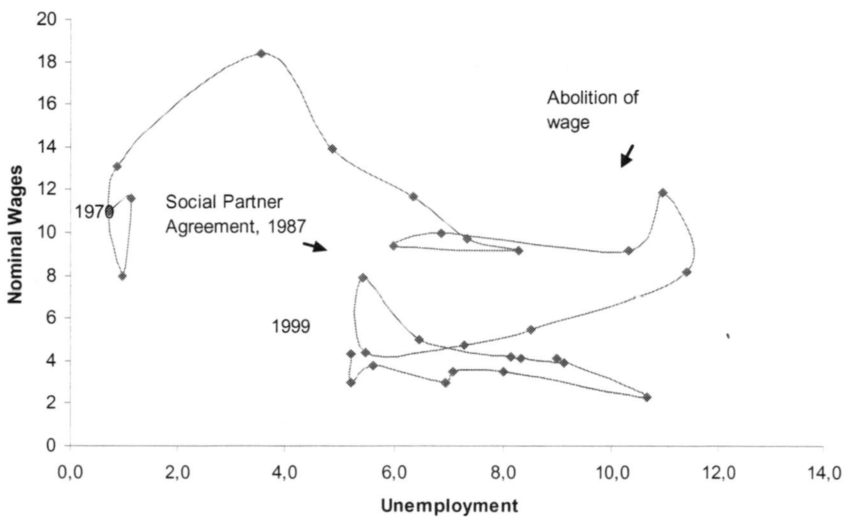

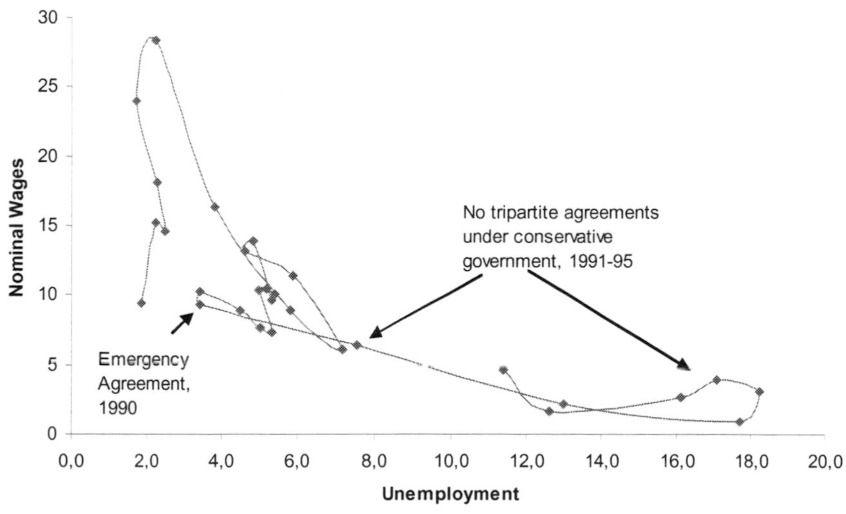

Figure A1 Evolution of wage formation, 13 Western European countries, continued

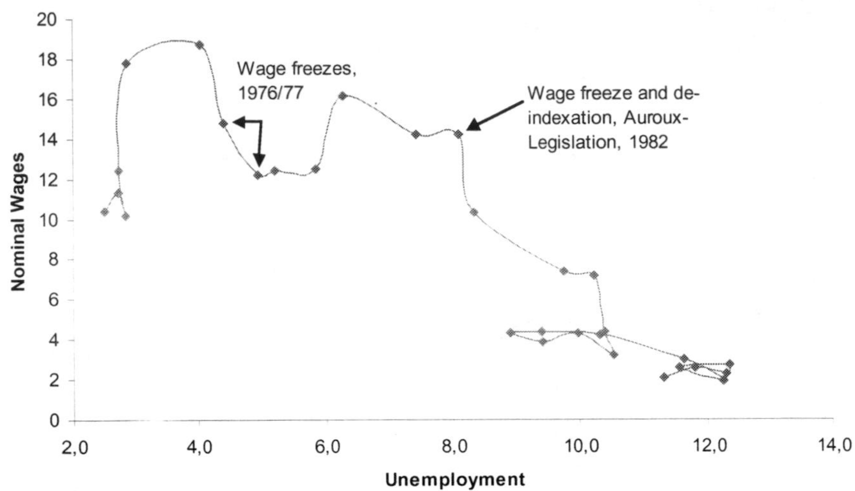

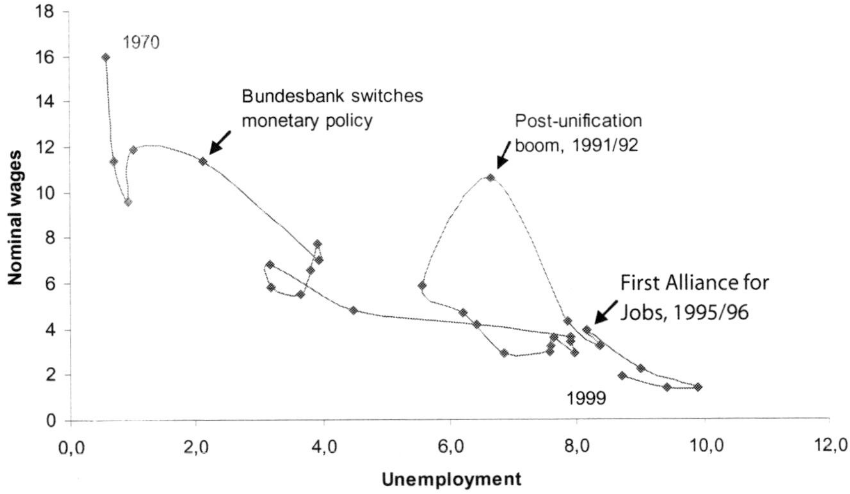

Figure A1 Evolution of wage formation, 13 Western European countries, continued

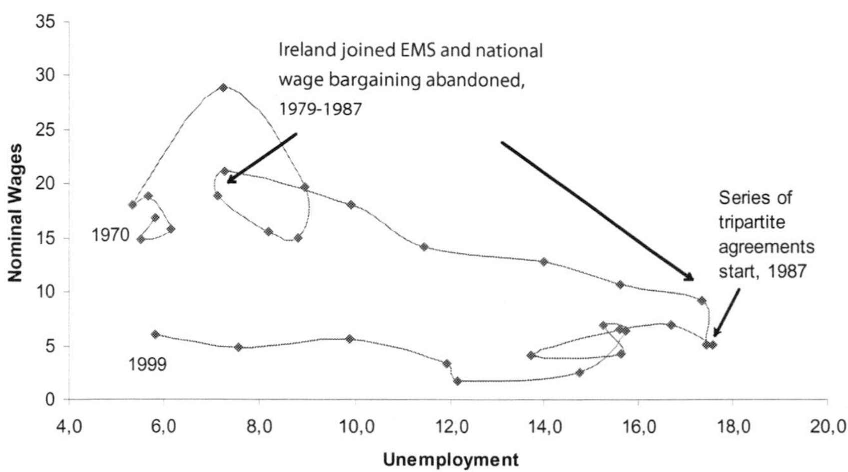

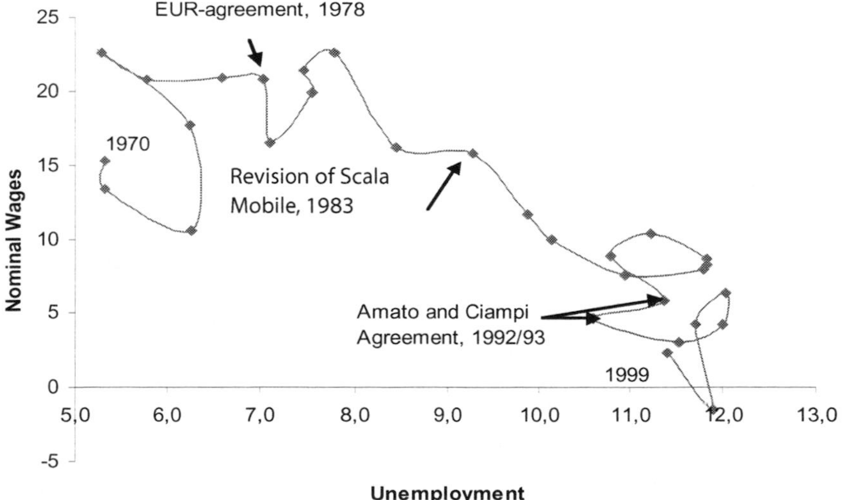

Figure A1 Evolution of wage formation, 13 Western European countries, continued

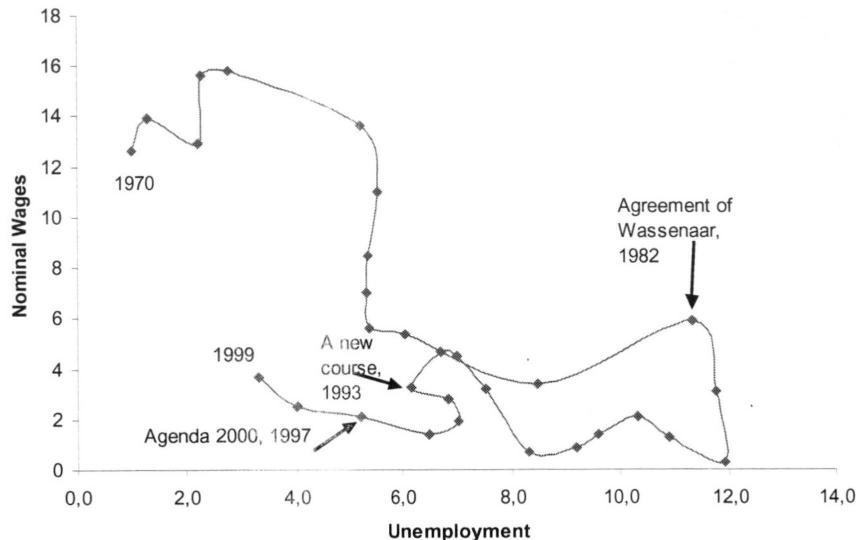

Evolution of wage formation in Portugal, 1970-99

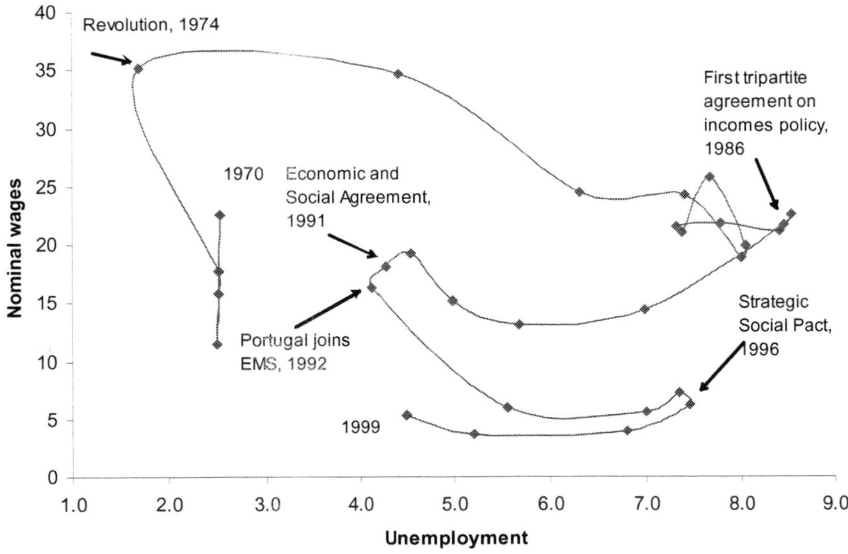

Figure A1 Evolution of wage formation, 13 Western European countries, continued

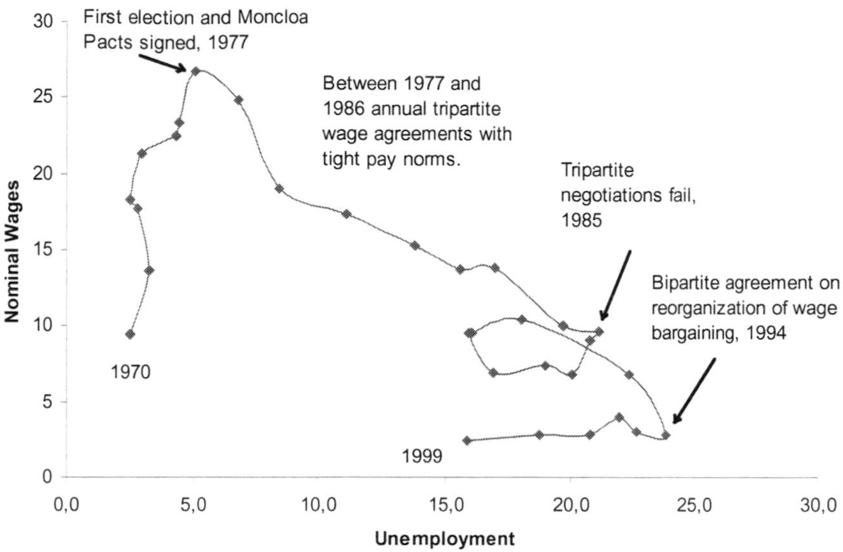

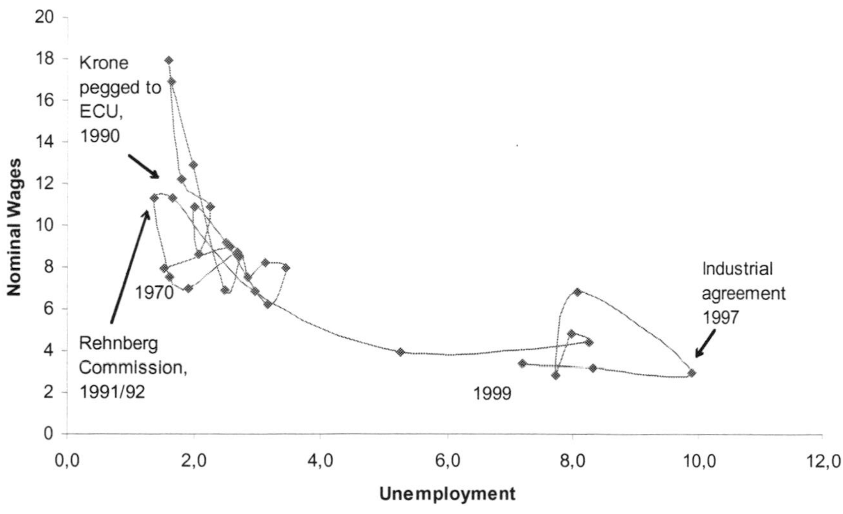

Figure A1 Evolution of wage formation, 13 Western European countries, continued

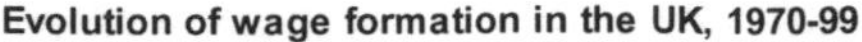

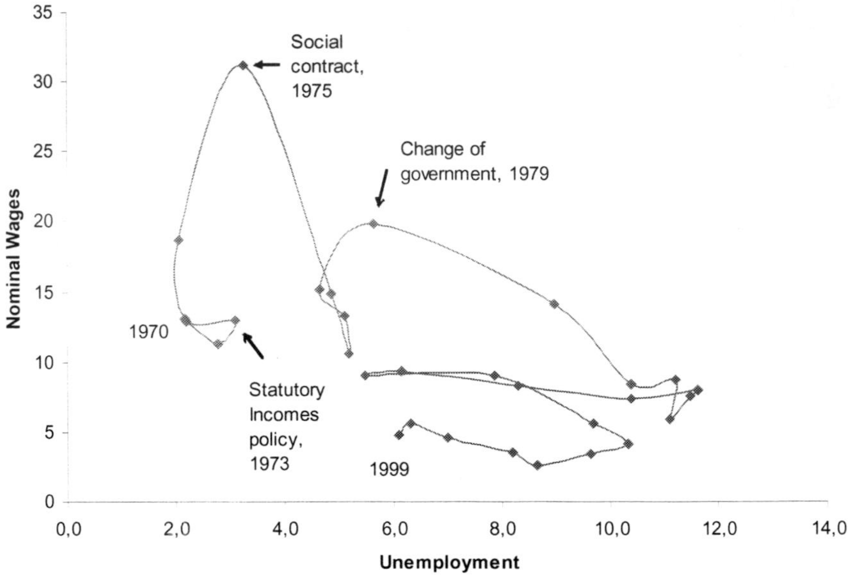

Notes

1 See McNamarra on the convergence of monetary policy (McNamarra 1998).

2 See on debate on EMU, wage bargaining and labour market regulation Calmfors (2001), Crouch (2000), Enderlein (2001), Hancké and Rhodes (2005), Hancké and Soskice (2005) and Soskice and Iversen (1998).

3 In particular Richard Layard (1982 and 1986), Layard *et al.* (1991) and David Soskice, based on Carlin and Soskice (1990), and Flanagan, Soskice *et al.* (1983).

4 On the emergence of new social pacts see Pochet and Fajertag (1997 and 2000), Hassel (2000), Regini (2000), Rhodes (1998 and 2001a), Schmitter and Grote (1997), Traxler (1997) and Visser (1999).

5 See on the evolution of wage bargaining structures in Scandinavia Iversen (1996), OECD (1997a), Wallerstein and Golden (1997), Wallerstein, Golden *et al.* (1997) and Chapter 7.

6 Tripartite concertation also became a major policy-making tool in the post-socialist political systems of Eastern Europe, mainly for reasons of increased legitimacy and policy implementation (Schmitter and Grote 1997).

7 See for an overview of corporatist theory Molina and Rhodes (2002) and Baccaro (2003). For the main contributions to the debate on neo-corporatism see Schmitter (1974 and 1981), Schmitter and Lehmbruch (1979), Berger (1981), Heinze (1981), Lehmbruch (1982), Lehmbruch and Schmitter (1982), Goldthorpe (1984), Streeck (1984), Streeck (2003). For finer distinctions within the neo-corporatist debate see Chapter 3.

8 Interpenetration of public policy and interest groups was to be found in other policy fields such as technical standardization or health policy. But it was the incorporation of trade unions into the political decision-making procedures that dominated the neo-corporatist literature.

9 For instance Nedelmann and Meier (1979), Lehmbruch (1984), Marin (1990 and 1991), Treu (1992), Regini (1997), Compston (2002). Lucio Baccaro has specifically addressed the emergence of concertation in countries that do not have corporatist structures of interest representation (Baccaro 2003). Bac-

caro emphasizes that inter-organizational coordination that is a prerequisite for concertation can take in fragmented organizational systems.

10 See on the notion of political exchange the seminal article by Pizzorno (1978). In later publications, political exchanges and generalized exchanges were developed (Marin 1990; Crouch 1993b and 1995; Streeck and Schmitter 1985).

11 See Chapter 2 for a summary of the political economy literature.

12 Own calculation based on data in table 4 (Armingeon 2001). The data is based on the International Social Survey 'Role of Government' (1996).

13 For studies in comparative political economy that focus on employers and firms see Swenson (1991), Hall and Soskice (2001) and Thelen (2003). A similar claim – that employers did not play an important role in the emergence of concertation – is made by Baccaro (2003: 701) for the cases of Ireland and Italy.

14 This omission might be a serious one. Recent literature on concertation has emphasized the close link between wage bargaining and social policy (Ebbinghaus and Hassel 1999 and 2000; Streeck and Hassel 2003). Moreover, studies on welfare reforms have pointed to the role of unions either as veto players in welfare reform (Pierson 1996; Schludi 2005) or as actors who fill the gap that is left by welfare privatization (Trampusch 2006). Wolfgang Streeck has pointed to welfare provisions as a functional equivalent to Keynesian economic policy (Streeck 2003). Nevertheless, in this book welfare is treated as one – though the most important – of many contextual factors that do not systematically enter the explanation.

15 For instance Siegel (2005), Donaghey and Teague (2005), Rhodes (2001a).

16 In line with for instance Hancké and Rhodes (2005).

17 For most recent contributions on this debate see Flanagan (2003), Traxler, Blaschke *et al.* (2001) and Traxler (2003).

18 Having a mixed approach of quantitative variables combined with case studies has become more popular in recent years. See for instance Iversen (1999), Scharpf and Schmidt (2000) and Enderlein (2001).

19 For instance, the view that governments are responsible for reducing unemployment is strongly shared in the EU member states (33 per cent agree) compared to the OECD countries outside Europe such as Japan, the US, Australia, Canada and New Zealand (16.4 per cent agree). Data from International Social Survey, Armingeon (2001, table 4).

20 On this point in general see Ebbinghaus (1998).

21 One could argue that the crudeness of the data does strictly speaking not allow for comparative means tests or bivariate correlations. However, I used these tools nevertheless, while being aware of the limitation. On the role of aggregate statistical data in the social sciences in general see Widmaier (1997).

22 This applies even to those cases where governments wished to delegate their control to independent monetary authorities such as independent central banks.

23 In the Anglo-Saxon countries, various economists were working on the design of tax-based incomes policies that had automatic tax incentives for wage restraint. See Blackwell and Santomero (1978) and Slitor (1979).

24 For an assessment of incomes policy during that period see Braun (1975), Soskice (1978), Flanagan, Soskice *et al.* (1983).

25 The report adds an interesting footnote when it states: "In this respect, things are very different than they were in, say, 1970, when it was possible to write: '...the fundamental problem is how to get people to exercise the moderation that they would do if they believed that a major recession was possible, without actually having to administer the lesson'" (OECD 1977: 215).

26 There have been many discussions about the short-term Phillips curve. While some economists argued that even in the short run people would adjust their expectations so that no relationship exists between the two (Lucas 1976), the mainstream in macroeconomics now assumes that there is a short-term trade-off, either based on the stickiness of wages and prices or on information asymmetries (Taylor 1997).

27 The political economy literature on the impact of wage bargaining institutions on economic performance is vast. See Flanagan (1999), Calmfors (1993) and Moene, Wallerstein and Hoel (1993) for the most comprehensive reviews of the impact of wage bargaining institutions on economic performance and for references. The most important references are Crouch (1985), Bruno and Sachs (1985), Calmfors and Driffil (1988), Soskice (1990) and more generally Olson (1990), and most recently Iversen (1999), Traxler; Blaschke *et al.* (2001) and Traxler (2003).

28 Iversen argues that industry level bargaining is most effective under restrictive monetary policy (Iversen 1999). See for a good overview of the different arguments Adolph (2004).

29 With the exception of Calmfors (2001) and Calmfors and Johansson (2001), who argued similarly with regard to the effects of EMU. The difference here, however, is that it is not EMU that prompts an incentive to increase coordination, but any disinflationary policy that is based on the credibility of the monetary regime.

30 For an overview of the economic literature on credibility see Cukierman (1998), Alesina and Summers (1993) and Rogoff (1985) and further references in Chapter 4.

31 See Chapter 4 for references to the literature on central bank independence.

32 See references in endnote 28.

33 The exact relationship between wage bargaining institutions and economic performance has been discussed extensively and many modifications can be found in the literature. For the latest assessment see Traxler, Blaschke *et al.* (2001) and Franzese (2001 and 2002). This, however, is not important for the argument presented here as long as one assumes that this approach as a whole is credible. It is only important to point out that different institutional properties are connected to different outcomes on the labour market.

34 Iversen (1999), however, uses a different argument to explain the lack of interaction of highly centralized wage bargaining systems. He argues that the responsive of highly centralized bargaining systems decreases due to the coalitions that highly centralized bargaining units have to engage in between the low paid and the high paid, which then leads to a higher degree of wage compression.

35 For a more formal economic treatment on the issue see Flanagan, Soskice *et al.* (1983). For the case of ERM and EMU see Hancké and Soskice (2003). Hancké and Soskice emphasize that "for governments (as well as unions and employers) the need to meet the Maastricht conditions meant that the coordinated bargaining was a valuable instrument in the development of social pacts" (Hancké and Soskice 2003: 152).

36 The argument in this section can also be found in Hassel (2003).

37 For a comprehensive overview, see Streeck and Kenworthy (2005).

38 Starting from Schmitter (1974) who introduced the role of organizational structures of interest associations for policy-making.

39 The use of the term 'accommodation' is owed to Gosta Esping-Andersen when he discusses the 'institutional accommodation to full employment' (Esping-Andersen 1990, Chapter 7). Esping-Andersen himself accredits it to the contribution originally made by Michael Kalecki, who anticipated the problems a democratic government might face in the pursuit of full employment if there was no institutional support for restraining expectations (Kalecki 1943).

40 In what follows, political and negotiated accommodation will be used synonymously.

41 In the UK, for instance, the attempts to create institutional structures that could accommodate trade union policy were half-hearted. The British unions refused to cooperate with two successive advisory bodies set up by Conservative governments in 1958 and 1962 to take evidence and issue reports on incomes, prices and productivity. In 1961, the TUC after much hesitation agreed to take part in the NEDC – a new consultative organization appointed by the government, with ministers as well as management, unions and independent experts among its members and with a strong staff. The purpose of

the NEDC was to promote economic growth and to elaborate a national plan; it was not, however, expected to concern itself in any detail with incomes policy. See Peter Hall on France and Great Britain (Hall 1986).

42 Incomes policies are all measures by government to restrain wage bargaining behaviour. The price that governments in some situations have to pay for wage restraint is expressed by the notion of political exchange. Obviously, there can be policies without compensation.

43 With the exception of the Golden-Lange-Wallerstein index as discussed below.

44 There have since been yardsticks proposed for ranking the degree of corporatism, which aimed at measuring something similar. For a ranking of consensual incomes policy see Marks (1986). For more descriptive studies see Armingeon (1982 and 1983), Braun (1975), OECD (1980) and United Nations (1967).

45 *Erga omnes* clauses are mechanisms for extending the terms and conditions of collective agreements to areas that are not covered by the agreement. They exist in most EU member states that are covered by this study with the exception of Italy, Sweden and the UK (EIROnline 2002a)

46 In the Golden-Lange-Wallerstein index, the Agreement of Wassenaar was categorized as 15 despite the fact that the government was not a signatory to the agreement.

47 More detailed periodization might mark the end of the 1970s in 1978 with the establishment of the EMS and begin the 1990s in 1991 with the Maastricht Treaty. Since the data should not be overemphasized, but only give a broad account of the attitudes of governments towards the organization of the labour market and the need for adjustment, the periodization in decades is equally acceptable.

48 A similar bargaining authority and coordination index has been developed by Calmfors (2001) that is not based on annual data points, but also covers Ireland, Portugal and Spain. It correlates with the Iversen index with 0.62.

49 For coding and sources see Appendix. For a thorough overview of the different measures see Kenworthy (2001a).

50 Other measures of corporatism, such as the one constructed by Siaroff (1999), which is more time-sensitive, also fail to correlate with the degree of government intervention as measured here.

51 The claim of the beneficial effects of central bank independence as claimed by Alesina and Summers (1993) has been strongly contested. See Forder (2001) for the theoretical criticism; Forder (1998 and 1999) and Mangano (1998) for conceptual criticism. Empirically, negative employment effects have been pointed out by Hall and Franzese (1998), Iversen (1999), Garrett

and Way (2002) and Posen (1998). Central bankers themselves have seriously questioned the assertion that politicians or politically controlled central bankers are more lenient towards inflation than independent central banks. After having served a term as Vice Chairman of the US central bank, the Federal Reserve, Alan Blinder argues that the policy-makers do not try to sacrifice price stability for employment (Blinder 1997). From a different position, but with a similar conclusion, Kathleen McNamara has argued that the spread of central bank independence across the developed and developing world is not due to narrow functional benefits but rather "because delegation has important legitimizing and symbolic properties which render it attractive in times of uncertainty or economic distress. The spread of central bank independence should be seen as a fundamentally social and political phenomenon, rooted in the logic of organizational mimicry and global norms of neo-liberal governance" (McNamara 2002: 48). Similarly, Adolph contests the assumption that central bankers value low inflation (Adolph 2004). Others have acknowledged the empirical relationship between central bank independence and low inflation, but questioned the mechanism of credibility. Posen, for instance, argues that central bank independence might more usefully be seen as a social preference for reacting strongly to inflationary shocks rather than as a credibility mechanism (Posen 1998: 357).

52 See, on the powerful role of economic ideas, the edited volume by Peter A. Hall (1989). On the role of ideas in the evolution of European monetary union see McNamara (1999).

53 See for a further discussion on the issue from a political science perspective and with respect to wage bargaining institutions Iversen (1999), Hall and Franzese (1998) and Franzese (2002).

54 That independent central bankers are more conservative than others is however empirically not the case as has been shown by Adolph (2004).

55 It is for this reason that empirical studies which, in researching the interaction between monetary policy and wage bargaining, focus solely on monetary policy seem to miss the point of the argument. For instance, Traxler, Blaschke *et al.* (2001) employ annual changes in money supply as their indicator of monetary policy. Iversen (1999) uses a combined index of Cukierman's legal independence and the changes in the real exchange rate of the national currency. Both studies are driven by the aim to have time-variant data for monetary conservatism used in cross-sectional time-series analysis.

56 The arguments are based primarily on the literature on optimum currency areas, which has defined criteria for the design of currency areas according to the incidence of economic disturbances across regions (Mundell 1961). Following on from here, many economists have judged the euro-zone to be

unsuitable as a currency area because of low-level factor mobility and labour market rigidities. For a common view see De Grauwe (2000).

57 Monetary union in the Werner report was identified with: (1) total and irreversible convertibility of currencies; (2) elimination of margins of fluctuation in exchange rates; (3) irrevocable fixing of parties; (4) elimination of restrictions on capital movement; and (5) coordination of aggregate demand policies (*The Economist* 1975c).

58 The snake was soon criticized by the All Saints' Day Manifesto, which proposed a European parallel currency held constant by exchange rate adjustments between national currencies and the EPC (Basevi *et al.* in *The Economist* 1975c). This would trigger an automatic and gradual integration as well as stability of the currencies.

59 'The currency chameleon', *The Economist* (1977).

60 On the evolution of the snake see McNamara (1998: 98ff.) and Gros and Thygesen (1992).

61 This was also due to the fact that the snake followed a functionalist logic that was the conventional wisdom about the process of EU integration at the time. It assumed that major political decisions could only be taken through a process of 'incremental decision-making'. The snake was therefore designed to develop and encourage a political climate that would be conducive to monetary unification (Cobham 1989: 207).

62 These efforts are well documented in McNamara (1998).

63 "The French tried to keep the franc in the snake right up to the last moment. When Mr Fourcade arrived at the snake ministers' meeting at 6 pm on Sunday evening, he was clutching a plan for reform of the snake which would allow the franc to stay. He proposed a devaluation of the franc by 3 per cent and an upvaluation of the D-mark by 3 per cent, as well as wider margins of permitted fluctuations and a more effective system of intervention, involving pooling of reserves..." (*The Economist* 1976).

64 'British woes help European unity', *Business Week* (1975).

65 'As Ireland stakes its shirt on EMS, Italy wants shorter odds', *The Economist* (1978b).

66 See for instance the portrait of Otmar Emminger as the new president of the Bundesbank in *Business Week* (1977).

67 A similar observation can be made when looking at inflation differentials over the three decades. Neither the average inflation differential with Germany nor the standard deviation was considerably lower during the 1980s compared with the 1990s.

68 The difference is twofold. Firstly, under fixed but adjustable exchange rates, an adjustment would have been possible in case of an external asymmetric

shock. Even without such a shock, a major adjustment of the exchange rates took place during the EMS crisis 1992. Secondly, monetary policy can still vary from country to country, even if it has to prioritize to diminish inflation differentials. Nevertheless, the principal theoretical implications are the same. See Calmfors (1998).

69 The implications for monetary policy of monetary integration under fixed exchange rates had been discussed under the notion of the Mundell Holy Trinity since the 1960s and were well known in the 1980s (Mundell 1961).

70 This argument follows standard economic discussion on the explanation of unemployment in Europe. In the account of economists, the degree of external shocks and the response of wages to these shocks are the main explanatory variables for unemployment, accounting for about half of the variance in the model proposed by Layard *et al.* (1991). Wage equations are usually estimated by three sets of parameters: the change in prices, the level of unemployment, and a third set that includes all other parameters such as trade union bargaining power, workers militancy, the reservation wage and the like. For an excellent overview of the literature up to the mid-1990s see Bean (1994).

71 Despite the predictions of theories of rational expectations, disinflation by means of tight monetary policies always has negative effects on output and employment. A credible announcement of monetary restrictions has never been good enough to lower inflationary pressures without additional costs (Ball 1988 and 1991).

72 In the economic literature, real wage rigidity (RWR) and the size of an external shock are the two major explanatory factors for the persistence of unemployment, explaining about 50 per cent of the variance of changes in unemployment (Layard *et al.* 1991; more generally, Bean 1994 and Layard 1986).

73 For a critical discussion of the central bank independence measure see Mangano (1998) and Forder (1999).

74 The Grilli *et al.* index does not include Portugal, Finland and Sweden. However, it should also be pointed out that the observed negative relationship between central bank independence and government intervention that will be reported below is weaker with the Grilli, Masciandaro and Tabellini index (using only nine countries) and not significant.

75 Scores for individual countries have been disputed in the literature. The low score for Japan was seen by Iversen not to reflect the monetary policy practice of Japan. Iversen actually ranked Japan higher (Iversen 1999). Also, with regard to Austria, the high score of independence has been criticized since the Austrian social partners are influential in the appointments of the governors (Straumann 2001).

76 Since both measures are not of a metrical scale and the Cukierman index is moreover time-invariant, no further statistical relationships could be reliably assessed.

77 The partial correlation coefficient for annual data changes from -0.28** to -0.27** when controlling for inflation.

78 The same is true when testing for the relationship between government intervention and unemployment. Government intervention is positively correlated with the degree of unemployment. This relationship, however, disappears when central bank independence is controlled for.

79 See for a sophisticated treatment of this very general point Immergut (1992) and Tsebelis (2002).

80 For a comprehensive treatment of different types of democracies see Schmidt (2000) and Lijphart (1999).

81 The most important contributions to the debate from the perspective of historical institutionalism can be found in Steinmo, Thelen and Longstreth (1992), but also Immergut (1992), Tsebelis (2002) and Schmidt (2000).

82 Immergut talks about veto points rather than veto players, since she identifies the mechanisms of blocking a political decision in the combination of political institutions and their locations of actors within these institutions rather than the number or position of specific actors (Immergut 1992). Nevertheless, for the sake of brevity, veto points and veto players are here lumped into one category.

83 Other measures of institutional constraints on governments, such as those compiled by Schmidt (1996), or of constitutional structures, as devised by Huber, Ragin and Stephens (1993), have not been pursued further because these constraint measures were specially designed to explain differences in public policy-making and are therefore not directly relevant to the questions pursued here.

84 Similarly, there has also been the claim that corporatism and consociationalism show affinities. In particular, Gerhard Lehmbruch has claimed: "The European consociationalist democracies all have strong neo-corporatist elements, and the evolution of both is closely related" (Lehmbruch 1992: 210-11). However, as Lane points out, with consensus democracies in general, not all consociationalist countries are corporatist (i.e. Switzerland) and not all corporatist countries are consociational. Nor do the two forms of power sharing have the same roots, because the one developed in response to the regulation of class conflict in the 1930s and the other grew out of ethnic or religious fragmentation in deeply divided societies (Lane 1997: 21).

85 The Lijphart variable on the federalism–unitary dimension is in effect a veto-player dimension (Schmidt 2000). Empirically, the executive dimension and the federalism dimension do not co-vary, but the combination of the two

dimensions presents different groups of democracies in which the degree of federalism (or other constraints in the political system) modifies the executive power axis. In fact, central bank independence is one indicator of the federalism dimension along with federalism *per se*. As was shown in Chapter 4, central bank independence reduces the propensity of governments to intervene in wage bargaining procedures rather than increases it. In the context of government intervention in wage bargaining, both dimensions have clearly opposing effects.

86 A similar argument has been made about the relationship between political institutions and the evolution of coordinated market economies by Hall and Soskice (2001). They argue that "political regimes characterized by coalition governments, multiple veto points, and parties that entrench the power of producer groups may be more conducive to co-specific assets than states that concentrate power in highly autonomous party leaders".

87 Principal component analysis was employed using the average for the number of effective parties, 1980-99, and the share of minimal winning one-party cabinets, 1971-96, as shown in tables 5.1 and 5.2.

88 See 'Why French Communists have refused to join a new Government', *Financial Times* (1984).

89 Redondo resigned his parliamentary seat in January 1988 in an argument over public sector pay (*Financial Times* 1988a).

90 The special powers of government effectively allowed the new centre-right government to introduce by 'decree' a range of measures aimed at reviving the economy without having to submit them for normal parliamentary debate (*Financial Times* 1982a).

91 With the possible exception of a very flexible law on working hours enacted in 1988.

92 For instance, the Schluter government in Denmark of 1982-1988 and the Lubbers government in the Netherlands, both of which were determined not to continue with the conflictual rounds of incomes policies that they inherited from their predecessors.

93 Important contributions are Hibbs (1977) Hicks and Swank (1992) Huber, Ragin *et al.* (1993).

94 There is, however, a short-term effect of partisanship on economic policy, as Alesina has shown using a 'rational partisan model'. Since there is a time lag between a change in policy and a catch-up movement by wage bargainers, left-wing governments can and do try to exploit the short-term trade-off (Alesina and Rosenthal 1995; Alesina *et al.* 1997).

95 'Dutch centre-right coalition agrees austerity programme', *Financial Times* (1982b), 'Wim Kok: Trade unions' uncrowned king', *Financial Times* (1982c).

96 'Budget Sinks Irish Coalition', *Financial Times* (1987a) and 'Economy Responds To Haughey Treatment', *Financial Times* (1987b).

97 Conservative governments might also have had less of a reputation problem when engaging in incomes policy with trade unions (in accordance with the so-called Nixon-goes-to-China phenomenon). After the 1970s had seen highly conflictual episodes of negotiations between social democratic governments and trade unions, the general public might have had severe reservations about further tripartite negotiations between left-wing governments and trade unions.

98 For a very broad literature see Calmfors (1993) Flanagan (1999 and 2003) and Crouch (1978). For empirical tests see Traxler, Blaschke *et al.* (2001) OECD (1994) and Iversen (1999).

99 This term was suggested by David Soskice (1990: 54), who also discussed the role of local pushfulness in counteracting coordination. In the discussion here, the two are taken together.

100 On the economic effects of wage indexation see Braun (1976) Gray (1976 and 1978), Blanchard (1979), Ball (1988), Milesi-Ferretti (1994) and Waller and VanHoose (1992).

101 See Western and Healy (1999 and 2001) for a discussion on the slowdown in real wage growth after the oil crisis.

102 See Appendix for further information on the wage equation.

103 Another factor that could be discussed here is the role of workplace trade union or workers' representation and the legal regulation of wage bargaining at the plant level. Workplace representation of trade unions can either support local wage assertiveness, as has been pointed out by David Soskice (1988), or plant-level representation can have beneficial effects on productivity enhancing measures. As has been pointed out many times with regard to the German model, the interaction between sectoral bargaining and company productivity pacts has contributed to wage restraint at the sectoral level and productivity increases locally, which have allowed for real wage increases (Streeck 1994). The legal regulation of wage bargaining as containing local wage assertiveness has been discussed by Traxler, Blaschke *et al.* (2001).

104 In the literature, the role of dissenting factions between different trade union organizations is frequently incorporated into the measurement of centralization or coordination, through the statement that wage bargaining institutions are less centralized or coordinated where local or sectoral factions are strong (see Crouch 1990, Iversen 1999, Traxler, Blaschke *et al.* 2001, Traxler 2003). This can be misleading, however. For instance, Finnish wage bargaining procedures have always been considered as highly centralized, although they

were influenced by the communist split during the 1960s. Dissenting factions do generally point, therefore, to competitive pressures within the trade unions, even though wage bargaining can be coordinated and comprehensive.

105 One important consequence of the coupling of wage bargaining for the sheltered service sectors is that wage increases in these sectors are frequently above the level of productivity increases in these sectors.

106 Union density rates in the public sector stand at roughly 60 per cent whereas overall union density has declined to less than 30 per cent (Ebbinghaus 2003, 190).

107 On the institutional foundations of Austrian Keynesian economic policy see in detail Katzenstein (1985) Scharpf (1991) Guger and Polt (1994) and Hemerijck, Unger et al (2000a); for more recent developments Pelinka (2002).

108 In 2003, Austria was hit by the first general strike in 50 years over issues of pension reforms. This has however not affected the patterns of wage bargaining (EIRR 2004; EIROnline 2004a).

109 At the same time, the employment crisis of the German welfare state had already been building up since the 1970s. See Manow and Seils (2000).

110 See for a more detailed account of the negotiations between the German government and trade unions over wages and social policy retrenchment Hassel (2001) and Streeck and Trampusch (2005).

111 For an overview on the failed first attempt to create an Alliance for Jobs in 1995/1996 see Bispinck (1997); for a more detailed account of the second Alliance for Jobs after 1998 see Bispinck and Schulten (2000), Hassel (2001), Heinze (2002) and Streeck and Hassel (2003).

112 Concession bargaining became a persistent feature in German industrial relations from the early 1990s onwards (Hassel and Rehder 2001; Rehder 2003; Streeck and Rehder 2005). The concessions by the unions made the call for more far-reaching reforms for business unnecessary.

113 The metal sector trade union had previously rejected early retirement policies and instead favoured a shorter working week for political reasons (Jacobs *et al.* 1991). The union therefore found it much more difficult to lobby for an extension of the existing part-time early retirement scheme.

114 Lorwin even described labour relations in Belgium as "over-institutionalized" (Lorwin 1975: 257).

115 Up until 1991, 49 agreements had been declared binding.

116 The Dutch case has been thoroughly analysed by Jelle Visser and Anton Hemerijck. See in particular Hemerijck (1995), Visser and Hemerijck (1997), Hemerijck and Visser (2000), Hemerijck; Unger *et al.* (2000a), Hemerijck, Van der Meer (2000b), Visser (1990, 1997 and 1998b) and Van den Toren (1997).

117 See on Denmark Elvander (1974), Flanagan, Soskice *et al.* (1983), Scheuer

(1992 and 1997), Boje and Madsen (1994), Due, Madsen *et al.* (1995), Iversen (1999), Benner and Bundgaard-Vad (2000) and Lind (2000).

118 For a detailed account on the negotiations of tripartite pacts in Belgium see Spineux (1990), Hemerijck, Unger *et al.* (2000), Hemerijck and Visser (2000), Vilrox and Leemput (1992: 372 and 1998) and Arcq and Pochet (2000). For general information on labour relations in Belgium see also Molitor (1978), Lorwin (1975) and Hancké (1991).

119 Nowadays, wages and salaries are automatically increased for around 80 per cent of public employees and workers across most sectors once the threshold or 'spill index' is reached. Wages are then automatically increased to keep up with the cost of living. In certain sectors there is an increase at fixed intervals, for example every quarter or every six months (EIROnline 1998).

120 Following the evaluation, CNT/NAR and CCE/CRB concluded that the "auspicious climate in which the execution of the intersectoral agreement and the conclusion of sectoral agreements took off was a major contribution to the achievement of social peace, and by that very fact, to stability at the level of sectors (...) The agreement appears to be making good progress in terms of concretization; consequently, and on the basis of currently available information, this first evaluation is positive" (Evaluation of trends in labour costs, employment and training efforts, Central Economic Council and National Labour Council, joint session, 20 September 1999). See EIROnline (1999).

121 An example of this dynamic can be seen in the discussion between the social partners on the issue of pay. For instance, Pieter Timmermans, director-general of the Federation of Belgian Enterprises (FEB/VBO), said in interviews in the run-up to the new central talks in 2002 that if the current 'pay norm', setting the limit for wage increases, were to be abolished, automatic pay indexation would have to be abolished as well: "If you break through the pay ceiling, why leave the floor as it is?" (EIROnline 2002b).

122 On 8 March 1997, eight unions and employers set up new procedure modelled on coordination of Metall, SIF und CF. They proposed mechanisms for elaborating a joint view and following new procedures (Martin 2000). See also Jochem (2003).

123 See National Mediation Office (2001). 'Mission Statement of the Medlingsinstitutet – A Short Presentation of a New Swedish Agency', Schulten (2002).

124 Elvander (2002a and 2002b), Sheldon and Thornthwaite (1999).

125 See on Finland Arter (1987), Lilja (1992), Kauppinen (1994) and (2000) and Pochet (1999b).

126 The militant communist trade unions were supported by the Soviet ambassador, who was asked to leave by the Finnish president in 1971 (Kauppinen 1994: 69).

127 Sectoral agreements were concluded in 1973, 1980, 1983, 1989, 1994 and 1995 (Kauppinen 2000: 176).

128 See also on the French case Reynaud (1975), Hege (1999) and Levy (2000).

129 There have been further attempts to reform collective bargaining recently. In April 2004, the French parliament passed a law that aimed to strengthen bargaining by requiring that agreements must have the support of the majority of either employees or unions in the firm and that company agreements can depart from sectoral agreements (EIROnline 2004b).

130 See on the United Kingdom Scharpf (1991), Hall (1986), Flanagan, Soskice *et al.* (1983), Clegg (1979), Edwards *et al.* (1992 and 1998), Crouch (1978 and 1993a).

131 Between 1975 and 1979, real wages in the United Kingdom grew by 1.4 per cent annually, compared to 2.8 on average in the other Western European countries. This figure was only matched by Denmark where real wages grew by 0.7 percent.

132 See on Italy Regini (1984), Lange and Regini (1989), Locke (1995), Ferner and Hyman (1992b), Regalia and Regini (1998 and 2004), Baccaro (2000 and 2002), Ferrera and Gualmini (2000a and b).

133 For each percentage point increase in the rate of inflation, all wages were to be increased by a flat rate (*punto unico di contigenza*) (Ferrara and Gualmini 2000b).

134 The Craxi government won the referendum with a majority of 54.3 per cent. The result was also seen as a success for the Government in general since it meant "the defeat of the unspoken veto that the Communist Party has always exercised over economic measures affecting the working class" (Financial Times 1985).

135 For details of the negotiation process behind the agreement see Regalia and Regini (2004) and Baccaro (2000).

136 These were followed by further pacts in 1996 (Pact for Employment) and 1998 (Social Pact for Development). These, however, were no longer focused on the issue of wage formation. The fundamental restructuring in pay bargaining took place in 1993.

137 The instrument of tripartite agreements has therefore persisted. In February 2000 another agreement was negotiated though not signed by the CGIL, while a similar agreement was signed by all three main trade unions, a range of employers' associations and regional authorities in May 2002 (EIRR 2002b).

138 See on the Irish case Browne (1965), Hardiman (1988 and 2002), von Prondzynski (1992 and 1998), Aust (1999), Visser (1998a), O'Donnell and O'Reardon (1997 and 2000).

139 The Employer-Labour Conference had 42 members, 21 from each side. It also had a steering committee with five members from each side (Hardiman 1988: 51).

140 The National Understanding also failed because the government was no longer able to deliver on its promises in exchange for wage restraint (von Prondzynski 1992: 80).

141 'A Strategy for Development 1986-1990' (NESC 1986).

142 Therefore, the course of government sponsored wage settlements has been upheld. Until the end of 2005, another two agreements were successfully negotiated, again including pay agreements and other labour market regulations (EIRR 2003a).

143 In contrast to the Portuguese case, tripartism in Spain is very well documented in the literature. For an overview see Hamann (1998 and 2001), Hamann and Lucio (2003), Royo (2000, and 2002a and b), Perez (2000a and b). For Spanish industrial relations in general see Lucio (1992 and 1998). On the transition to democracy see Heywood (1996) and Van der Meer (1996).

144 'Signs of wear and tear in Spanish Socialist Party clothes, *Financial Times* (1988b).

145 In the national election in 1993, the PSOE had lost its majority and formed an alliance with the centre-right Catalan nationalist Party. The Catalan party insisted on the devolution of bargaining to the regional level.

146 Information on Portugal is considerably rarer than on any other Western European country. Good descriptions on concertation in Portugal are provided by Royo (2002a and b), Barreto (1992), Barreto and Naumann (1998), Pinto (1990). On Portuguese trade unions see Stoleroff (1992) and Stoleroff and Naumann (1994), on collective bargaining see Menezes Leitào (2001).

147 The late Caetano regime granted trade unions some limited bargaining rights. Collective bargaining in the early 1970s, although compulsory, was ineffective (Barreto and Naumann 1998).

148 'Portuguese Unions Protest at Reforms', *Financial Times* (1988c); see also Royo (2002b: 86).

149 The CGTP, however, remained part of the bargaining set-up and has since signed two sub-agreements on safety at work and training (Royo 2002b, 86).

150 'Public Sector Deal in Portugal', *Financial Times* (1996).

151 Differences of the role of concertation and government-trade union interaction in Western and Eastern Europe can be primarily explained by the different role of trade unions in the political economies in Eastern Europe. Union weakness leads to an instrumental and strategic use of union support by governments for reasons for legitimacy with largely meaningless processes of concertation (Hassel 2005; Ost 2000).

152 'Europe's painful inflation exorcism', *The Economist* (1975b).

153 On the challenges of EMU to national economic policy-making see Soskice and Iversen (1998), Calmfors (2001), Calmfors and Johansson (2001), Crouch (2000) and Enderlein (2001).

154 See for further information on recent developments on the Netherlands EIRR (2003b), Donaghey and Teague (2005: 489), EIRR (2005), on Denmark Donaghey and Teague (2005: 481), on Belgium Donaghey and Teagaue (2005: 483), EIRR (2001b and 2003c), on Finland EIRR (2003d) and on Ireland EIRR (2003a). On social pacts in the post-Euro period see Donaghey and Teague (2005).

Bibliography

Adolph, Christopher Alan (2004). *The Dilemma of Discretion: Career Ambitions and the Politics of Central Banking*. Cambridge, PhD Thesis, Department of Government, Harvard University.

Alesina, Alberto and Howard Rosenthal (1995). *Partisan Politics, Divided Government, and the Economy*. Cambridge, Cambridge University Press.

Alesina, Alberto, Roubini, Nouriel and Cohen, Gerald D. (1997). *Political Cycles and the Macroeconomy*. Cambridge, MIT Press.

Alesina, Alberto and Lawrence H. Summers (1993). "Central Bank Independence and Macroeconomic Performance." *Journal of Money, Credit and Banking* 25 (2): 151-163.

Alogoskoufis, George S. (1994). "On Inflation, Unemployment, and the Optimal Exchange Rate Regime." Van Der Ploeg, F. ed. *Handbook of International Macroeconomics*. Oxford and Cambridge, Blackwell: 192-223.

Alogoskoufis, George S. and Manning, Alan (1988). "On the Persistence of Unemployment." *Economic Policy* 7: 427-469.

Alogoskoufis, George S. and Ron Smith (1991). "The Phillips Curve, the Persistence of Inflation, and the Lucas Critique: Evidence from Exchange Rate Regimes." *The American Economic Review* 81 (5): 1254-1275.

Alvarez, R. Michael, Geoffrey Garrett, *et al.* (1991). "Government Partisanship, Labor Organization, and Macroeconomic Performance." *American Political Science Review* 85 (2): 539-556.

Anderson, Liam (2001). "The Implications of Institutional Design for Macroeconomic Performance. Reassessing the Claims of Consensus Democracy." *Comparative Political Studies* 34 (4): 429-452.

Andrews, David M. (1994). "Capital Mobility and Monetary Adjustment in Western Europe, 1973-1991." *Policy Sciences* 27: 425-445.

Arcq, Etienne and Philippe Pochet (2000). "Toward a new social pact in Belgium?" G. Fajertag and P. Pochet eds. *Social Pacts in Europe – New Dynamics*. Brussels, ETUI: 113-134.

Armingeon, Klaus (1982). "Determining the Level of Wages: the Role of Parties and Trade Unions." F.G. Castles ed. *The Impact of Parties: Politics and Policies in Democratic Capitalist States.* London, Beverley Hills, Sage Publications: 225-282.

Armingeon, Klaus (1983). *Neo-korporatistische Einkommenspolitik.* Frankfurt, Haag + Herchen Verlag.

Armingeon, Klaus (2001): "Institutionalising the Swiss Welfare State." J.-E. Lane ed. *The Swiss Labyrinth. Institutions, Outcomes and Redesign* Special Issue West European Politics, Vol. 24, April London, Frank Cass: 145-168.

Armingeon, Klaus (2002a). "Interest Intermediation: The Cases of Consociational Democracy and Corporatism." H. Keman ed. *Comparative Democratic Politics.* London, Sage: 143-165.

Armingeon, Klaus (2002b). "The Effects of Negotiation Democracy: A Comparative Analysis." *European Journal of Political Research* 41: 81-105.

Armingeon, Klaus (2003). "OECD and National Welfare State Development." K. Armingeon and M. Beyeler eds. *The OECD and National Welfare States, 1970-2000.* London, Edward Elgar, forthcoming.

Armingeon, Klaus, Michelle Beyeler, *et al.* (2002). *Comparative Political Data Set 1960-2001.* Berne, Institute of Political Science, University of Berne.

Armingeon, Klaus and Michelle Beyeler eds. (2003). *The OECD and National Welfare States, 1970-2000.* London, Edward Elgar.

Arter, David (1987). *Politics and Policy-Making in Finland.* Brighton, Wheatsheaf.

Aust, Andreas (1999). "The 'Celtic Tiger' and its beneficiaries. 'Competitive corporatism' in Ireland." Paper presented at the *ECPR Joint Sessions of Workshops* in Mannheim, March 26-31, 1999.

Baccaro, Lucio (2000). "Centralized collective bargaining and the problem of 'compliance' – Lessons from the Italian experience." *Industrial and Labor Relations Review* 53 (4): 579-601.

Baccaro, Lucio (2002). "The Construction of 'Democratic' Corporatism in Italy." *Politics and Society* 30 (2): 327-357.

Baccaro, Lucio (2003). "What is Alive and What is Dead in the Theory of Corporatims." *British Journal of Industrial Relations* 41 (1) December: 683-706.

Ball, Laurence (1988). "Is Equilibrium Indexation Efficient?" *The Quarterly Journal of Economics*: 299-311.

Ball, Laurence (1991). "The Genesis of Inflation and the Costs of Disinflation." *Journal of Money, Credit and Banking* 23 (3): 439-452.

Barbash, Jack (1972). *Trade Unions and National Economic Policy.* Baltimore, London, The Johns Hopkins Press.

Barreto, José (1992). "Portugal: Industrial Relations under Democracy." A. Ferner and R. Hyman eds. *Industrial Relations in the New Europe.* Oxford, Blackwell Business: 445-481.

Barreto, José and Reinhard Naumann (1998). "Portugal: Industrial Relations under Democracy." A. Ferner and R. Hyman eds. *Changing Industrial Relations in Europe*. Oxford, Blackwell: 395-425.

Bayoumi, Tamim and Barry Eichengreen (1993). "Shocking Aspects of European Monetary Integration." F. Torres and G. Francesco eds. *Adjustment and Growth in the European Monetary Union*. Oxford, New York, Melbourne, Cambridge University Press: 193-229.

Bean, Charles R. (1994). "European Unemployment: A Survey." *Journal of Economic Literature* 32 (2): 573-619.

Benner, Mats and Torben Bundgaard-Vad (2000). "Sweden and Denmark – Defending the Welfare State." F.W. Scharpf and V.A. Schmidt eds. *Welfare and Work in the Open Economy. Volume II*. Oxford, Oxford University Press: 399-466.

Berger, Suzanne ed. (1981). *Organizing Interests in Western Europe: Pluralism, Corporatism and the Transformation of Politics*. Cambridge, Cambridge University Press

Birchfield, Vicki. and Markus M. L. Crepaz (1998). "The impact of constitutional structures and collective and competitive veto points on income inequality in industrialized democracies." *European Journal of Political Research* 34 (2): 175-200.

Bispinck, Reinhard (1997). "The chequered history of the Alliance for Jobs." G. Fajertag and P. Pochet eds. *Social Pacts in Europe*. Brussels, ETUI: 63-78.

Bispinck, Reinhard and Thorsten Schulten (2000). "Alliance for Jobs – is Germany following the path of competitive corporatism?" G. Fajertag and P. Pochet eds. *Social Pacts in Europe – New Dynamics*. Brussels, OSE-ETUI: 187-218.

Blackwell, Norman R. and Anthony M. Santomero (1978). "Incomes Policy and Tax Rates – an Innovative Policy Attempt in the United Kingdom." *Economica*, 45 (178): 153-164.

Blanchard, Olivier Jean (1979). "Wage Indexing Rules and the Behavior of the Economy." *Journal of Political Economy* 87 (4): 798-815.

Blinder, Alan (1997). "What central bankers can learn from academics – and vice versa." *Journal of Economic Perspectives* 11: 3-19.

Boje, Thomas P. and Per Kongshoj Madsen (1994). "Wage Formation and Incomes Policy in Denmark in the 1980s." R. Dore, R. Boyer and Z. Mars eds. *The Return to Incomes Policy*. London and New York, Pinter: 94-117.

Braun, Anne Romanis (1975). "The Role of Incomes Policy in Industrial Countries since World War II." *IMF Staff Papers* 23 (1): 1-36.

Braun, Anne Romanis (1976). "Indexation of Wages and Salaries in Developed Economies." IMF *Staff Papers* 23 (2): 226-271.

Brittan, Samuel (1970). *Steering the Economy*. Harmondsworth, Penguin.

Browne, M.H. (1965). "Industrial labour and incomes policy in the Republic of Ireland." *British Journal of Industrial Relations* 3 (1): 46-66.

Bruno, Michael and Jeffrey D. Sachs (1985). *Economics of Worldwide Stagflation.* Cambridge, Harvard University Press.

Business Week (1975). "British Woes Help European Unity." *Business Week* 26 May 1975.

Business Week (1977). "A hard-liner takes over at the Bundesbank." *Business Week* 20 June. 1977.

Calmfors, Lars ed. (1990). *Wage Formation and Macro-Economic Policy in the Nordic Countries.* Oxford, Oxford University Press.

Calmfors, Lars (1993). "Centralisation of Wage Bargaining and Macroeconomic Performance – A Survey." OECD *Economic Studies* 21 (Winter): 161-191.

Calmfors, Lars (1998). "Macroeconomic Policy, Wage Setting, and Employment – What Difference does the EMU make?" *Oxford Review of Economic Policy* 14 (3): 125-151.

Calmfors, Lars (2001). "Wages and Wage-Bargaining Institutions in the EMU – A Survey of the Issues." *Empirica* 28: 325-351.

Calmfors, Lars, Alison Booth, *et al.* (2001). "The Future of Collective Bargaining in Europe." T. Boeri, A. Brugiavini and L. Calmfors eds. *The Role of Unions in the Twenty-First Century.* Oxford, Oxford University Press: 1-134.

Calmfors, Lars and J. Driffil (1988). "Bargaining Structure, Corporatism and Macroeconomic Performance." *Economic Policy* (6): 14-47.

Calmfors, Lars and Asa Johansson (2001). *Nominal Wage Flexibility, Wage Indexation and Monetary Union.* Stockholm, Institute for International Economic Studies, unpublished manuscript.

Cameron, David R. (1984). "Social Democracy, Corporatism, Labour Quiescence, and the Representation of Economic Interest in Advanced Capitalist Society." J.H. Goldthorpe ed. *Order and Conflict in Contemporary Capitalism.* Oxford, Oxford University Press: 143-178.

Carlin, Wendy and David Soskice (1990). *Macroeconomics and the Wage Bargain. A Modern Approach to Employment, Inflation, and the Exchange Rate.* Oxford, Oxford University Press.

Clegg, Hugh A. (1979). *The Changing System of Industrial Relations.* Oxford, Blackwell.

Cobham, David (1989). "Strategies for Monetary Integration Revisited." *Journal of Common Market Studies* 27 (3): 203-218.

Compston, Hugh (2002). "The strange persistence of policy concertation." S. Berger and H. Compston eds. *Policy Concertation and Social Partnership in Western Europe.* New York and Oxford: Berghahn: 1-16.

Corden, Max W. (1972). *Monetary Integration.* Princeton, New York, Princeton University Press.

Corricelli, Fabrizio, Alex Cukierman, *et al.* (2000). *Monetary Institutions, Monopolistic Competition, Unionized Labor Markets and Economic Performance.* University of Sienna, unpublished manuscript.

Crouch, Colin (1978). "The Intensification of Industrial Conflict in the United Kingdom." C. Crouch and A. Pizzorno eds. *The Resurgence of Class Conflict in Western Europe since 1968.* 191-256.

Crouch, Colin (1985). "Conditions for Trade-Union Wage Restraint." L.N. Lindberg and C.S. Maier eds. *The Politics of Inflation and Economic Stagnation.* Washington DC, Brookings Institutions.

Crouch, Colin (1990). "Trade Unions in the Exposed Sector: Their Influence on Neo-Corporatist Behaviour." R. Brunetta and C. Dell'Aringa eds. *Labour Relations and Economic Performance. Proceedings of a conference held by the International Economic Association in Venice, Italy.* London, Macmillan: 68-91.

Crouch, Colin (1993a). "United Kingdom: The Refection of Compromise." G. Baglioni and C. Crouch eds. *European Industrial Relations. The Challenge of Flexibility.* London, Sage Publications: 326-355.

Crouch, Colin (1993b). *Industrial Relations and European State Traditions.* Oxford, Clarendon Press.

Crouch, Colin (1995). "Reconstructing Corporatism? Organized Decentralization and Other Paradoxes." C. Crouch and F. Traxler eds. *Organized Industrial Relations. What Future?* Aldershot and Brookfield, Ashgate Publishing: 311-330.

Crouch, Colin (2000). "National Wage Determination and European Monetary Union." C. Crouch ed. *After the Euro. Shaping Institutions for Governance in the Wake of European Monetary Union.* Oxford, Oxford University Press, 203-226.

Cukierman, Alex (1998). *Central Bank Strategy, Credibility, and Independence. Theory and Evidence.* Cambridge, MIT Press.

Cukierman, Alex and Francesco Lippi (1999). "Central Bank Independence, Centralization of Wage Bargaining, Inflation and Unemployment: Theory and some Evidence." *European Economic Review* 43 (7): 1395-1434.

Currie, David (1991). "European Monetary Union: institutional structure and economic performance." *Economic Journal* 102 (411): 248.

Cusack, Thomas R. (1995). "Politics and Macroeconomic Performance in the OECD countries" *WZB Discussion Paper* FS I: 95-315.

Dancet, Guy (1988). "Wage Regulation and Complexity: The Belgian Experience." R. Boyer ed. *The Search for Labour Market Flexibility.* Oxford, Clarendon Press: 212-237.

De Grauwe, Paul and Wim Vanhaverbeke (1990). "Exchange Rate Experience of Small EMS Countries: Belgium, Denmark and the Netherlands." V. Argy and P. De Grauwe eds. *Choosing an Exchange Rate Regime: The Challenge for Smaller Industrial Countries.* Washington, International Monetary Fund.

De Grauwe, Paul (2000). "Monetary Policies in the Presence of Asymmetries." *Journal of Common Market Studies* 38 (4): 593-612.

De Wolff, P. (1965). "The OECD-Contribution to the Development of Incomes Policy as an Economic-Policy Instrument of Central Governments." E. Schneider ed. *Probleme der Einkommenspolitik. Vorträge auf der Round-Table-Konferenz des Instituts für Weltwirtschaft an der Universität Kiel vom 17.-19. Mai 1965.* Tübingen, J.C.B. Mohr (Paul Siebeck): 191-215.

Deutsche Bundesbank (1998). *Monatsbericht.* Frankfurt: 1.

Donaghey, Jimmy and Paul Teague (2005). "The persistence of social pacts in Europe." *Industrial Relations Journal* 36 (6): 478-493.

Due, Jesper, Jorgen Steen Madsen, *et al.* (1995). "Adjusting the Danish Model: Towards Centralized Decentralization." C. Crouch and F. Traxler eds. *Organized Industrial Relations. What Future?* Aldershot and Brookfield, Ashgate Publishing: 121-150.

Ebbinghaus, Bernhard (1993). *Labour Unity in Union Diversity. Trade Unions and Social Cleavages in Western Europe, 1890-1989.* Phd Dissertation Florence, European University Institute.

Ebbinghaus, Bernhard (1998). "Europe Through the Looking-Glass: Comparative and Multi-Level Perspectives." *Acta Sociologica* 41 (4): 301-313.

Ebbinghaus, Bernhard (2003). "Die Mitgliederentwicklung deutscher Gewerkschaften im historischen und internationalen Vergleich." Wolfgang Schroeder and Bernhard Weßels eds. *Die Gewerkschaften in Politik und Gesellschaft der Bundesrepublik Deutschland.* Opladen: Westdeutscher Verlag: 174-203.

Ebbinghaus, Bernhard and Anke Hassel (1999). "The role of tripartite concertation in the reform of the welfare state." *Transfer* 1-2: 64-81.

Ebbinghaus, Bernhard and Anke Hassel (2000). "Striking Deals – Concertation in the Reform of the Continental European Welfare States." *Journal of European Public Policy* 7 (1): 44-62.

Ebbinghaus, Bernhard and Jelle Visser (1999). "When Institutions Matter – Union Growth and Decline in Western Europe, 1950-1995." *European Sociological Review* 15 (2): 135-158.

Ebbinghaus, Bernhard and Jelle Visser (2000). *Trade Unions in Western Europe Since 1945.* London, Macmillan.

Economist (1975a). "Some Rabbit." *The Economist* London. 22 March 1975.

Economist (1975b). "Europe's Painful Inflation Exorcism." *The Economist* London. 10 May 1975.

Economist (1975c). "The All Saints' Day Manifesto for European Monetary Union." London. *The Economist* 01 November 1975.

Economist (1976). "Italy; Communist Jitters." *The Economist* London. 20 March 1976.

Economist (1977). "The Currency Chameleon." *The Economist* London. 09 April 1977.

Economist (1978a). "Europe's Incomes Policies." *The Economist* London. 11 February 1978.

Economist (1978b). "As Ireland Stakes its Shirt on EMS, Italy Wants Shorter Odds." *The Economist* London. 04 November 1978.

Edwards, Paul, Mark Hall, *et al.* (1992). "Great Britain – Still Muddling Through." A. Ferner and R. Hyman eds. *Industrial Relations in the New Europe.* Oxford, Blackwell: 1-69.

Edwards, Paul, Mark Hall, *et al.* (1998). "Great Britain: From Partial Collectivism to Neo-liberalism to Where?" A. Ferner and R. Hyman eds. *Changing Industrial Relations in Europe: Traditions and Transitions.* Oxford, Blackwell: 315-347.

EIROnline (1998). "Belgium: Belgium revises its consumer prices index." *EIROnline* 22 February 98.

EIROnline (1999). "Belgium: The 1999-2000 Intersectoral Agreement, One Year on." *EIROnline* 28 December 99.

EIROnline (2002a). "Collective bargaining coverage and extension procedures." *EIROnline* 18 December 02

EIROnline (2002b). "Belgium: Debate resurfaces on automatic pay indexation." *EIROnline* 13 August 02.

EIROnline (2002c). "Belgium: Central talks get off to difficult start." *EIROnline* 11 September 02.

EIROnline (2004a). "2004 Annual Review for Austria." *EIROnline* 20 January 05.

EIROnline (2004b). "Collective bargaining reform law passed." *EIROnline* 10 April 04.

EIRR (1990). "New Industrial Relations Bill." *European Industrial Relations Review* 192: 6-7.

EIRR (1992). "Collective bargaining in 1991." *European Industrial Relations Review* 227: 20-24.

EIRR (1994a). "Change at DA and LO." *European Industrial Relations Review* 242: 4-5.

EIRR (1994b). "Central agreement on company-level representation." *European Industrial Relations Review* 241: 19-22.

EIRR (1995). "Agreements on working time and bargaining." *European Industrial Relations Review* 263, December: 14-17.

EIRR (1997). "Government urges social partners to agree bargaining formula." *European Industrial Relations Review* 277, February: 17-18.

EIRR (2001). "Mediation accord hailed as a success." *European Industrial Relations Review* 325: 17-18.

EIRR (2002a). "Sweden. Successful First Year for Mediation Institute." *European Industrial Relations Review* 340, May: 21-24.

EIRR (2002b). "Italy. Social partners sign employment pact." *European Industrial Relations Review* 341, June: 7.

EIRR (2003a). "Ireland. New national agreement." *European Industrial Relations Review* 351, April: 15-16.

EIRR (2003b). "Netherlands. Wage freeze agreed." *European Industrial Relations Review* 359, December: 16-17.

EIRR (2003c). "Belgium. New national agreement." *European Industrial Relations Review* 348, January: 4.

EIRR (2003d). "Finland. New national incomes policy accord." *European Industrial Relations Review* 348, January: 24-26.

EIRR (2004). "Austria. Review of main collective bargaining trends." *European Industrial Relations Review* 368, September: 17-21.

EIRR (2005). "New social agreement in place." *European Industrial Relations Review* 374, March: 28-31.

Elvander, Nils (1974). "Collective bargaining and incomes policy in the Nordic countries: a comparative analysis." *British Journal of Industrial Relations*: 417-437.

Elvander, Nils (2002a). "The New Swedish Regime for Collective Bargaining and Conflict Resolution: A Comparative Perspective." *European Journal of Industrial Relations* 8 (2): 197-216.

Elvander, Nils (2002b). "The labour market regimes in the Nordic countries: A comparative analysis." *Scandinavian Political Studies* 25: 117-137.

Elvander, Nils and Bertil Holmlund eds. (1997). *The Swedish Bargaining System in the Melting Pot. Institutions, Norms and Outcomes in the 1990s*. Solna, Arbetslivinstitutet.

Enderlein, Henrik (2001). *Wirtschaftspolitik in der Währungsunion: Die Auswirkungen der Europäischen Wirtschafts- und Währungsunion auf die finanz- und lohnpolitischen Institutionen in den Mitgliedsländern*. Frankfurt, Campus.

Esping-Andersen, Gosta (1990). *The Three Worlds of Welfare Capitalism*. Oxford, Polity Press.

Estivill, Jordi and Josep M. de la Hoz (1990). "Transition and Crisis: The Complexity of Spanish Industrial Relations." G. Baglioni and C. Crouch eds. *Euro-*

pean Industrial Relations. The challenge of flexibility. London, Sage Publications: 265-300.

European Monetary Institute (1999). *Annual Report 1998*. Frankfurt/Main, European Monetary Institute.

Fajertag, Giuseppe and Philippe Pochet eds. (2000). *Social Pacts in Europe – New Dynamics*. Brussels, OSE-ETUI.

Ferner, Anthony and Richard Hyman eds. (1992a). *Industrial Relations in the New Europe*. Oxford, Basil Blackwell.

Ferner, Anthony and Richard Hyman (1992b). "Italy: Between Political Exchange and Micro-Corporatism." A. Ferner and R. Hyman eds. *Industrial Relations in the New Europe*. Oxford, Basil Blackwell: 524-601.

Ferner, Anthony and Richard Hyman eds. (1998a). *Changing Industrial Relations in Europe*. Oxford, Basil Blackwell.

Ferner, Anthony and Richard Hyman (1998b). "Introduction – Towards European Industrial Relations." A. Ferner and R. Hyman eds. *Changing Industrial Relations in Europe*. Oxford, Blackwell: xi-xxvi.

Ferrera, Maurizio and Elisabetta Gualmini (2000a). "Reforms Guided by Consensus – The Welfare State in the Italian Transition." *West European Politics* 23 (2): 187-208.

Ferrera, Maurizio and Elisabetta Gualmini (2000b). "Italy – Rescue from without." F.W. Scharpf and V.A. Schmidt eds. *Welfare and Work in the Open Economy Volume II*. Oxford, Oxford University Press: 351-398.

Financial Times (1982a). "Belgium acts to create more jobs." *Financial Times* London. 04 February 1982.

Financial Times (1982b): "Dutch centre-right coalition agrees austerity programme." *Financial Times* London 27 October 82.

Financial Times (1982c): "Wim Kok; Trade unions' uncrowned king." *Financial Times* London 16 November 82.

Financial Times (1984). "Why French Communists have refused to join a new Government." *Financial Times* London. 20 July 1984.

Financial Times (1985). "Craxi wins key referendum on wage indexation." *Financial Times* London 11 June 1985.

Financial Times (1987a). "Budget Sinks Irish Coalition." *Financial Times* London 21 January 1987.

Financial Times (1987b). "Economy Responds To Haughey Treatment." *Financial Times* London 04 August 1987.

Financial Times (1988a). "Magic Starts To Wear Thin." *Financial Times* London. 18 January 1988.

Financial Times (1988b). "Signs of wear and tear in Spanish Socialists' Party clothes." *Financial Times* London. 21 January 1988.

Financial Times (1988c). "Portuguese Unions Protest at Reforms." *Financial Times* London. 08 February 1988.

Financial Times (1989a). "Portugal Labours to Lift Clouds over the Economy." *Financial Times* London. 23 March 1989.

Financial Times (1989b). "Trade Union Groups Draw Closer." *Financial Times* London. 11 October 1989.

Financial Times (1991). "Swedish trade unions divided over wage agreement." *Financial Times* London. 09 January 1991.

Financial Times (1996). "Public Sector Deal in Portugal." *Financial Times* London. 12 January 1996.

Fischer, Stanley and Lawrence H. Summers (1989). "Should Governments Learn to Live with Inflation?" *AEA Papers and Proceedings* 79 (2): 383-387.

Fitoussi, Jean Paul (1993). *Competitive disinflation: the mark and budgetary politics in Europe*. Oxford, Oxford University Press.

Flanagan, Robert J. (1999). "Macroeconomic Performance and Collective Bargaining: An International Perspective." *Journal of Economic Literature* 37 (3): 1150-1175.

Flanagan, Robert J. (2003). "Collective Bargaining and Macroeconomic Performance." John T. Addison and Claus Schnabel eds. *International Handbook of Trade Unions*. London, Edward Elgar: forthcoming.

Flanagan, Robert J., David W. Soskice, *et al.* (1983). *Unionism, Economic Stabilization, and Incomes Policies: European Experience*. Washington D.C., The Brookings Institution.

Forder, James (1998). "Central bank independence – conceptual clarifications and interim assessment." *Oxford Economic Papers* 50 (3): 307-334.

Forder, James (1999). "Central Bank Independence: Reassessing the Measures." *Journal of Economic Issues* 33 (1): 23-40.

Forder, James (2001). "The Theory of Credibility and the Reputation-bias of Policy." *Review of Political Economy* 13 (1): 5-25.

Franzese, Robert J. (2001). "Monetary Policy and Wage/Price Bargaining – Macro-Institutional Interactions in the Traded, Public, and Sheltered Sectors." P. Hall and D. Soskice eds. *Varieties of Capitalism: the Institutional Foundations of Comparative Advantage*. Cambridge, Cambridge University Press: 104-144.

Franzese, Robert J. (2002). *Macroeconomic policies of developed democracies*. Cambridge, Cambridge University Press.

Friedman, Milton (1968). "The Role of Monetary Policy." *The American Economic Review* 58 (1): 1-17.

Fulcher, James (1991). *Labour Movements, Employers and the State. Conflict and Co-operation in Britain and Sweden*. Oxford, Clarendon Press.

Ganghof, Steffen (2003). *Parties, power and progressivity. On the political economy of income taxation in open states.* Dissertation, Bremen.

Garrett, Geoffrey and Christopher R. Way (2000). "Public Sector Unions, Corporatism, and Wage Determination." T. Iversen, J. Pontusson and D. Soskice eds. *Unions, Employers, and Central Banks.* Cambridge, Cambridge University Press: 267-291.

Garrett, Geoffrey and Christopher R. Way (2002). *Why do Independent Central Banks Require so Much 'Sacrifice'?* Unpublished paper.

Gillespie, Richard (1990). "The Break-up of the 'Socialist Family' – Party-Union Relations in Spain, 1982-89." *West European Politics* (January): 47-62.

Goetschy, Janine (1997). "France – The Limits of Reform." A. Ferner and R. Hyman eds. *Changing Industrial Relations in Europe.* Oxford, Blackwell: 357-395.

Golden, Miriam, Peter Lange and Michael Wallerstein (2002). "Union Centralization among Advanced Industrial Societies: An Empirical Study." Dataset available at *http://www.shelley.polisci.ucla.edu/data.* Version dated 19 September 2002.

Goldthorpe, John H. (1984). "The End of Convergence – Corporatist and Dualist Tendencies in Modern Western Societies." J.H. Goldthorpe ed. *Order and Conflict in Contemporary Capitalism.* Oxford, Oxford University Press: 315-343.

Gray, Jo Anna (1976). "Wage Indexation: A Macroeconomic Approach." *Journal of Monetary Economics* 2: 221-235.

Gray, Jo Anna (1978). "On Indexation and Contract Length." *Journal of Political Economy* 86 (1): 1-18.

Grilli, Vittorio, Donato Masciandaro, *et al.* (1991). "Political and Monetary Institutions and Public Financial Policies in the Industrialised Countries." *Economic Policy* 13: 42-92.

Gros, Daniel and Nils Thygesen (1992). *European Monetary Integration – From the European System to European Monetary Union.* London, Longham.

Grubb, Dennis, Richard Jackman and Richard Layard (1983). "Wage rigidity and unemployment in OECD countries." *European Economic Review* 21: 11-39.

Guger, Alois and Wolfgang Polt (1994). "Corporatism and Incomes Policy in Austria – Experiences and Perspectives." R. Dore, R. Boyer and Z. Mars eds. *The Return to Incomes Policy.* London/New York, Pinter: 151-160.

Hall, Peter A. (1986). *Governing the Economy: The politics of State Intervention in Britain and France.* Cambridge, Polity Press.

Hall, Peter A. ed. (1989). *The Political Power of Economic Ideas.* Princeton, New Jersey, Princeton University Press.

Hall, Peter A. and Robert J. Franzese (1998). "Mixed Signals: Central Bank Independence, Coordinated Wage Bargaining, and European Monetary Union." *International Organization* 52 (3): 505-535.

Hall, Peter A. and David Soskice (2001). "An Introduction into Varieties of Capitalism." P. A. Hall and D. Soskice eds. *Varieties of Capitalism. The Institutional Foundations of Comparative Advantage* Oxford, Oxford University Press: 1-71.

Hamann, Kerstin (1998). "Spanish Unions: Institutional Legacy and Responsiveness to Economic and Industrial Change." *Industrial and Labor Relations Review* 51 (3): 424-444.

Hamann, Kerstin (2001). "The resurgence of national-level bargaining: union strategies in Spain." *Industrial Relations Journal* 32 (2): 154-172.

Hamann, Kerstin and Miguel Martinez Lucio (2003). "Strategies of union revitalization in Spain. Negotiating change and fragementation." *European Journal of Industrial Relations* 9 (1): 61-78.

Hancké, Bob (1991). "The Crisis of National Unions: Belgian Labor in Decline." *Politics and Society* 19 (4): 463-487.

Hancké, Bob and Martin Rhodes (2005). "EMU and Labor Market Institutions in Europe: The Rise and Fall of National Social Pacts." *Work and Occupations* 32 (2): 196-228.

Hancké, Bob and David Soskice (2003). "Wage-setting and inflation targets in EMU." *Oxford Review of Economic Policy* 19 (1): 149-160.

Hardiman, Niamh (1988). *Pay, Politics and Economic Performance in Ireland, 1970-1987*. Oxford, Clarendon Press.

Hardiman, Niamh (2002). "From Conflict to Co-ordination: Economic Governance and Political Innovation in Ireland." *West European Politics* 25 (4): 1-24.

Hassel, Anke (2000). "Bündnisse für Arbeit. Nationale Handlungsfähigkeit im Europäischen Regimewettbewerb." *Politische Vierteljahresschrift* (3): 498-524.

Hassel, Anke (2001). "The Problem of Political Exchange in Complex Governance Systems: The Case of Germany's Alliance for Jobs." *European Journal of Industrial Relations* 7 (3): 305-323.

Hassel, Anke (2003). "The Politics of Social Pacts." *British Journal of Industrial Relations* 41 (4): 707-726.

Hassel, Anke (2005). "Policy- und Machtinteressen in Sozialpakten in Europa." F. Karlhofer and E. Tálos eds. *Sozialpartnerschaft – eine Europäische Perspektive?* Hamburg, LIT-Verlag: 109-134.

Hassel, Anke and Britta Rehder (2001). "Institutional Change in the German Wage Bargaining System – The Role of Big Companies." *MPIfG Working Paper 01/9* Köln.

Headey, Bruce W. (1970). "Trade Unions and National Wage Policies." *Journal of Politics* 32 (2): 407-439.

Hege, Adelheid (1999). "Collective Bargaining in Germany in the Age of Monetary Union." P. Pochet ed. *Monetary Union and Collective Bargaining in Europe.* Brussels, P.I.E. Lang: 41-84.

Heinze, Rolf G. (1981). *Verbändepolitik und "Neokorporatismus": Zur politischen Soziologie organisierter Interessen.* Opladen, Westdeutscher Verlag.

Heinze, Rolf G. (2002): *Die Berliner Räterepublik: viel Rat – wenig Tat?* Wiesbaden: Westdeutscher Verlag.

Hemerijck, Anton (1995). "Corporatist Immobility in the Netherlands." C. Crouch and F. Traxler eds. *Organized Industrial Relationships in Europe: What Future?* Aldershot, Avebury: 183-226.

Hemerijck, Anton, Brigitte Unger, *et al.* (2000). "How small countries negotiate change – twenty-five years of policy adjustment in Austria, the Netherlands, and Belgium." F.W. Scharpf and V.A. Schmidt eds. *Diverse Responses to Common Challenges.* Oxford, Oxford University Press: 175-263.

Hemerijck, Anton, Marc Van der Meer, *et al.* (2000). "Innovation through Coordination – Two Decades of Social Pacts in the Netherlands." G. Fajertag and P. Pochet eds. *Social Pacts in Europe – New Dynamics.* Brussels, OSE-ETUI: 257-278.

Hemerijck, Anton and Jelle Visser (2000). "Change and Immobility – Three Decades of Policy Adjustment in the Netherlands and Belgium." *West European Politics* 23 (2): 229-256.

Heywood, Paul (1996). "The Emergence of New Party Systems and Transitions to Democracy: Spain in Comparative Perspective." G. Pridham and P. G. Lewis eds. *Stabilising Fragile Democracies. Comparing New Party Systems in Southern and Eastern Europe.* London and New York, Routledge: 145-166.

Hibbs, Douglas A. (1977). "Political Parties and Macroeconomic Policy." *The American Political Science Review* 71: 1467-1487.

Hicks, J.R. (1955). "Economic Foundations of Wage Policy." *The Economic Journal* 65 (259): 389-404.

Hicks, Alexander and Duane Swank (1992). "Politics, Institutions, and Welfare Spending in Industrialized Democracies, 1960-82." *American Political Science Review* 86 (3): 658-74.

Huber, Evelyne, Charles Ragin, *et al.* (1993). "Social Democracy, Christian Democracy, Constitutional Structure, and the Welfare State." *American Journal of Sociology* 99: 711-749.

Huber, Evelyne and John D. Stephens (2001). *Development and Crisis of the Welfare State. Parties and Policies in Global Markets.* Chicago and London, University of Chicago Press.

Immergut, Ellen (1992). *Health Politics: Interests and Institutions in Western Europe.* Cambridge, Cambridge University Press.

Iversen, Torben (1996). "Power, Flexibility, and the Breakdown of Centralized Wage Bargaining – Denmark and Sweden in Comparative Perspective." *Comparative Politics* 28 (4): 399-436.

Iversen, Torben (1998). "Wage Bargaining, Central Bank Independence, and the Real Effects of Money." *International Organization* 52 (3): 469-504.

Iversen, Torben (1999). Contested Economic Institutions – The Politics of Macroeconomics and Wage Bargaining in Advanced Democracies. Cambridge, Cambridge University Press.

Iversen, Torben and Niels Thygesen (1998). "Denmark – From External to Internal Adjustment." J. Frieden, D. Gros and E. Jones eds. *Joining Europe's Monetary Club*. New York, Macmillan: 62-81.

Jacobs, Klaus, Martin Kohli, *et al.* (1991). "Germany – The Diversity of Pathways." M. Kohli, M. Rein, A.-M. Guillemard and H. van Gunsteren eds. *Time for Retirement: Comparative Studies of Early Exit from the Labor Force*. Cambridge, New York, Port Chester, Melbourne, Sydney, Cambridge University Press: 181-221.

Jochem, Sven (2003). "Konzertierung und Parteienwettbewerb – Das schwedische Modell im Wandel." S. Jochem and N. Siegel eds. *Konzertierung, Verhandlungsdemokratie und Reformpolitik im Wohlfahrtsstaat. Das Modell Deutschland im Vergleich*. Opladen, Leske + Budrich: 271-310.

Kästner, Erich (1998 [1933]). *Das fliegende Klassenzimmer. Ein Roman für Kinder*. Hamburg, Dressler Verlag.

Kalecki, Michal (1943). "Political Aspects of Full Employment." *Political Quarterly* 14.

Katz, Harry C. (1993). "The Decentralization of Collective Bargaining – A Literature Review and Comparative Analysis." *Industrial and Labor Relations Review* 47 (1): 3-22.

Katzenstein, Peter J. (1985). *Small States in World Markets. Industrial Policy in Europe*. Ithaca and London, Cornell University Press.

Kauppinen, Timo (1994). *The Transformation of Labour Relations in Finland*. Helsinki: Ministry of Labour.

Kauppinen, Timo (2000). "Social Pacts in Finland." G. Fajertag and P. Pochet eds. *Social Pacts in Europe – New Dynamics*. Brussels, OSE-ETUI: 161-186.

Kavanagh, Ella, John Considine, *et al.* (1998). "The Political Economy of EMU in Ireland." J. Frieden, D. Gros and E. Jones eds. *Joining Europe's Monetary Club*. New York, Macmillan: 123-148.

Keman, Hans and Paul Pennings (1995). "Managing Political and Societal Conflict in Democracies: Do Consensus and Corporatism Matter?" *British Journal of Political Science* 25 (2): 271-281.

Kenworthy, Lane (2001). "Wage-Setting Measures: A Survey and Assessment." *World Politics* 54 (1): 57-98.

Kenworthy, Lane (2003). "Quantitative Indicators of Corporatism." *International Journal of Sociology*, 33 (3): 10-46.

Kindleberger, Charles (1965). "Germany's Persistent Balance of Payment Disequilibrium." R.E. Baldwin ed. *Trade, Growth and the Balance of Payments.* Chicago, Amsterdam, Rand McNally: 230-248.

Kittel, Bernhard (2000). "Trade Union Bargaining Horizons in Comparative Perspective: The Effects of Encompassing Organization, Unemployment and the Monetary Regime of Wage-Pushfulness." *European Journal of Industrial Relations* 6 (2): 181-202.

Kjellberg, Anders (1998). "Sweden – Restoring the Model?" A. Ferner and R. Hyman eds. *Changing Industrial Relations in Europe.* Oxford, Blackwell: 74-117.

Korpi, Walter (1983). *The Democratic Class Struggle*. London, Routledge.

Kurzer, Paulette (1988). "The Politics of Central Banks: Austerity and Unemployment in Europe." *Journal of Public Policy* 7 (1): 21-47.

Kurzer, Paulette (1993). "The European Community and the Postwar Settlement. The Effect of Monetary Integration on Corporatist Arrangements." D. L. Smith and J.L. Ray eds. *The 1992 Project and the Future of Integration in Europe*. Armonk, London, M.E. Sharpe: 126-142.

Kydland, Finn and Edward C. Prescott (1977). "Rules rather than Discretion: The Inconsistency of Optimal Plans." *Journal of Political Economy* 85: 473-490.

Laakso, Markku and Rein Taagepera (1979). "Effective Number of Parties: A Measure with Application to West Europe." *Comparative Political Studies* 12 (1): 3-27.

Lane, Jan-Erik (1997). "The Institutions of Koncordanz and Corporatism." *Schweizerische Zeitschrift für Politische Wissenschaften* 3 (1): 5-30.

Lange, Peter and Geoffrey Garrett (1985). "The Politics of Growth – Strategic Interaction and Economic Performance, 1974-1980." *Journal of Politics* 47: 792-827.

Lange, Peter and Marino Regini (1989). "Introduction – interests and institutions – forms of social regulation and public policy-making." P. Lange and M. Regini eds. *State, Market, and Social Regulation: New perspectives on Italy.* Cambridge, Cambridge University Press: 1-25.

Lange, Peter, Michael Wallerstein, *et al.* (1995). "The End of Corporatism? Wage Setting in the Nordic and Germanic Countries." Sanford M. Jacoby ed. *The Workers of Nations – Industrial Relations in a Global Economy*. New York and Oxford, Oxford University Press: 76-100.

Layard, Richard (1982). "Incomes Policies to Answer Unemployment?" *Economica* 49: 219-239.

Layard, Richard (1986). *How to Beat Unemployment.* Oxford, Oxford University Press.

Layard, Richard, Stephen Nickell and Richard Jackman (1991). *Unemployment. Macroeconomic Performance and the Labour Market.* Oxford, Oxford University Press.

Lehmbruch, Gerhard (1979). "Consociational Democracy, Class Conflict and the New Corporatism." P.C. Schmitter and G. Lehmbruch eds. *Trends Towards Corporatist Intermediation.* Beverly Hills, Sage. 1.

Lehmbruch, Gerhard (1982). "Introduction – Neo-Corporatism in Comparative Perspective." Gerhard Lehmbruch and Philippe C. Schmitter eds. *Patterns of Corporatist Policy-Making.* London, Sage: 1-28.

Lehmbruch, Gerhard (1984). "Concertation and the Structure of Corporatist Networks." J.H. Goldthorpe ed. *Order and Conflict in Contemporary Capitalism.* Oxford, Clarendon Press: 60-80.

Lehmbruch, Gerhard (1992). "Konkordanzdemokratie." M.G. Schmidt ed. *Lexikon der Politik: Die westlichen Länder.* München, Beck: 206-211.

Lehmbruch, Gerhard (2000). "Institutionelle Schranken einer ausgehandelten Reform des Wohlfahrtsstaates – das Bündnis für Arbeit und seine Erfolgsbedingungen." R. Czada and H. Wollmann eds. *Von der Bonner zur Berliner Republik.* Opladen, Westdeutscher Verlag: 89-112.

Lehmbruch, Gerhard and Philippe C. Schmitter (1982). *Patterns of Corporatist Policy-Making.* Gerhard Lehmbruch. London, Sage.

Levy, Jonah (2000). "France." F.W. Scharpf and V.A. Schmidt eds. *Welfare and Work in the Open Economy Volume 2.* Oxford, Oxford University Press: 308-350.

Lijphart, Arend and Markus M.L. Crepaz (1991). "Corporatism and Consensus Democracy in Eighteen Countries: Conceptual and Empirical Linkages." *British Journal of Political Science* 21: 235-256.

Lijphart, Arend (1999). *Patterns of Democracy. Government Forms and Performance in Thirty-Six Countries.* New Haven, London, Yale University Press.

Lijphart, Arend (2001). "The pros and cons – but mainly pros – of consensus democracy" *Acta Politica* 36 (2): 129-139.

Lijphart, Arend (2002). "Negotiation democracy versus consensus democracy: parallel conclusions and recommendations." *European Journal of Political Research* 41: 107-113.

Lilja, Kari (1992). "Finland: No Longer the Nordic Exception." A. Ferner and R. Hyman eds. *Industrial Relations in the New Europe.* Oxford, Blackwell Business: 198-217.

Lind, Jens (2000). "Recent Issues on the Social Pact in Denmark." G. Fajertag and P. Pochet eds. *Social Pacts in Europe – New Dynamics.* Brussels, OSE-ETUI: 135-160.

Locke, Richard M. (1995). *Remaking the Italian Economy.* Ithaca, Cornell University Press.

Lorwin, Val R. (1975). "Labor Unions and Political Parties in Belgium." *Industrial and Labor Relations Review* 28 (2): 243-263.

Lucas, Robert (1976). "Econometric Policy Evaluation: A Critique." *Journal of Monetary Economics* 1 (2), Supplementary Series: 19-46.

Lucio, Miguel Martinez (1992). "Spain: Constructing Institutions and Actors in a Context of Change." A. Ferner and R. Hyman eds. *Industrial Relations in the New Europe.* Oxford, Blackwell: 482-523.

Lucio, Miguel Martinez (1998). "Spain: Regulating Employment and Social Fragmentation." A. Ferner and R. Hyman eds. *Changing Industrial Relations in Europe.* Oxford, Blackwell: 426-458.

Lutz, Burkart (1984). *Der kurze Traum immerwährender Prosperität. Eine Neuinterpretation der industriell-kapitalistischen Entwicklung im Europa des 20. Jahrhunderts.* Frankfurt and New York: Campus Verlag.

Magone, José M. (2001). *Iberian Trade Unionism. Democratization under the Impact of the European Union.* New Brunswick and London, Transaction Publishers.

Mangano, Gabriel (1998). "Measuring Central Bank Independence: A Tale of Subjectivity and of its Consequences." *Oxford Economic Papers* 50: 468-492.

Manow, Philip and Eric Seils (2000). "The Employment Crisis of the German Welfare State." *West European Politics* 23 (2): 137-160.

Marin, Bernd (1990). "Generalized Political Exchange: Preliminary Considerations." B. Marin ed. *Generalized Political Exchange.* Frankfurt / Main, Campus Verlag: 37-66.

Marin, Bernd (1991). "Introduction – Studying Policy Networks." B. M. Marin and R. Mayntz eds. *Policy Networks. Empirical Evidence and Theoretical Considerations.* Frankfurt / Main, Campus Verlag and Boulder, Colorado, Westview Press: 11-24.

Marks, Gary (1986). "Neocorporatism and Incomes Policy in Western Europe and North America." *Comparative Politics*: 253-277.

Marshall, Matt (1999). *The Bank: The Birth of Europe's Central Bank and the Rebirth of Europe's Power.* London, Random House.

Martin, Andrew (1985). "Wages, Profits, and Investment in Sweden." L. N. Lindberg and C. S. Maier eds. *The Politics of Inflation and Economic Stagnation.* Washington D.C., The Brookings Institution: 403-466.

Martin, Andrew (1995). "The Swedish Model: Demise or Reconfiguration?" T. Kochan, R. Locke and M. Piore eds. *Employment Relations in a Changing World Economy.* Cambridge, MIT Press: 263-296.

Martin, Andrew (2000). "The Politics of Macroeconomic Policy and Wage Negotiations in Sweden." T. Iversen, J. Pontusson and D. Soskice eds. *Unions, Employers, and Central Banks*. Cambridge, Cambridge University Press: 232-266.

McMorrow, Kieran (1996). "The Wage Formation Process and labour Market Flexibility in Labour Market Flexibility in the Community, the US and Japan." *Working Paper No. 118*. Brussels, European Commission, Directorate-General for Economic and Financial Affairs.

McNamara, Kathleen R. (1998). *The Currency of Ideas. Monetary Politics in the European Union*. Ithaca, Cornell University Press.

McNamara, Kathleen (1999). "Consensus and Constraint: Ideas and Capital Mobility in European Monetary Integration." *Journal of Common Market Studies* 37 (3): 455-476.

McNamara, Kathleen (2002). "Rational Fictions: Central Bank Independence and the Social Logic of Delegation." *West European Politics* 25 (1): 47-76.

Menezes Leitào, Maria Josefina (2001). "General Features of Collective Bargaining in Portugal." *The International Journal of Comparative Labour Law and Industrial Relations* 17 (4): 441-459.

Milesi-Ferretti, Gian Maria (1994). "Wage Indexation and Time Consistency: Note." *Journal of Money, Credit and Banking* 26 (4): 941-950.

Mitchell, Daniel J.B. (1993). "Keynesian, Old Keynesian, and New Keynesian Wage Nominalism." *Industrial Relations* 32 (1): 1-29.

Moene, Karl Ove, Michael Wallerstein, *et al.* (1993). "Bargaining Structure and Economic Performance." R.J. Flanagan, K.O. Moene and M. Wallerstein eds. *Trade Union Behaviour, Pay-Bargaining, and Economic Performance*. Oxford, Clarendon Press: 63-131.

Molina, Oscar and Martin Rhodes (2002). "Corporatism: The Past, Present and Future of a Concept." *Annual Review of Political Science* 5: 305-331.

Molitor, Michel (1978). "Social Conflicts in Belgium." C. Crouch and A. Pizzorno eds. *The Resurgence of Class Conflict in Western Europe Since 1968*. London, Macmillan : 21-51.

Mundell, Robert A. (1961). "A Theory of Optimum Currency Areas." *The American Economic Review* 51 (4): 657-665.

National Mediation Office (2001). *Mission Statement of the Medlingsinstitutet – A Short Presentation of a New Swedish Agency*. Stockholm.

Naumann, Reinhard (2000). "Portugal." G. Fajertag ed. *Collective Bargaining in Europe, 1998-99*. Brussels, OSE-ETUI: 369-384.

NESC (1986). *A Strategy for Development, 1986-1990*. Dublin, National Economic and Social Council.

Nedelmann, Birgitta and Kurt G. Meier (1979). "Theories of Contemporary Corporatism: Static or Dynamic?" P.C. Schmitter and G. Lehmbruch eds. *Trends*

Towards Corporatist Intermediation. Contemporary Political Sociology. Beverly Hills, Sage: 95-119.

Nickell, Stephen (1998). "Unemployment: Questions and Some Answers." *The Economic Journal* 108 (May): 802-816.

Nordhaus, William D. (1975). "The Political Business Cycle." *The Review of Economic Studies* 42 (2): 169-190.

O'Donnell, Rory and Colm O'Reardon (1997). "Ireland's experiment in social partnership 1987-96." G. Fajertag and P. Pochet eds. *Social Pacts in Europe*. Brussels, OSE-ETUI: 79-95.

O'Donnell, Rory and Colm O'Reardon (2000). "Social Partnership in Ireland's Economic Transformation." G. Fajertag, P. Pochet eds. *Social Pacts in Europe – New Dynamics*. Brussels, OSE-ETUI: 237-257.

OECD (various years). *National Accounts*. Paris, OECD.

OECD (various years). *Historical Statistics*. Paris, OECD.

OECD (1962). *Policies for Price Stability*. Paris, OECD.

OECD (1977). *Towards Full Employment and Price Stability. A Report to the OECD by a Group of Independent Experts (McCracken Report)*. Paris, OECD.

OECD (1980). "Incomes Policy in Theory and Practice." *Economic Outlook*. Paris, OECD: 33-50.

OECD (1994a). *The OECD Jobs Study: Evidence and Explanations. Part I: Labour Market Trends and Underlying Forces of Change*. Paris, OECD.

OECD (1994b). *The OECD Jobs Study: Evidence and Explanations. Part II: The Adjustment Potential of the Labour Market*. Paris, OECD.

OECD (1997a). "Economic Performance and the Structure of Collective Bargaining." *Employment Outlook 1997*. Paris, OECD: 63-92.

OECD (1997b). *Labour Force Statistics* 1976-1996. Paris, OECD.

OECD (2000). "Spain." *OECD Economic Surveys*. Paris, OECD.

Olson, Mancur (1990). *The Rise and Decline of Nations: Economic Growth, Stagflation, and Social Rigidities*. New Haven and London, Yale University Press.

Ost, David (2000). "Illusory Corporatism in Eastern Europe: Neoliberal Tripartism and Postcommunist Class Identities." *Politics & Society*, 28 (4), 503-530.

Page, S.A.B. and Sandra Trollope (1974). "An international survey of indexing and its effects." *National Institute Economic Review* 70 (4): 46-60.

Pelinka, Anton (2002). "Consociational Democracy in Austria: Political Change, 1968-1998." J. Steiner and T. Ertman eds. *Consociationalism and Corporatism in Western Europe: Still the Politics of Accommodation. Acta Politica special 1/2*: 139-157.

Pen, J. (1964). "Income Policy in the Netherlands." *Scottish Journal of Political Economy* 11: 179-193.

Perez, Sofia A. (2000a). "From Decentralization to Reorganization. Explaining the Return to National Bargaining in Italy and Spain." *Comparative Politics* (July): 437-458.

Perez, Sofia A. (2000b). "Social Pacts in Spain." G. Fajertag and P. Pochet eds. *Social Pacts in Europe – New Dynamics*. Brussels, OSE-ETUI: 343-365.

Phelps, Edmund S. (1967). "Phillips Curves, Expectations of Inflation and Optimal Unemployment over Time." *Economica* 34: 254-281.

Pierson, Paul (1996). "The new politics of the welfare state." *World Politics* 48 (January): 143-179.

Pierson, Paul (2000). "Increasing Returns, Path Dependence, and the Study of Politics." *American Political Science Review* 94 (2): 251-267.

Pinto, Mario (1990). "Trade Union Action and Industrial Relations in Portugal." G. Baglioni and C. Crouch eds. *European Industrial Relations: The Challenge of Flexibility*. London, Sage Publications: 243-265.

Pizzorno, Alessandro (1978). "Political Exchange and Collective Identity in Industrial Conflict." C. Crouch and A. Pizzorno eds. *The Resurgence of Class Conflict in Western Societies since 1968*. London, Macmillan: 277-298.

Pochet, Philippe (1999a). "Monetary Union and Collective Bargaining in Belgium." P. Pochet ed. *Monetary Union and Collective Bargaining in Europe*. Brussels, P.I.E. Lang: 187-218.

Pochet, Philippe (1999b). "Monetary Union and Collective Bargaining in Finland." P. Pochet ed. *Monetary Union and Collective Bargaining in Europe*. Brussels, P.I.E. Lang: 219-244.

Pochet, Philippe and Giuseppe Fajertag (1997). "Social Pacts in Europe in the 1990s. Towards a European Social Pact?" G. Fajertag and P. Pochet eds. *Social Pacts in Europe*. Brussels, OSE-ETUI: 9-25.

Pochet, Philippe and Guiseppe Fajertag (2000). "A New Era for Social Pacts in Europe." G. Fajertag and P. Pochet eds. *Social Pacts in Europe – New Dynamics*. Brussels, OSE-ETUI: 9-40.

Pontusson, Jonas and Peter Swenson (1996). "Labor Markets, Production Strategies and Wage Bargaining Institutions. The Swedish Employer Offensive in Comparative Perspective." *Comparative Political Studies* 29 (2): 223-250.

Posen, Adam (1998). "Central bank independence and disinflationary credibility: a missing link." *Oxford Economic Papers* 50: 335-359.

Postan, Michael M. (1967). *An Economic History of Western Europe*. London, Methuen.

Regalia, Ida and Marino Regini (1998). "Italy – The Dual Character of Industrial Relations." A. Ferner and R. Hyman eds. *Changing Industrial Relations in Europe*. Oxford, Blackwell: 459-500.

Regalia, Ida and Marino Regini (2004). "Collective Bargaining and Social Pacts in Italy." H. Katz ed. *The New Structure of Labor Relations: Tripartism and Decentralization*. Ithaca, New York, Cornell University Press: 59-83.

Regini, Marino (1984). "The condition for political exchange – How concertation emerged and collapsed in Italy and Great Britain." J.H. Goldthorpe ed. *Order and Conflict in Contemporary Capitalism*. Oxford, Oxford University Press: 124-142.

Regini, Marino (1997). "Still engaging in corporatism? Recent Italian experience in comparative perspective" *European Journal of Industrial Relations* 3: 259-78.

Regini, Marino (2000). "Between Deregulation and Social Pacts – The Responses of European Economies to Globalization." *Politics & Society* 28 (1): 5-33.

Rehder, Britta (2003). *Betriebliche Bündnisse für Arbeit in Deutschland. Mitbestimmung und Flächentarif im Wandel*. Frankfurt am Main, New York, Campus Verlag.

Reynaud, Jean-Daniel (1975). "Trade unions and political parties in France: some recent trends." *Industrial and Labor Relations Review* 28 (2): 208-225.

Rhodes, Martin (1998). "Globalization, Labour Markets and Welfare States. A Future of 'Competitive Corporatism'?" M. Rhodes and Y. Mény eds. *The Future of European Welfare – A New Social Contract?*. Houndsmill, Macmillan: 178-203.

Rhodes, Martin (2000a). "Desperately Seeking a Solution – Social Democracy, Thatcherism and the 'Third Way' in British Welfare." *West European Politics* 23 (2): 161-186.

Rhodes, Martin (2000b). "Restructuring the British Welfare State – Between Domestic Constraints and Global Imperatives." F.W. Scharpf and V.A. Schmidt eds. *Welfare and Work in the Open Economy. Volume II*. Oxford, Oxford University Press: 19-68.

Rhodes, Martin (2001a). "The Political Economy of Social Pacts – Competitive Corporatism and European Welfare Reform." Paul Pierson ed. *The New Politics of the Welfare State*. Oxford, Oxford University Press: 165-194.

Rhodes, Martin (2001b). "Why EMU is (or May Be) Good for European Welfare States." K. Dyson ed. *The European State and the Euro: Playing the Semi-Sovereignty Game*. Oxford, Oxford University Press.

Roche, William K. (1997). "Between regime fragmentation and realignment: Irish industrial relations in the 1990s." *Industrial Relations Journal* 29 (2): 112-125.

Rogoff, Kenneth (1985). "The Optimal Degree of Commitment to an Intermediate Monetary Target." *The Quarterly Journal of Economics* 100 (4): 1169-1189.

Royo, Sebastián (2000). *From Social Democracy to Neoliberalism: The Consequences of Party Hegemony in Spain, 1982-1996*. New York, St. Martin's Press.

Royo, Sebastián (2002a). "A New Century of Corporatism?" *Corporatism in Southern Europe – Spain and Portugal in Comparative Perspective*. Westport, Connecticut, London, Praeger.

Royo, Sebastián (2002b). "A New Century of Corporatism?' Corporatism in Spain and Portugal." *West European Politics* 25 (3), 77-104.

Sachverständigenrat zur Begutachtung der gesamtwirtschaftlichen Entwicklung (1987). *Weiter auf Wachstumskurs. Jahresgutachten 1986/87*. Stuttgart and Mainz, Verlag W. Kohlhammer GmbH.

Scharpf, Fritz W. (1991). *Crisis and Choice in European Social Democracy*. Ithaca, Cornell University Press.

Scharpf, Fritz W. (2000). "Economic Changes, Vulnerabilities, and Institutional Capabilities." F.W. Scharpf and V.A. Schmidt eds. *Welfare and Work in the Open Economy. Volume I. From Vulnerability to Competitiveness*. Oxford, Oxford University Press: 21-120.

Scharpf, Fritz W. and V.A. Schmidt (eds.) (2000). *Welfare and Work in the Open Economy. Volume 1. From Vulnerability to Competitiveness*. Oxford, Oxford University Press. Volume 1 and 2.

Scheuer, Steen (1992). "Denmark – Return to Decentralization." A. Ferner and R. Hyman eds. *Industrial Relations in the New Europe*. Oxford, Blackwell: 143-167.

Scheuer, Steen (1997). "Denmark – Return to Decentralization." A. Ferner and R. Hyman eds. *Changing Industrial Relations in Europe: Traditions and Transitions*. Oxford, Blackwell: 315-347.

Schludi, Martin (2005). *The Reform of Bismarckian Pension Systems. A Comparison of Pension Politics in Austria, France, Germany, Italy and Sweden*. Amsterdam, Amsterdam University Press.

Schmidt, Manfred G. (1996). "When parties matter: A review of the possibilities and limits of partisan influence on public policy." *European Journal of Political Research* 30 (3): 155-183.

Schmidt, Manfred G. (2000). *Demokratietheorien*. Opladen, Leske + Budrich.

Schmidt, Manfred G. (2002a). "The Impact of Political Parties, Constitutional Structures and Veto Players on Public Policy." H. Keman ed. *Comparative Democratic Politics*. London, Sage: 166-184.

Schmidt, Manfred G. (2002b). "Political performance and types of democracy. Findings from comparative studies." *European Journal of Political Research* 41: 147-163.

Schmitter, Philippe C. (1974). "Still the Century of Corporatism?" *Review of Politics* 36: 85-131.

Schmitter, Philippe C. (1977). "Modes of Interest Intermediation and Models of Societal Change in Western Europe." *Comparative Political Studies* (10): 7-38.

Schmitter, Philippe C. (1979). "Still the Century of Corporatism?" P. C. Schmitter and G. Lehmbruch eds. *Trends Towards Corporatist Intermediation.* Contemporary Political Sociology. Beverly Hills, Sage: 7-52.

Schmitter, Philippe C. (1981). "Interest Intermediation and Regime Governability in Contemporary Western Europe and North America." Suzanne Berger ed. *Organizing Interests in Western Europe: Pluralism, Corporatism and the Transformation of Politics.* Cambridge, Cambridge University Press: 285-327.

Schmitter, Philippe C. and Jürgen R. Grote (1997). "Der korporatistische Sysiphus – Vergangenheit, Gegenwart und Zukunft." *Politische Vierteljahresschrift* 38 (3): 530-554.

Schmitter, Philippe C. and Gerhard Lehmbruch eds. (1979). *Trends Towards Corporatist Intermediation.* Contemporary Political Sociology. Beverly Hills, Sage.

Schulten, Thorsten (2002). *Tarifpolitik in Europa 2001/2002. 2. Europäischer Tarifbericht.* Duesseldorf, Wirtschafts- und Sozialwissenschaftliches Institut.

Schulten, Thorsten and Angelika Stueckler (2000). *Wage policy and EMU.* Dublin, European Industrial Relations Observatory.

Sheldon, Peter and Louise Thornthwaite (1999). "Swedish engineering employers: The search for industrial peace in the absence of centralised collective bargaining." *Industrial Relations Journal* 30 (5): 514-532.

Shonfield, Andrew (1965). *Modern Capitalism. The Changing Balance of Public and Private Power.* Oxford, Oxford University Press.

Siaroff, Alan (1999). "Corporatism in 24 industrial democracies: Meaning and measurement." *European Journal of Political Research* 36 (2): 175-206.

Siegel, Nico (2005). "Social Pacts Revisited: 'Competitive Concertation' and Complex Causality in Negotiated Welfare State Reforms" *European Journal of Industrial Relations* 11 (1): 107-126.

Simmons, Beth A. (1994). *Who Adjusts? Domestic Sources of Foreign Economic Policy During the Interwar Years.* Princeton, New Jersey, Princeton University Press.

Slitor Richard E (1979). "Implementation and Design of Tax-Based Incomes Policies." *American Economic Review* 69 (2), 212-15.

Soskice, David (1978). "Strike Waves and Wage Explosions, 1968-1970: An Economic Interpretation." C. Crouch and A. Pizzorno eds. *The Resurgence of Class Conflict in Western Europe Since 1968.* New York, Holmes and Meyer: 221-246.

Soskice, David (1988). Industrial Relations and Unemployment – The Case for Flexible Corporatism. J.A. Kregel, E. Matzner and A. Roncaglia eds. *Barriers to Full Employment.* London, Macmillan Press: 212-226.

Soskice, David (1990). "Wage Determination – The Changing Role of Institutions in Advanced Industrialized Countries." *Oxford Review of Economic Policy* 6 (4): 36-61.

Soskice, David and Torben Iversen (1998). "Multiple Wage-Bargaining Systems in the Single European Currency Area." *Oxford Review of Economic Policy* 14 (3): 110-124.

Spineux, Armand (1990). "Trade Unionism in Belgium: The Difficulties of a Major Renovation." G. Baglioni and C. Crouch eds. *European Industrial Relations: The Challenge of Flexibility*. London, Sage Publications: 42 - 70.

Steinmo, Sven, Kathleen Thelen and Longstreth Frank H. (eds.) (1992). *Structuring Politics: Historical Institutionalism in Comparative Analysis.* Cambridge, Cambridge University Press.

Stephens, John D., Evelyne Huber, *et al.* (1998). "The Welfare State in Hard Times." G. Marks, J.D. Stephens, H. Kitschelt and P. Lange eds. *Continuity and Change in Contemporary Capitalism*. Cambridge, Cambridge University Press: 164-193.

Stoleroff, Alan (1992). "Between Corporatism and Class Struggle: the Portuguese Labour Movement and the Cavaco Silva Governments." *West European Politics* 15 (4): 118-150.

Stoleroff, Alan and Reinhard Naumann (1994). "Der Fall Portugal." *WSI Mitteilungen* (2): 134-139.

Straumann, Tobias (2001). "Old Reactions to New Challenges: Small European States and the EMS Crisis in 1992/93." Paper Presented at the Conference *Small States in World Markets: Fifteen Years Later*, Gothenburg.

Streeck, Wolfgang (1984). "Neo-Corporatist Industrial Relations and the Economic Crisis in West Germany." J.H. Goldthorpe ed. *Order and Conflict in Contemporary Capitalism – Studies in the Political Economy of West European Nations*. Oxford, Clarendon Press: 291-314.

Streeck, Wolfgang (1992). "From National Corporatism to Transnational Pluralism – European Interest Politics and the Single Market." Tiziano Treu ed. *Participation in Public Policy-Making. The Role of Trade Unions and Employers' Association*. Berlin, De Gruyter: 97-126.

Streeck, Wolfgang (1993). "The Rise and Decline of Neocorporatism." L. Ulman, B. Eichengreen and W. T. Dickens eds. *Labor and an Integrated Europe*. Washington D.C., The Brookings Institution: 80-101.

Streeck, Wolfgang (1994). "Pay Restraint without Incomes Policy – Institutionalized Monetarism and Industrial Unionism in Germany." R. Dore, R. Boyer and Z. Mars eds. *The Return to Incomes Policy*. London, New York, Pinter: 117-140.

Streeck, Wolfgang (2003). "From State Weakness as Strength to State Weakness as Weakness: Welfare Corporatism and the Private Use of the Public Interest." Cologne, *MPIfG Working Paper 03/2*.

Streeck, Wolfgang and Anke Hassel (2003). "Trade Unions and the Political Process." J.T. Addison and C. Schnabel eds. *International Handbook of Trade Unions*. London, Edward Elgar: 335-365.

Streeck, Wolfgang and Lane Kenworthy (2005). "Theories and Practices of Neo-Corporatism" T. Janoski, R. Alford, A. Hicks, M. Schwartz eds. *Handbook of Political Sociology*. New York, Cambridge University.

Streeck, Wolfgang and Britta Rehder (2005). "Institutionen im Wandel. Hat die Tarifautonomie eine Zukunft?"H.-W. Busch, H.-P. Frey, M. Hüther, B. Rehder, W. Streeck eds. *Tarifpolitik im Umbruch*, Köln, Deutscher Instituts-Verlag: 49-82.

Streeck, Wolfgang and Philippe C. Schmitter eds. (1985). *Private interest government. Beyond Market and State*. London, Sage Publications.

Streeck, Wolfgang and Philippe C. Schmitter (1991). "From National Corporatism to Transnational Pluralism. Organized Interests in the Single European Market." *Politics and Society* 19 (29): 133-164.

Streeck, Wolfgang and Christine Trampusch (2005). "Economic Reform and the Political Economy of the German Welfare State." *German Politics* 14 (2): 174-195.

Strom, Kaare (1984). "Minority Governments in Parliamentary Democracy. The Rationality of Non-winning Cabinet Solutions." *Comparative Political Studies* 17 (2): 199-227.

Swenson, Peter A. (1991). "Bringing capital back in, or social democracy reconsidered: employer power, cross-class alliance, and centralization of industrial relations in Denmark and Sweden" *World Politics* 43: 513-544.

Suppanz, Hannes and Derek Robinson (1972). *Prices and Incomes Policy. The Austrian Experience*. Paris, OECD.

Tálos, Emmerich and Bernhard Kittel (1996). "Roots of Austro-Corporatism: Institutional Preconditions and Cooperation Before and After 1945." G. Bischof and A. Pelinka eds. *Austro-Corporatism; Past, Present, Future. (Contemporary Austrian Studies Vol. 4)*. New Brunswick, London, Transaction Publishers: 21-52.

Tálos, Emmerich and Bernhard Kittel (1999). "Sozialpartnerschaft und Sozialpolitik." F. Karlhofer and E. Tálos eds. *Zukunft der Sozialpartnerschaft: Veränderungsdynamik und Reformbedarf*. Wien, Signum Verlag: 137-164.

Taylor, John B. (1982). "Establishing Credibility: A Rational Expectations Viewpoint." *The American Economic Review* 72 (2): 81-85.

Taylor, John B. (1997). "A Core of Practical Macroeconomics." *The American Economic Review* 87 (2): 233-235.

Thelen, Kathleen (2000). "Why German Employers Cannot Bring Themselves to Dismantle the German Model." T. Iversen, J. Pontusson and D. Soskice eds. *Unions, Employers, and Central Banks*. Cambridge, Cambridge University Press: 138-172.

Thelen, Kathleen (2003). "The political economy of business and labour in the developed democracies" I. Katznelson and H. Milner eds. *Political Science: the State of the Discipline*. New York, W.W. Norton.

Trampusch, Christine (2006). "Industrial Relations and Welfare States. The Different Dynamics of Retrenchment in the Netherlands and Germany." *Journal of European Social Policy*, (2): 121-133.

Traxler, Franz (1982). *Evolution gewerkschaftlicher Interessenvertretung. Entwicklungslogik und Organisationsdynamik gewerkschaftlichen Handelns am Beispiel Österreich*. Frankfurt, Campus.

Traxler, Franz (1997). "The Logic of Social Pacts." G. Fajertag and P. Pochet eds. *Social Pacts in Europe*. Brussels, OSE-ETUI: 27-36.

Traxler, Franz (1998). "Austria – Still the Country of Corporatism." A. Ferner and R. Hyman eds. *Changing Industrial Relations in Europe*. Oxford, Blackwell: 239-261.

Traxler, Franz (2001). "Die Metamorphosen des Korporatismus: Vom klassischen zum schlanken Muster." *Politische Vierteljahreschrift* 42 (4): 590-623.

Traxler, Franz (2003). "Bargaining institutions and the monetary regime: a cross-national comparison and its implications for European monetary union." *Journal of European Public Policy* 10 (4): 596-615.

Traxler, Franz, Sabine Blaschke, *et al.* (2001). *National Labor Relations in Internationalized Markets*. Oxford, Oxford University Press.

Treu, Tiziano (1992). "Tripartite Social Policy Making – An Overview." T. Treu ed. *Participation in Public Policy-Making: The Role of Trade Unions and Employers' Associations*. Berlin, Walter de Gruyter: 1-25.

Tsebelis, George (1995). "Decision making in Political Systems – Veto Players in Presidentialism, Parliamentarism, Multicameralism and Multipartyism." *British Journal of Political Science* 25: 289-325.

Tsebelis, George (1999). "Veto Players and Law Production in Parliamentary Democracies: An Empirical Analysis." *The American Political Science Review* 93 (3): 591-608.

Tsebelis, George (2002). *Veto Players. How Political Institutions Work*. New York, Russell Sage Foundation.

Ulman, Lloyd and Robert J. Flanagan (1971). *Wage Restraint. A Study of Incomes Policies in Western Europe*. Berkeley, University of California Press.

United Nations (1967). *Incomes in Postwar Europe: A Study of Policies, Growth and Distribution*. Economic Survey of Europe in 1965: Part 2. Geneva, Secretariat of the Economic Commission for Europe.

Van der Meer, Marc (1996). "Aspiring Corporatism? Industrial Relations in Spain." J. van Ruysseveldt and J. Visser eds. *Industrial Relations in Europe. Traditions and Transitions*. London, Sage: 310-336.

Van den Toren, Jan Peter (1997). "A 'Tripartite Consensus Economy': the Dutch Variant of a Social Pact." G. Fajertag and P. Pochet eds. *Social Pacts in Europe*. Brussels, OSE-ETUI: 181-194.

Van Ruysseveldt, Joris and Jelle Visser (1996). "Weak Corporatisms going Different Ways? Industrial Relations in the Netherlands and Belgium." J. van Ruysseveldt and J. Visser eds. *Industrial Relations in Europe. Traditions and Transitions*. London, Sage: 205-264.

Vilrokx, Jacques and Jim Van Leemput (1998). "Belgium: The Great Transformation." A. Ferner and R. Hyman eds. *Changing Industrial Relations in Europe: Traditions and transitions*. Oxford, Blackwell: 315-347.

Visser, Jelle (1990). "Continuity and Change in Dutch Industrial Relations." G. Baglioni and C. Crouch eds. *European Industrial Relations. The Challenge of Flexibility*. London, Sage Publications: 199-242.

Visser, Jelle (1997). "The Netherlands: The Return of Responsive Corporatism." R. Hyman and A. Ferner eds. *Changing Industrial Relations in Europe*. Oxford, Oxford University Press: 283-314.

Visser, Jelle (1998a). *Social Dialogue and Industrial Relations in Austria, Denmark, Ireland and the Netherlands*. Amsterdam, Report prepared for the ILO Country Employment Policy Review in selected OECD countries. Geneva, ILO.

Visser, Jelle (1998b). "Two Cheers for Corporatism, One for the Market: Industrial Relations, Wage Moderation and Job Growth in the Netherlands." *British Journal of Industrial Relations* 36 (2): 269-292.

Visser, Jelle (1999). "Concertation and the art of making social pacts." E. Gabaglio and R. Hoffmann eds. *European Trade Union Yearbook*. Brussels, European Trade Union Institute: 217-232.

Visser, Jelle (2002). "Why Fewer Workers Join Unions in Europe: A Social Custom Explanation of Membership Trends." *British Journal of Industrial Relations* 40 (30): 403-430.

Visser, Jelle and Anton Hemerijck (1997). *'A Dutch Miracle.' Job Growth, Welfare Reform and Corporatism in the Netherlands*. Amsterdam, Amsterdam University Press.

von Prondzynski, Ferdinand (1992). "Ireland: Corporatism Revived?" A. Ferner and R. Hyman eds. *Industrial Relations in the New Europe*. Oxford, Blackwell: 69-87.

von Prondzynski, Ferdinand (1998). "Ireland: Corporatism Revived?" A. Ferner and R. Hyman eds. *Changing Industrial Relations in Europe: Traditions and transitions*. Oxford, Blackwell: 55-73.

Waller, Christopher J. and David D. VanHoose (1992). "Discretionary Monetary Policy and Socially Efficient Wage Indexation." *The Quarterly Journal of Economics* (November): 1451-1460.

Wallerstein, Michael and Miriam Golden (1997). "The Fragmentation of the Bargaining Society. Wage Setting in the Nordic Countries, 1950 to 1992." *Comparative Political Studies* 30 (6): 699-731.

Wallerstein, Michael, Miriam Golden, *et al.* (1997). "Unions, Employers' Associations, and Wage-Setting Institutions in Northern and Central Europe, 1950-1992." *Industrial and Labor Relations Review* 50 (3): 379-401.

Western, Bruce (1997). *Between Class and Market: Postwar Unionization in the Capitalist Democracies.* Princeton, Princeton University Press.

Western, Bruce and Kieran Healy (1999). "Explaining the OECD Wage Slowdown – Recession or Labour Decline?" *European Sociological Review* 15 (3): 233-249.

Western, Bruce and Kieran Healy (2001). "Wage Growth, Recession, and Labor Decline in the Industrialized Democracies, 1965-1993." N. Bermeo ed. *Unemployment in the New Europe.* Cambridge, Cambridge University Press: 121-144.

Widmaier, Ulrich (1989). *Endogene Grenzen des Wachstums. Eine politisch-ökonomische Analyse von Verteilungskonflikten in demokratischen Staaten.* Baden-Baden, Nomos Verlagsgesellschaft.

Widmaier, Ulrich (1997). Vergleichende Aggregatdatenanalyse: Probleme und Perspektiven. D. Berg-Schlosser and F. Müller-Rommel eds. *Vergleichende Politikwissenschaft.* Opladen, Leske + Budrich: 103-118.

Wilensky, Harold J. (1976). *The New Corporatism, Centralization and the Welfare State.* London, Sage Publications.

Wilensky, Harold J. (2002). *Rich Democracies: Political Economy, Public Policy, and Performance.* Berkeley, University of California Press.

Windmuller, John P. (1969). *Labor Relations in the Netherlands.* Ithaca, NY, Cornell University Press.

Wolinetz, Steven B. (1989). "Socio-economic Bargaining in the Netherlands – Redefining the Post-war Policy Coalition." *West European Politics* 12 (1): 79-98.

Index of Names

Index of Subjects